Michael Eskin, Karen Leeder and Marko Pajević (Eds.)
Paul Celan Today

Companions to Contemporary German Culture

Edited by
Michael Eskin · Karen Leeder · Christopher Young

Volume 10

Paul Celan Today

A Companion

Edited by
Michael Eskin, Karen Leeder and Marko Pajević

DE GRUYTER

ISBN 978-3-11-065340-3
e-ISBN (PDF) 978-3-11-065833-0
e-ISBN (EPUB) 978-3-11-065861-3
ISSN 2193-9659

Library of Congress Control Number: 2021936048

Bibliographic information published by the Deutsche Nationalbibliothek
The Deutsche Nationalbibliothek lists this publication in the Deutsche Nationalbibliografie; detailed bibliographic data are available on the Internet at http://dnb.dnb.de.

Cover image: Paul Celan, 1938. Public domain/wikipedia/redesigned.
Printing and binding: CPI books GmbH, Leck

www.degruyter.com

Table of Contents

A Note on Translations

Quotations are generally given only in English, except where a particular linguistic or formal point is being made, or when a reader who has German might particularly benefit from having the original. In the case of quotations from Paul Celan himself quotations are given in German and English. Contributors have given sources for published translations used or have provided new translations. These follow the relevant German in square brackets and the primary aim is to provide an accessible working translation. Unless otherwise specified, all other translations are by the author of the chapter.

To avoid unnecessary repetition, however, the titles of Paul Celan's poetry collections are given in the German only. The titles of individual poems are given both in German and English throughout. For ease of reference a list of translations of these main works is included here, and a fuller Select Bibliography is given at the end of the volume.

Poetry collections

Der Sand aus den Urnen (1948)	[The Sand from the Urns]
Mohn und Gedächtnis (1952)	[Poppy and Memory]
Von Schwelle zu Schwelle (1955)	[From Threshold to Threshold]
Sprachgitter (1959)	[Speechgrille]
Die Niemandsrose (1963)	[The No-One's-Rose]
Atemwende (1967)	[Breathturn]
Fadensonnen (1968)	[Threadsuns]
Lichtzwang (1970)	[Lightduress]
Schneepart (1971)	[Snowpart]
Zeitgehöft (1976)	[Timestead]

Essays

Der Meridian (Rede anlässlich der Verleihung des Georg-Büchner Preises 1960)	[The Meridian]
Rede anlässlich der Entgegennahme des Literaturpreises der Hansestadt Bremen (1958)	[Bremen Speech]

https://doi.org/10.1515/9783110658330-001

Michael Eskin
Introduction

2020 marked the centennial of Paul Celan's birth and the semi-centennial of his death by suicide.

Paying tribute to the late poet in the 1970 commemorative issue of *Études germaniques*, renowned twentieth-century French Germanist Claude David famously called Celan 'le plus grand poète français de langue allemande' – the greatest French poet of the German language.[1] David's dual superlative assessment of Celan's stature as a poetic giant slyly obviates the pitfalls of having to measure his legacy against the achievements of his peers in the German and French languages, respectively, casting him as a bi-national, bi-cultural phenomenon *sui generis*, a literary-historical singularity. In a pinch, Rilke and Heine may come to mind as foils for David's characterization: the former having lived in France and written poetry in both French and German, and, arguably, the undisputed modern global superstar of German poetry, especially in the popular imagination (even Woody Allen quotes him at length in one of his movies); the latter, who spent the second half of his life in Paris, having been viewed by some in his adoptive country as 'the greatest German poet, and indeed one of the greatest French authors'.[2] Yet neither Rilke nor Heine, their ties to France and French culture notwithstanding, can 'officially' lay claim to the title of 'greatest French poet of the German language': for unlike Celan, neither ever became a *French* citizen; and Heine, for one, considered himself emphatically a *German* rather than French poet ('Ich bin ein deutscher Dichter'[3]).

What, then, does it mean to be 'the greatest French poet of the German language'?

A complex and perhaps unanswerable question – a question, in fact, that might be best left alone, in the abeyance of its own suggestiveness, the reflected glow of the ennobling aura and intuitive pathos of David's praise – but a question that implies, or contains, a handful of further, interrelated, questions that *are* worth pursuing in their own right, such as: what does it mean to be the 'greatest' poet *tout court?* The 'greatest' to and for whom? The 'greatest' in perpetuity or merely for a time – be it a historical period, a generation, the lifespan

1 Claude David, 'Préambule', Études Germaniques ('Hommage à Paul Celan') 25, no. 3 (1970), 239–241 (p. 239).

2 John A. Hess, 'Heine and the French', The Modern Language Journal 16, no. 3 (Dec. 1931), 193–203 (p. 193).

3 Heinrich Heine, Buch der Lieder (Hamburg: Hoffman und Campe, 1827), p. 192.

https://doi.org/10.1515/9783110658330-002

of a political system? Think of such 'greatest' authors – pardon the paradox of plurality here – as William Shakespeare, Friedrich Hölderlin or Maxim Gorky: the former two having gone through long periods of eclipse until the full-fledged rediscovery of their genius by the Romantics (especially, the German Romantics) in Shakespeare's and by early twentieth-century German literary scholar Norbert von Hellingrath in Hölderlin's case, respectively; the latter having been demoted until further notice from his empyreal status as the 'greatest' Soviet writer following the irreversible demise of *Realsozialismus* in the late 1980s.

Thus, being the 'greatest' poet (or artist of any kind) reveals itself as historically relative at best, and indicative, above all, of the critical attitude of the one(s) declaring 'greatness'. This being the case, the real question can be said to be *not* what it *is* to be the 'greatest' poet or artist so much as what it *means* to be *dubbed* or *considered* such in a given historical situation or context. What is it about a poet's or artist's project or legacy that elicits such superlative praise? What is it about a poet's or artist's oeuvre that ostensibly meets certain aesthetic and socio-cultural needs, responds to certain pressing cultural-political questions and concerns, encapsulates and articulates 'in a nutshell' the spirit or zeitgeist of an epoch or historical moment, intimates possible, hitherto untrodden paths of addressing the present and conceiving of past and future in creative and novel ways – all of which might then warrant the moniker 'greatest'?

Again, I don't think that a clear-cut answer to these queries is feasible. But an approximation ought perhaps to be ventured, if only to better understand our desire ever so often to lavish the attribute 'greatest' on certain poets and artists, while withholding it from others.

To begin with, then, let us agree to rephrase 'greatest' in terms of the less exuberantly absolute and somewhat more sober and hands-on 'most significant', which I take to constitute its core meaning, especially when applied to art and its makers. We can now more concretely ask: 'most significant' in respect to what? And that is a question that, I believe, can indeed be plausibly answered on the basis of cultural-historical, thematic, socio-political and aesthetic argument, which may or may not be accepted by some and rejected by others, but which will, if seriously and cogently presented, have to be reckoned with beyond intuition, taste and pathos above all. If 'greatest' beckons towards the *absolute* and is *a fortiori* a function of a certain *je ne sais quoi*, then 'most significant' is decidedly *relative* and squarely a function of (ever-changing) consensus.

And such precisely is the goal of the volume you are about to embark on: thinking through the knotty question as to whether and, if so, why Paul Celan might *actually* and *justifiably* be considered if not *the* then at least *one of the* most significant poets not only of the modern and, in particular, post-war era, but of our budding twenty-first century and beyond.

The contributions gathered in this volume, ranging from scholarly articles to genuine artistic responses and meditations on Celan's life and poetry, probe and illuminate his legacy from as wide an array of perspectives as possible (pragmatic constraints permitting) – historical, biographical, cultural, political, philosophical, aesthetic, poetological, linguistic, visual-cinematic and personal – with a view to striking the balance, as it were, of what it *has singularly meant* and suggesting or intimating what it might *yet*, or ought to, *singularly mean* for current and future generations.

Eschewing, for reasons of nugatory redundancy, to summarize the individual chapters that follow – the chapter headings themselves eloquently indicate what each contribution is about – suffice it to highlight that in addition to expert scholarly treatments of the above-listed aspects of Celan's life and art (e.g., his multilingualism and multiculturalism, the politics of his aesthetics, his poetics' philosophical paradigmaticity, etc.) the reader will also be treated to a choice of more personal, emphatically subjective engagements with Celan by five outstanding contemporary artists: Peter Waterhouse, Edmund de Waal, Ulrike Draesner, Anselm Kiefer and Durs Grünbein (the latter in conversation), which testify to the poet's wider cultural-historical impact and import beyond the (permeable) walls of the academy, where the majority of his readers and critics have hitherto tended to congregate. Taken together, the editors hope that all of the contributions here gathered may enable you to form your own opinion on the continued significance of, arguably, one of the 'greatest poet[s] of the German language' – both today and for future generations...

Amy-Diana Colin and Andrei Corbea-Hoisie

Paul Celan's Bukovina-Meridians

In his seminal poetological text *Der Meridian* [*The Meridian*], Paul Celan invokes a journey in light of 'u-topia' but back in time. It is a search for both a historical and imaginary 'topos' (τόπος): a 'World of Yesterday':

> From this point of 'comfort', but also in the light of utopia, let me now undertake a bit of topological research. I shall search for the region [...] for my own place of origin.
>
> None of these places can be found. They do not exist. But I know where they ought to exist, especially now, and... I find something else.[1]

Celan's place of origin, in both a literal and metaphorical sense, was Czernowitz, capital of the Bukovina, a region located between the Bessarabian steppe, the northern Carpathian Mountains and Moldavia (Romania). There, Romanians, Ruthenians, Germans, Austrians, Jews, Poles, Armenians, Hungarians, Slovenes, Turks, Greeks, Hutsuls, Lipovans, Roma and several different religious denominations coexisted relatively peacefully for centuries despite ethnic and religious prejudices and conflicts. Their interaction contributed to the development of a multifaceted culture that produced Romanian, Ukrainian, Austro-German, Austro-Jewish and Yiddish literature as well as authors fluent in many different languages. Jewish writers and poets had a seminal role in the flowering of Bukovina's culture, in particular its Austro-German literature. The latter emerged in the Habsburg Bukovina of the nineteenth century, paradoxically reaching its culmination in the 1920s and early 1930s when the region was part of the Romanian Kingdom. World War II and the Holocaust destroyed Bukovina's Austro-Jewish and Yiddish culture, while putting a temporary end to all other intellectual, literary and artistic activities. After 1944/1945, some aspects of Bukovina's culture were resuscitated but declined again during subsequent Soviet rule. Today, the Bukovina is split into two different predominantly monocultural worlds: the Ukrainian in the north and the Romanian in the south.

As the pre-World War II multi-ethnic sociotope Bukovina vanished, its memory and myths became increasingly powerful tropes in a variety of literary, his-

1 Paul Celan, 'Der Meridian', in Celan, *Gesammelte Werke in fünf Bänden*, ed. by Beda Allemann and Stefan Reichert in collaboration with Rolf Bücher (Frankfurt a.M.: Suhrkamp, 1983), henceforth abbreviated as GW5, vol. III, p. 202 (this edition corresponds to the first five volumes of *Gesammelte Werke in sieben Bänden*); Celan, *Collected Prose*, trans. by Rosmarie Waldrop (Manchester: Carcanet Press, 1985), p. 54.

https://doi.org/10.1515/9783110658330-003

torical, ethnographic and theoretical writings, including Celan's *Der Meridian.* In this programmatic text, initially a speech held on the occasion of receiving the Georg Büchner Award (22 October 1960), Celan's imaginary return to his homeland leads him to a discovery: 'a meridian',[2] a key concept of his work. In its multiplicity of meanings, a 'meridian' indicates both the link and the distance between the places and poles that it connects: in Celan's case, his situation as a post-Holocaust Jewish poet writing in German and his distant Bukovina; his biographical itinerary and the genesis of his work; his early poems written in Czernowitz and his late, almost hermetic works.

This chapter explores the ways in which Celan's 'meridian' discloses itself in several nodal 'topoi' on the trajectory of his poetic development. The first part gives an insight into Celan's Bukovina and its impact upon the poet's education, experiences and poetic aspirations. The second part explores other 'meridians' connecting Celan's poetry to his Bukovina: the multilingual character of his poetic language; the mediation between cultures as a salient feature of both Bukovina's literature and Celan's own work; Celan's poetics of upheaval as a response to the Nazi abuse and destruction of the German language.

This chapter is based on the work of two scholars who have written about Celan and the Bukovina from different perspectives.[3] By mapping out the intricate relationship between Celan's poetry and his native contextuality, we will provide an insight into the genesis of his work in its relationship to the Bukovina.

I Celan's Bukovina: A world of yesterday

An exceptional place

Time and again, authors from the Bukovina invoked their place of origin, imbuing the reminiscences of the past with new meanings that disclose the relevance of this multi-ethnic sociotope for later generations. Reflecting on the Bukovina

2 Celan, GW5, vol. III, p. 202; Celan, *Collected Prose*, p. 54.

3 Publications include: Amy-Diana Colin, *Paul Celan. Holograms of Darkness* (Bloomington: Indiana University Press, 1991) and 'Czernowitz/Cernăuţi/Chernovtsy/Chernivtsi/Czerniowce: A Testing Ground for Peaceful Coexistence in a Plural Society", in *Journal of Austrian Studies* 53, no. 3 (2020), 17–44, henceforth abbreviated as 'Czernowitz'; Andrei Corbea-Hoisie, *Czernowitzer Geschichten. Über eine städtische Kultur in Mittel(Ost)-Europa* (Vienna: Böhlau, 2002), pp. 29–42; and *La Bucovine. Éléments d'histoire politique et culturelle* (Paris: Institut d'Études Slaves, 2004).

as a 'haven of peace and mutual understanding', Rose Ausländer (1901–1988), in her series of numbered 'Bukowina' poems, writes: 'Vier Sprachen | Viersprachenlieder || Menschen | die sich verstehen' [Four languages | Fourlanguagesongs || people | understanding one another].[4] By contrast, other authors such as Alfred Gong (1920–1981), Edgar Hilsenrath (1926–2018) and Gregor von Rezzori (1914–1998) showed that peaceful coexistence in the Bukovina was as much a myth as a reality. According to Gregor von Rezzori, Bukovina's main characteristic was a precarious balance between tolerance and intolerance, respect and hatred: 'A dozen different nationalities and half a dozen fiercely fighting religious denominations coexisted there in the cynical harmony of mutual animosity and business deals. Nowhere were the fanatics more tolerant and the tolerant people more dangerous'.[5] For a long time, such balance safeguarded peace in the Bukovina.

Yet Celan had a different interpretation of his own 'world of yesterday'. In a speech held in Bremen (1958) on the occasion of receiving the Literary Award of the Hanseatic city, the poet referred to his homeland as 'a region, where people and books lived'.[6] This image, both vivid and concise, became so famous that literary studies of Celan's work have cited it time and again. This excessive repetition has turned Celan's significant 'topos of memories' into a commonplace and a commemorative cliché. Still, despite the use and abuse, Celan's metaphor has retained its initial meaning and sense: it invokes the 'meridian' that links the power of literature to Celan's own life and to the 'people of the book' in his Bukovina. The spiritual force of books had nourished, motivated and inspired a community of Jewish intellectuals, writers and artists in his homeland. Many years after the war, in Paris, Celan still felt close to them.

In the same passage from his *Bremer Rede* [*Bremen Speech*], Celan associates his Bukovina with the 'Hassidic tales' collected and translated into German by Martin Buber. These stories about the wise 'Wunderrabbiner' [miracle rabbis] from Sadagora, a small town close to Czernowitz, disclose a belief in the magic power of the words cherished not only by Baal Shem Tov, the founder of Chassidism, but also by Jewish writers from the Bukovina as well as by European poets in the orphic tradition. The meridian connecting Celan's Bukovina to Chassidic storytelling lends his native contextuality a mystical aura, turning it into a source of fiction and poetry. At the same time, Celan points to three aspects of an

4 Rose Ausländer, 'Bukowina III', in Rose Ausländer: *Gesammelte Werke in 8 Bänden* (Frankfurt a.M.: S. Fischer, 1984), vol. IV, p. 130 (translation by Amy-Diana Colin).

5 Gregor von Rezzori, *Ein Hermelin in Tschernopol* (Hamburg: Rowohlt Verlag, 1958), p. 17 (translation by Amy-Diana Colin).

6 Celan, GW5, vol. III, p. 185; Celan, *Collected Prose*, p. 33.

important historical and biographical context: Buber's efforts to build bridges between Jews and Germans as well as between enlightened, orthodox and Chassidic German-speaking Jews by telling and retelling Hassidic stories; the Jewish belief in the fruitfulness of a 'German-Jewish symbiosis' as advocated by authors such as Rudolf Borchardt (1877–1944), an antimodernist and conservative German-Jewish author who was so fascinated by Mussolini's fascism that he visited the Duce;[7] and, last but not least, German 'inner immigration' as a response to Nazi barbarism – a form of resistance practiced by poets such as Rudolf Alexander Schröder (1878–1962), co-founder of the Bremer Presse and member of the Confessing Church that opposed Hitler's regime.[8] The adolescent Paul Antschel was quite familiar with the ideas of these different authors representing heterogeneous but interrelated traditions.

In *Der Meridian*, written two years after the *Bremer Rede*, Celan further develops the link between his reminiscences of the Bukovina and the allusion to the German-Jewish symbiosis, referring explicitly to another of its main advocates: Karl Emil Franzos (1848–1904), a Galician Jew educated at the Middle School of Czernowitz who became a well-known German novelist. Franzos, who regarded himself as a German national of Jewish faith,[9] believed in the ideals of the Austrian Enlightenment in the tradition of Joseph II. It is from this perspective that the series of his 'Kulturbilder' from 'Halb-Asien' [half-Asia] describe Franzos's journey through Eastern Europe. These books combine essays on the history and socio-political situation in Galicia, Russia, Romania and the Bukovina with ironic sketches, presenting Eastern Europe as a 'melange' between 'European' and 'Asiatic' civilization. Franzos held the latter responsible for all social, economic, and political problems. As a result, he labelled most Eastern-European regions 'half-Asia', meaning for him 'half-civilized'.[10] According to Franzos,

7 The Nazis shattered his illusions, for the SS arrested him. He died heartbroken after his release. In his *Bremer Rede*, Celan mentions that he had read Borchardt's 'Ode with a Pomegranade', see: Celan, GW5, vol. III, p. 185; Celan, *Collected Prose*, p. 33.

8 Ibid., pp. 33–34.

9 In the introduction to his novel *Der Pojaz*, Franzos mentions the source of his self-interpretation. It was his father's conviction that he was a German in terms of nationality and a Jew in terms of faith: 'Du bist deiner Nationalität nach kein Pole, kein Ruthene, kein Jude – du bist ein Deutscher, aber deinem Glauben nach bist du ein Jude.' Cited after: Karl Emil Franzos, *Der Pojaz. Eine Geschichte aus dem Osten* [Vorwort] (Berlin: J.G. Cotta, 1905), p. 6.

10 For detailed interpretations of 'Halb-Asien', see: Colin, *Paul Celan. Holograms*, p. 13, and 'Karl Emil Franzos, die Bukowina und Europa', in *Spuren eines Europäers. Karl Emil Franzos als Mittler zwischen den Kulturen*, ed. with E. V. Kotowski and A. D. Ludewig. (Hildesheim: Georg Olms Verlag, 2007), pp. 55–71; as well as Corbea-Hoisie, 'Halb-Asien', in *Habsburg neu*

there was only one radically different region: the Bukovina. The source of such difference was the Austro-German 'Geist' that had transformed the Bukovina into Franzos's ideal of a European cultural state: 'the German spirit [der deutsche Geist], the most benevolent and powerful wizard under the Sun turned the Bukovina into a flourishing piece of Europe'.[11]

Many Bukovinians, regardless of their ethnicity, shared Franzos's understanding of their homeland as an example of 'exceptionalism': a *Kronland* [crownland] pursuing a 'Sonderweg' in the Austro-Hungarian Empire. Like Franzos, Bukovinian representatives of the Jewish middle-class in the Haskala tradition believed in the benefits of a 'German-Jewish symbiosis' for the 'exceptionalism' of both their homeland and their own communities. Despite the rise of violent nationalism and anti-Semitism in the 1920s and 1930s, they continued to share these convictions. But Celan, a German-speaking European-Jewish poet deeply scarred by the Holocaust, rejected such views inscribing his criticism not only in *Der Meridian* but also in his late poem 'Eine Gauner- und Ganovenweise' ['A Rogues and Ganif's Ditty'],[12] which he reworked several times over the course of almost two years (from February 1961 to November 1962). The poem's subtitle introduces its author's identity-marker, thereby reversing a traditional hierarchy: 'sung [...] by Paul Celan of Czernowitz near Sadagora'.[13] For Celan, Sadagora is no longer the shtetl in the vicinity of Bukovina's capital. Rather, Czernowitz, once regarded as the metropolis of Jewish assimilation or acculturation, acquired the status Sadagorian suburb. Despite the irony inherent in this poem, Czernowitz retains its significance for Celan, prompting readers to explore the uniqueness of his real and imaginary homeland.

The Bukovina: Historical and cultural aspects (1774–1919)

On 23 November 1920, when Paul Antschel was born in Czernowitz, the former Habsburg province had been part of the Kingdom of Romania for almost two years. Over the course of its tumultuous history, the Bukovina, located at the

---

denken. Vielfalt und Ambivalenz in Zentraleuropa. 30 kulturwissenschaftliche Stichworte, ed. by Johannes Feichtinger and Heidemarie Uhl (Vienna: Böhlau, 2016), pp. 73–81.

11 Karl Emil Franzos, *Aus Halb-Asien. Culturbilder aus Galizien, der Bukowina, Südrussland und Rumänien* (Leipzig: Duncker & Humblot, 1876), p. 113.

12 Celan, 'Eine Gauner- und Ganovenweise gesungen zu Paris emprès Pontoise von Paul Celan aus Czernowitz bei Sadagora', in GW5, vol. I, pp. 229–30; Celan, *Selected Poems and Prose*, trans. by John Felstiner (New York: Norton, 2001), pp. 161–63.

13 Ibid.

crossroads of its neighbours' political interests, had become a target of their conquests: its territories, comprising about 10,500 km^2, belonged to the rulers of the Kiev Empire, the dukedom of Halicz and, finally, to the Moldavian duchy that was first part of the Kingdom of Hungary. After a short period of independence, the Principality of Moldavia (including the Bukovina) became a vassal state of Poland and in 1514 of the Ottoman Empire. During the Russian-Turkish War (1766–1774), as a result of peace negotiations between Sultan Abdul Hamid I and Joseph II of Austria, Russia's ally at that time, the Bukovina was integrated into the Habsburg Empire.

The Habsburg administration turned the region into a buffer zone in order to protect its Empire from Russian and Ottoman expansion, thereby changing Bukovina's ethnic and demographic composition. Prior to 1774, the scarce population of the region was predominantly of Romance origin. The Habsburg officials promoted the settlement of German colonists (both Catholics and Protestants) from Bohemia, Swabia and the Spiš (mostly farmers, craftsmen or miners) as well as Ukrainians from Galician villages. In the first decades of their rule, the profoundly anti-Jewish Habsburg military administrators forced Jews either to leave the region or face tough professional restrictions. Emperor Joseph II promoted more liberal policies towards religious minorities (by issuing the Patent of Toleration in 1782). Eventually Jews also benefited from it. As a result, many Jews settled in the Bukovina around 1800.

In 1857, the Austrian census recorded 455,800 inhabitants: 44.6% Romanians, 38% Ruthenians, 6.4% Germans, 6.4% Jews, 3% Poles, 1.6% Magyars and 0.57% Russians. By 1910, the Austrian census counted 794,945 inhabitants: 237,216 (34.4%) Romanians, 305,222 (38.4%) Ruthenians, 95,706 (12%) Jews, 73,073 (9.2%) Germans and 47,728 (6%) belonging to other ethnic groups (i.e. Lipovans, Poles, Hungarians, Slovaks and Armenians). In addition, several religious denominations coexisted in the Bukovina.[14]

The growth of Bukovina's population fostered the demographic development of its capital Czernowitz. In 1787, imperial officials documented 153 Romanians, 84 Germans, 76 Jews and a small number of other ethnicities. On 2 August 1786, Czernowitz received a new constitution that granted Christian inhabitants the opportunity to obtain citizenship by taking an oath of allegiance, as well as the right to elect the town's council. By 1848, the multi-ethnic population of Czernowitz increased to 20,000 inhabitants. By 1900, the size of Bukovina's cap-

14 The adherents of different religious communities included: Greek-Catholics, Armenian Catholics, Armenian Gregorians, Protestants, Old Believers (adherents of the Lipovan Orthodox Old-Rite Church) and Jews.

ital was comparable to that of other provincial cities in the Austro-Hungarian Empire such as Innsbruck or Brünn.

The Habsburg officials promoted the acculturation of Romanians and Ukrainians, the two largest ethnic groups, by admitting them into civil service and the administration. Jews were excluded, although they had to pay high taxes. In the late nineteenth and twentieth centuries, Habsburg officials gradually changed their policy towards Bukovinian Jews. By the late nineteenth and early twentieth centuries, the ethnic plurality was mirrored in the administration of the Bukovina and its capital, whose mayors included the Armenian Jacob Ritter von Petrowicz (mayor, 1864–1866), the Pole Anton Freiherr Kochanowski von Stawczan (mayor, 1866–1874, 1887–1905), the Austro-German Wilhelm von Klimesh (mayor, 1881–1887), and the Austro-Jews Eduard Reiß (mayor, 1905–1907) and Salo Weisselberger (mayor, 1912–1914).

The German language played a crucial part in the process of acculturation, for Habsburg officials turned the knowledge of German into a precondition for getting jobs, presenting it as people's entry ticket into society. In the case of Jews, Habsburg policies were more radical: in the eighteenth century, the Imperial administration required Jews who wished to marry and/or attend Talmud schools to provide a school certificate proving that they had learned German. Initially, only soldiers, public officials and Viennese teachers sent to Czernowitz mastered German. But over time, German became the lingua franca of the Bukovinians. According to the 1910 Austrian census, 20% of Bukovina's inhabitants (around 12% Jews and 9% ethnic Germans) declared German to be their mother tongue.[15] But Ukrainians, Romanians and Poles were also fluent in German. The notion of a 'homo bucovinensis' became inextricably linked to the knowledge of the German language,[16] acquiring a 'national' and 'supra-national' character.[17]

Some orthodox Jewish communities and the Bukovinian bastions of Chassidism in Sadagora, Bojan and Vizhnits resisted the process of acculturation and Germanization set in motion by the Imperial administration. After 1848, the *Haskalah* (Jewish Enlightenment) also gained increasing significance in the Bukovina, in particular in Czernowitz. It reinforced the process of acculturation into Austro-German society, especially affecting the Jewish middle class.

---

15 'Die Ergebnisse der Volks- und Viehzählung vom 31. Dezember 1910 im Herzogtum Bukowina', *Mitteilungen des statistischen Landesamtes des Herzogtums Bukowina* 17 (1913), 54, 80.

16 Andrei Corbea-Hoisie, *La Bucovine*; Corbea-Hoisie, 'Czernowitz. Modernisierung an der Schwelle zur Moderne', in *Laboratorien der Moderne. Orte und Räume des Wissens in Mittel- und Osteuropa*, ed. by Bernd Stiegler and Sylwia Werner (Paderborn: Fink, 2016), pp. 133–50.

17 Amy-Diana Colin, 'An den Schnittpunkten der Tradition – Deutsch in der Bukowina', *Neue Deutsche Hefte* 4 (1983), 739–69; and Colin, *Paul Celan. Holograms*, pp. 3–50.

Moreover, in 1867, a new constitution granted Jews full citizenship rights in Austria. The new political developments enabled Jews from the Bukovina, in particular representatives of the middle class, not only to gain civil rights but also to consolidate their economic position and to take an active part in a variety of political, administrative, governmental and educational institutions.[18]

At the end of the nineteenth century and beginning of the twentieth century, Czernowitz had turned into a remarkable cultural metropolis.[19] It had schools for different ethnic groups, hospitals, a major library (opened in 1851), theatres, including the impressive, City Theatre, which still exists today, built by the Viennese architects Hermann Helmer and Ferdinand Fellner in 1904–1905; a *Landesmuseum*; a *Musikverein*; printing and publishing houses; civic buildings in Vienna's Ringstrasse style; and the remarkable Greek Orthodox Episcopal residence designed by Joseph Hlavka from Prague and decorated by historicist painters from Vienna.[20] In 1875, the Franz-Josephs-Universität Czernowitz [University of Czernowitz] was inaugurated. Around 1900, the prosperous and cosmopolitan Czernowitz had electric streetlights (introduced in 1895), a canalization system with water pipes and drainage (begun in 1890), several well-kept parks, a *Kursalon* with a bath house in the Volkspark, beautiful Art Nouveau edifices such as the Savingsbank on the Ringplatz, the German House, a richly adorned train station, the elegant shopping street Herrengasse and residential areas with multilevel buildings in Biedermeier (historicist) and Art Nouveau style. Last but not least, Czernowitz had Viennese-style coffee houses such as Café Europe, described in the ads of the time as the '*rendez-vous* place' of the *haute volée:* high state officials, university professors, representatives of the arts, music and the press, members of the state theatre, physicians and lawyers. Its reading room displayed dozens of different national and international newspapers.

The development of Czernowitz as a city was inextricably linked to its cultural flowering after 1848. The liberalization of the Habsburg monarchy in the

18 Martin Broszat, 'Von der Kulturnation zur Volksgruppe. Die nationale Stellung der Juden in der Bukowina im 19. und 20. Jahrhundert', *Historische Zeitschrift* 200 (1965), 572–605; Michael John and Albert Lichtblau, 'Mythos "deutsche Kultur". Jüdische Gemeinden in Galizien und der Bukowina. Zur unterschiedlichen Ausformung kultureller Identität', in *Studien zur Geschichte der Juden in Österreich*, ed. by Martha Keil and Eleonore Lappin-Eppel (Bodenheim: Philo, 1997), pp. 81–121; Andrei Corbea-Hoisie, *Czernowitzer Geschichten*, pp. 29–42; David Rechter, *Becoming Habsburg: The Jews of Austrian Bukovina 1774–1914* (London: Littman, 2013).

19 For detailed descriptions see: Colin, 'Czernowitz' and Corbea-Hoisie, *Czernowitzer Geschichten.*

20 The Greek Orthodox Episcopal residence was built between 1864 and 1882.

mid–nineteenth century and the relative political independence of the Bukovina enhanced the cultural activities of all ethnic groups and stimulated the flowering of Bukovina's Romanian, Ukrainian, Yiddish and Austro-German literature. Writers and artists gathered in literary societies such as the *Areopag über Schönheit, Kunst und Wissen* [Areopagus for Beauty, Art and Knowledge], the Ukrainian *Ruska Besida* [Ukrainian Tongue] and a Romanian reading circle. The first newspaper, *Bucovina* (1848 – 1850), published by the brothers Hurmuzachi[21] in Romanian and German, featured articles on politics, religion and literature. A few years later, the Austro-German writer Ernst Rudolf Neubauer (1828 – 1890) started the German newspaper *Bukowina. Landes- und Amtszeitung* [*Bukovina. Official State Newspaper*] (1862 – 1868). It printed not only news but also literary, ethnographic and historical texts by Bukovinian writers, including the Romanian Iancu Lupul (1836 – 1922), the Rutheno-Romanian Ludwig Adolf Simiginowicz-Staufe (1831 – 1897) and the Ruthenian Osip Yurii Fed'kovych (1834 – 1888), as well as the Austrian-Jewish author Moritz Amster (1831 – 1903). Bukovinian journalists and writers could publish their texts in newspapers such as *Czernowitzer Zeitung* [*The Czernowitz Newspaper*] (1868 – 1914), *Bukowinaer Rundschau* [*The Bukovinian Review*] (1882 – 1907), *Bukowiner Nachrichten* [*Bukovinian News*] (1888 – 1914), *Bukowiner Post* (1893 – 1914), the *Buchenblätter* (1864, 1870, and 1871), *Czernowitzer Tagblatt* (1903 – 1919) and the *Czernowitzer Allgemeine Zeitung* (1903 – 1940).[22] The Eckhardt publishing house printed the Babylonian Talmud (1839 – 1848), a Bible with standard commentaries (1839 – 1842), the Mishnah (1840 – 1846) and other rabbinical works.

In the last decades of the nineteenth century and at the beginning of the twentieth century, Bukovinian Jews who believed in their Austro-German cultural identity and the benefits of the 'German-Jewish cultural symbiosis' enhanced Austria's 'cultural mission' in Eastern Europe. Moreover, intellectuals from different ethnic groups in the Bukovina identified their notions of 'homo bucovinensis' with 'homo austriacus'. As the Rutheno-Romanian Konstantin Tomaszczuk, rector of the University of Czernowitz, pointed out, Bukovinian scholars and scientists, regardless of their ethnicity, felt deeply rooted in Austrian culture and German *Wissenschaft* because they believed that it had acquired a universal character:

21 Constantin (1811 – 1869), Eudoxiu (1812 – 1874), Gheorghe (1817 – 1882), Alexandru (1823 – 1871) and Nicolae (1826 – 1909) Hurmuzachi.

22 For more information, see: *Prolegomene la un dicționar al presei de limbă germană din Bucovina istorică. 1848 – 1940*, ed. by Andrei Corbea-Hoisie, Ion Lihaciu, Markus Winkler (Jassy: Editura Universității Alexandru Ioan Cuza, 2012).

> German *Wissenschaft* has universal validity. It is only because German culture has universal significance that the non-German sons of the Bukovina establish a German university. [...] We are not just Poles, Germans, Romanians, we are primarily human beings, who are rooted in the same soil, from which we derive our strength. I mean Austria.[23]

The University of Czernowitz played a crucial part in the city's cultural flowering, being the first in the region to offer a programme in Eastern and South-Eastern European history. Among the prominent professors at this university were the historians Ion Nistor and Wladimir Milkowicz, the legal scholar Eugen Ehrlich, founder of the sociology of law, the criminologist Hans Gross, the leading economist Joseph Schumpeter, the mathematician Hans Hahn, member of the Vienna circle, the Slavist Stefan Smal-Stocki, the Germanist Wilhelm Kosch, as well as the philosophers Carl Siegel, who taught traditional idealistic philosophy, and the agnostic Richard Wahle, who opposed metaphysics. The university both motivated and justified interpretations of the Bukovina as an example of middle-European 'exceptionalism'.

Although Austro-German traditions played a crucial role in the Bukovina, in the beginning of the twentieth century, Czernowitz also became a centre of Yiddish education and culture promoted by the Yidisher Schul-Farayn [Yiddish School Union]. As a result, in 1908 the city was selected as the site of the first international Yiddish Language Congress initiated by the scholar Nathan Birnbaum and organized by a New York committee. The conference brought together many eminent Yiddish writers, including Schalom Asch, Hirsch David Nomberg, I. L. Peretz and Abraham Reisen.

World War I put a temporary end to all cultural endeavours in the Bukovina as the region became a battleground and as Russian soldiers occupied Czernowitz three times. During the 4 October 1918 session of the Viennese parliament, the Bukovinian Jewish delegate Benno Straucher (1854–1940) voted for his homeland to join Austria. Ukrainians and their political representatives sought the union of the Bukovina with the Ukraine. There was dissent among Romanian political figures: Constantin Isopescu-Grecul (1871–1938) pleaded for the preservation of Bukovina's bond to Austria, Aurel Onciul (1864–1921) wished to see the region divided along ethnic lines (Ukrainian in the north, Romanian in the south), but Iancu Flondor (1865–1924) and his supporters demanded a union with the Romanian Kingdom. As the tensions between different ethnic groups turned into riots, the Romanian 8th Division entered the Bukovina and incorpo-

23 Cited in Franz H. Riedl, 'Die Universität Czernowitz als völkerverbindende Institution 1875–1919', *Der Donauraum* 15, nos. 3–4 (1970), 216–28; Colin, *Paul Celan. Holograms*, pp. 8–11, 174.

rated it into the Romanian Kingdom.[24] On 10 September 1919, the Treaty of Saint-Germain sanctioned this incorporation, but the Soviet Union rejected it.

Under Romanian rule from 1919 to 1940, the Bukovina and its capital Czernowitz underwent major transformations. Romanian officials occupied all key positions in the administration, and Romanian was declared the official language of the Bukovina. Czernowitz was now once again called Cernăuţi, and its streets received either Romanian translations of their German names or new Romanian names. All emblems recalling the Habsburg era were destroyed. In the 1920s and early 1930s, the Romanian regime was relatively liberal. As a result, Romanian officials remained somewhat receptive to the needs of the various ethnic groups and tolerated existing German, Ukrainian and Jewish schools. Moreover, in 1923, the Romanian regime finally granted Jews citizenship. This new policy was a requirement of the Allied Powers for their acceptance of Romania's territorial expansion after World War I. But in 1924, the Romanian government passed additional laws which caused 80,000 Jews to become stateless. In subsequent years, in particular in the 1930s, the Romanian regime became increasingly nationalistic. In the name of the country's majority, meaning the Romanian 'nation',[25] the regime tried to transform the Bukovina into a monocultural province but did not manage to erase its receptivity to other cultures inherent in the mentality of the Bukovina's inhabitants.

Celan's Czernowitz in the roaring 1920s

In the 1920s and early 1930s, the Bukovina and Cernăuţi re-established their reputation as centres of intense cultural activity.[26] The stars of the Viennese and Berlin theatres came on tour to Cernăuţi. Famous Romanian actors such as Constantin Nottara and Ronald Bulfinski, the tragedians Paul Baratov and Rudolf Schildkraut, as well as the Vilna Troupe, all performed in the capital of the Bukovina. The eminent Jewish actors Hertz Grosbard, Jehuda Ehrenkranz and Leibu Levin gave readings of Yiddish literature. The sculptor Bernard Reder and the painters Oskar Laske and Arthur Kolnik created and exhibited their works in

---

24 As a state Romania had emerged from the Union of the Principalities of Moldavia and Wallachia, a union established in 1859–1862 and later turned into a kindgdom. The Kingdom of Romania (proclaimed in 1881) therefore claimed its historical ownership of the territories belonging to the two principalities.

25 Mariana Hausleitner, *Die Rumänisierung der Bukowina. Die Durchsetzung des nationalstaatlichen Anspruchs Grossrumäniens 1918–1944* (Munich: Oldenbourg, 2001).

26 For more information see: Colin, 'Czernowitz', and Corbea-Hoisie, *Czernowitzer Geschichten*.

the Bukovina. The Jewish philosopher Constantin Brunner had a deep impact on the Bukovinian intellectuals who gathered in the Ethisches Seminar Platonica [the Platonic Seminar on Ethics] for discussions.[27] After World War I, the Expressionist literary and political journal *Der Nerv* (1919)[28] became an organ of Bukovinian intellectuals. The journal's founder was Albert Maurüber, a friend of Martin Buber and an admirer of Karl Kraus, Kurt Hiller and Ludwig Rubiner. Like his models, Maurüber demanded moral integrity in politics, economics, culture, literature and journalism. His later, more radical journal, *Die Gemeinschaft* (1928–1930), fostered both social-democratic ideas and the avant-garde rejection of traditional aesthetics. At the same time, the Yiddish Workers' Cultural Union Morgenroit organized lectures and recitals. The famous fable writer Eliezer Stejnbarg (1880–1932), who moved to the Bukovina in 1919, played a crucial part in promoting Yiddish language and culture. In addition, the Yiddish theatre Chameleon attracted the youth.

But the rise of nationalism and fascism also left its imprint upon Bukovina's literature of the inter-war period. Some of the main representatives of the new generation of Romanian writers – Mircea Streinul, Traian Chelariu and Iulian Vesper – became increasingly nationalistic; Streinul even supported the fascist Legion of Archangel Michael. German ethnic poets such Heinrich Kipper and Alfred Klug were attracted by the 'völkische' ideology, Klug later becoming a Nazi.

At the beginning of the century and during World War I, some Bukovinian writers, artists and scholars who had left the Bukovina became well-known to a broader public: Joseph Gregor, the last librettist of Richard Strauß and author of *Weltgeschichte des Theaters* [*World History of Theatre*] (1933), held key positions in Vienna, including the directorship of the National Library and a professorship at the University of Vienna. Rudolf Kommer, who lived in Vienna, London and later New York, made a name for himself as the author of *Stories from the Vienna Café* (1915) and *Der österreichische Staatsgedanke* [*The Austrian Conception of State*] (1917). Victor Wittner became the editor of the leading Viennese literary journal *Die Bühne* and of the Berlin-based *Der Querschnitt*; he authored collections of poems such as *Klüfte, Klagen, Klärungen* [*Fissures, Lamen-*

---

27 Eli Rottner, *Das ethische Seminar in Czernowitz. Die Wiege des Internationalen Constantin-Brunner-Kreises* (Dortmund: Selbstverlag, 1973). Among his young 'admirers and followers' was Rose Ausländer, see: 'Erinnerungen an eine Stadt', in *Grüne Mutter Bukowina. Ausgewählte Gedichte und Prosa*, ed. by Helmut Braun (Aachen: Rimbaud, 2004), p. 115.

28 *Der Nerv. Eine expressionistische Zeitschrift aus Czernowitz*, ed. by Ernest Wichner and Herbert Wiesner (Berlin: Literaturhaus, 1997). See also: Corbea-Hoisie, *Czernowitzer Geschichten*, pp. 149–84.

tations, Clarifications] (1914) and *Der Sprung auf die Straße* [*Leap onto the Street*] (1924) that anticipated the literary movement that would be called *Neue Sachlichkeit* [New Objectivity]. The poet Alfred Margul-Sperber (1898–1967) had moved to Vienna during World War I, and to Paris and then New York in the early 1920s, but he returned to the Bukovina in 1924. As the editor of the 'Feuilleton' [literary section] of the *Czernowitzer Morgenblatt*, he published Jean Cocteau, Max Jacob, Henri Michaux, Yvan Goll and Guillaume Apollinaire, introducing these and other avant-garde authors of the time to the broader Bukovinian public. Moreover, he promoted Alfred Kittner, Rose Ausländer and Moses Rosenkranz, as well as a much younger generation of poets that included Immanuel Weißglas and Paul Celan.

In the late 1920s and the 1930s, the political situation in Romania changed. The extreme nationalist and anti-Semite Alexandru Constantin Cuza (1857–1947),[29] a professor of economics at the University of Jassy, was spreading hate and anti-Semitism. He did not permit Jewish students to enrol in his classes, demanded a numerus clausus for all Jewish students and incited the anti-Jewish animosity of Christian students. One of Cuza's students, Corneliu Zelea Codreanu (1899–1938), helped spread the anti-Semitic ideology of his teacher. In 1927, Codreanu founded the Legion of the Archangel Michael and later also established its political and paramilitary arm: the notorious Eiserne Garde [Iron Guard] that attacked Jewish communities, assassinated Jews and organized the atrocious pogrom in Bucharest (January 1941). In December 1937, an anti-Semitic and nationalist government under the leadership of the political figure Octavian Goga (1881–1938) came to power in Romania. Goga appointed Cuza as a member of his cabinet. Although the Goga-Cuza government lasted only a few weeks (until 10 February 1938), it changed laws in order to launch a mass persecution of Jews. King Charles (Carol) II ousted this government and implemented his 'royal dictatorship' but did not abolish the anti-Semitic laws.

These political developments affected the Bukovina as well. In the late 1930s, the government tried to force the population of the Bukovina to speak only Romanian in public spaces but could not implement this policy and therefore had to change it within a few weeks. Yet high school teachers had to offer all courses in Romanian, for it had become the only official language of instruction. In 1940, Jewish students were forced out of Romanian public schools. Leftist newspapers published by German-speaking Jews were censored and required

---

29 Together with the historian and writer Nicolae Iorga (1871–1940) he founded the anti-Semitic 'Partidul Naționalist-Democrat' [National Democratic Party] in 1910, but he left it a decade later. In 1923, he established the anti-Semitic 'Liga Apărării Național-Creștine' [League for the Christian National Defence].

to print the front page in Romanian. Moreover, the change in political climate found support among nationalist Romanian and German intellectuals but triggered opposition among the liberal Bukovinians. In reaction to the rise of fascism, Jewish intellectuals increasingly turned towards Zionism, Bundism[30] or Communism.

The political changes left their imprint on the German-Jewish literature of the Bukovina. The increasing isolation of German-speaking Jewish authors in Romanian society manifested itself in their emphasis on social, political, cultural and literary alienation.[31] In addition, the developments also affected Alfred Margul-Sperber's planned publication of an anthology of poems written by Jewish poets from the Bukovina. In the mid-1930s, German publishing houses rejected this book.[32] The Schocken Verlag offered to print it but was closed down prior to realizing the project.[33] By contrast, in 1939, Alfred Klug published his anthology of German poetry from the Bukovina in Nazi Germany. It included poems (with little or no artistic value) exclusively by ethnic German authors.[34]

In 1938–1940, the windows of Norbert Niedermayer's Czernowitz bookstore *Literaria* were still displaying new poetry volumes by Alfred Kittner, Rose Ausländer, Alfred Margul-Sperber, Moses Rosenkranz and David Goldfeld. Their works illustrated an extraordinary flourishing lyrical production in German. Although they were aware of the political changes, Jewish intellectuals, including writers and poets, continued to believe in the Bukovina as a special creative space precisely because the region's Austro-German and Austro-Jewish literature reached its zenith precisely in the inter-war period. In a 1928 series of articles published in the *Czernowitzer Morgenblatt* under the title 'The Invisi-

---

30 Social democratic Jewish labour movement established in the Russian Empire in 1897: Algemeyner Yidisher Arbeter Bund in Liteh, Poyln un Rusland.

31 For further information see: Amy-Diana Colin, 'Einleitung', in *Versunkene Dichtung der Bukowina. Eine Anthologie deutschsprachiger Lyrik*, ed. by Amy-Diana Colin and Alfred Kittner (Munich: Wilhelm Fink Verlag, 1994), pp. 13–24; Andrei Corbea-Hoisie, 'Das Fremde in der Fremde. Zur Typologie einer Literatur des Deutschtums im Ausland', in *Begegnung mit dem Fremden. Akten des VIII. Internationalen Germanisten-Kongresses Tokyo 1990*, ed. by Eijiro Ivasaki and Yoshinori Shichiji (Munich: Iudicium, 1991), pp. 171–78.

32 See: Margul-Sperber's correspondance with editors (1935/36) mentioned in Colin's 'Vorwort', in *Versunkene Dichtung der Bukowina*, pp. 10–11, and George Guțu and Peter Motzan, 'Nachwort', in *Die Buche. Eine Anthologie deutschsprachiger Judendichtung aus der Bukowina. Zusammengestellt von Alfred Margul-Sperber*, ed. by George Guțu, Peter Motzan and Stefan Sienerth (Munich: IKGS, 2009), pp. 425–69. Margul-Sperber's anthology included texts by thirty-two authors from the Bukovina.

33 Colin, 'Vorwort', in *Versunkene Dichtung der Bukowina*, p. 10.

34 *Bukowiner deutsches Dichterbuch*, ed. by Alfred Klug (Stuttgart: Wahl, 1939).

ble Choir'[35] and in a later open letter dated 1930, Alfred Margul-Sperber underlined the *exceptional* flowering of German literature in the Bukovina in spite of its increasing isolation within Romanian surroundings.[36]

Paul Antschel's world of people and books

This political turmoil overshadowed Paul Antschel's childhood and youth.[37] Born into an observant yet acculturated middle class Jewish family, he experienced some of the conflicts marking Jewish communities in the Bukovina even during his childhood. His father, Leo Antschel, a Zionist, insisted that his son leave the Meisler School, a primary school where German was the language of instruction, and enrolled him in the private Hebrew school Safa Ivria. His mother Friederike, whose maiden name was Schrager, taught him German and familiarized him with the Austro-German culture that she cherished. Paul disliked the Safa Ivria and gradually developed a rather ambivalent relationship towards his father. He felt close to his mother and shared her interest in German literature. He left the Safa Ivria after three years, but continued to take Hebrew lessons privately. In the public Romanian high school, Paul further advanced his knowledge of both Romanian and French, while deepening his insight into German literature on his own and in discussions with his friends, who included Edith Horowitz. Paul and Edith fell in love, and it was the very first love for both of them. They shared literary and artistic interests as well as political convictions. Paul was fifteen/sixteen years old when he wrote some of his early poems for Edith. Many years later, Edith Horowitz, later Edith Silbermann (1921–2008),

---

35 Alfred Margul-Sperber, 'Der unsichtbare Chor. Entwurf eines Grundrisses des deutschen Schriftums in der Bukowina' ['The invisible choir. An Outline of German Writing in the Bukovina'], in *Czernowitzer Morgenblatt*, 2 August 1928, p. 6, and 3 August 1928, p. 2.

36 'In the Bukovina, it is precisely now that a branch of the German language becomes creative independently, without any connection to the territories of origin, and within the borders of a strongly assimilationist Greater Romania', wrote Alfred Margul-Sperber in 'Brief an einen Dichter', in *Czernowitzer Morgenblatt*, 21 December 1930, p. 13.

37 For more information see Celan's biographies: Israel Chalfen, *Paul Celan. Eine Biographie seiner Jugend* (Frankfurt a.M.: Suhrkamp, 1983); Chalfen, *Paul Celan. A Biography of His Youth*, trans. by Maximilian Bleyleben (New York: Persea Books, 1991); Wolfgang Emmerich, *Paul Celan* (Hamburg: Rowohlt, 1999); John Felstiner, *Paul Celan. Poet, Survivor, Jew* (New Haven: Yale University Press, 1995); Peter Rychlo, 'Neue Angaben zu Paul Celans Gymnasialjahren aus dem Czernowitzer Bezirksarchiv', in *Kulturlandschaft Bukowina. Studien zur deutschsprachigen Literatur des Buchenlandes nach 1918*, ed. Andrei Corbea, Michael Astner (Iași/Konstanz: Editura Universității/Hartung-Gorre 1990), pp. 205–210.

wrote about their life-long friendship and published their correspondence.[38] Paul and Edith's mutual friends included his classmate Gustav (called Gustl) Chomed, his cousin Erich Einhorn and Immanuel Weißglas, nicknamed Oniu, a talented poet and translator. Oniu was sixteen when he made a name for himself through his translation of Mihai Eminescu's poem 'Luceafărul'. In Czernowitz, Paul and Oniu were inseparable. They shared a passion for German literature and competed with one another by writing poems on similar themes.[39]

Paul and the friends of his youth were avid readers. Edith's home with her father's fantastic private library became a magnet for the young poets and their friends. Karl Horowitz, Edith's father, was a bibliophile who had studied German, Greek and Latin at the University of Vienna and had brought his large book collection from Vienna to Czernowitz when he decided to resettle in his hometown in 1920. Edith described his library as a 'Fundgrube' [a treasure chest] for the young poet Antschel. He spent many hours in Karl's home in order to read and to discuss poetry with him and Edith. Many decades later, in October 1964, in his handwritten dedication for Karl Horowitz on the first page of the volume *Mohn und Gedächtnis*, Celan wrote: 'For Karl Horowitz, in grateful memory of his house, his books, and everything which is still present.'[40] Karl Horowitz had introduced him to works by Eduard Mörike, Theodor Storm, Conrad Ferdinand Meyer, Gottfried Keller, Jakob Wassermann and Leonhard Frank. He awakened Paul Antschel's enthusiasm for both Middle High German and Expressionist poetry. They spent hours reading poems together by Klabund, Georg Heym and Georg Trakl. He also sparked Paul's interest in Hermann Hesse, whose

38 *Paul Celan – Edith Silbermann. Zeugnisse einer Freundschaft. Gedichte, Briefwechsel, Erinnerungen*, ed. by Amy-Diana Colin and Edith Silbermann (Munich: Wilhelm Fink Verlag, 2010), henceforth abbreviated as *Paul Celan – Edith Silbermann*; Edith Silbermann, *Czernowitz – Stadt der Dichter. Geschichte einer jüdischen Familie aus der Bukowina (1900–1948)*, ed. by Amy-Diana Colin (Paderborn: Wilhelm Fink, 2015). From the early 1960s to almost the end of her life, Edith Silbermann, an acclaimed actress, gave numerous recitals of Celan's poetry, mostly in Germany and Austria, but also in The Netherlands, France, Israel and the United States. She also set his poem 'Espenbaum' to music and performed it time and again.

39 Edith Silbermann, *Begegnung mit Paul Celan. Erinnerung und Interpretation* (Aachen: Rimbaud, 1993, 1995), pp. 41–70; Silbermann, *Czernowitz – Stadt der Dichter*, pp. 91–93; Ilana Shmueli, *Ein Kind aus guter Familie. Czernowitz 1924–1944*, ed. by Andrei Corbea-Hoisie (Aachen: Rimbaud, 2006), pp. 46, 74.

40 'Für Karl Horowitz, in dankbarer Erinnerung an sein Haus, seine Bücher, an vieles noch immer Gegenwärtiges', in *Czernowitz – Stadt der Dichter*, ed. by Colin, pp. 248–58.

later wife Ninon Ausländer, the daughter of a renowned lawyer in Czernowitz, was Karl's classmate and childhood friend.[41]

Among the older friends who played a key part in Antschel's youth was Jacob Silbermann (1907–1979), a known Czernowitz lawyer and the co-author of a timely study,[42] detailing legal strategies for Jews to prove their claims to Romanian citizenship at a time when the anti-Semitic regime was contesting them. Silbermann had a large book and record collection, including disks with readings by Alexander Moissi and Karl Kraus, whom he greatly admired. Silbermann introduced his younger friend Antschel to Hugo von Hofmannsthal's *Chandos-Brief* [*Chandos Letter*] and engaged in discussions with him about the critique of language prevalent in 1900. It was Silbermann who gave Antschel the idea to change his name, drawing his attention to the importance of the aura of a writer's name and arguing that nobody would have remembered the name 'Gundelfinger', whereas 'Gundolf' entered literary history. In subsequent years, Silbermann would help Antschel time and again.

Since the age of fifteen or sixteen, Paul Antschel had been a great admirer of Hölderlin and Rilke, one of the 'cult authors' in Czernowitz. Paul frequently entertained his friends by reading to them Rilke's *Cornett*, his poems from *Stundenbuch* and *Buch der Bilder* as well as *Sonette an Orpheus*. Moreover, he shared his friends' interest in Manfred Hausmann's novel *Lampion küsst Mädchen und kleine Birken* (1928) and his dramatic ballad *Lilofee* (1929). Knut Hamsun's novel *Mysterien* [*Mysteries*] (1982), cherished by Edith and the Czernowitz youth, also had a deep impact on the poet. In school, students read Victor Hugo and Alfred de Vigny, but Celan and his friend Oniu (Immanuel) Weißglas were passionate about Paul Verlaine, Stéphane Mallarmé and Guillaume Apollinaire.[43] At that time, Paul Antschel also read W. B. Yeats, Rupert Brook and Shakespeare, whom he greatly admired. In her memoirs, Edith Silbermann recalls that he loved to recite Ophelia's and Julia's parts. Antschel's world of books also included Yiddish literature, in particular Eliezer Stejnbarg's innovative fables.[44] Gustav Chomed, in a letter to Edith Silbermann, underlined that Paul not only read

---

41 Ninon and Karl, both teenagers, were Hesse fans. Ninon was so fascinated by Hesse's first novel *Peter Camenzind* (1904) that she sent him a letter which marked the beginning of their friendship. See: Gisela Kleine, *Ninon und Hermann Hesse: Leben als Dialog* (Sigmaringen: Thorbecke, 1982).

42 Nicu Adelstein, Jacob Silbermann, *Comentarul la Decretul-Lege pentru Reviziunea Cetățeniei* (Commentary to the Decree Law Regarding the Revision of Citizenship), prefaced by Eugen Herovanu (Czernowitz: Tipografia şi Editura Eminescu, 1939).

43 Silbermann, *Czernowitz – Stadt der Dichter*, pp. 88–99.

44 *Paul Celan – Edith Silbermann*, pp. 29–30.

Stejnbarg's fables to him, but also performed them. Paul's friends nourished his interest in Yiddish. Antschel's new love, Ruth Kraft (1916–1998), aspired to become a Jewish actress. Edith, who remained a close friend, pursued a similar objective, later becoming the star of the Yiddish theatre in Bucharest. Their mutual friend Hersch Segal (1905–1982) co-edited the Yiddish poetry collections *Naje Jidise Dichtung. Klejne Antologie* (1934) and *Zeks Shloflider* (1939).

In the 1930s, Antschel and his Jewish friends were in a vulnerable position, for they were confronted with growing anti-Semitism. 'Well, regarding anti-Semitism in our school, I could write a book three hundred pages thick', remarked Antschel in 1934.[45] He moved to another school, originally a Ukrainian gymnasium, attended by Jewish students. Similar to his friends, Antschel became deeply aware of his Jewishness. He witnessed repressive anti-Jewish measures such as the closure of Morgenroit[46] and Jewish efforts to organize self-defence groups against the anti-Semitic excesses that often turned bloody. Yet unlike his own father, Moshe Barash[47] and other Czernowitz youth, he did not embrace Zionism. Rather, when he was just a high-school student, he joined the illegal communist youth organization in the Bukovina. Although there were severe reprisals against communist activities, Antschel and his friends secretly brought out a leftist pamphlet, *Elevul Roșu* [*The Red Student*], and distributed it among high-school students and workers. It included Paul Antschel's Romanian translations of passages from Marxist writings and texts about the situation of the working class. Among these young political activists were Paul, Edith and Gustav, as well as Ilse Goldmann (1921–1983) and Ruth Kissmann (1921–1999); the latter was the daughter of Leah and Joseph Kissmann, the founders of Morgenroit. Time and again they met in Ilse's home in order to read and discuss Marx's *Capital*, the *Communist Manifesto* and Bucharin's *ABC*. They later shared an interest in Rosa Luxemburg, Karl Kautsky, Werner Sombart, Gustav Landauer and Kropotkin. But after reading André Gide's *Retouches à mon Retour de l'U.R.S.S.* (1937), they started to have doubts about their previous political convictions.[48]

---

45 Cited after Chalfen, *Paul Celan*, p. 51

46 Joseph Kissman, 'Zur Geschichte der jüdischen Arbeiterbewegung "Bund" in der Bukowina', in *Geschichte der Juden in der Bukowina*, ed. Hugo Gold, 2 vols (Tel Aviv: Olamenu, 1958, 1962), vol. I, pp. 143–44.

47 'Moshe Barash über Paul Celan. Interview von Cord Barkhausen', in *Sprache und Literatur in Wissenschaft und Unterricht* 55 (1985), 93–107.

48 *Paul Celan – Edith Silbermann*, pp. 33–37.

In *Ein Kind aus guter Familie. Czernowitz 1924–1944* (2006),[49] Liane Schindler, later Ilana Shmueli (1924–2011), describes her first encounters with the poet in Czernowitz. Looking back at her childhood, she notes that Bukovina's Jewish middle class engaged in a 'Kultur-Kult'.[50] She criticizes its artificiality, saying that it was based on a mimicry of Western European, in particular Viennese models. But she also recounts how the Bukovinian desire to be 'exceptional' and 'different' by striving to be educated and to meet 'high intellectual standards' became the source of an 'unusual and remarkable personal development'[51] for some Bukovinians.

In 1938, Antschel graduated from high school. Under the influence of his parents, he decided to study medicine. But Czernowitz did not have a medical school. After Hitler's rise to power and the Nazi occupation of Austria, Jewish parents sent their sons and daughters to French universities, for they believed that the French republic was an undeniable pillar of democracy. Antschel's parents followed their example and Paul enrolled in a pre-medical programme at the University of Tours. On 8 November 1938, on his journey from Czernowitz to Paris, he passed through Nazi Germany and stopped for a change of trains at the station Anhalter Bahnhof in Berlin. In a letter to Edith written and mailed that day, he describes the smoke hovering over the beech tree woods and asks whether it was the smoke of books or perhaps of people set on fire.[52]

In Tours, Antschel studied not only medicine but also French surrealism. When he returned from Tours to Czernowitz in the summer of 1939, he had read Breton's *Manifesto* and was familiar with avant-garde literary experiments. With the advent of World War II, he could no longer return to Tours and he remained in Czernowitz.

In Soviet Czernowitz (1940–1941)

On 26 June 1940, the Soviet Union, following the Molotov-Ribbentrop Pact (a non-aggression pact with Nazi Germany), issued an ultimatum demanding that Romania cede Bessarabia and the northern Bukovina, including Czernowitz, within forty-eight hours. Two days later, the Red Army occupied the territories. Some Romanians, in particular administrators and other officials, fled to the

49 Shmueli, *Ein Kind*. In Israel, she met Celan once again, and their later romantic relationship inspired some of his late poems.
50 Ibid., p. 9.
51 Ibid., p. 10.
52 *Paul Celan – Edith Silbermann*, p. 38.

southern Bukovina. As the Romanian troops withdrew, they attacked Jewish communities, robbing and murdering many Jews in the southern Bukovina. On 1 July 1940, they organized a terrible pogrom in the city of Dorohoi (northern Romania).

At first, politically left-oriented intellectuals and many Jews in the northern region welcomed the Soviet occupation because it marked an end to the anti-Semitic Romanian regime.[53] But the realities of the regime soon became apparent. The Soviets took over every aspect of life in the northern Bukovina. Following the agreement between the Soviet Union and Nazi Germany, Germans from both the northern and southern Bukovina returned to the German Reich, leaving behind everything they had worked for during the past decades. By November 1940, these returnees numbered almost 80,000.[54] At the same time, special units of the NKVD implemented 'Sovietization' through expropriation and nationalization. Their main targets were the alleged 'enemies of the people': former businessmen, landowners, politicians, journalists, activists of the associations, national parties, Zionist organizations and potential opponents, including leftist intellectuals and social democrats. In addition, northern Bukovina and Czernowitz underwent a process of Russification: streets were given Russian names, monuments were replaced, and the theatre only presented performances in either Russian or Ukrainian. German-speaking newspapers, mostly published by Jews, had to close. Only Soviet publications were accessible and available. The Soviets also reorganized the school system and the university. Russian became the sole language of instruction and the ideological indoctrination of students the main goal of most teachers.[55] Since the Soviets regarded Yiddish as the 'national' language of the Jews, they funded a Yiddish theatre and permitted Yiddish cultural and educational activities, but they prohibited Zionist organizations and religious schools such as the Cheder.

In this period, Paul Antschel, Erich Einhorn and Gustav Chomed were studying at the University of Czernowitz. Paul focused on French literature,[56] since he wished to obtain a degree in Romance language and literature, but he also learned Russian. As his later correspondence with his friend Erich shows, he

---

53 Silbermann, *Czernowitz – Stadt der Dichter*, pp. 126–27.

54 The movement back to the 'Reich' also included Germans from Southern Bukovina, see: Mariana Hausleitner, *'Viel Mischmasch mitgenommen'. Die Umsiedlungen aus der Bukowina 1940* (Berlin: De Gruyter Oldenbourg, 2018).

55 Manfred Reifer, *Menschen und Ideen. Erinnerungen* (Tel Aviv: Olympia, 1952), pp. 222–37; Alfred Kittner, *Erinnerungen 1906–1991*, ed. by Edith Silbermann (Aachen: Rimbaud, 1996), pp. 47–54; Shmueli, *Ein Kind*, pp. 69–72.

56 Chalfen, *Paul Celan*, pp. 94–95.

shared a strong interest in Russian poetry, in particular in Sergei A. Yesenin.[57] It was at that time that he also translated Shakespeare's sonnets into German.

In September 1940, General Ion Antonescu came to power in Romania. He forced King Charles II to abdicate in favour of his son Mihai. The young King Mihai I became a marionette in the hands of the fascist dictator, who had absolute power and proclaimed himself as Romania's state leader ('Conducător al Statului'). Antonescu included members of the Iron Guard in his newly established government, but a few months later, in January 1941, they staged a rebellion against him. Antonescu crushed it and consolidated his relationship with Nazi Germany. Under his leadership, Romania joined the Axis powers that were planning to attack the Soviet Union.

As war loomed, the NKVD organized massive deportations of all potentially 'hostile' elements in sealed train cars to Siberia; among the deportees were thousands of Romanians, Ukrainians and Jews, along with their families.[58] At the same time, in the summer of 1941, the Soviets withdrew from the Bukovina and Bessarabia. Political events separated Paul, Erich and Gustav, but their friendship lasted a lifetime. Gustav and Erich, along with other students, were evacuated, sent to the Soviet Union and drafted into the Red Army. Paul Antschel remained in Czernowitz. After the war, in Vienna, Paul met Erich once again, who was working as a translator for the Soviet militaries.[59] Later, when Erich was back in the Soviet Union, Celan corresponded with him and immortalized his friend's family name in the poem 'Schibboleth': 'Einhorn: du weißt um die Steine'.[60] Like Erich, Gustav – who served in a Soviet storm battalion and was the one to identify Joseph Goebbels's corpse in the bunker of the Berlin Reichskanzlei – became a translator for the Soviet military at the Nuremberg trials. After his return to the Soviet Union, he also corresponded with Celan. 'I need your letters', wrote Celan to Gustav, and this powerful statement summarized Celan's relationship to Gustav and other friends from his youth.[61]

57 See: *Paul Celan – Erich Einhorn. Einhorn: du weißt um die Steine... Briefwechsel*, ed. by Marina Dmitrieva-Einhorn (Berlin: Friedenauer Presse, 2001); 'Paul Celan-Erich Einhorn: Briefe', ed. Dmitrieva-Einhorn, *Celan-Jahrbuch*, ed. by Hans-Michael Speier, 7 (1997/1998), 23–49.

58 Manfred Reifer, 'Geschichte der Juden in der Bukowina (1919–1944)' in *Geschichte der Juden in der Bukowina*, ed. Hugo Gold, vol. 2, p. 13; Stefan Purici, 'Represiunile sovietice în regiunea Cernăuţi (anii '40–'50 ai secolului al XX-lea)', *Analele Bucovinei* 2 (2001), 249–68.

59 Erich Einhorn served as an interpreter for the Soviet military in Berlin (1945–1946) and Vienna (1946–1949). He returned and remained in the Soviet Union.

60 Celan, GW5, vol. I, pp. 131–132. See also footnote 57.

61 See: *Paul Celan – Gustav Chomed: 'Ich brauche Deine Briefe'. Der Briefwechsel*, ed. by Jürgen Köchel and Barbara Wiedemann (Frankfurt a.M.: Suhrkamp, 2010). In 1972, Gustav immigrated with his family to Israel.

During the Holocaust (1941–1944)

On 22 June 1941, without making a declaration of war, the Axis powers launched an attack on the Soviet Union in order to annihilate it. In the notorious Operation Barbarossa, as Hitler and the Nazis called it, the Axis powers deployed four million men. The 11th Wehrmacht (with 100,000 soldiers) and the III and IV Romanian Army (with 200,000 soldiers) conquered the northern Bukovina and Bessarabia. The Nazi Einsatzgruppe D (mobile killing squads), led by SS Standartenführer Otto Ohlendorf, marched into the Bukovina in their wake. Einsatzgruppe D (comprising 600 men) controlled five Sonderkommandos (subgroups with a total of 3,000 men). The main objective of these paramilitary death squads was the mass murder of Jews.[62] In cooperation with Romanian soldiers as well as anti-Semitic followers ranging from gangs to neighbours, the perpetrators plundered, tortured and massacred the Jewish population of the Bukovina.

On 8 July 1941, the fascist dictator Ion Antonescu decided to 'cleanse' the Bukovina of Jews. On 4 October 1941, he issued an order to deport all Jews from the Bukovina to Transnistria, an area located between the rivers Dnjestr (west) and Bug (east) as well as between the northern border of the Hotin district and the Black Sea (south-west). Based on a treaty between Hitler and Antonescu, the region was placed under Romanian administration. From 9 to 13 October 1941, thus within just four days, the large majority of Bukovina's Jewish population was deported to Transnistria.[63] By the summer of 1942, German Nazis and Romanian fascists had deported 96,135 Jews from the Bukovina and the district of Dorohoi.[64]

When Czernowitz was occupied on July 5, the Einsatzkommando 10b, Romanian soldiers and policemen, Ukrainian volunteers and even local residents plundered Jewish homes and shops, raped Jewish women and massacred Jews. Within the next few days, 3,000 Jews were arrested, including Jewish dignitaries. Rabbi Abraham Mark, two cantors and the synagogue caretaker were forced into the shaft of the elevator in the hotel 'Der schwarze Adler' [The Black Eagle]. On 9 July 1941, the fascist perpetrators drove them along with 600 Jews to the River Pruth and shot them there. According to Mayor Traian Popovici, about 2,000 Czernowitz Jews were murdered in July. The count of the Jew-

62 Following Hitler's order, Himmler established four Einsatzgruppen and several Sonderkommandos. Genocide was their only objective.

63 Jean Ancel, *The History of the Holocaust in Romania*, trans. by Yaffah Murciano, ed. by Leon Volovici with the assistance of Miriam Caloianu (Lincoln: Nebraska University Press, Jerusalem: Yad Vashem, 2011), pp. 289–91.

64 Ibid., pp. 544, 559.

ish community was considerably higher. On 1 August 1941, the Einsatzgruppe D arrived in Czernowitz, murdering 682 Jews in one day.

Following the fascist occupation of Czernowitz in July, Jews were deprived of their civil rights; their movements in the city was restricted; synagogues and Jewish schools were closed; banks and post offices were barred from delivering money to Jews; and Jewish shops, businesses and factories were 'romanianized'. In September 1941, German Nazis and Romanian fascist forced about 50,000 Jews into a ghetto surrounded by a three-metre-high fence and guarded by Romanian gendarmes and regular soldiers. Following an order by dictator Ion Antonescu, on 11 October 1941, German Nazis and Romanian fascists began deporting Jews from the Czernowitz ghetto in cattle wagons to the ghettos, forced labour camps and the death camps in Transnistria. By mid-November, 28,391 Jews from Czernowitz had been deported in cattle wagons to Transnistria.

Traian Popovici, Mayor of Czernowitz, rescued about 17,000 Jewish citizens by convincing the dictator Ion Antonescu and his collaborator Mihai Antonescu, the Vice-President of the Council of Ministers, to exempt so-called 'economically useful' Jews from deportation. Several thousand Jews received exemption permits signed by the Romanian general Corneliu Calotescu. They could return to their homes, which they often found looted or destroyed. When the trains could no longer run owing to the harsh winter, those who had remained in the ghetto were also permitted to leave it. Mayor Popovici issued them his own exemption permits. At the start of the following year, the Mayor lost his power. When the deportations to Transnistria resumed in March and April 1942, Jews holding exemption permits signed by the Mayor were among the 4,700 to 5,000 deportees.

In Transnistria, Jews were forced into ghettos, hard labour camps or death camps. Thousands died due to starvation, forced marches, their brutal treatment by Romanian gendarmes and Ukrainian auxiliary troops, typhoid fever and other epidemics, or were murdered by the perpetrators. In some areas under Romanian administration, Jews had a slim chance of survival. But on the other side of the river Bug, German Nazis controlled the regions. They murdered Jews right away or as soon as they could longer work. According to a German-Romanian agreement, all Jewish deportees to Transnistria were supposed to be sent to German controlled territories on the other side of the river Bug. At the end of the war, the Jews who were able to remain in Czernowitz and about 35,000 Jewish deportees to Transnistria survived.[65]

---

65 Jean Ancel, *Contribuții la istoria României. Problema evreiască*, trans. by Carol Bines (Bucharest: Hasefer, 2001), vol. I.2, pp. 111–99, 230–77; and the vol. II.1.

Following the occupation of Czernowitz by Romanian troops in July 1941, the Antschel family, who had decided – in the spite of the foreseeable dangers – to remain in Czernowitz, lived through the nightmare experienced there by the Jewish population: robberies, assassinations, racial laws similar to those of Nazi Germany, the forced wearing of the yellow star and the evacuation to the ghetto. The Anschel family escaped the deportations to Transnistria in the autumn of 1941 and received Traian Popovici's exemption permits. Like so many other Jews, Antschel's parents believed that the Mayor had adequately protected them, but their son recognized the looming danger. On the night of 28 June 1942, Paul had a disagreement with his father regarding their safety. He begged his parents to go into hiding, but they stayed. Paul left them, finding shelter in the home of Karl Horowitz, who held Calotescu permits.[66] When Paul returned to his parental apartment next morning, it was boarded up. Like many other Jews, his parents had been deported in a cattle wagon to Ataki in Bessarabia and thereafter to Moghilev in Transnistria. From Moghilev they were sent to Schmerinka, then to the camp of Ladijin on the bank of the Bug River, in an area controlled by the Romanian administration. In August, they were deported to Michailowka, an even more horrible camp in an area occupied by German troops. In the autumn of 1942, Leo Antschel either died of typhus or was killed by the guards because he could no longer work. Antschel's mother Friederike was shot dead, in the neck.[67]

When the deportations from Czernowitz stopped, all Jewish men who had escaped them, including Paul Antschel, were sent to forced labour camps in Romania, where they shovelled stones and built roads. 'I have seen life exchanged for utmost bitterness',[68] he wrote from the labour camp in Tăbăreşti (Southern Moldavia) on 2 August 1942. In spite of it all, he continued to write poems in German, sending some of his love poems to Ruth Kraft, who had managed to remain in Czernowitz.

---

66 See: Silbermann, *Czernowitz – Stadt der Dichter*, pp. 153–55.

67 In a letter dated 1 July 1944 and sent from Kiev to his friend Erich Einhorn, Paul Antschel writes that his parents were deported to and murdered in Krasnopolska on the river Bug. Paul Antschel's letter to Erich Einhorn, in Emmerich, *Paul Celan*, p. 46 and in *Paul Celan – Erich Einhorn*, *Celan-Jahrbuch* 7 (1997/1998), 23–24. According to some survivors, Leo Antschel, Celan's father, perished in a camp or area near Gaissin, and Friederike Antschel, the poet's beloved mother, was murdered in Michailowka. Definitive information regarding the places of their murder is still missing.

68 Chalfen, *Paul Celan. Eine Biographie*; John Felstiner, 'Paul Celan. The Strain of Jewishness', *Commentary* (April 1985), 44–53.

In December 1942, Romanian officials permitted Paul to visit Czernowitz and again stayed at the house of Edith's parents. In February 1944, the Romanian labour camp was closed down owing to the harsh winter storms, and Paul was allowed to return to Czernowitz. Upon his arrival, his friends Jacob Silbermann and Hersch Segal[69] presented him with a special gift: a bound edition of his early poetry. It contained ninety-nine poems which they had collected. Since paper was a scarce item during the war, they were able to produce only three copies. When the poet returned to Czernowitz from the forced labour camp in February 1944, they gave him this volume. It was their way of encouraging him to continue to write poetry.[70]

In Soviet Czernowitz again

In March 1944, the Red Army re-conquered the northern Bukovina, but the southern Bukovina remained under Romanian control. The Soviets were preparing a massive attack on Romania. On 23 August 1944, King Mihai I, supported by a coalition of members of the Romanian historical political parties, the Communist Party and the military, ousted the fascist dictator Ion Antonescu, had him arrested along with Mihai Antonescu and publicly announced that Romania had joined the Allied forces. A few days later, Soviet troops marched into Romania and its capital. For decades, the country was to remain within the Soviet sphere of influence.

The response of Bukovinian Jews to the Soviet of occupation was mixed. On the one hand, they were grateful because the Red Army had saved them from extermination, but, on the other hand, they had not forgotten the harshness of the Soviet regime during its first occupation of the city in 1940–1941. They feared new food shortages, the Soviet rejection of the free practice of religion, forced conscription either to the army or to work detachments in the coalmines of the Donbas, and further persecutions. After 23 August 1944, many Jews from the northern Bukovina (around 12,000 people) therefore defied all dangers and illegally crossed the border into Romania.[71]

---

69 Decades later, Segal was the first to publish a collection of poems entitled *Blütenlese* (1976) by Selma Meerbaum-Eisinger (1924–1942), Celan's talented cousin, regarded today as the second Anne Frank.

70 For more information about this first volume, later called *Typoskript 1944*, see: *Paul Celan – Edith Silbermann*, pp. 234–38.

71 Mordechai Altshuler, 'The Soviet "Transfer" of Jews from Chernovtsy Province to Romania', *Jews in Eastern Europe* 2 (1998), 54–75.

In the autumn of 1944, the University of Czernowitz reopened. Antschel enrolled in its English programme while simultaneously working as a nurse in a psychiatric clinic under the directorship of Pinkas Meyer, the brother-in-law of Hersch Segal. According to Paul Antschel's own statements, at the start of July 1944, he was part of a medical team sent to Kiev.[72] Upon his return, he wrote the poem 'Nähe der Gräber'. At that time, he also created his own collection of early poems, recording them in his beautiful handwriting in a small booklet. At the start of 1945, Ruth Kraft had the opportunity to leave Soviet Czernowitz for Romania, crossing the border illegally in the disguise of a Red Cross nurse. Paul Antschel gave her his collection of poems, asking her to bring it to Alfred Margul-Sperber, the 'Doyen of Bukovina's Literature', who was in Bucharest. Antschel hoped that Margul-Sperber would help him to publish his poems. Many years after Celan's death, Ruth Kraft published this booklet with a facsimile in *Gedichte 1938–1944*.[73]

The Soviet regime distrusted Romanians because their country had been an ally of Nazi Germany. As a result, the Soviet authorities decided to permit former holders of Romanian citizenship to repatriate to Romania. There was no official information, but in early spring of 1945 rumours spread in Czernowitz letting people know the locations of makeshift offices that would accept requests for repatriation.[74] It was difficult and costly to obtain such permissions, but many Jews used the opportunity to leave for Romania, hoping to continue their travel to Western Europe, Palestine or the United States. By the end of April 1945, the borders were closed again but reopened in the summer to let other former Romanian citizens repatriate, this policy change being attributed to an intervention by Nikita Khrushchev, head of the Ukrainian Communist Party at the time.[75] By April 1946, about 22,307 people from Czernowitz officially crossed the border to Romania.[76]

Antschel also tried to leave Soviet Czernowitz, but he had no means to pay the authorities for a permit and to purchase a ticket. In spite of his own financial hardship, Jacob Silbermann gave Antschel the necessary financial support. To-

---

72 Celan's reference to this trip in his letter to Erich Einhorn, Emmerich, *Paul Celan*, p. 33. See also: Marc Sagnol, 'Celan, les eaux du Boug', *Temps Modernes* 690 (2016), 1–27.

73 Celan, *Gedichte 1938–1944* (Frankfurt a.M.: Suhrkamp, 1985).

74 Vadim Altskan, 'The Closing Chapter. Northern Bukovinian Jews 1944–1946', *Yad Vashem Studies* 2/43 (2015), 51–81; Silbermann, *Czernowitz – Stadt der Dichter*, pp. 185–87.

75 Altskan, Ibid.

76 Jean Ancel, 'The New Jewish Invasion – The Return of the Survivors from Transnistria', in *The Jews are Coming Back. The Return of the Jews to Their Countries of Origin After WW II*, ed. by David Banker (New York/Oxford: Berghahn, 2005), pp. 231–56; Altskan, Ibid., pp. 51–81.

gether they boarded the train to Romania. After crossing the border, Antschel continued to Bucharest, while Jacob Silbermann went to meet his family and Edith Horowitz, who had left the Soviet Bukovina via a different route. Rose Ausländer, Alfred Kittner and Immanuel Weißglas were also able to leave the Soviet Bukovina. In Bucharest, the Czernowitz friends reunited. Their life in the Romanian capital was overshadowed by economic and financial hardships as well as the threats of the looming Stalinist-style dictatorship. In spite of his own precarious situation, Silbermann stood by his young friend Ancel (alias Antschel) when he became ill.[77] In 1947, Paul Ancel managed to leave Romania, crossing the border illegally into Hungary and continuing his journey to Vienna. A few months later, he left for Paris, which became the poet's new adopted home. Margul-Sperber wrote letters of introduction to Otto Basil in Vienna and Yvan Goll in Paris, drawing their attention to Antschel's talent.[78] Margul-Sperber, who had become Ancel's mentor, tried to open doors for him in the 'Golden West', as Eastern Europeans under the communist dictatorship called Western European democracies. But in Vienna and Paris, the poet was once again confronted with the harshness of émigré life. When he finally succeeded in making a name for himself as a German-speaking Jewish poet, unjustified accusations of plagiarism and anti-Semitic attacks darkened his life. Looking back, the world of 'people and books' experienced in Czernowitz acquired a new sense and significance for him.

---

77 When Antschel contracted a life-threatening disease in Bucharest and had no means to pay for medical treatment, it was again Silbermann who gave him the funding for the urgently needed medical care. When Edith and Jacob Silbermann finally succeeded in leaving Romania, Celan reciprocated their help. In the early 1960s, the friends met again in Düsseldorf, and Celan bitterly complained about the libel campaign against him. Silbermann, a lawyer, offered to help Celan. But the poet did not wish to pursue legal action. In a phone call to Silbermann in the spring of 1970, Celan asked him whether he could come to Paris. Shortly thereafter, Edith and Jacob Silbermann learned of his suicide. See: Silbermann, *Begegnung mit Paul Celan*, pp. 68–69; Jacob Silbermann's correspondence with Celan appeared in *Paul Celan – Edith Silbermann*, pp. 253–64.

78 For more information about other Czernowitz friends and classmates see: Silbermann, *Czernowitz – Stadt der Dichter*, pp. 85–196. Among them were Marcel Pohne (1913–1964), who later became a journalist working for the *Deutsche Welle*, and the poet Alfred Gong (1920–1981), a classmate, but not a close friend. In Czernowitz, Antschel also met and engaged in a dialogue with Rose Ausländer (1901–1988) and Alfred Kittner (1906–1991).

II Other 'meridians'

Translation as cultural mediation

One of the main characteristics of Bukovina's multilingual literature was the receptiveness of its representatives towards various cultures and their strong interest in different languages. In the nineteenth century, poets and prose writers like Ludwig Adolf Simiginowicz-Staufe (1831–1897) wrote in Romanian, Ruthenian and German; Osip Yurii Fed'kovych (1834–1888) in German and Ruthenian; Olha J. Kobylanska (1836–1942) in German and Ukrainian; and Eliazar Ladier (1873–1932) and Manfred Winkler (1922–2014) in German and Hebrew. Klara Blum (1904–1971) integrated motifs from Romanian, Russian and Chinese literature into her novels and poems written in German.

Interest in foreign languages and an openness towards other cultures motivated their activities as translators. Joseph Kalmer (1899–1959) published his translations of poems from thirty-three different languages into German in his *Anthologie Europäischer Lyrik der Gegenwart, 1900–1925, in Nachdichtungen* [*Anthology of Contemporary European Poetry, 1900–1925, in Adaptations*] (1927), while Alfred Margul-Sperber translated poems by Robert Frost, Nicholas Vachel Lindsay, Wallace Stevens, Edna St. Vincent Millay and e.e. cummings, as well as Native American texts, into German. He was the first German translator of Guillaume Apollinaire's *Calligrammes*, T.S. Eliot's *The Waste Land* and Gérard de Nerval's works. Many years after the war, in Bucharest, Immanuel Weißglas translated Grillparzer's *Der arme Spielmann*, Stifter's *Nachsommer* and both parts of Goethe's *Faust* into Romanian, a remarkable achievement considering the poet's native tongue was German.

Already in Czernowitz, Paul Celan translated into German some of Shakespeare's sonnets and poems by A. E. Housman, W. B. Yeats, Rupert Brooke, Sergei A. Yesenin and Guillaume Apollinaire. In Bucharest, he continued his work as translator for the publishing house The Russian Book. In Paris, Celan taught courses on translation at the École Normale Supérieure and produced a considerable number of German adaptations of Romanian, Hebrew, French, Russian, English, Portuguese and Italian poems. Among the authors translated by Celan were Alexander Blok, Emily Dickinson, Stéphane Mallarmé, Osip Mandelstam, Fernando Pessoa, Arthur Rimbaud, William Shakespeare, Giuseppe Ungaretti, Paul Valéry and Sergei A. Yesenin – to name just a few. Celan's 'Nachdichtungen' disclosed his interpretations of the texts whose meanings he carried over into his own world of thought, while simultaneously leading readers into the poetic universe of these different authors. In this respect, Celan continued a Bukovinian tradition of translation as cultural mediation.

Celan's multilingual German

The impact of Austro-German culture upon the multi-ethnic sociotope Bukovina was so strong that Ukrainian, Romanian and Jewish poets wrote in German prior to turning to their own native tongues. In the nineteenth century, the Ukrainian writers Osip Yurii Fed'kovych, Isidor Felix Niemchevski, Alexander Popovych and Isidor Vorobkevych composed their first poems in German. Under the impact of rising nationalism, they turned to their native tongue. Olga Kobylanska, a major Ukrainian author, wrote her diary and first novella in German. The Romanian poet Iancu Lupul and his brother Theodor Lupul chose German as their poetic idiom and wrote all their works in German.

Prior to the Holocaust, the fascination with and love for the German language was a main characteristic of Jewish writers and poets from the Bukovina. These authors from Karl Emil Franzos to Alfred Margul-Sperber and Moses Rosenkranz made a substantial contribution to the flowering of Bukovina's Austro-German literature. Most of them displayed a strong preference for traditional means of poetic expression and forms. Like his model Karl Kraus, a master of the German language, Alfred Margul-Sperber regarded himself as one of the 'epigones who live in the ancient house of language' (Karl Kraus).[79] Kraus's literary tenets justified and reinforced the attachment of Jewish poets from the Bukovina to tradition.

In the 1930s, Nazi poets abused classical linguistic and artistic forms in order to propagate their murderous ideology while trying to prove themselves the heirs of German cultural traditions. Despite the rise of Nazism, Jewish poets from the Bukovina remained faithful to both their German mother tongue and the classical poetic style. They wanted to prove that they, the persecuted Jews and outcasts of Nazi Germany, were the true heirs of German culture.[80] Even in Transnistria's death ghettos and death camps, Immanuel Weißglas and Alfred Kittner wrote ballads and rhymed poems in German. After the Holocaust, some of these surviving Jewish poets from the Bukovina continued to write in German: Manfred Winkler published poems in German and Hebrew,

79 Karl Kraus, *Ausgewählte Gedichte* (Zurich: Oprecht, 1939), p. 24.
80 Further information in Colin, *Paul Celan. Holograms*, pp. 19–40.

and others such as Aharon Appelfeld and Dan Pagis turned to Hebrew, becoming leading Israeli authors.

In Czernowitz, as a teenager and young adolescent, Paul Antschel (Celan) wrote German verses imbued with images drawn from a variety of literary traditions ranging from Romanticism to Expressionism, in particular Georg Trakl's style. In the labour camp, Paul also continued to use traditional means of poetic expression. After the experience of the Holocaust, the deportation and murder of his parents, and his own sufferings in a forced labour camp, Celan's main objective was to inscribe the memory of the genocide into his poems. In his early poems, including 'Mutter', 'Espenbaum', 'Chanson Juive' and in his famous 'Todesfuge' ['Death Fugue'], he thematized the persecution and annihilation of the Jewish people. His early poem 'Es fällt nun Mutter, Schnee', written after receiving the news of his mother's murder in the winter of 1942/1943, includes the image of a loud harp with strings torn apart. The harp, the world's oldest known instrument, is a symbol of musicality. But a harp with broken strings produces only dissonance. In his first manuscript of this poem, Antschel even wrote the word 'zerrissen' [torn-apart] in bold letters in order to stress its importance.[81] 'Es fällt nun Mutter, Schnee' is Antschel's first poem signalling his distancing himself from his own previous melodious verses and the traditional poetic style cherished by his literary compatriots. In his poem 'Nähe der Gräber' (1944), Celan thematized his critique of language by asking the crucial question: 'Und duldest du, Mutter, wie einst, ach, daheim, | den leisen, den deutschen, den schmerzlichen Reim?' [And mother, you bear it, as once, oh, at home, | the gentle, the German, the heart-wrenching rhyme?][82] Still, Antschel continued to write in German, but his relationship to his mother tongue and his poetic development differed substantially from that of most other German-speaking Jewish poets from the Bukovina.

In a letter dated 3 November 1946 and sent from Bucharest to the Swiss critic Max Rychner, Paul Celan (then Ancel) underlined: 'it is so hard, as a Jew, to write poems in German.'[83] In Bucharest, Paul Ancel wrote several Romanian texts, but he did not wish to become a Romanian poet. From 1948 to 1970, Celan lived in France and was fluent in French, but he did not consider becoming a French poet. Time and again, he insisted upon the significance of his German mother tongue for his own poetic tenets. When asked how he could still write in a language abused by the Nazis, he replied: 'Nur in der Muttersprache

81 *Paul Celan – Edith Silbermann*, p. 179.

82 Celan, 'Nähe der Gräber', in GW5, vol. 3, p. 20; Celan, *Selected Poems and Prose*, p. 11.

83 Celan, 'Brief an Max Rychner von 3.11.1946', in *Paul Celan: "etwas ganz und gar Persönliches". Briefe 1934–1970*, ed. Barbara Wiedemann (Berlin: Suhrkamp 2019), p. 27.

kann man die eigene Wahrheit aussagen', [Only in the mother tongue can one state one's truth].[84] In 1948, after leaving Bucharest for Vienna, he told a relative who had settled in Palestine that he had decided to remain in Europe precisely because it was only in Europe that he could follow his destiny as a Jew and German language poet.[85] Many years later, he was still convinced that 'this is my destiny: I must write poetry in the German language. And if poetry is my destiny, then I consider myself happy.'[86] But Celan suffered deeply from survivor's guilt and his dilemma of being a Jewish poet writing in German after the Holocaust. It motivated his incessant search for a different poetic idiom in German.

One of Antschel's early strategies of alienating his poetic language from his previous style of writing was the fusion of poetic forms and images from different literary traditions. His poems 'Nähe der Gräber' and 'Espenbaum' are written in the style of a Romanian folk elegy, called 'doina', which begins with an allocution to a leaf or a flower and then conveys the speaker's sorrow. Later the avant-garde, in particular Franco-Romanian Surrealism, provided Celan with the means of alienating words from familiar contexts, breaking them apart and combining their residues with words from other languages (Hebrew, Spanish, French) and terms from different fields (medicine, geology, and botany). He created innovative 'multilingual gratings', 'Sprachgitter', which could well be read as enacting linguistically one of the main characteristics of the Bukovina: its receptiveness to different cultural and literary traditions and languages.

Following Dylan Thomas's poetic idea that images bear the seeds to their own destruction, Celan later conceived his poems in such a way as to allow language itself to perform a movement from 'a still being' to a 'ceasing-to-be', carrying itself to the margins of silence but pulling itself back from it. It is through such an oscillatory movement that his poems disclose the wounds that the Holocaust burned into words. As Celan points out in his *Bremer Rede*, German language had gone 'through the thousand darkness of death-bringing speech' without providing 'words for that which happened'. It went through such darkness but resurfaced 'enriched by it all'.[87] It is precisely through the movement from 'a still being' to a 'ceasing-to-be' that Celan's poems disclose the traces of death-bringing speech within language. They destruct familiar syntactic and

84 Cited in Chalfen, *Paul Celan*, p. 148; Chalfen's source of information was Ruth Kraft.

85 Bianca Rosenthal, 'Quellen zum frühen Celan', *Monatshefte* 4 (1983), 402–3.

86 Beda Allemann, 'Max Rychner – Entdecker Paul Celans. Aus den Anfängen der Wirkungsgeschichte Celans im deutschen Sprachbereich', in *'Wir tragen den Zettelkasten mit den Steckbriefen unserer Freunde'. Beiträge jüdischer Autoren zur deutschen Literatur seit 1945*, ed. by Jens Stüben and others (Darmstadt: Häusser, 1994), p. 283. See also: Celan, *Briefe 1934–1970*, p. 27.

87 Celan, 'Ansprache', in GW5, vol. III, p. 186.

metaphoric structures in order to create an innovative idiom into which he could inscribe his memories of and response to the Holocaust. In the final lines of the poem 'Welchen der Steine du hebst' ['Whichever Stone you Lift'] from the volume *Von Schwelle zu Schwelle* [*From Threshold to Threshold*], Celan vivifies this idea: 'Whichever word you speak – you owe | to destruction'.[88]

Celan's later poem 'Engführung' ['Stretto'], which ends the volume *Sprachgitter* [*Speech-Grille*],[89] explodes not only the language of German poetic traditions but also Celan's own poetic idiom as conveyed in his early poetry. In a fugue, a stretto is the rapid overlapping of voices concluding the musical composition, thereby generating a contrapuntal superimposition of the main theme upon itself. Like the German 'Engführung', the English term stretto denotes a narrowing, tightening and closing. In Celan's linguistic stretto, a whirl of 'linguistic particles' narrows and tightens the German language, pushing it to the border of silence, but recalling it again and setting its messages free: the poet's rejection of the artistry and musicality marking his previous famous fugue, the 'Todesfuge';[90] the transformation of its language into another poetic idiom, a 'greyer' language, more adequate to convey his response to the Holocaust; and the enactment of an imperative expressed in his speech *Der Meridian:* 'geh mit der Kunst in deine allereigenste Enge. Und setze dich frei' [go with art into your very self-most straits. And set yourself free].[91] In its multiplicity of meanings, Celan's powerful imperative suggests that the journey into one's innermost self – a journey undertaken through a linguistic stretto – leads to self-liberation and personal freedom.

'Roots in the German-Jewish symbiosis' versus 'roots in the air'

There is yet another meridian that both connects and separates Celan and the Jewish poets from the Bukovina who believed themselves rooted in a German-Jewish symbiosis.

In his childhood, Celan had experienced belief in the fecundity of the German-Jewish symbiosis, for his own mother and some of his friends shared this belief and influenced him in turn. But even when he was just a teenager Antschel was confronted with the rise of anti-Semitism in the Romanian Kingdom. The

88 Celan, 'Welchen der Steine du hebst', in GW5, vol. I, p. 129; Celan, *Selected Poems and Prose*, p. 71.
89 Celan, 'Sprachgitter', in GW5, vol. I, pp. 147–204.
90 Celan, 'Todesfuge', in GW5, vol. I, pp. 41–42.
91 Celan, 'Der Meridian', in GW5, vol. III, p. 200; Celan, *Selected Poems and Prose*, p. 410.

persecution of Jews in the 1930s, their deportation to the death camps in Transnistria and the murder of his parents traumatized him. After World War II, as a German-speaking Jewish poet living in Paris, he was still confronted with anti-Semitism, becoming the target of anti-Semitic attacks masked as scathing reviews of his work. Some of these critics were left-wing journalists and writers. In a letter to his friends Edith and Jacob Silbermann, Celan bitterly complained about anti-Semitism in Germany, in particular left-wing anti-Semitism.[92]

In *Der Meridian*, Celan criticized Karl Emil Franzos because he had pleaded for Jewish acculturation into Austro-German traditions. Celan reproached him for having misread a key term in the original manuscript of Georg Büchner's *Leonce und Lena*[93]: the adjective 'commode' [accommodating or comfortable] which he mistook for 'ein Kommendes' [a coming thing].[94] Celan's comments are full of bitter irony as he asks himself whether such 'accommodation' dissimulates Franzos's apostolate in favour of the cultural 'Germanization' of the Jews. For Celan, the German-Jewish symbiosis was fertile soil for self-deception, rather than Jewish roots. He came to regard the belief in a German-Jewish symbiosis as the seed of the future tragedy of European Jews.

As an uprooted Jewish poet writing in German after the Holocaust, Celan anchored himself in a different way. 'Wer (das Gedicht) schreibt, bleibt ihm mitgegeben' [whoever writes, remains with it],[95] wrote Celan, who believed that poets engraved their signature into their poems. One of the many features of his own 'signature' was his self-interpretation as a modern Villon 'from Czernowitz near Sadagora' in his previously mentioned poem 'Eine Gauner- und Ganovenweise'. Celan's linguistic self-portrait invokes a link between wandering medieval European poets and wandering Jews, disclosing yet another meridian that connects Celan's early poetry written in Czernowitz and his late innovative texts: his notion of displacement.

In his early poems such as 'Chanson Juive', Antschel vivifies a condition of being uprooted as the result of the violent persecution, expulsion and deportation of the Jewish people throughout their history. These early poems emphasize the continuity of such displacement from antiquity to modern times, yet without drawing parallels, thus without undermining the uniqueness of each traumatic

---

92 *Paul Celan – Edith Silbermann*, p. 269.

93 Celan, 'Der Meridian', GW5, vol. III, p. 202.

94 Georg Büchner, *Sämmtliche Werke und handschriftlicher Nachlaß. Erste kritische Gesammt-Ausgabe*, ed. by Karl Emil Franzos (Frankfurt a. M.: Sauerländer, 1879), p. 157. For a detailed discussion of the difference between 'das Commode' and 'das Kommende' see: Colin, *Paul Celan. Holograms*, p. 12.

95 Celan, GW5, vol. III, p. 198; Celan, *Collected Prose*, p. 49.

event that contributed to the uprooting of the Jews. In his late poem 'In der Luft' ['In the Air'], which concludes the volume *Die Niemandsrose* [*No One's Rose*], Celan further develops this idea, suggesting that the Jewish condition of being displaced and uprooted has turned into a *condition humaine*, the condition of all victims of violence and war, symbolized in this poem by the 'Pomeranian', whose homeland was devastated during the Thirty Years' War: 'Tall | he walks, the banished one up there, the | burnt one: a Pomeranian, at home | in the may-bug song'.[96]

The powerful images in the poem's opening lines invoke yet another basic idea: being uprooted does not imply a lack of roots or an annihilation of these roots. Rather, it conveys a displacement of the roots into a different sphere: 'In the air, there your root lives on, there, | in the air [...]'.[97] Roots in the air are portable roots. They travel with the burned and 'banned Pomeranian' at home in a folk and children's song about violence and war. In the subsequent stanza, the poem points to the meridians that accompany the traveller: 'With him | the meridians walk [...]'.[98] Celan's verses can be interpreted as dramatizing Celan's own precarious situation as an Eastern European Jewish poet with roots in the air and a home in his poems. The latter disclose the meridians travelling with the poet on his journey back to a 'world of yesterday': the region of 'Menschen und Bücher', translated by Rosemarie Waldrop as 'people and books'.[99] Unlike 'people', however, the word 'Menschen' recalls the Yiddish 'Mensch' which denotes humanness. The conjunction 'and' links 'humanness' to 'books', invoking not only a humane 'people of the book' but also a humane world of books. Faced with his troubling experiences in the 'golden Western European democracies', Celan was longing for those 'Menschen' he once knew in Czernowitz and the world of books he had enjoyed in his youth. But his images go far beyond the biographical allusion. For Celan, the return to the past – invoked in *Der Meridian* – is a movement towards 'u-topia',[100] an imaginary future time when humanity and books will be linked. It is a time similar to Immanuel Kant's 'time of eternal peace'. It ought to exist but remains utopian and the objective of an existential search that becomes a categorical imperative in the Kantian sense.

96 Celan, GW5, vol. I, p. 290; Celan, *65 Poems*, trans. by Brian Lynch and Peter Jankowsky, p. 41.
97 Ibid.
98 Ibid.
99 Celan, *Collected Prose*, p. 33.
100 Celan, GW5, vol. III, p. 202; Celan, *Collected Prose*, p. 54.

Helmut Böttiger

A 'Poet in Destitute Times'. Paul Celan and the West German Literary Scene of the 1950s and 1960s

Moving from Vienna to Paris in June 1948, Paul Celan left the German-speaking world for good, abandoning his long-running attempts to establish closer ties to the West German literary establishment. In one telling example, illustrating his efforts to gain recognition as a poet, Celan wrote to Ernst Jünger on 11 June 1951,

> Wie schwer ist es doch, diesen Zeilen die Richtung zu geben, die in Ihre Nähe weist! Im Grunde können sie wohl nur die Hoffnung umschreiben, Sie möchten das beigeschlossene Manuskript an einer Stelle aufschlagen, die Ihrem Entgegenkommen zu danken weiß.
>
> [How difficult it is to give these lines a route that points in your direction! They likely can only approximate the hope that you might open the enclosed manuscript which is able to express gratitude for your goodwill.][1]

Celan must have known what to expect of Jünger, initially one of the most radical intellectual trailblazers of National Socialist ideology, but by this point more concerned with upholding an aristocratic elite culture over that of the common plebs. The rejection of both Nazis and Democrats alike, stemming from this ostensibly elite position, was a German trademark at the time, for which Ernst Jünger rapidly became one of the major spokesmen. His influence on the cultural landscape of the nascent Federal Republic was accordingly formidable.

It is a difficult, tortuous letter, in which Celan attempts to reconcile the motives that drive him:

> Auf vielerlei Wegen habe ich zu Ihrer Welt hinübergedacht und Ihnen zu begegnen versucht – aber das Zeichen, unter das ich mich stellte, schien mir nicht recht zu denjenigen zu gehören, die es vermocht hätten, Ihr Auge auch für die Gestalt unter ihm zu gewinnen.
>
> [In many ways, I have thought my way over to your world and attempted to encounter you – but the sign under which I've placed myself did not really seem to belong to those who would have been able to win your eye for the figure underneath it as well.]

1 Tobias Wimbauer, 'In Dankbarkeit und Verehrung. Hilfe kommt aus Wilflingen; Ein Brief von Paul Celan an Ernst Jünger wurde im Marbacher Literaturarchiv entdeckt', *Frankfurter Allgemeine Zeitung*, 8 January 2005.

https://doi.org/10.1515/9783110658330-004

He had 'faltered every time', as he 'groped his way forward towards the words' that he 'was forced to send ahead' of his poems. Celan signed the letter, 'With gratitude and admiration.'

Celan heard nothing from Jünger. He would ultimately gain access to the German literary scene through his Viennese friend, Ingeborg Bachmann. On a trip to Vienna to look for fresh contacts, Hans Werner Richter, then head of the Gruppe 47, a loose association of writers, had encountered Ingeborg Bachmann and invited her to a conference in May 1952 in Niendorf, a Baltic seaside resort. Bachmann quickly succeeded in getting Paul Celan involved as well: 'It will be important for you, because the entire German press corps has been invited, the literature editors from the German broadcasters etc., who immediately purchase the best stories, poems etc.'[2]

That assessment was a bit of an exaggeration: at that time, Gruppe 47 exerted nowhere near the influence it would enjoy a decade later. The common ground that the mostly young and unknown group of writers shared was a comparatively clear anti-fascism along with a kind of atmospheric opposition at the outset of the Konrad Adenauer era in West Germany. The Gruppe 47 gathered together a wide variety of characters and biographies yet did not pursue a pronounced aesthetic; their literary positions were far too diverse for that. Celan had nothing in common with the radically sober style espoused by the older core around Hans Werner Richter, grounded in the tough, realistic language of Hemingway, but he could relate to the rising younger faction and their enthusiasm for Kafka. As the conference drew nearer, Bachmann wrote Celan with portentous advice, 'And you absolutely must read the 'Todesfuge' ['Death Fugue'] – despite everything – because I think I know a thing or two about the Gruppe 47.'[3]

Celan's performance at the Gruppe 47 meeting has become the subject of numerous legends. It has long since been established that Celan was rejected by the group and that he was even unanimously laughed at. In a documentary feature broadcast in 2016 by the TV station arte, the only information about Celan's appearance were photos of the Gruppe 47 members juxtaposed with a contemptuous studio-produced laugh track.[4] A polemical essay by Germanist Klaus Briegleb with the charged subtitle, 'Wie antisemitisch war die Gruppe 47?' ['How

---

2 *Herzzeit. Ingeborg Bachmann-Paul Celan. Der Briefwechsel*, ed. by Bertrand Badiou and others (Frankfurt a.M.: Suhrkamp, 2008), p. 40.

3 Ibid., p. 49.

4 *Paul Celan. Dichter ist, wer menschlich spricht*, broadcast on arte on 16 October 2016.

antisemitic was Gruppe 47?'] also promoted the automatic association of the Gruppe 47 with antisemitism, using Celan's reading as its main argument.[5]

Contemporary documents suggest nothing of the sort. The Group 47 Prize, which was awarded during the conference based on a vote by all members in attendance, sends a clear message: Celan took third place among more than twenty participants. First place was awarded to Ilse Aichinger, also an author of Jewish ancestry with an advanced aesthetic. Crucially for Celan, the outcome of the conference was a concrete deal from a publishing house. After his reading, the editor-in-chief of the Deutsche Verlags-Anstalt, Willi A. Koch, immediately made him an offer. Furthermore, Celan received a few commissions from magazines and radio stations which had rejected his submissions years earlier. He would also remain in contact with some of the participants, including Heinrich Böll.

In his rather officious conference report, Hans Georg Brenner wrote that an 'occasionally indulgent leniency' had prevailed in the critiques 'although, during the reading of a *homo novus*, whose work either pushed the unexpected vehemence of the critique beneath its level or raised it far beyond its actual meaning, they sometimes remembered their previous quick-wittedness and sharpness.' A conflict between the established members of the group and the younger newcomers – and a competition for market share – had seemingly been ignited. Brenner clearly emphasizes poetry in this regard:

While poetry rarely led to critical discussions in these circles, this time around, the nature and form of the assertions gave rise to lively voices, which – proceeding from Karl Krolow's flawless imaginary richness – committed themselves to the intense lyrical restraint of the young Austrian poet Ingeborg Bachmann. Here, as in the *poésie pure* of the Austrian Paul Celan, the unobtrusively powerful eloquence and the precision of the images surprised.[6]

In a newspaper article, founding member Heinz Friedrich, one of the older knights in Hans Werner Richter's inner circle, reported:

The reading of the poems of the Romanian-German Paul Celan, who, following in the footsteps of Mombert and Else Lasker-Schüler, was striving to find his own voice, sparked a fierce debate over the old controversy: *poésie pure* versus *poésie engagée*, which – as in all such debates – did not lead to a satisfying answer. Nonetheless, the choice of the Gruppe 47 prize-winner demonstrated that

---

5 Klaus Briegleb, *Missachtung und Tabu. Eine Streitschrift zur Frage: 'Wie antisemitisch war die Gruppe 47?'* (Berlin: Philo, 2003).

6 Hans Georg Brenner, 'Ilse Aichinger – Preisträgerin der Gruppe 47', in *Die Gruppe 47: Bericht, Kritik, Polemik; Ein Handbuch*, ed. by Reinhard Lettau (Neuwied: Luchterhand, 1967), pp. 72–77 (p. 75).

the composition of this year's conference participants forced a shift away from the realistic novel towards the poetic statement.[7]

Here, too, the generational conflict was made manifest. The founding fathers surrounding Hans Werner Richter and Heinz Friedrich, who advocated an 'engaged', realistic understanding of literature, were suddenly confronted with younger authors inspired by Western modernism. Over the course of the two or three previous conferences, it had already become apparent that the advocates of a clear-cut sober prose were on the defensive. Many years later, Friedrich looked back on his 'incomprehension' at Celan's reading: 'Surely, it also had to do with the author's lachrymose recitation style',[8] simultaneously illuminating the particular reservations Celan encountered among some of the old group members. His recitation style had its origins in interwar Czernowitz and was influenced by the formidable tone of the Burg Theatre and the declamations of a certain Alexander Moissi, whose recitations – read in an Italian accent which caused him to sing rather than speak – had also gained acclaim in Czernowitz. Listening to Celan's radio and vinyl recordings, it is easy to hear the echoes of Moissi's style. Conversely, Hans Werner Richter, Heinz Friedrich and Walter Kolbenhoff – shaped by their experience of the war – had no connection to this tradition.

Considering the success and renown that Celan ultimately attained on the German literary scene, the question arises as to how the accusation of antisemitism and the legend of Celan's being laughed at came about. Unsurprisingly, the first reference dates back to an interview with Walter Jens, an influential professor of rhetoric, in 1976. Jens was speaking within a particular context, wherein Celan had long emerged as the most widely interpreted contemporary lyricist, but who remained a mythical, mysterious poet about whom little was known, except that he had committed suicide a few years earlier at the age of 50 and that 'Todesfuge' was included in all the textbooks. For Jens, these fragments were part of a much larger German tradition of the poetic genius which is both doomed to tragic failure and painfully revered. Jens noted:

When Celan appeared for the first time, people said, 'Nobody can hear that!' He read very pathetically. We laughed about it. One of them said that, 'He reads just like Goebbels!' He was laughed at; a speaker from the Gruppe 47, Walter Hilsbecher from Frankfurt, had to recite the poems all over again. The 'Todesfuge'

7 Heinz Friedrich, 'Die Gruppe 47', quoted in ibid., pp. 77–79 (p. 78).

8 Heinz Friedrich, quoted in Peter Engel, 'Die Sekunde des Umschlags. Die Niendorfer Tagung der "Gruppe 47"', *Neue Zürcher Zeitung*, 6 September 1997.

was a flop in the group! That was a completely different world – the Neorealists, who had grown up with this program, so to speak, could not follow along.[9]

Jens' intention in 1976 was clearly to rise above the contemptible practices of the post-war period. By the seventies, the Gruppe 47 was almost exclusively seen as a business phenomenon, to which the old truism of literature applied: greatness is always misunderstood while mediocrity rules the day. From that standpoint, Jens stylized the consternation that Celan triggered in certain people more than twenty years earlier. Jens did not mention antisemitism. But in the midst of Celan's reception as a great, albeit hermetic poet, the twice-repeated 'He was laughed at' fell on fertile soil.

The comparison of Celan to the Nazi propaganda minister Joseph Goebbels, however, weighed heavily upon Celan; the source of this comparison was Hans Werner Richter, who made it during lunch as he and his inner circle recalled the event. Long after his death, a diary of Richter's was discovered which included an entry written after he had learned of Celan's suicide and which offers the most concrete reconstruction of that moment:

I didn't know at the time that Ingeborg had been Paul Celan's lover, that he'd in fact substantially influenced her poetry. This led to certain odd moments. After Celan's reading, I unintentionally mentioned during lunch – as an aside – that Celan's voice reminded me of Joseph Goebbels'. Given that both Celan's parents had been killed by the SS, a dramatic confrontation ensued. Paul Celan wanted to hold me to account and tried to push me into the position of a former National Socialist. Ilse Aichinger and Ingeborg Bachmann wept and, tears gushing, begged me to apologize, which I eventually did. Paul Celan never forgave me.[10]

Inherent to Richter's sense of self was his opposition to National Socialism, yet he denied that his comparison of Celan to Goebbels was anything short of outrageous. Nonetheless, between the lines, his difficulty in dealing with the challenge is unmistakeable; the distance between these worlds in conflict seems grotesque. Richter says 'Goebbels' and means everything he rejects linguistically: hollow pathos, emotionally charged recitation filled with ornamentation and theatricality – the whole arsenal of National Socialist furore. But he could not recognize the scandal in associating Goebbels with a Jewish poet, who had barely escaped death at the hands of by Goebbels' henchmen. Richter expresses a specific kind of denial here, connected to his position as a German and a former Wehrmacht soldier. It is apparent from several of his texts that the

---

9 Walter Jens, 15 October 1976, quoted in Heinz Ludwig Arnold, *Die Gruppe 47* (Reinbek bei Hamburg: Rowohlt, 2004), p. 76.

10 Hans Werner Richter, *Mittendrin. Die Tagebücher, 1966–1972* (Munich: C.H. Beck, 2012), p. 158.

mass murder of Europe's Jews by Germans played a role in Richter's thinking, but he was not interested in lyric poetry. Celan's performance as such seems to have caused a mental short circuit in Richter.

There is some indication that Celan shared Richter's political outlook and was able to compartmentalize his derailment as an expression of his aesthetic limitations. Richter's papers include a volume of poems by Alexander Block translated by Celan, which he dedicated, on 1 June 1962, 'For Hans Werner Richter, in memory of Niendorf, May '52, and Frankfurt, May '62. Warmly, Paul Celan.'[11] In September 1962, he also expressed his regret at having to decline the invitation to the next Gruppe 47 meeting because of his duties at the École Normale Supérieure: 'It is not a pleonasm to repeat here once again that I really would have liked to come to Berlin.'[12] Klaus Voswinckel, who wrote one of the first dissertations on Celan and visited the poet several times in Paris in the sixties, recalls: 'He spoke about Hans Werner Richter as about someone who was the antithesis of an enemy.'[13]

Celan's own perception of the Gruppe 47 conference in Niendorf is reflected in his correspondence, published decades later. On 31 May 1952, Celan wrote to his wife:

> Erster Waffengang. Lesungen, dann Stellungnahme der ‚Kritik'. Worte, mit oder ohne inneren Horizont. Aber zumindest gutgesagt, an diesem ersten Tag. [...] Um neun Uhr abends war die Reihe an mir. Ich habe laut gelesen, ich hatte den Eindruck, über diese Köpfe hinaus – die selten wohlmeinend waren – einen Raum zu erreichen, in dem die ‚Stimmen der Stille' noch vernommen wurden... Die Wirkung war eindeutig. Hans Werner Richter, der Chef der Gruppe, Initiator eines Realismus, der nicht einmal erste Wahl ist, lehnte sich auf. Diese Stimme, im vorliegenden Falle die meine, die nicht wie die der andern durch die Wörter hindurchglitt, sondern oft in einer Meditation bei ihnen verweilte, an der ich gar nicht anders konnte, als voll und von ganzem Herzen daran teilzunehmen – diese Stimme musste angefochten werden, damit die Ohren der Zeitungsleser keine Erinnerung an sie behielten... Jene also, die die Poesie nicht mögen – sie waren in der Mehrzahl – lehnten sich auf.
>
> [First armed encounter. Readings, then the critiques. Words, with or without an inner horizon. But at least well-articulated, on this first day. [...] At nine in the evening, it was my turn. I read loudly; I had the impression, over these heads – which were seldom well-meaning – to reach a space in which the 'voices of silence' were still heard... The effect was clear. Hans Werner Richter, the head of the group, initiator of a realism that was not even the first choice, revolted against it. This voice, in this case mine, which, unlike those of the others, did not glide through the words, but often lingered with them in a meditation in which

11 Nachlass Hans Werner Richter, Archiv der Akademie der Künste, Berlin.
12 Hans Werner Richter, *Briefe*, ed. by Sabine Cofalla (Munich: Hanser, 1997), p. 407.
13 Interview with Klaus Voswinckel, in Helmut Böttiger, *Wir sagen uns Dunkles. Die Liebesgeschichte zwischen Ingeborg Bachmann und Paul Celan* (Munich: DVA, 2017), p. 127.

> I could not help but to fully and wholeheartedly participate – this voice had to be challenged, so that the ears of the newspaper readers would not keep any memory of it... That is to say, those who do not like poetry – they were the majority – revolted.][14]

Richter 'revolted', those who do not like poetry 'revolted'. Twice, Celan uses this word to describe the reaction to his reading – a rather unusual verb in this context. It describes his perception of the ritual of critique, the discussion of the text that took place directly after the reading. Celan was wholly unprepared for it. He was used to reciting his poems as a kind of song, allowing them to reverberate through the room. Relativizing, classifying or even critical words had no place there. Instructive is an anecdote once recounted by Günter Grass: during a visit with Celan, Grass had spied a volume of poetry on the table, taken it into his hand and was leafing through it. Celan took the book away from him and said: 'That's no way to read my poems!'[15] There was a huge gulf between Celan's approach to literature and the practice of the Gruppe 47.

Celan's first official volume of poems, *Mohn und Gedächtnis* [*Poppy and Memory*], a partial run printed for Christmas 1952 as a gift for the friends of the publishing house, was very well received. When the Süddeutsche Rundfunk in Stuttgart broadcast a reading of Celan's poems on 15 June 1954, editor Karl Schwedhelm introduced him as a matter of course: 'Paul Celan is a household name for anybody who enjoys German poetry.'[16]

In addition to the reading by the author, this broadcast is of particular interest, since Schwedhelm and Celan engaged in a short conversation, marking the only interview Celan ever gave on radio or television and thus the only recording of his voice in conversation. It is revealing how Celan behaved in such a vulnerable situation: on an influential West German radio station, on a prestigious stage of the literary scene. It must be noted that at the time, the mass murder of the Holocaust played almost no role in Germany's public discourse. Where Celan came from and the fate he endured were relegated to an intangible, existential realm.

The stress Celan was under is palpable. To be sitting in a German broadcast studio, just a few years after the murder of his parents, was obviously at the forefront of his mind. When the conversation turned to poetry, Schwedhelm asked his questions in a manner typical of West Germany at the time: when the conver-

---

14 *Herzzeit*, p. 22.

15 Interview with Günter Grass, in Böttiger, *Wir sagen uns Dunkles*, p. 131.

16 Karl Schwedhelm, interview with Paul Celan on Süddeutscher Rundfunk, 15 June 1954. A transcript is reprinted in Paul Celan, *Mikrolithen sinds, Steinchen. Die Prosa aus dem Nachlass*, ed. by Barbara Wiedemann and Bertrand Badiou (Frankfurt a. M.: Suhrkamp, 2005), pp. 188–93.

sation turned to poetry, it was always about something higher, something dreamlike. Remarkable was how Celan began to laugh, even giggle, as the broadcast progressed – a side of him that was invisible in his poetry. This laughter countered the pressure Celan was under – an artificial media situation on the one hand, a personal trial on the other.

One can quite clearly identify the moment when Celan's self-identificatory preoccupation with Jewish tradition comes to the fore. In May 1957, he bought the works of Osip Mandelstam, in the original Russian, from one of the bookstalls along the Seine in Paris. In Mandelstam, he discovered a kindred spirit, an Eastern Jewish equivalent. Like Celan, Mandelstam was marked by the totalitarian experiences of the twentieth century, having died in a Stalinist camp in the early 1940s. Celan's volume of poems *Die Niemandsrose* [*No One's Rose*] from 1963 is 'In memory of Osip Mandelstam'; the book itself contains many echoes of Mandelstam's writing. In that sense, the poem 'Und mit dem Buch aus Tarussa' ['And with the book from Tarussa'] has a motto, abbreviating and concentrating a line by the Russian poet Marina Tsvetaeva ['In this most Christian of worlds | poets are Jews.'[17]] – 'All poets are Jews.'[18] In so doing, his poetic existence was fused with the fate of the Jews.

Over the course of the sixties, it would become his life's motto, directly related to the increase in antisemitic incidents in West Germany in the late 1950s. In parallel, the 'Goll affair' began to take up more space Celan's letters. After Celan became known for *Mohn und Gedächtnis*, Claire Goll perfidiously accused him of having plagiarized the late Yvan Goll's later work.[19] Another important incident occurred during Celan's reading in Bonn on 17 November 1958. Jean Firges, a well-meaning student, who would soon thereafter write the first dissertation about Celan, mentioned that several people were of the opinion that Celan's introductions 'contained much of Heinz Erhardt's humour'. A caricature had also been passed around with the image of a shackled, stooped slave, with the caption 'Hosiannah the son of David!'[20] Against the political backdrop of West Germany's accelerated post-war restoration, this was more than just a student prank. Many colleagues in West Germany would receive an excerpt

---

17 Translation from Christine Ivanovic, *'Kyrillisches, Freunde, auch das...'. Die russische Bibliothek Paul Celans im Deutschen Literaturarchiv Marbach* (Marbach am Neckar: Deutsche Schillergesellschaft, 1996), p. 47

18 Paul Celan, 'Und mit dem Buch aus Tarussa', in Paul Celan, *Die Niemandsrose. Gedichte* (Frankfurt a.M.: S. Fischer, 1963), p. 85.

19 On this, see *Paul Celan. Die Goll-Affäre; Dokumente zu einer 'Infamie'*, ed. by Barbara Wiedemann (Frankfurt a.M.: Suhrkamp, 2000).

20 *Herzzeit*, p. 99.

from the student's account with a request that had begun to appear more often in letters to friends during this period: 'Please, tell me what you think.'[21]

What he longed for was connected to deep wounds. In Paris, Celan obsessively bought German newspapers; he wanted to know what was being written there, especially about him. And if he came across something that was personally unpleasant, it became an occasion to find out more. 'Celan returned damaged from every trip to West Germany', recalled Günter Grass, who lived in Paris from 1956 to 1959. Celan's wife Gisèle once stopped by and asked Grass to accompany her to Celan's apartment – 'Paul is very ill' – where they found Celan sitting on the sofa with a compress on his head, a newspaper in his hand hanging off the edge of the sofa. Celan would only say, 'Read that!'[22] The most painful review came from critic Günter Blöcker, who described Celan's poems as mere 'graphic constructs'. The author, the review insinuated, was not a real German: 'Celan has greater freedom with regard to the German language than most of his poet-colleagues. This may be due to his origins. The role of language as a tool of communication inhibits and burdens him less than it does others. Admittedly, it is precisely that which often seduces him to act in a void.[23]

When Celan engages with the mass murder of the Jews by the Germans, Blöcker sees him 'acting in the void', laying bare an enormous desire to repress and a catalogue of antisemitic clichés. Essential for his classification within the context of literary history, Blöcker was also a major opponent of the Gruppe 47. As was Hans-Egon Holthusen: he wrote a critique of Celan's *Niemandsrose* in 1964, wherein he described Celan's image of 'mills of death' as a 'genitive metaphor indulging in arbitrariness to the nth degree'.[24] Holthusen seems to have been unaware that Adolf Eichmann had spoken of letting the 'mill in Auschwitz do its work', or that the 'mill' was a longstanding metaphor for Auschwitz. Holthusen's critique proved to be a major topic of discussion when Celan and Peter Szondi visited the classical philologist Jean Bollack in the Dordogne in late August 1964. A note, written by Bollack's wife Mayotte about the conversation, describes Celan's condition at the time: 'One evening in the Dordogne, while he was preoccupied with Hölderlin's figures and memories, he said: "Je suis la poé-

21 Ibid.

22 Interview with Günter Grass, in Böttiger, *Wir sagen uns Dunkles*, pp. 205–6.

23 Günter Blöcker, 'Gedichte als graphische Gebilde', *Der Tagesspiegel*, 11 October 1959.

24 Hans Egon Holthusen, 'Das verzweifelte Gedicht. 'Die Niemandsrose' – nach vier Jahren ein neuer Gedichtband von Paul Celan', *Frankfurter Allgemeine Zeitung*, 2 May 1964.

sie." That evening he was agitated [on the other days rather closed off and evasive]. Silently, we listened to him as he recited these pathetic sentences.'[25]

The poet and the Jew had become one and the same for Celan: 'All poets are Jews.' This fusion would also become an important catalyst for his contentious relationship with the German philosopher Martin Heidegger. Traces of Celan's reading of Heidegger, whose ideas he grappled with extensively, are unavoidable in Celan's library – including a spontaneously drafted letter of admiration to the philosopher. From the Mediterranean village of La Ciotat, in the autumn of 1954, Celan tentatively wrote to: 'Herrn Martin Heidegger | dem Denk-Herrn' [the thought-master] and noted further: 'vom Meer her | dieses Zeichen der Verehrung | aus einer kleinen fernen | wunschdurchklungenen | Nachbarschaft' [from the sea | this sign of devotion | from a small distant | wish-riddled proximity].[26]

The essay 'Wozu Dichter?' ['What are poets for?'] in Heidegger's 1950 volume *Holzwege* [*Off the Beaten Track*] spoke directly to Celan: he highlighted one passage, 'Die Sprache ist der Bezirk (templum), d. h. das Haus des Seins' [Language is the precinct (templum)', i.e. the house of being], and marked it with a bracket.[27] There was, however, one decisive difference for Celan: language as the 'house of being' was by no means a safe harbour; German, his mother tongue, had become something different than it was in Heidegger's conception of German as a secure and untouchable refuge – a homeland. What Heidegger regarded, despite the cataclysmic evidence to the contrary, as a stable starting point, had been transformed for Celan through his specific personal historical experiences into something unstable, insecure and open. Inevitably, his German was forced to assume a different character than Heidegger's; the 'unlost' had to be searched for and located again and again.

The poet Hölderlin represents a possible bridge between the two, as Hölderlin provided a reference point throughout Celan's oeuvre, while also being foundational to Heidegger's view of language and poetry. Heidegger connected Hölderlin's key poetic-political question – '[...] und wozu Dichter in dürftiger Zeit?' [(...) and what are poets for in destitute times?], from his elegy *Brod und Wein* [*Bread and Wine*] – to his immediate present, and in so doing purposefully transformed it into a supra-temporal truth that transcends concrete historical experiences.

---

25 Jean Bollack, *Herzstein. Über ein unveröffentlichtes Gedicht von Paul Celan* (Munich: Hanser, 1993), p. 11.
26 Quoted in André Robert, *Gespräche von Text zu Text. Celan – Heidegger – Hölderlin* (Hamburg: Felix Meiner, 2001), p. 224.
27 Ibid.

Heidegger's comment about 'Andenken' [remembrance] as the 'source of poetry', which Celan underlined, naturally also refers to Hölderlin's poem of the same title, with the famous final line: 'But the poets found what lasts.' This verse marks the last horizon of knowledge in Heidegger's philosophy. In Celan's work, too, this sentence becomes an irrevocable global formula. His own existence had become indistinguishable from poetry. In the imaginary intersection between Celan and Heidegger, Hölderlin would be at its centre with this – at first unambiguous, but then increasingly enigmatic and ever more difficult to explain – thought.

Celan always held out the hope of engaging Heidegger in a conversation about their different perspectives on poetry. On 25 July 1967, he set foot in the location that Heidegger had created for that purpose: the *Denkklause* [thinking-hermitage], close to Todtnauberg in the Black Forest. Afterwards, he wrote inside the hut's guestbook: 'Into the Hütte-book, while gazing on the well-star, with a hope for a word to come in the heart'. Shortly thereafter, Celan wrote his poem 'Todtnauberg', which reads: 'Written in the book | – whose name did it record | before mine? –, | in this book | the line about | a hope, today | for a thinker's | word | to come | in the heart.'[28] The hoped-for word never came. The inherent conflict between Celan and the West German literary scene in the fifties and sixties is thus clearly demarcated. While he had initially found support and friends in the – for the most part politically left-leaning – Gruppe 47, he operated within a line of tradition, in terms of his literary style, which the most important protagonists of the Gruppe 47 had curtailed for political reasons; the strikingly satirical Heidegger passages in Günter Grass's novel *Hundejahre* [*Dog Years*] offer a telling example. This specific political constellation led to many misunderstandings that could not be resolved within the framework of the era.

Celan justified his refusal to take part in a planned Heidegger Festschrift by arguing that he did not want to be placed next to names he considered unacceptable. In a letter to Ingeborg Bachmann, however, this rejection takes an unexpected turn:

> Ich bin, Du weißts, sicherlich der letzte, der über die Freiburger Rektoratsrede und einiges andere hinwegsehen kann; aber ich sage mir auch, zumal jetzt, da ich meine höchst konkreten Erfahrungen mit so patentierten Antinazis wie Böll oder Andersch gemacht habe, dass derjenige, der an seinen Verfehlungen würgt, der nicht so tut, als habe er nie gefehlt, der den Makel, der an ihm haftet, nicht kaschiert, besser ist als derjenige, der sich in seiner

---

28 Paul Celan, 'Todtnauberg', *Breathturn Into Timestead. The Collected Later Poetry*, trans. by Pierre Joris (New York: Farrar Straus and Giroux, 2014).

seinerzeitigen Unbescholtenheit (war es, so muss ich, und ich habe Grund dazu, fragen wirklich und in allen Teilen Unbescholtenheit?) auf das bequemste und einträglichste eingerichtet hat, so bequem, dass er sich jetzt und hier – freilich nur ‚privat' und nicht in der Öffentlichkeit, denn das schadet ja bekanntlich dem Prestige – die eklatantesten Gemeinheiten leisten kann. Mit anderen Worten: ich kann mir sagen, dass Heidegger vielleicht einiges eingesehen hat, ich SEHE, wieviel Niedertracht in einem Andersch oder Böll steckt.

[I am, you know, the last person to look beyond the Rector of Freiburg's (Heidegger's) inaugural address and a few other things; but I also tell myself, especially now that I have had several very concrete experiences with such patented anti-Nazis like Böll or Andersch, that the one who chokes on his own transgressions, who does not pretend to have never committed wrong, who does not conceal the flaw that clings to him, is better than the one who, in his blamelessness at the time (and was it – I have to ask, and have every reason to ask – really blamelessness in all ways?) arranged himself in the most comfortable and lucrative fashion, so comfortable that he can afford, here and now – admittedly only 'privately' and not in public, for as we all know, that damages the prestige – the most blatant vulgarities. In other words: I can tell myself that Heidegger may have realized a few things; I can SEE how much malice there lies in an Andersch or a Böll.][29]

Celan would eventually experience for himself, however, that Heidegger was in fact pretending to the very end that 'he had never committed wrong'. It is thus all the more striking how aggressively he reacted to the 'patented anti-Nazis'. The fact that he doubted Heinrich Böll, of all people, came in response to the reading in Bonn, during which an antisemitic caricature had been passed around. Celan had written to Böll about the matter and received a brief answer by postcard four months later: 'Dear Paul, I hope you aren't angry or impatient that I haven't answered yet. I am buried under an avalanche of resignation that I am slowly freeing myself from. The novel will soon be finished and will also contain an answer to your letter.'[30]

Consequently, Celan moved Böll into the sphere of anti-Semites, replying that he, Celan, had made the 'antediluvian' assumption that an 'engaged' writer would share his opinion that 'Nazism concerns not only the Jews.' Celan concluded: 'A bitter letter – you deserve it.'[31] Böll replied:

I can take your letter for nothing more than an affront, in light of the fact that you yourself confess to leisurely conversations about literature with Mohler, and that you cultivate friendships with people whose pasts you know NOTHING about – professional conversations among the unengaged, I assume.[32]

---

29 *Herzzeit*, p. 118.

30 Paul Celan, *Briefwechsel mit den rheinischen Freunden. Heinrich Böll, Paul Schallück und Rolf Schroers*, ed. by Barbara Wiedemann (Berlin: Suhrkamp, 2011), p. 358.

31 Ibid., p. 359.

32 Böll, ibid., p. 360

'Engaged' apparently had a slightly different connotation for Celan than for Böll, exposing differences stemming from their divergent processes of socialization. Celan considered himself a leftist – his points of reference were anarchists such as Pjotr Kropotkin or Gustav Landauer, but his self-identification as a leftist was fundamentally different from the process that an initially hesitant and then increasingly engaged 'Left' had undergone in West Germany. Above all, he was distinctly interested – beyond concrete political classifications – in protagonists that embodied a German 'spirit' that attempted to rise above quotidian political affairs. Armin Mohler, Ernst Jünger's friend and secretary and avowed 'right-winger', lived near Paris for a while and did, as Böll stated, occasionally engage in conversations with Celan. The 'friendship' that Celan had 'cultivated' must have particularly troubled Böll, who vehemently opposed the activities of ex-Nazis in West Germany, since the friend was Rolf Schroers.

The son of an SS Brigade Leader, Schroers was ultimately promoted to Senior Lieutenant in the Wehrmacht and served as leader of a Military Reconnaissance commando in Italy. In short: he held a leading position in the military secret service, and his activities blatantly differed from those of ordinary Wehrmacht soldiers. Active in the fight against partisans, Schroers would have had to prove his suitability and political reliability to his Nazi superiors. Ultimately, he is an example of the continuities between the Nazi regime and post-war West Germany, which continued to employ certain experts – including Schroers, whose involvement with North Rhine-Westphalia's Office for the Protection of the Constitution (a domestic intelligence agency) has been confirmed. According to contemporary witnesses, his habitus clearly betrayed his past, including when he appeared at Gruppe 47 conferences. Eventually, Hans Werner Richter would see Schroers as an opponent pursuing his own interests and ended up fighting vehemently against him. After a scandal with Richter over the anti-nuclear movement, Schroers, whose excellent contacts within the ruling power structure were striking, served as editor-in-chief of the Free Democratic Party (FDP) magazine, *Liberal*, and later as director of the FDP's Theodor-Heuss-Akademie.

Celan first met Schroers at the Gruppe 47 conference in Niendorf. As a staff member at Deutsche Verlags-Anstalt, Schroers played a role in the publication of Celan's *Mohn und Gedächtnis*. Shortly after the conference, Celan visited Schroers in Bergen near Frankfurt and wrote about the visit to his wife:

> Er bewohnt ein kleines Bauernhaus, es ist zugleich nett und unerquicklich, sehr deutsch, deutsch in einem Sinne, der einen zuerst abstößt und einen dann zum Nachdenken veranlasst. Obgleich Schroers sehr liebenswürdig, sehr zuvorkommend gewesen ist – er hatte mich schon in Hamburg eingeladen, bei ihm zu wohnen –, habe ich es doch abgelehnt, bei ihm zu bleiben, unter dem Vorwand, dass es zu weit sei, in Wirklichkeit aber, weil ich hier allzuviele Spuren einer Vergangenheit voller schrecklicher Dinge bemerkt hatte.

> [He lives in a small farmhouse; it is nice and unedifying and very German, German in a sense that first repels you and then makes you think. Although Schroers was very kind, very obliging – he had already invited me to stay at his place in Hamburg – I refused to stay with him, on the pretext that it was too far away, but in reality because I had noticed too many traces of a past full of atrocities.][33]

Here, Celan appears incorruptible and clear-eyed, yet he would come to trust Schroers, likely because Schroers provided him with contacts and advice, as well as greatly admiring him. In Schroers' mind, Celan embodied precisely the same high tone that he also claimed for himself. Schroers' long and frequent letters to Celan display not only practical expressions of friendship but also how much he laboured with his German self-identity, between agonizing feelings of guilt and self-aggrandizement. Schroers incessantly attempted to find an elitist, poetic similitude. Without reflection, he placed himself on equal footing with Celan and his experiences: 'As human beings, Paul, there are always just a few who, Jew or not, are scorned by the pack.'[34]

Celan noted Schroers political activities, including the initiative 'Fight Nuclear Death'. Given his sensitivity to modes of speaking, however, it is surprising how close a contact with Schroers Celan maintained over the years, offering him the informal 'du' [you] and inviting him to Paris. Nonetheless, when Schroers sent him an essay on the subject of 'Jews', Celan initially reacted with shock before enquiring further. In a letter, Schroers pursued the subject: he wrote of a 'tolerant defence against the Jewish', which was 'perhaps no longer antisemitic', evoking the 'pitiful reality of a calloused Polish village blacksmith'.[35] Schroers' texts are often characterized by such a convoluted mixture of guilt and self-justification. Such a question from a former senior lieutenant of the German military intelligence about a new 'defence against the Jewish' horrified Celan; in that very moment, he felt he was being addressed as a Jew and no longer as a poet. When Schroers sent Celan his book *Der Partisan. Ein Beitrag zur politischen Anthropologie* [*The Partisan. A Contribution to Political Anthropology*] at the end of 1961, Celan abruptly dropped all contact. In Celan's copy, he underlined words such as 'artfremd' [foreign to the species] and 'Mischpoke' [family – from the Yiddish].[36]

---

33 Celan and Celan-Lestrange, ibid., p. 24.

34 Schroers, ibid., p. 125.

35 Ibid., p. 178.

36 *Briefwechsel mit den rheinischen Freunden*, pp. 228. It should be noted that in her afterword, Wiedemann paints a more empathic picture of Schroers. She emphasizes, 'the effect Richter's slander against Schroers must have had on Celan' as the main reason for the end of the relation-

Schroers, Ernst Jünger, Heidegger – for Celan, these contemporaries and intellectuals obviously meant something different than they did to those in the opposition during the early years of the Federal Republic. Against this backdrop, Celan's quarrel with Heinrich Böll seems almost tragic. In his preference for Heidegger over 'critical' fellow writers, a cataclysmic gulf opened up between him and the West German literary landscape, across which no communication was possible at the time.

It was an enormous blow to Celan when, after receiving painful critiques, his friends did not support him as much as he had expected. Desperate and upset, he lumped reviews like Günter Blöcker's together with the casually neglectful or hurriedly busy reactions from friends like Heinrich Böll or Günter Grass. Celan was unwilling and unable to differentiate any longer, suffering under a wide variety of attacks: malicious gossip, envy from colleagues or attempts from young poets to make their mark, like Peter Rühmkorf, who attempted to sharpen his own aesthetic position in relation to Celan.[37] The usual mechanisms of the literary world are most difficult to endure when ambitious and intelligent competitors realize that somebody might be superior to them, making them act in particularly perfidious, malicious and snide ways. Celan soon interpreted any critical comment as antisemitic. Especially unpleasant was a breach of trust by the ambitious writer Peter Jokostra towards the poet Johannes Bobrowski: Bobrowski very much admired Celan,[38] but in a careless moment, had made a negative comment to Jokostra about Celan's success, which Jokostra immediately relayed back to Celan.[39]

Aside from the speculations about the state of his mental health, it is clear that Celan increasingly occupied an isolated outsider position in the West German literary landscape. It is striking how well his poetry was received in Martin Heidegger's academic environment, yet how it was simultaneously regarded as a marginal phenomenon within a literary business world dominated by the Gruppe 47. This coincidence is significant. Ever since his performance at the Gruppe 47, Celan had the support of a segment of the critical public. His cries for help in the face of Claire Goll's plagiarism accusations were heard above all by his old Viennese friends and by left-wing colleagues from West Germany.

---

ship between Celan and Schroers (ibid., p. 452). Also of note is her assessment that Celan's 'friendships with Schroers and with Bachmann' were comparable to an 'exemplary constellation' (ibid., p. 453 ff).

37 On this, see Paul Celan, 'Die Goll-Affäre', ibid. p. 662 ff.

38 Johannes Bobrowski to Fritz Schaumann, 26 April 1954, after reading Celan's poems, in Bobrowski, *Briefe*, ed. by Jochen Meyer, 4 vols. (Göttingen: Wallstein, 2007), vol. 1, p. 351.

39 Johannes Bobrowski to Peter Jokostra, 5 May 1959, ibid., vol. 2, pp. 57–58.

Throughout the sixties, however, an increasing number of voices misappropriated him for the still very powerful tradition of Stefan George's circle, interpreting his 'high tone' and his search for the roots of language from a culturally conservative perspective without considering the political and historical implications of doing so. Celan remained a stranger to the literary trends in Germany emerging in the lead-up to the 1968 movement. Literary critic Peter Hamm recalled a reception for literary critics organized by Suhrkamp publisher Siegfried Unseld at the 1968 Book Fair: 'Celan sat alone and isolated on the stairs to the garden; nobody talked to him.'[40]

All the more astonishing was his prominence in a university milieu that sought to rise above the crude politics of the day and engage in the spirit of a humanistic aristocracy. At the invitation of Gerhart Baumann, professor of German literature, for example, Celan gave a reading on 24 July 1967 in the crowded Auditorium Maximum of the University of Freiburg. It was the most important of his extremely rare public appearances. Baumann was deeply influenced by Stefan George's pupil Ernst Bertram, who was compromised by his active support of National Socialism; in Freiburg, Heidegger was one of his closest associates. Celan's relationship to Gerhart Baumann, like his relationship to Heidegger, reveals a contradiction that cannot be fully resolved: on the one hand, the Jewish survivor, on the other, a German academic, who at no time connected his past to any expression of guilt. Nevertheless, Baumann seems to have embodied something that attracted Celan, namely the professor's habitus when it came to poetry. Baumann placed Celan squarely within the tradition of the German visionary, which must have at least somewhat resonated with Celan. In his letters, which grew longer and longer, Baumann wove garlands of praise that drove even the conventions of the George circle into undreamt-of levels of ornamentation. In response to Celan's mention of Rilke, Baumann wrote: '"Malte Laurids Brigge" has gained an additional dimension through your allusions: complete time has thus fully revealed itself, the relationship between prelude and epilogue, the suspenseful simultaneity of Then and Now, of real fictions and fictive reality.' This was Baumann's speciality: a constant exchange and shifting of opposites in Goethe's sense of *Permanence in Change*. Baumann did not write: 'He could not decide', rather, he wrote: 'In the undecided, he perhaps sought the temporary solution. The decided remained unspoken.'[41]

---

40 Peter Hamm, conversation with the author.

41 Arno Barnert, Chiara Caradonna, Annika Stello, '"Im Reich der mittleren Dämonen". Paul Celan in Freiburg und sein Briefwechsel mit Gerhart Baumann', *Textkritische Beiträge*, (2016), 15–115 (pp. 46 and 72).

Celan's behaviour in response is fascinating: writing about his stay in Freiburg, he noted twice in his workbook, as if to isolate himself from his own receptivity: 'Im Reich der mittleren Dämonen' [In the realm of the middle demons], a referenceto the National Revolutionary Ernst Niekisch's reckoning with the National Socialists, under the title *Im Reich der niederen Dämonen* [*In the Realm of the Lower Demons*].[42] By making the connection to an ironically diluted National Socialism he felt was palpable in Freiburg, Celan was expressing this personal dichotomy. Conversely, Celan's relationship to Baumann's disciple Gerhart Neumann was clearer: in 1970, Neumann published an essay on the 'absolute Metapher' [absolute metaphor] in which he compared Stéphane Mallarmé to Celan[43] – an interesting academic exercise that missed the point of Celan's intentions. Upon reading the essay, the poet broke off the relationship; the academic experienced this as a tremendous 'offense'.[44] Neumann, after all, was the only witness to the historical encounter between Celan and Heidegger in his Black Forest hut. He was the driver – 'he who drives us, the mensch, he also hears it' in 'Todtnauberg'.[45]

Much has been speculated about what exactly occurred during the encounter between Celan and Heidegger. Neumann revealed nothing during his lifetime, but in his autobiographical *Selbstversuch* [*Self-experiment*] published after his death, Celan's 'offense' forms the cornerstone. Decades later, with great combinatorial effort in a kind of act of revenge, Neumann interprets Celan's 'Todtnauberg', defiantly insisting on the set of tools he had already deployed in his text on the 'absolute metaphor'. But that approach already had failed: as early as 1959, Ingeborg Bachmann argued that Celan was 'treading new territory. The metaphors have completely disappeared' as new connections were being made between 'word and world'.[46]

Neumann's Aristotelian concept of metaphor, the interplay between imitation and likeness, or a poetology of 'absolute metaphor' have nothing whatsoever in common with a poem like 'Todtnauberg'.[47] Celan's isolation within Germa-

---

42 Ibid., p. 15

43 Gerhard Neumann, 'Die 'absolute' Metapher. Ein Abgrenzungsversuch am Beispiel Stéphane Mallarmés und Paul Celans', *Poetica*, 3 (1970), 188–225.

44 Gerhard Neumann, *Selbstversuch* (Freiburg: Rombach, 2018), p. 13.

45 Paul Celan, 'Todtnauberg', *Breathturn Into Timestead. The Collected Later Poetry*, trans. by Pierre Joris (New York: Farrar Straus and Giroux, 2014).

46 Ingeborg Bachmann, 'Frankfurter Vorlesungen. Probleme zeitgenössischer Dichtung', Ingeborg Bachmann, *Werke*, ed. by Christine Koschel, Inge von Weidenbaum, and Clemens Münster (Munich: Piper, 1982), vol. 4, p. 216.

47 Neumann, *Selbstversuch*, p. 303.

ny's cultural milieu becomes crystal clear: the interpreter, Neumann, is not interested in the biographical and historical conditions inscribed in Celan's late poems. The lack of interest in the evolution of his aesthetics on the part of those who claimed him for themselves, who stood for a conservative cosmos of values, intersected with an unfortunate distance from his increasingly politically engaged fellow writers.

Neumann's preoccupation with Celan's 'Todtnauberg' demonstrates the drama of this poet even more radically: he begins with the scene in the car, where he is also present, portraying himself as a witness and leading to the core of his deliberations: the witness is 'burdened with the role of guilty party, effectively participating in an act of surveillance and blackmail.'[48] In the language of one of the most influential and powerful German literary scholars of the previous decades, Celan's 'poetic communication strategy' is aimed at 'extorting a confession from the communication partner as the culprit, the confession of his guilt.'[49] It is an unusually concise and extremely eloquent attempt at a specifically German form of repression. It is also the same constellation Celan experienced during the encounter with Heidegger in the hut.

Within the German literary-political debates of his time, Celan was seen as a monolith, struck from afar. Following his suicide in the Seine in 1970, however, it was precisely for this reason that he became the highlight of German literary studies, a nearly inexhaustible object of interpretation, his own genre in the academic world. In literary debates, conversely, he mostly remained a unique case, at times admired, but usually considered incompatible with current styles of writing. Strictly speaking, owing to his biography only, it was impossible for Celan to have 'disciples' (in the strictest sense) in West Germany. Of the contemporary poets making links to Celan, they are another matter entirely: their quotations and appeals are justified by their own poetology. When successfully executed, they orient themselves on Celan's linguistic consistency and style, as Marcel Beyer's engagement with Celan's poem 'DU LIEGST' ['You Lie']. What interested him in the process is reflected directly in the epistemological interests of the present day: 'Ich lausche hier einer Reflexion über den Klang, nicht in Begriffen, sondern in Form von Klängen selbst.' [I am listening here to a reflection on the sound, not in words, but in the form of the sounds themselves.][50]

48 Ibid., p. 302.

49 Ibid., p. 14.

50 Marcel Beyer, 'Andere Echos', *die horen*, 205 (2002), 93–108 (p. 104).

Thomas C. Connolly

Translating the Night. On Paul Celan and Fragment 178 of René Char's *Feuillets d'Hypnos*

Une fois de plus j'ai vérifié que les purs sentiments ne sont pas sans mélange, et que le cercle ne va pas sans la fourche...[1]

'One of the greatnesses of Char', asserted Maurice Blanchot in 1946, 'one that is unequalled in our time, is that his poetry is a revelation of poetry, poetry of poetry, and as Heidegger almost says of Hölderlin, poem of the essence of the poem'.[2] When Paul Celan addressed the first of many letters to René Char (1907–1988) on 21 July 1954, it was this statement he chose to echo: 'In addressing these lines to you, I recover all the anguished hope that governs my rare encounters with Poetry'.[3] Char replied the next day – 'You are among the very rare poets whom I wished to meet'[4] – and the two met for the first time at Char's home on the rue de Chanaleilles on 26 July. In the days and weeks that followed, Char, Paul and his wife – the graphic artist, Gisèle de Lestrange (1927–1991) – struck up a close relationship. The Celans in particular were very taken with their new friend.[5] Sending new year's wishes that December, Paul exclaims: 'Dear René Char, we are so happy to know you!'[6] At around the same time, he wrote – idealistically – to Gisèle: 'One day, we will only see people like Char'.[7]

Celan's enthusiasm would soon cool, but in these early days, Char was an example of how resistance against oppression could be persuasively married

1 Letter from Char to Celan dated 15 August 1963 (Paul Celan, René Char, *Correspondance. 1954–1968: avec des lettres de Gisèle Celan-Lestrange, Jean Delay, Marie-Madeleine Delay et Pierre Deniker. Suivie de la Correspondance René Char – Gisèle Celan-Lestrange, 1969–1977*, ed. by Bertrand Badiou (Paris: Gallimard, 2015), pp. 159–60.

2 Maurice Blanchot, *La Part du feu* (Paris: Gallimard, 1949), p. 105. Unless otherwise stated, all translations are my own.

3 Celan, Char, *Correspondance*, p. 53.

4 Ibid., p. 54.

5 Lefebvre notes that Celan refers to their meetings in his personal notes, while Char does not (Jean-Pierre Lefebvre, 'La Correspondance entre René Char et Paul Celan', *Études Germaniques*, 71.1 [2016], 159–64 [p. 160]).

6 Letter dated 28 December 1954 (Celan, Char, *Correspondance*, p. 64).

7 Paul Celan, Gisèle Celan-Lestrange, *Correspondance 1951–1970. Avec un choix de lettres de Paul Celan à son fils Eric*, ed. by Bertrand Badiou with Eric Celan, 2 vols (Paris: Seuil, 2001), I, p. 63.

https://doi.org/10.1515/9783110658330-005

to poetic language. Where Celan had been unable to prevent the deportation of his parents from Czernowitz in June 1942 and their subsequent death in camps in Ukraine, here was a poet of action, a leader in the underground resistance, a man who had killed and who had allowed others to be killed, in the pursuit of his country's liberation. In the wake of the accusations levied by Claire Goll (1890–1977) that Celan had plagiarized the German poems of her late husband Yvan (1891–1950), Char's 'double-edged resistance',[8] as Maulpoix calls it, contrasted with Celan's purely poetic praxis.[9] As Bertrand Badiou says, Char was the poet for whom 'action had preceded, accompanied and ultimately added ballast to poetic speech'.[10] Char also knew the limits of the poetic word, opting not to publish during the occupation, 'as long as nothing is produced which would entirely overturn the unnameable situation in which we find ourselves'.[11] After meeting Char, Celan wrote to Christoph Schwerin (1933–1996),[12] who had introduced the poets: 'He is exactly as you described him to me, so totally in the centre, in the heart of his language, a language that seems never to refuse him. Strange, how, even where it speaks of the most objective, concrete things, this language can surround itself with the aura of the universal!'[13]

Celan began to translate Char soon after meeting him. We know from his mostly unsuccessful attempts to translate the American poems of Marianne Moore (1887–1972) that for Celan, translation is often experimental, an attempt to obtain entry or 'Zugang' to what is poetic in the poem.[14] Celan translated 'À la

---

8 Jean-Michel Maulpoix, *Pour un lyrisme critique. En lisant en écrivant* (Paris: José Corti, 2009), p. 157.

9 See *Die Goll-Affäre. Dokumente zu einer 'Infamie'*, ed. by Barbara Wiedemann (Frankfurt a. M.: Suhrkamp, 2000).

10 Bertrand Badiou, '*D'une main – de l'autre main. Préface*', in Paul Celan, René Char, *Correspondance. 1954–1968: avec des lettres de Gisèle Celan-Lestrange, Jean Delay, Marie-Madeleine Delay et Pierre Deniker. Suivie de la Correspondance René Char – Gisèle Celan-Lestrange, 1969–1977*, ed. by Bertrand Badiou (Paris: Gallimard, 2015), pp. 9–31 (p. 16).

11 René Char, *Œuvres complètes* (Paris: Gallimard, 1983), p. 632.

12 Schwerin was the son of Ulrich-Wilhelm Graf von Schwerin von Schwanenfeld, one of the German officers behind the failed attempt on Adolf Hitler's life on 20 July 1944.

13 'Er ist ganz, wie Sie ihn mir geschildert haben, so völlig im Mittelpunkt, im Herzen seiner Sprache, die sich ihm nie zu verweigern scheint. Seltsam, wie diese Sprache noch da, wo sie das Gegenständlichste, Konkreteste zitiert, es mit der Aura des Universalen zu umgeben weiß!' Quoted in Christoph Graf von Schwerin, *Als sei nichts gewesen. Erinnerungen* (Berlin: edition ost, 1997), p. 199.

14 See Celan's letter to Max Niedermayer, dated 16 July 1953 ('*Fremde Nähe*'. *Celan als Übersetzer*, ed. by Axel Gellhaus et al. [Marbach am Neckar: Deutsche Schillergesellschaft, 1997], p. 400).

santé du serpent'[15] in the summer and fall of 1954, surprising Char with the typed manuscript on 18 November.[16] In 1958, he completed translations of both *À une Sérénité crispée*[17] and *Les Feuillets d'Hypnos.*[18] Celan's last known translation of Char – the poem 'Dernière marche'[19] – was sent to Char on 21 July 1966, shortly after Celan's release from a prolonged period of psychiatric hospitalization.[20] With the exception of the freer, more poetic rendition of 'À la santé du serpent', Celan does not adhere to Novalis's call for the true translator to be 'der Dichter des Dichters', the poet's poet.[21] His translations of this poetry are mostly quite literal. They are marked by what the late Bernhard Böschenstein calls 'austere precision' and a 'will to greater brittleness'.[22] As a result, and in contrast to his translations of Shakespeare, Valéry, Mandelstam and Rimbaud, Celan's versions of Char have provoked less critical excitement. Beese sidelines them in her study of 'Nachdichtung' [paraphrastic translation] in Celan, as does Olschner in his major work on Celan as translator.[23] Febel argues that the experience of translating Char will only manifest itself in Celan's own poetic language in *Atemwende* [*Breathturn*] (1968).[24] Sanmann – writing before the publication of the poets' correspondence – scrutinizes each translation in turn, as well as 'Argumentum e silentio', the poem Celan dedicated to Char in 1954.[25]

---

15 Char, *Œuvres complètes*, pp. 262–67.

16 'Die Schlange zum Wohl' was first published in *Texte und Zeichen* 1 (1955): 81–83. Char did not speak German and could neither read these translations nor respond with translations of Celan's work.

17 Char, *Œuvres complètes*, pp. 747–62.

18 Ibid., pp. 171–233.

19 Ibid., p. 438. Translation first published in: Celan, Char, *Correspondance*, pp. 193–94.

20 On this hospitalization see: Thomas C. Connolly, *Paul Celan's Unfinished Poetics. Readings in the Sous-Œuvre* (Cambridge: Legenda, 2018), p. 16.

21 Novalis, *Novalis Schriften*, ed. by Ludwig Tieck and Fr. Schlegel, 3 vols (Berlin: Verlag von G. Reimer, 1837), II, p. 187.

22 Bernhard Böschenstein, 'Anmerkungen zu Celans letzter Übersetzung. Jean Daive: Weisse Dezimale', *Text + Kritik*, 53/54 (1977), 69–73 (pp. 69, 71).

23 Henriette Beese, *Nachdichtung als Erinnerung. Allegorische Lektüre einiger Gedichte von Paul Celan* (Darmstadt: Agora, 1976), p. 9; Leonard Moore Olschner, *Der feste Buchstab. Erläuterungen zu Paul Celans Gedichtübertragungen* (Göttingen: Vandenhoeck & Ruprecht, 1985).

24 Gisela Febel, 'Gibt Paul Celans *Sprachgitter* wirklich nur den Blick auf einen hermetischen René Char frei? Überlegungen zur Wirkung von Übersetzungen und zur Macht von Rezeptionsmustern', in *Literarische Übersetzung. Formen und Möglichkeiten ihrer Wirkung in neuerer Zeit*, ed. by Wolfgang Pöckl (Bonn: Romantischer Verlag, 1992), pp. 179–209 (p. 202).

25 Angela Sanmann, *Poetische Interaktion. Französisch-deutsche Lyrikübersetzungen bei Friedhelm Kemp, Paul Celan, Ludwig Harig, Volker Braun* (Berlin/Boston: De Gruyter, 2013), pp. 167–215.

Here, I focus on Celan's translation of *Les Feuillets d'Hypnos*, written mostly between the summers of 1943 and 1944, when Char was a resistance fighter in the south of France,[26] and first published in full in 1946.[27] *Feuillets* consists of two hundred thirty-nine short passages in prose, consecutively numbered much in the style of the fragments of Heraclitus.[28] The 'feuillets' [leaflets or notes] recall Rimbaud's description of *Une Saison en enfer* (1873) as a 'few hideous leaflets from my notebook of the damned',[29] but encompass a broad range of registers and themes. Some appeal to Greek myth – Hypnos is the god of sleep, brother of Thanatos, the god of death, and both are sons of Nox, the night. Linda Orr notes that the characters in *Feuillets* – The Pruner, Sparrow, Friend of the Wheat – seem to emerge from a medieval romance.[30] A number of fragments deal explicitly with the war as experienced in the Maquis. 53 is an account of a nocturnal arms drop that goes wrong, setting the countryside ablaze.[31] In 87, we learn that Hypnos was Char's wartime code name.[32] 121 describes the ambush of a small column of 'Schutzstaffel', or SS troops.[33] The SS also features

---

26 Char was a captain in the 'Forces Françaises Libres' and responsible for the 'Section Atterrissage Parachutage' of the southern region (R2) (Jean-Claude Mathieu, *La Poésie de René Char ou Le Sel de la splendeur*, 2 vols [Paris: José Corti, 1985], II, pp. 201–2).

27 Excerpts had been published in *Fontaine* 45 (October 1945) and *Poésie* 28 (October 1945). Camus writes the introduction for the first German edition of Char's poetry, dubbing him 'our greatest living poet' (Albert Camus, *Œuvres complètes*, 4 vols (Paris: Gallimard, 2008), IV, pp. 617–18); 'Vorwort' in René Char, *Poésies/Dichtungen* (Frankfurt a.M.: Fischer, 1959), pp. 5–8. Translated by Kurt Leonhard.

28 See: *Héraclite d'Éphèse*, trans. by Yves Battistini, preface René Char (Paris: Cahiers d'Art, 1948). In his preface, Char speaks of Heraclitus as being 'ce génie fier, stable et anxieux,' not quite 'a very stable genius' but a 'proud, stable and anxious genius' (ibid., p. 14).

29 Arthur Rimbaud, *Œuvres complètes*, ed. by André Guyaux and Aurélia Cervoni (Paris: Gallimard, 2009), p. 246.

30 Linda Orr, 'The Limit of Limits. Aphorism in Char's *Feuillets d'Hypnos*', in *Symbolism and Modern Literature. Studies in Honor of Wallace Fowlie*, ed. by Marcel Tetel (Durham: Duke University Press, 1978), pp. 248–63 (p. 257).

31 Char, *Œuvres complètes*, pp. 187–88. The codeword for this arms drop was 'La bibliothèque est en feu' [the library is on fire], which became the title for a collection of poems (ibid., pp. 375–93). This episode is central to Hamacher's reading of Char: 'Language and everything coming into contact with it burns and this is no metaphor. [...] This poem is also an arms delivery; it too should push the resistance forward, even though it too runs the risk of exploding upon impact, upon being read by its readers – its philologists – and thereby obliterating the resistance, itself, and its password, its *parole*' (Werner Hamacher, *Minima Philologica*, trans. by Catharine Diehl and Jason Groves [New York: Fordham University Press, 2015], pp. 136–37).

32 Char, *Œuvres complètes*, p. 196.

33 Ibid., p. 203.

in 128, when troops briefly occupy the village of Céreste where Char is hiding.[34] 138 recounts how Char and his fighters look on, guns in hand, as Germans execute B., a fellow poet and resistance fighter.[35]

Celan began work on a literal translation of the first edition of *Feuillets* in early 1958. As he writes in a letter to his fellow translator, Kurt Leonhard: 'I have striven for literalness, have tried to convey the meaning…'.[36] Jean Bollack saw this approach as an inevitable response to the text itself, which 'did not lend itself to any sort of transposition. There was no choice but to repeat the content unchanged in the other language'.[37] When Celan experienced frustration in his pursuit of literal meaning, he wrote to the poet to ask for help.[38] He also asked other translators of Char if there was a key to reading him.[39] As he explains to Leonhard:

> It was difficult to translate this text, there are countless ellipses in it, it's basically a single ellipsis, German is, in such cases, as you well know, slower, signifiers hang for longer onto the signifieds, (and how much is not also implied when something is 'signified'!), syntax obeys other laws, besides, Char has these extremely idiosyncratic phrases – but I don't want to go on about my own (so questionable) business any longer.[40]

When broaching the question of translation with regard to Heraclitus – a key figure for Char – Martin Heidegger (1889–1976) asks us to imagine translation not as *setting* across ('Über*setzen*'), but as setting *across* ('*Über*setzen') onto the other, barely-known bank of a broad current. He does this because there is no guarantee translation will succeed: 'It could easily lead to an odyssey and usu-

---

34 Ibid., pp. 205–6.

35 Ibid., p. 208.

36 'Ich habe mich um Wörtlichkeit bemüht, den Sinn wiederzugeben versucht…' (Char, Celan, *Correspondance*, pp. 257–58).

37 Jean Bollack, *Poésie contre poésie. Celan et la littérature* (Paris: Presses universitaires de France, 2001) p. 169.

38 Celan, Char, *Correspondance*, p. 118.

39 Lother Klünner, 'Schritte mit René Char', *Die neue Rundschau*, 90.3 (1979): 361–70 (p. 361). When Franz Wurm complains that translating Char is harder than translating Rimbaud, Char replies: 'Have you never before tried to photograph lightning?' (Franz Wurm, 'Blitz Licht. Beim Übersetzen einer Zeile von René Char', *Neue Zürcher Zeitung* [18./19. April 1998], p. 69).

40 'Es war schwer diesen Text zu übersetzen, die Ellipsen darin sind ohne Zahl, es ist im Grunde eine einzige Ellipse, das Deutsche ist in solchen Fällen, Sie wissen es ja, langsamer, das Meinende bleibt länger am Gemeinten hängen (und wieviel ist nicht mitgemeint, wo etwas "gemeint" ist!), die Syntax gehorcht anderen Gesetzen, bei Char gibt es überdies recht eigenwillige Wortfolgen – nun, ich will nicht länger in eigener (und so fragwürdiger) Sache reden' (Celan, Char, *Correspondance*, pp. 257–58).

ally it ends in shipwreck'.[41] Here, Celan indicates that his attempts to reach the other bank are repeatedly interrupted. The distended, paratactic shape of his phrase – punctuated by commas, a dash, parentheses and underscoring – gives form to the 'anguished hope' that presides over this intimate encounter with Char's most famous text. Celan even admits to Leonhard that he is unable to translate fragment 215.[42] Its translation was only added at the very last moment: a scrap of paper bearing a typed version is stapled to the final proofs.

Celan's translation of Char's *Feuillets* was published in the fall of 1958 as 'Hypnos. Aufzeichnungen aus dem Maquis (1943/44)'.[43] An identical version, this time alongside the original French, was published the following spring as part of a selection of poems chosen by the author.[44] A modified translation appeared in 1963.[45]

I analyze here Celan's translation of fragment 178 as published in 1959. This fragment stands out in *Feuillets* both as the only instance of ekphrasis and as the only fragment to mention explicitly the seventeenth-century French painter Georges de la Tour (1593–1652). La Tour is a major source of inspiration for Char, above all as an example of vigilance, of resistance against the darkness of night.[46] As such he can be considered a manifestation of Hypnos, the god who sleeps with his eyes open, so as to always keep watch. In an interview with Raymond Jean in January 1969, Char states: 'The painter knows. The painter and the man. I say: knows, and not knew. Baudelaire is also one who knows. What God and Satan are to him, so day and night are to La Tour'.[47] When

41 Martin Heidegger, *Heraklit. I. Der Anfang des abendländischen Denkens. Freiburger Vorlesung vom Sommersemester 1943. Gesamtausgabe Bd. 55* (Frankfurt a. M.: Klostermann, 1979), p. 45.
42 Celan, Char, *Correspondance*, p. 258.
43 René Char, 'Hypnos. Aufzeichnungen aus dem Maquis (1943/44)', *Die neue Rundschau*, 69.4 (1958), 565–601.
44 René Char, *Poésies/Dichtungen*, ed. by Jean-Pierre Wilhelm (Frankfurt a. M.: Fischer, 1959), pp. 117–201. This edition includes Celan's translation of 'À une sérénité crispée' as 'Einer harschen Heiterkeit' (ibid., pp. 267–97).
45 René Char, *Hypnos und andere Dichtungen. Eine Auswahl des Autors*, trans. by Paul Celan, Johannes Hübner, Lothar Klünner, Jean-Pierre Wilhelm, and Franz Wurm (Frankfurt a. M.: S. Fischer, 1963). This edition is edited entirely by Celan. See: John Voellmy, 'Paul Celan révise les traductions allemandes des poèmes de René Char', *Colloquium Helveticum*, 33 (2002), 325–51.
46 For other references to La Tour, see: 'A deux mérites' (Char, *Œuvres complètes*, p. 157); 'Justesse de Georges de la Tour' (ibid., p. 455); 'Arthur Rimbaud' (ibid., p. 731); 'Madeleine à la veilleuse *par Georges de La Tour*' (ibid., p. 276); '*Une communication ?* Madeleine qui veillait' (ibid., pp. 663–65).
47 Quoted in Raymond Jean, 'Ne nous montrons pas diseurs d'apocalypse', *Le Monde* (11 January 1969). See also Char, *Œuvres complètes*, pp. 1256–57.

Henri Meschonnic describes Char's syntax and rhetoric as neo-classical – '(the 'que' with the imperative, the exclamatory 'ô,' the rhetorical question addressed to one's self or to an entity)'[48] – he also evokes the balance of forces that make Char's work simultaneously transparent and difficult, the baroque balance between the obscurity of what is represented and the clear mode of that representation in language.[49] Meschonnic finds visual parallels for this in the work of de Chirico, Magritte, Tanguy and Dalí. In 178, Char invites us to read him more accurately – with a greater sense of his poetic project – through the contemplation of a painting by La Tour he calls 'The Prisoner', now known as 'Job Scolded by his Wife'.[50] The painting can be seen in the museum at Épinal, but the reproduction referred to by Char was published as a colour plate in the 1935 edition of *Minotaure* (see Fig. 1):

> [178]
> La reproduction en couleur du 'Pri-
> sonnier' de Georges de la Tour, que
> j'ai piquée sur le mur de chaux de la pièce
> où je travaille, semble, avec le temps,
> réfléchir son sens dans notre condition.
> Elle serre le cœur mais combien désal-
> tère! Depuis deux ans, pas un réfractaire
> qui n'ait, passant la porte, brûlé ses yeux
> aux preuves de cette chandelle. La femme
> explique, l'emmuré écoute. Les mots qui
> tombent de cette terrestre silhouette d'ange
> rouge sont des mots essentiels, des mots qui
> portent immédiatement secours. Au fond
> du cachot, les minutes de suif de la clarté
> tirent et diluent les traits de l'homme
> assis. Sa maigreur d'ortie sèche, je ne vois
> pas un souvenir pour la faire frissonner.
> L'écuelle est une ruine. Mais la robe
> gonflée emplit soudain tout le cachot.
> Le Verbe de la femme donne naissance à
> l'inespéré mieux que n'importe quelle
> aurore.

48 Henri Meschonnic, *La Rime et la vie* (Paris: Éditions Verdier, 2006), p. 374.
49 What Char calls 'clarté énigmatique' [enigmatic clarity] (Char, *Œuvres complètes*, p. 743).
50 Demonts is the first to imply that the picture should be attributed to La Tour (Louis Demonts, 'Georges du Ménil de La Tour, peintre lorrain au début du xviie siècle', *Chronique des arts et de la curiosité. Supplément à la Gazette des beaux-arts* (30 April 1922), pp. 60 – 61).

Fig. 1: Georges de La Tour, 'Job Scolded by his Wife', late 1640s/early 1650s, Musée départemental des Vosges, Épinal. As Reproduced in *Minotaure* 7 (1935), n.p.

Reconnaissance à Georges de La Tour
qui maîtrisa les ténèbres hitlériennes avec
un dialogue d'êtres humains.[51]

[The colour reproduction of the *Prisoner* by Georges de La Tour, which I have pinned on the whitewashed wall of the room where I work, seems, with time, to reflect its meaning back into our condition. It grips the heart but quenches it too! For two years, there has not been a single *réfractaire* who, passing the door, has not burned his eyes on the proofs of this candle. The woman explains, the immured one listens. The words that fall from this terrestrial silhouette of the red angel are essential words, words that immediately bring succour. At the back of the cell, the tallow-minutes of clarity draw out and dilute the features of the seated man. His dry-nettle thinness, I see no memory to make him shudder. The bowl is a ruin. But the swollen gown suddenly fills the entire cell. The Word of the woman gives birth to the unhoped for better than any dawn. Recognition to Georges de La Tour, who mastered the Hitler shadows with a dialogue between human beings.]

Although fragments in *Feuillets* adopt various forms, the dimensions of this short passage of prose, as well as its unity of theme, and its gratuitousness, align the fragment with the French prose poem as defined by Suzanne Bernard.[52] Its internal coherence is suggested by the repetition of the painter's name in the first and the final sentence, as well as by the echo of the opening 'reproduction' in the closing 'Reconnaissance'. The structural juxtaposition of representation and gratitude or recognition highlights a striking feature of the text – that representation is consistently presented as unproblematic, a given, possible because non-reciprocal. The colour reproduction – pinned to the wall of the speaker's room – is (contra Benjamin) entirely adequate to the task of communicating La Tour's picture. Nothing is lost in representation as it 'reflects its meaning into our condition', and as it simultaneously 'grips' and 'quenches' the viewer's heart. The candle in the woman's right hand 'burns' the eyes of those who look at it, despite being several times removed from the original candle, which is depicted in the painting, reproduced in the colour print and then translated into Char's poem.

This model of transparent representation is echoed in the way opposite forces are balanced throughout the text. The woman explaining finds its complement in the man listening. The ruined bowl is repaired by the woman's red robe, which suddenly fills the entire cell.[53] Signifiers are easily married to signifieds.

---

51 René Char, *Feuillets d'Hypnos* (Paris: Gallimard, 1946), pp. 75–76.
52 Suzanne Bernard, *Le poème en prose de Baudelaire jusqu'à nos jours* (Paris: Librarie Nizet, 1959), pp. 11–15.
53 178 bears comparison with Baudelaire's 'Sur *Le Tasse en Prison* d'Eugène Delacroix', which begins: 'Le poète au cachot, débraillé, maladif...' (Charles Baudelaire, *Œuvres complètes*, ed. Claude Pichois, 2 vols [Paris: Gallimard, 1975–1976], I, pp. 168–69).

The words that fall from the woman are 'essential', that is to say, 'immediately' effective. As Char says in a letter sent to Gisèle from Lunéville – the town in Lorraine where La Tour worked and died – the language of his paintings is 'beneficial and secret'.[54] If the poem contains a model for its own translation, then it is one where the original lends itself to its copy – in a gesture of selfless nobility, of natural grandeur – and where the interlocutor gratefully listens. Literal translation is prescribed almost as a moral imperative.

In his translation, Celan identifies, reiterates, but also quietly dislocates, this model of reproduction:

> 178
> Die farbige Reproduktion des 'Gefangenen' von Georges de la Tour, die ich an die weißgetünchte Wand des Raumes geheftet habe, in dem ich arbeite: je mehr die Zeit verstreicht, desto stärker scheint sie ihren Sinn auf unsere Lage zurückzustrahlen. Sie schnürt das Herz zusammen, gewiß, doch wie löscht sie den Durst! Kein einziger Widerstandskämpfer seit zwei Jahren, der, zur Tür hereingekommen, sich nicht die Augen verbrannt hätte an den Beweisen dieser Kerze. Die Frau erklärt, der Ummauerte lauscht. Die Worte, die von dieser irdischen Engelsgestalt herabfallen, sind die wesentlichen, unverzüglich bringen sie Hilfe. Die Züge des in der Tiefe des Kerkers Sitzenden: die Talgminuten des Lichts dehnen sie, lassen sie verfließen. Der Mann ist ausgetrocknet wie eine welke Nessel – keine Erinnerung, bei der er erschauern könnte. Die Schüssel ist eine Ruine. Aber das gebauschte Kleid füllt plötzlich den ganzen Kerker aus. Das WORT der Frau setzt das Unverhoffte in die Welt – keine Morgenröte, die es ihr hierin zuvortun könnte.
> Dank sei Georges de la Tour, der die Hitlernacht bezwang mit einem Gespräch von Menschen![55]

In keeping with the model of reproduction prescribed by the original, there are multiple concessions made here to Char's neo-classical, if not noble, style. Contrary to common perceptions of Celan's method of translation, the syntax of Char's prose is mostly maintained, only interrupted by dashes and colons on a couple of occasions.[56] Much of the vocabulary deployed here is alien to Celan's

54 Celan, Char, *Correspondance*, p. 174.
55 Char, *Poésies/Dichtungen*, pp. 179, 181.
56 Febel, 'Überlegungen', p. 187.

poetic practice. Consider the formulations 'Reproduktion' [reproduction] and 'Dank sei...' [thanks to...], for which there are no parallels in Celan's own work. The name 'Hitler' never appears in Celan's published collections.[57] Forms of 'Kerker' [prison] occur in only two poems, on one occasion in the context of Celan's enforced hospitalization for psychosis.[58] The adjective 'gebauscht' [puffy, bouffant], adopted to describe the poem's most dynamic moment – when the woman's dress swells throughout the room – is also foreign to Celan's poetic lexicon.[59] Despite the occurrence of certain key Celanian terms such as 'Herz' [heart], 'Nessel' [nettle] and 'Gespräch' [speech], there can be no accusation here – as in certain cases – of the poet having 'Celanized' Char's text.[60] Instead, Celan appears to respect the setting without seeking to change it, as if taken aback by the strange integrity of another person's religious devotion.

Alongside the literalness-in-translation that Char's text demands and which Celan largely privileges, there remain traces of the translator's presence. In a letter sent to the translator Karl Dedecius (1921–2016) in January 1960 – in response to Dedecius's veiled criticism of his free translations of Sergei Yesenin[61] – Celan will articulate a concept of translation in which 'Textnähe' [proximity to the text] and 'Texttreue' [fidelity to the text] remain central, alongside the alterity of the translator, that is – to borrow a line from Celan's response to a questionnaire by the Librairie Flinker – 'the angle of inclination'[62] from which the translator approaches the work: 'Even in a very literal repetition of the prescribed text

---

57 See the uncollected poems: 'Wenn es einen Gott gibt' (Celan, *Die Gedichte*, p. 433); 'Die ihn bestohlen hatten' (ibid., pp. 452–54), also the only poem by Celan in which the word 'Auschwitz' appears.

58 'Lebe-Käuzchen' (ibid., p. 472); 'Wasser und Feuer' (ibid., p. 59).

59 See the poem, written ten years later, that begins: 'VON QUERAB | komm ein, als die Nacht, | das Notsegel | bauscht sich, [...]' (ibid. p. 491).

60 See Dedecius's public evaluation of Celan's translation of Yesenin: 'a West-German poetic variation, which totally fails to capture the popular, entirely unintellectual Yesenin, and which, fundamentally – above all syntactically – alters, alienates (in this case, Celanizes) him' (Karl Dedecius, 'Slawische Lyrik – übersetzt – übertragen – nachgedichtet', *Osteuropa. Zeitschrift für Gegenwartsfragen des Ostens*, 11.3 [1961], 165–78 [p. 174]).

61 They are described as 'very particular, [...] unusually expressive.' (Qtd. in Matthias Zach, *Traduction littéraire et création poétique. Yves Bonnefoy et Paul Celan traducteurs de Shakespeare* (Tours: Presses universitaires François-Rabelais, 2018), p. 145.

62 Paul Celan, *Gesammelte Werke in sieben Bänden* (Frankfurt a.M.: Suhrkamp, 2000), III, p. 168. Hamacher appropriates this turn of phrase to describe the intellectual bearing of the philologist: 'Philology is the passion of those who speak. It indicates the angle of inclination of linguistic existence' (Hamacher, *Minima Philologica*, p. 24).

[...] it remains, to all intents and purposes, a repetition, a second enunciation...'[63] Celan appears to confirm this to the Swiss scholar Werner Weber (1919–2005) the following March: 'Yes, the poem, the translated poem must, if it wants to *be* in the second language, remain mindful of this being-other, this being-different, this being-separate'.[64]

Curiously, however, the self that Celan imprints upon Char's poem is not that of the late 1950s. In this translation, Celan deploys a number of German terms that he himself only used when writing poems in his early to mid-twenties, poems that are contemporaneous with the composition of Char's text. 'Morgenröte' [dawn, lit. morning redness] not only adds more red to a poem and a picture in which the colour is already prominent, but forges a link to the only poem written by Celan in which the term appears, from sometime in the 1940s.[65] 'Talgminuten' [tallow minutes] may recall the poem 'Talglicht' [tallow light], written in 1945 or 1946.[66] When Celan uses the adjective 'welk' [withered] to translate 'ortie sèche' [dry nettle] as 'welke Nessel' – and with which he replaces 'trockene' [dry] (see Fig. 3) – he self-consciously references a period of his own work in which the term, and its derivatives, appear repeatedly, namely between 1940 and 1944.[67] In the phrase 'Sie schnürt das Herz zusammen...' [It binds the heart up...], there is a precise echo of a prose poem written by Celan in Romanian after the war.[68] When 'von dieser irdischen Engelsgestalt' [from this earthly angel] in the 1958 version becomes 'von dieser so irdischen roten Engelsgestalt' [from this so earthly red angel] in 1963, some relation to the half line:

---

63 'Noch beim [allerwörtlichsten] Nachsprechen des Vorgegebenen – [...] es bleibt, faktisch, immer ein Nachsprechen, ein zweites Sprechen...' ('List Paula Celana do Karla Dedeciusa z 31 stycznia 1960 r.' Translated by Przemysław Chojnowski. *Z problemów przekładu i stosunków międzyjęzykowych III.* Pod redakją Marii Piotrowskiej i Tadeusza Szczerbowskiego [Kraków: Wydwnictwo Naukowe AP, 2006], pp. 152–57 [p. 152]). Transcription amended by Sanmann (p. 202).

64 'Ja, das Gedicht, das übertragene Gedicht muss, wenn es in der zweiten Sprache noch einmal dasein will, dieses Anders- und Verschiedenseins, dieses Geschiedenseins eingedenk bleiben' (*Fremde Nähe*, p. 397).

65 'Aubade' (Celan, *Die Gedichte*, p. 345).

66 Ibid., p. 35.

67 See 'Ballade' (probably 1940) (ibid., p. 321); 'Sonnenwende' (probably 1941) (ibid., p. 332); 'Beieinander' (unknown date) (ibid., p. 336); 'Ich weiss' (unknown date) (ibid., p. 341); 'Ferne' (unknown date) (ibid., p. 344); 'Schlummermännlein' (1942) (ibid., p. 365); 'Schöner Oktober' (probably October 1944) (ibid., p. 367).

68 'Sub picioare simții șinele, auzii șueratul unei locomotive, foarte aproape, inima mi se încleștă. Trenul trecu deasupra capetelor noastre' [Under my feet, I could feel the rails, I could hear the whistle of a locomotive, very close, my heart was clenched [das Herz schnürte sich mir zusammen]. The train passed over our heads] (ibid., p. 386).

'O Eis von unirdischer Röte' [Oh ice of unearthly redness] in 'Schwarze Flocken' ['Black Flakes'], a poem from the early 1940s, cannot be dismissed.[69] These are all elements of what George Steiner calls the 'artifice of retrospection'.[70] They dislocate Char's text from the eternal present his language covets – note the predominance of the present tense throughout his work – and relegate it to a particular historical moment.

There are other small but telling indications of Celan's intervention through translation, of the 'knowing' that Char attributes to La Tour and Baudelaire. Acoustically, Char's text coheres around the voiceless fricative /ʃ/, which occurs in the poem's major terms – 'de chaux' [whitewashed], 'réfléchir' [reflect], 'chandelle' [candle], 'cachot' [cell] (twice) and 'sèche' [dry]. Besides being Char's aural signature, the sound 'ch' multiplies and diversifies the 'chandelle' which, as Finck suggests, is the symbol *par excellence* of Char's poetic resistance.[71] Just as the visual logic of La Tour's paintings derives from the depiction of artificial light in darkness,[72] so too here, the amplified presence of the candle provides an acoustic structure for the poem. This acoustic structure is approximated, and perhaps even enhanced, through the repetition of the letter 'k' in Celan's German. 'Kerker' [prison] is repeated and echoed in 'Kerze' [candle], as well as 'welke', 'keine' [none] and 'Kleid' [dress]. Drafts show that Celan was initially minded to translate 'mur de chaux' [whitewashed wall] as 'Kalkwand'. His decision to replace this with the more prosaic 'weißgetünchte Wand' is intriguing and warrants closer attention (see Fig. 2).

I suggest that this particular intervention has broader consequences – intended and unintended – both for the translation and for the original text. As an instance of Celan's active intervention, it is aimed specifically at reminding the reader of Martin Luther's translation of the Old Testament, where 'getüncht' appears with some frequency. See, for instance, the description of the walls of Belshazzar's palace in Daniel 5, on which the 'menetekel' appears to pronounce the king's death.[73] Consider also the parable of the whitewashed wall built by

69 Ibid., p. 19.

70 George Steiner, *After Babel. Aspects of Language and Translation* (Oxford: Oxford University Press, 1981), p. 334.

71 Michèle Finck, 'René Char et Georges de La Tour: la peinture au secours de l'action poétique dans le feuillet 178 des *Feuillets d'Hypnos*'. Presented at the Université de Strasbourg, 18 October 2016. Available at https://lettres.unistra.fr/uploads/media/Finck_Char.pdf, p. 11.

72 Quignard perceives the halos that traditionally encircle the heads of gods and saints as recovered in La Tour's candlelight (Pascal Quignard, *La Nuit et le silence* [Paris: Flohic, 1997], p. 35).

73 Martin Luther, *Lutherbibel (Textfassung 1912)* (Altenmünster: Jazzy Bee Verlag Jürgen Beck, 2016), p. 617. Celan returns to Daniel in 1965 and 1966, in 'All deine Siegel', 'Bedenkenlos'

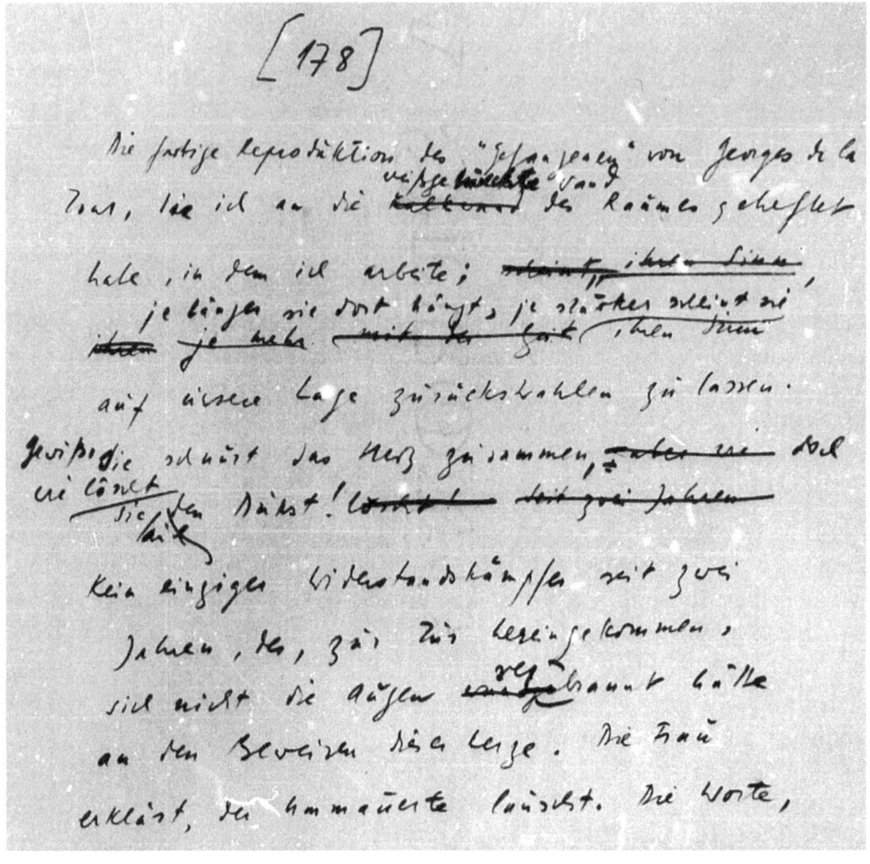

Fig. 2: Draft of Fragment 178 (first page), 'Hypnos. Aufzeichnungen aus dem Maquis 1943/44', 1958. German Literature Archive, Marbach am Neckar.

the false prophets in Ezekiel 13.[74] In both biblical texts, the wall sets the scene for the performance of retributive justice against those who misuse language to speak untruths. Where 'Kalkwand' adhered to a defining structure of the original poem – the repetition of the letter 'k' in imitation of the sound 'ch' – 'weißgetüncht' hints at the operation of an alternative logic, of a logic that draws at-

and 'Vom Hochseil'... For readings of these poems see: Connolly, *Unfinished Poetics*, pp. 165 and 168–84.

74 Luther, *Lutherbibel*, p. 581.

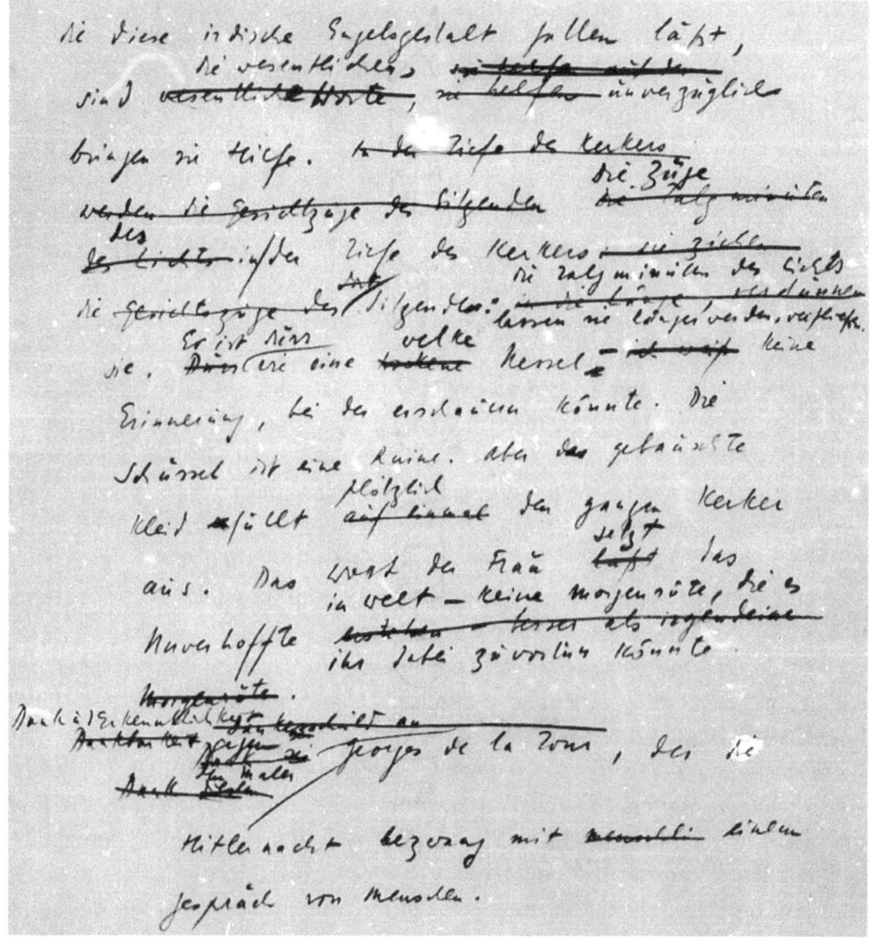

Fig. 3: Draft of Fragment 178 (second page), 'Hypnos. Aufzeichnungen aus dem Maquis 1943/44', 1958. German Literature Archive, Marbach am Neckar.

tention to something known or suspected and, in particular, to a crime that has been obscured.

Celan provides us with a broader definition of this same counter-logic in his response to the Librairie Flinker, when he says that – compared to contemporary French poetry – the language of German poetry 'has become more sober, more factual. It treats the 'beautiful' with suspicion, it tries to be true'.[75] 'Weißgetüncht' points towards this sober, greyer language, towards a language more aware of the role that poetry might play in bringing about justice, towards a poetry that 'knows'. 'Weißgetüncht' may also be a sign of the translator's resistance to Char's poetics. As Böschenstein notes: 'Char's pathetic aphorisms [...] have little in common with Celan's experience of a destruction of language which founds language anew'.[76] It may even contain a hidden reproach to Char, as by this stage Celan's enthusiasm had given way to a brooding discontent caused by the French poet's lacklustre support against Goll's accusations.[77]

But beyond any intention of the translator, 'weißgetüncht' challenges the reader in the here and now to consider what might have remained hidden in this poem about a picture and to exercise the attention to detail, to the real and to the true, which Celan repeatedly enjoins. As he says in the response to Flinker, poetic language 'does not transfigure or "poeticize", it names and sets, it tries to measure out the domain of the given and of the possible'.[78] Celan's discreet dislocations – the replacement of 'Kalkwand' with 'weißgetünchte Wand' as well as the retrospective choice of vocabulary – should encourage us to examine whether the nature of the 'given' and of the 'possible' is as Char says it is.

To identify the weakness that Celan seems to sense in Char's poem but which he cannot fully articulate, I propose to go back to the moment when Char first encountered La Tour, at an exhibition held at the Orangerie des Tuileries of the Musée du Louvre between November 1934 and March 1935. This exhibition, called 'Painters of Reality in Seventeenth-Century France,' was the first time La Tour's paintings – thirteen of the fifteen then known – had been exhibited together. Although the existence of a painter named Georges du Mesnil de La Tour had been established in the 1860s,[79] no works were attributed to him until 1915, when the prominent German art critic and museum curator Hermann Voss (1884–1969) identified him as the author of two paintings in the gallery at

75 'ist nüchterner, faktischer geworden. Sie misstraut dem 'Schönen', sie versucht, wahr zu sein' (Celan, *Gesammelte Werke*, III, p. 167).

76 Bernhard Böschenstein, 'Paul Celan und die französische Dichtung', in Bernhard Böschenstein, *Leuchttürme. Von Hölderlin zu Celan. Wirkung und Vergleich* (Frankfurt a.M.: Insel, 1977), pp. 307–30 (p. 310).

77 Badiou, 'D'une main...', p. 23.

78 'verklärt nicht, "poetisiert" nicht, sie nennt und setzt, sie versucht, den Bereich des Gegebenen und des Möglichen auszumessen' (Celan, *Gesammelte Werke*, III, p. 167).

79 Alexandre Joly, 'Du Mesnil-la-Tour, peintre', *Journal de la Société d'archéologie lorraine*, 12 (1863).

Nantes and one in Rennes.[80] Voss would lead the way in recovering La Tour from the shadows of history. He was the first to define his style. He was the first to propose that the Lorrainian must have spent time in Rome – where he would have encountered influential Caravaggisti such as Hendrick ter Brugghen and Gerrit van Honthorst (whom the Italians called Gherardo delle Notti).[81] In 1931, he was the first to attribute diurnal scenes to the painter of the night, suggesting that the nocturnal works dated from late in the painter's career.[82] As Cuzin and Salmon note: 'these findings and intuitions would go on to mark research on La Tour for years to come'.[83] Just as in Char's reading of La Tour's painting the red woman leads the prisoner out into the light of liberation, so too Voss rescues La Tour from the night of oblivion. As a result of the exhibition of 1934, La Tour rapidly became not only a leading example of the genius of seventeenth-century French painting but also a vehicle for French pride and national identity.

It is in the historical context of Char's appropriation of La Tour that I turn to the single text that did most to introduce La Tour to the twentieth century. It is a text which Char read.[84] In his preface to the exhibition catalogue, Paul Jamot (1863–1939) claims that the revelation of La Tour is proof that French painting has always been concerned with the 'real', even at those moments when other tastes seemed to prevail. The metaphor he uses to describe how this interest in the 'real' was always present – although not always visible – will be familiar to readers of René Char:

> *Like one of these rivers that run partly underground which, precisely, are one of the natural curiosities of certain French regions. It disappears into an abyß between two rocks & we forget its presence; but it is still there, & we soon see it emerging, more powerful [plus puißant], from the deep shadows to spread its liquid sheets out under the light of the sky. It prevents imaginatives & poets from getting lost in abstraction or in the clouds. And, as if along this route in the shadows, it had collected, in its water, some glitter of mystery, it spreads a subtle poetry in the simple & frank style of Le Nain, Chardin, Corot, Courbet, Manet, this style that*

80 Hermann Voss, 'Georges du Mesnil de La Tour', *Archiv für Kunstgeschichte*, 2 (1914–1915), plates 121–23.

81 Hermann Voss, 'Georges du Mesnil de la Tour. A Forgotten French Master of the Seventeenth Century', *Art in America*, 17 (1928–1929), 40–48 (pp. 40, 47).

82 Hermann Voss, 'Tableaux à éclairage diurne de G. de La Tour', *Formes*, 16 (1931), pp. 97–100.

83 Jean-Pierre Cuzin et Dimitri Salmon, *Georges de La Tour. Histoire d'une redécouverte* (Paris: Gallimard, 1997), p. 27.

84 Martine Créac'h, 'LA TOUR, Georges de', in *Dictionnaire René Char*, ed. by Danièle Leclair and Patrick Née (Paris: Classiques Garnier, 2015), pp. 337–38, (p. 337).

> *has nothing to do with the realism of the Flemish and the Dutch, full of verve, overflowing with sensuality & carried away by a sort of Bacchic lyricism.*[85]

Char was born in L'Isle-sur-la-Sorgue, an island on the river Sorgue, a few miles downstream from Fontaine de Vaucluse, where the water surges from under the ground, much as in Jamot's analogy. Both channels are sources of poetry. For Jamot, the river brings forth the subtle poetry and simple art of French genius. For Char, the Sorgue is the source of metaphors that irrigate his poetics. In 1945, he describes one of his early collections as '*this river hardly seen that ran inland* [...] *this radiant and enigmatic river*'.[86] In a later poem called 'La Sorgue', he writes: 'River too soon departed, all of a sudden, without company, | Give the children of my country the traits of your passion'.[87] Maulpoix describes the Sorgue in Char's work as 'a river that emerges from the night, leaping from the rock like an "ineffable beast"',[88] and applies it metaphorically to the powerful but sometimes hidden presence of Rimbaud, Heraclitus and La Tour.[89]

Both Jamot's and Char's subterranean streams carry La Tour into the present. But in passing through the underground night, there is evidence to suggest that they do more than acquire the 'glitter of mystery'. Namely, that they also expose themselves to the possibility of contamination. A curious characteristic of Jamot's seminal text is that all instances of double 's' are rendered 'ß'. We encounter phrases such as 'paßionné pour Georges de la Tour' [excited by Georges de La Tour] and 'le grand Poußin' [the great Poussin],[90] as well as 'sortir plus puißant des ténèbres inférieures' [emerge, more powerful, from the deep shadows]. Although legible, the 'ß' lends an unusual aspect to the French text, one that might be compared to the strange posture – particularly the loosely cocked wrist – of the red woman in La Tour's painting. 'ß' occasionally appears in seventeenth-century French texts – primarily in the case of the adverb 'außi' [also] – and it may be this phenomenon that Jamot (or his typesetter) aims to mimic.[91] But 'ß' is more commonly found in German texts, where it is known as the

85 Paul Jamot, 'Préface', in *Les Peintres de la réalité en France au xvii*e *siècle* (Paris: Édition des musées nationaux, 1934), pp. xv–xxvii (p. xvii).
86 Char, *Œuvres complètes*, p. 3.
87 Ibid., p. 274. See also 'Aux Riverains de la Sorgue' (ibid., p. 412).
88 Jean-Michel Maulpoix, *Fureur et Mystère de René Char* (Paris: Gallimard, 1996), p. 28.
89 Maulpoix, *Pour un lyrisme critique*, p. 169.
90 Jamot, 'Préface', p. xviii.
91 '... *Et comme ton Amour merite Celanire, | Fay voir que ton courage à vaincre si constant, | Merite außi sa part du Sceptre qu'elle attend*' (Pierre Du Ryer, *Le Cléomédon. Trage-Comédie* [Paris: Sommaville, 1638], p. 28).

'scharfes S' [sharp s] or the 'esszet' [s-z]. Given the political climate in Europe in late 1934 and the context of a preface that aims to promote the glory of the French nation through the recovery of its forgotten masters, I propose to read 'ß' as the trace of an unexpected presence.

Specifically, 'ß' is a vehicle that bears the name of the art critic Hermann Voss, here spelled Voß.[92] In spite of the nationalist thrust of his preface, Jamot will later merit his German colleague with being 'a critic who has contributed more than any other to the resurrection of Georges de La Tour, and who cannot be suspected of indulgence, as might happen in the case of a Frenchman'.[93] Besides being a leading art historian of the Italian Renaissance and German Baroque, a recent study has detailed how Voss became closely aligned with the National Socialists.[94] At around the time Jamot wrote this text, Voss – first as director of the Kaiser-Friedrich-Museum in Berlin and from 1935 as director of the museum at Wiesbaden – benefitted from the illegal appropriation of works of art from Jewish owners. At Wiesbaden, he fashioned the collection to suit the National Socialist doctrine, selling or exchanging works considered out of keeping with the preferred aesthetic. In March 1943, after private meetings with Joseph Goebbels and Adolf Hitler, he was appointed director of the Museum at Dresden.[95] He was also entrusted with the task of creating a collection for the planned museum at Linz, the so-called 'Jugendstadt des Führers' [the Führer's hometown],[96] which Hitler wanted to make the most important cultural centre of the Third Reich.

Georges de La Tour re-emerges in the twentieth century through the efforts of an art critic subsequently implicated in propagating the same 'Hitlerian shadows' that Char merits La Tour with mastering in fragment 178. The revelation of Voss – and something of National Socialism – in the shadows of La Tour's painting may not challenge the integrity of the works themselves, but it does raise questions about how these works are appropriated and redeployed. It is probable that neither Char nor Celan knew much of the debt French cultural history owed to Voss. It is also unlikely that they could have known of his role in the Third Reich, as Voss enjoyed a successful career in Munich following the war

92 Jamot, 'Préface', p. xix.

93 Paul Jamot, 'Georges de La Tour. A propos de quelques tableaux nouvellement découverts', *Gazette des beaux-arts*, 81.6.21 (1939), 243–86 (p. 280).

94 Kathrin Iselt, *'Sonderbeauftrager des Führers'. Der Kunsthistoriker und Museumsmann Hermann Voss (1884–1969)* (Cologne: Böhlau Verlag, 2010).

95 Voss met with Goebbels in Berlin on 3 February 1943, and with Hitler in Rastenburg (now Kętrzyn) on 16 February (ibid., pp. 186–96).

96 Ibid., p. 161.

and died – unperturbed by his past – in 1969.[97] But in light of Voss's presence, the models of transparent representation and of literal translation that Char promotes in his poem suddenly seem insufficiently critical, lacking in the very vigilance that La Tour is meant to exemplify. There is little in Char's text that prepares its reader for the devious twists of history, such as those that implicate a National Socialist in the discovery of a painter whose work was thought – albeit anachronistically and poetically – to master the 'Hitler night'.

There are signs that the same contaminated current that bears La Tour into contemporary consciousness also runs through Char's ekphrasis and even its translation. The double 's' of Voss's name – which Jamot unwittingly highlights – persists in Char's poem as: 'passant la porte' [passing the door], 'des mots essentiels' [essential words], 'l'homme assis' [the seated man], 'donne naissance' [give birth] and 'Reconnaissance...'. In the line: 'je ne vois pas un souvenir pour la faire frissonner' [I see no memory to make him shudder], 'je ne vois pas' not only articulates the limits of what is seen and known. It also imperfectly articulates Voss's name – 'vois' – the revelation of which may well make us 'shudder'. Initially, this current seems to run into Celan's translation too. Celan maintains the double 's' (or 'ß') in 'gewiß [certainly], 'lassen sie verfließen' [let them flow by], 'Nessel' and 'Schüssel' [bowl], and perhaps above all in 'weißgetünchte Wand' [white-washed wall]. Crucially, he replaces the negative verbal form 'je ne vois pas' with a dash or 'Gedankenstrich'. Although typical of his translation method, in this particular instance the dash removes – at a stroke – both the notions of 'not seeing' and of 'not knowing', as well as the trace of Voss's name. It introduces in its stead what Febel calls 'a quasi-gestural space for reflection'.[98] The dash becomes an emblem not only for those things we do not yet know and which we may yet identify in the shadows of a painting, or of a poem, or of its translation. It also reminds us that a work of art might be changed by historical events and how we must be alert to these changes. It is a reminder to read – and to translate – with vigilance, and specifically with what Celan calls – in his 1960 speech *Der Meridian* – 'the grave accent of the historical'.[99]

If we are right to detect Voss's presence in the shadows of La Tour's painting, as well as in Char's poem and even Celan's translation, then – at the very least – there are grounds to re-evaluate Heidegger's model of translation. In translation, not all elements are exposed to the risk of odyssey or shipwreck. In some cases, the river will refuse to run within the banks set out in parallel, and will instead

97 A Festschrift from 1966 makes no mention of Voss's wartime activities (ibid., p. 452).
98 Febel, 'Überlegungen', p. 187.
99 Celan, *Gesammelte Werke*, III, p. 190.

undercut what is visible, freely flowing where it cannot be seen. This suggests that where we are used to seeing separation – of original and copy, of poet and translator, of one language and other – we should also be on the lookout for continuities. In the case of Char's resistance poetry, it perhaps points to the deep and obscured continuity of nationalisms – cultural as well as political, French as well as German – and to the ways they feed off and depend on each other, even at those moments when they appear to meet in antagonistic opposition. The small dislocations in Celan's literal translation – the historical displacement of its vocabulary as well as the decisive introduction of 'weißgetüncht' where 'Kalkwand' would have been in keeping with the poem's structure – are indices of discomfort, of misgivings that cannot yet be put into words, but which are always on the verge of bursting into the open.

This reading may therefore help explain the unease that quickly developed between the French war hero and the Jewish survivor of the Shoah. Shortly after meeting Celan in 1954, Char became close friends with Heidegger. Celan's difficult relationship with the German philosopher has been the focus of multiple studies. Unbeknownst to Celan, Char also maintained cordial relations with Claire Goll. Celan's translation of 178 discreetly indicates that the 'Hitlerian shadows' were never mastered as Char claimed in his poem, even in the mystical encounter with La Tour, and that his poem may even propagate them, although Char would have been unaware of this. They are the shadows of a time that – for Celan – will continue to contaminate even those most intimate, aesthetic and mystical of moments, moments which nevertheless remain essential or, as Char says, 'secret and beneficial'.

Camilla Miglio

Translating in a 'Wholly Other' German. 'Ricercar'

Coming from a multilingual and multicultural Eastern-European setting, Celan takes upon himself the legacy of German as a 'minor'[1] language. Foreignness and proximity, perceived both in his own cultural field at home and during his emigration, are carved into a hybridized identity where each language resonates with the whole. His language(s) and poetics run parallel. The polyphonic texture of the voices of his literary interlocutions in time and space, both inter- and intralinguistic, calling to each other and merging in his poetic other-voicedness, are expressed both in poetry and translation.[2]

I will focus on *exempla* of translations and original poems written between the end of the 1950s and the early 1960s.[3] In those intense and dramatic[4] years he came to poetic and existential self-awareness, poised between two linguistic and cultural worlds (without prejudice to the broader, complex original polyphony experienced since his childhood): the 'Cyrillic' world and his new home on

1 See Gilles Deleuze and Félix Guattari, *Kafka. Toward a Minor Literature*, trans. by Dana Polan (Minneapolis: University of Minnesota Press, 1986). N.B.: throughout the text, translations not attested by references are mine.

2 Following Eskin's and May's inputs, I extend Bakhtinian patterns to Celan's relational poetry, going beyond the Bakhtinian distinction between polyphonic prose and monologic poetry – e. g. in Mikhail M. Bakhtin, *Dialogic Imagination. Four Essays*, ed. by Michael Holquist (Austin: University of Texas Press, 1981), p. 328; see Michael Eskin, 'Bakhtin on Poetry', in *Poetics Today,* 1.21.2 (June 2000), 379 – 91, but see also below, note 6; Markus May *'Ein Klaffen, das mich sichtbar macht'. Untersuchungen zu Paul Celans Übersetzungen amerikanischer Lyrik* (Heidelberg: Winter 2004), pp. 100 – 12 (p. 105).

3 For a synoptic study of Celan's different translations and their contexts (irreducible to a single coherent picture), see the seminal study of Leonard M. Olschner, *Der feste Buchstab. Erläuterungen zu Paul Celans Gedichtübertragungen* (Göttingen: Vandenhoeck & Ruprecht, 1985); *'Fremde Nähe'. Eine Ausstellung des Deutschen Literaturarchivs im Schiller-Nationalmuseum Marbach am Neckar und im Stadthaus Zürich*, ed. by Axel Gellhaus und Rolf Bücher, Sabria Filali, Peter Goßens, Ute Harbusch, Thomas Heck, Christine Ivanovic, Andreas Lohr and Barbara Wiedemann with Petra Plättner (Marbach am Neckar: Deutsche Schillergesellschaft, 1987); *Stationen. Kontinuität und Entwicklung in Paul Celans Übersetzungswerk*, ed. by Jürgen Lehmann and Christine Ivanovic (Heidelberg: Winter, 1997); *Celan-Handbuch*, ed. by Markus May, Peter Goßens and Jürgen Lehmann (Weimar: Metzler, 2008), pp. 180 – 14.

4 The devastating 'Goll-Affair', begun in the early 1950s, exploded in 1959 (indeed, as a matter of translation); see Barbara Wiedemann, *Die Goll-Affäre. Dokumente zu einer 'Infamie'* (Frankfurt a. M.: Suhrkamp, 2000).

https://doi.org/10.1515/9783110658330-006

the Seine.[5] The tension between a figure of close 'poethic'[6] dialogue, such as Ossip Mandelstam, and a poetological counterpart in matters of 'obscurity', such as Paul Valéry, provides evidence of the new *meta-discursive*, ethical space of Celan's translations, exposing his 'Gesamtdeutsch'[7] [pan-German] readers to the experience of estrangement from their own supposed monolingualism. Celan's translational writing is based on an ethical commitment: 'repeating' lost and scattered voices, names and memories from and in different places, times and languages, Celan indicates a possibility of disclosing a traumatic past 'in the Light of U-topia'.[8] There, anything seemingly wholly other, lost or mute can be rewritten and performed[9] otherwise, as a speaking, translated voice.

Born in translation

Paul Pessach Antschel, born into a Jewish family at the outer reaches of the former Habsburg Empire, came from what we might call a 'translation zone'[10] in the

---

5 See 'Und mit dem Buch aus Tarussa', in Paul Celan, *Gesammelte Werke in fünf Bänden*, ed. by Beda Allemann, with Stefan Reichert and Rolf Bücher [GW] (Frankfurt a. M.: Suhrkamp, 1983), I, p. 288; Paul Celan, *Speech-Grille and Selected Poems*, trans. by Joachim Neugroschel (New York: Dutto, 1971), pp. 207–9.

6 See Michael Eskin, *Ethics and Dialogue. In the Works of Levinas, Bakhtin, Mandel'shtam, and Celan* (Oxford: Oxford University Press, 2000): a reading of Celan as 'poetologically complementing and poetically staging and illuminating both Levinas's correlation of Saying and Said and Bakhtin's claim that dialogic-existential relations 'pervade utterances from within' (pp. 11–12); he also reads Celan alongside their 'preoccupation with dialogue and otherness' (p. 66), their 'calling for interpretation of their writings in conjunction with others' writings' (p. xiii). See Eskin's careful analysis of the poems from the cycle *Die Niemandsrose* (1963), in which dialogical responsiveness to Mandelstam strongly resounds.

7 Celan's sense of estrangement towards 'Gesamtdeutsch' in Paul Celan, *'Mikrolithen sind's, Steinchen'. Die Prosa aus dem Nachlaß*, ed. by Barbara Wiedemann and Bertrand Badiou (Frankfurt a. M.: Suhrkamp, 2005), p. 28.

8 GWIII, p. 199. 'Im Lichte der Utopie'; Paul Celan, *Selected Poems and Prose*, trans. by John Felstiner (New York: Norton, 2001), p. 411.

9 'Das Mimische' (the mimetic aspect) of the poem in Paul Celan, *Der Meridian. Vorstufen – Textgenese – Endfassung. Tübinger Ausgabe*, ed. by Jürgen Wertheimer, Bernhard Böschenstein and Heino Schmull (Frankfurt a. M.: Suhrkamp 1999), p. 112.

10 I am here borrowing and adapting Emily Apter's formulation in *The Translation Zone. A New Comparative Literature* (Princeton: Princeton University Press, 2006). The situation of Celan's native town resonates in his linguistic and poetic awareness: it was a place in which political transformation run parallel to a struggle for linguistic dominance. Between the late 1920s and the end of the second world war, the normalization of a multilingual situation towards a national(ized) monolingualism in fact scattered and destroyed its transnational and translingual cultural mi-

former Czernowitz, capital of the *Kronland* [crownland] Bukovina. The town at the time of his birth in 1920 had already been renamed, or rather translated, into Rumanian as Cernăuţi and then, in 1941, into Černivci as a part of the Soviet Ukraine.[11] Antschel learned to live surrounded by interlinguistic and intercultural conflicts. Although his father Leo identified closely with the Zionist Jewish tradition, and his mother Friederike was more inclined towards the lay German tradition of *Humanität*,[12] which likely represented, for the modest social condition of the family, a way of attaining a higher symbolic cultural capital.

Paul's education was ultimately a result of his mother's influence. His curriculum records the fluctuating fortunes of the Jewish population in Cernăuţi in the 1920s, poised between a permanent plurilingualism and the acquisition of a sound classical, humanist education: primary education in German and Hebrew; 'liceul' [high school] in Rumanian and French (the new *langue de culture* in the Rumanian Cernăuţi, which replaced German, the *Bildungssprache* of the former Habsburg Czernowitz); his final years of high school education in German and Rumanian, but also Italian and English, Latin and Greek; French at the Faculty of Medicine in Tours;[13] then French and English during his further academic studies in Cernăuţi-Černivci.[14] Moreover, during his time spent in a Rumanian labour camp, he was able to take a notebook with him where he recorded his poems and translations of Shakespeare's sonnets.[15] In Bucharest[16] he translated into Russian and published under different pseudonyms: Aurel, Ancel, Celan, A. Pavel, writing in Rumanian, a language which was both foreign and familiar.

---

lieu. Celan's construction of different voices in his writing and translation practice can be represented as poetic creation of a 'zone' recalling yet different from the lost time and space: 'a broad intellectual topography that is neither property of a single nation, nor an amorphous condition associated with postnationalism, but rather a zone of critical engagement that connects the "l" and the "n" of transLation and transNation' (Apter, *The Translation Zone*, p. 5).

11 On Celan's youth in Cernăuţi see Israel Chalfen, *Paul Celan. Eine Biographie seiner Jugend* (Frankfurt a.M.: Insel, 1979).

12 In the sense given to the term during the 'Age of Goethe', from Herder to Goethe and Schiller, passing through Lessing and Mendelssohn.

13 See Amy-Diana Colin and Edith Silbermann, eds., *Paul Celan – Edith Silbermann. Zeugnisse einer Freundschaft. Gedichte, Briefwechsel, Erinnerungen* (Munich: Fink, 2010), p. 53.

14 See documentation with reproductions of the original School and University reports in Axel Gellhaus, ed., 'Paul Antschel/Paul Celan in Czernowitz', *Marbacher Magazin*, Sonderheft 90 (2000), 25–33.

15 See Chalfen, *Paul Celan*, p. 138; Colin/Silbermann, *Zeugnisse*, p. 125; Gellhaus, ed., *Marbacher Magazin*, pp. 68–69; Gellhaus et al. (eds), *'Fremde Nähe'*, p. 419.

16 See *Zeitschrift für Kulturaustausch. Vj. Bukarester Celan Kolloquium* 1981. *Texte zum frühen Celan*, ed. by Uwe Martin, 3, 32 (1982/3).

However, in the end he opted for German, his mother('s) tongue, the language of the destroyed 'minor culture' of Cernăuţi's Jewish bourgeoisie.

Celan witnessed the definitive loss of the linguistic and cultural milieu into which he had been born, taking his 'minor' language, German, as his only baggage to post-war Vienna, where German, however, was saturated with the anti-Semitic violence of a past that had not yet been dealt with. Celan's German was very different from any 'Bundesdeutsch';[17] borrowing an expression from Apter, we can say that he 'breaks the isomorphic fit between the name of a nation and the name of a language'.[18] All these tensions appear in his name: Paul was the *goijm* name usually associated with the Hebrew name Pessach, which he inherited from his paternal great-grandfather. His father's surname, first changed to Anczel and then recomposed into Celan, was passed down to Paul's son Eric, for 'Celan' was a name easily pronounced in Rumanian, German and French. In France, Celan continued to write in his German as a 'minor' language while using French in his everyday life;[19] his surname was Frenchified, and his first name became a source of support for his son: 'ton père | t'épaule'[20] [your father | will support you] wrote Celan on a 'Blatt' [sheet of paper] on which he had traced the shape of a 'Blatt' [leaf] from the Paulownia tree, thus playing on the triple meanings of the word in both German and French, in which the sonorous element of his proper name (epaule/Paul) also resonates.

---

17 I am using the term 'Bundesdeutsch' to refer to the uncomfortable mood Celan felt when he had to stay in the 'Bundesrepublik' and to a particular, actually 'national' self-awareness of the young generation of 'German' authors after the war. This is documented in his *Correspondance* with his wife, but also in an episode that occurred during his reading at the Gruppe 47 encounter in 1952. His German colleagues felt the strangeness and what they believed was the almost uncanny sound of his voice; H. Werner Richter's wife thought he was a French guest speaking very good German; other authors were confused by his intonation, some of them even comparing it with the voice of Goebbels [sic!], others – on the other hand – to a sort of synagogue sound. Further reports define him as a 'Rumäniendeutscher' poet. See Paul Celan – Gisèle Celan Lestrange, *Correspondance (1951–1970). Avec un choix de lettres de Paul Celan à son fils Eric*, ed. by Bertrand Badiou and Eric Celan (Paris: Seuil, 2001), I ('Lettres'), N. 14, 31 May 1952, p. 27 and II ('Commentaires et Illustrations'), pp. 61–63.
18 Apter, *The Translation Zone*, p. 243.
19 For a discussion on poetical and biographical-existential geography and topography by Celan, see Marko Pajević, 'Erfahrungen, Orte, Aufenthalte und die Sorge um das Selbst', *arcadia*, 32. 1 (1997), 148–61. On Celan's early years in Paris: Andrei Corbea-Hoise, *Paul Celans 'unbequemes Zuhause'. Sein erstes Jahrzehnt in Paris* (Aachen: Rimbaud, 2017).
20 Paul Celan, 'Ô les hâbleurs' [1968] in Paul Celan, *Die Gedichte. Neue kommentierte Gesamtausgabe in einem Band*, ed. by Barbara Wiedemann (Berlin: Suhrkamp, 2018), p. 536; see Michael G. Levine, *A Weak Messianic Power. Figures of a Time to Come in Benjamin, Derrida, and Celan* (New York: Fordham University Press, 2014).

Starting from an objective polyphony and based on his own aesthetic and existential development through language, Celan developed an idea of heteroglossia in which the different voices inside him were consciously modulated, going from a natural state of entropy (in which he could always *czernowitzeln* anyway)[21] to a 'negentropic' cultural translation.[22] This issue entails a crucial political turn, if we think, with Agamben (and Apter), that 'it is only by breaking at any point the nexus between the existence of language, grammar, people and state that thought and praxis will be equal to the tasks at hand'.[23]

'Fremde Nähe'

Celan's 'meta-German'[24] harked back both to his lost origins and to the shadows of LTI.[25] His interlinguistic polyphony was thus 'enriched'[26] by a painful intralinguistic dialogue, whose ethical and political dimension coalesced after 1945. The authors and the texts he translated had to 'pass through'[27] this experience.

In 'Dein vom Wachen'[28] ['Your Dream'[29]] (written 1963, published 1967 as part of *Atemwende* [*Breathturn*]) the trace of a word is carved, like a wound, into the 'horn' of a hurting dream. That wound needs to be 'translated' (transferred) – in a scene of physical pain. But language for Celan constitutes not only the space of physical suffering, as in Kafka; it is also a vast space where different voices gather and are set free. Translation creates this space, 'is' this space. All the voices, including those in German, that come from a 'no longer', tend to materialize in

---

21 Ilana Shmueli, *Sag, daß Jerusalem ist. Über Paul Celan: Oktober 1969 – April 1970* (Eggingen: Isele, 2000), p. 24.
22 See Michael Cronin, *Translation and Identity* (London: Routledge, 2006); Federico Italiano, *Translation and Geography* (London: Routledge, 2016), pp. 5–9.
23 Giorgio Agamben, *Means without Ends. Notes on Politics*, trans. by Vincenzo Binetti and Cesare Casarino (Minneapolis: University of Minnesota Press, 2000), p. 69. Discussed also by Apter, *The Translation Zone*, p. 244.
24 George Steiner, *After Babel. Aspects of Language and Translation* (Oxford: Oxford University Press, 1975), p. 409.
25 Victor Klemperer, *The Language of the Third Reich,* trans. by Martin Brady (London: Bloomsbury, 2010).
26 GWIII, pp.185–186. See May, *Ein Klaffen,* p. 109.
27 GWIII, p. 186. 'Hindurchgehen'. Celan, *Selected Poems and Prose*, p. 395.
28 GWII, p. 24. Also in Celan, *Die Gedichte*, p. 182, and Wiedemann's Commentary, p. 853.
29 Paul Celan, *Breathturn into Timestead. The Collected Later Poetry: A Bilingual Edition*, ed. and trans. by Pierre Joris (New York: Farrar, Straus & Giroux 2014), p. 12.

written form, in a word yet to come, which is 'ever-yet'[30] and manifests itself in a state of expectation, tension and search for direction, lighting up when it comes into contact with an 'Other'. See, e.g. the 'ferry' travelling back and forth between two poles:

> Die in der senk-
> rechten, schmalen
> Tagschlucht nach oben
> stakende Fähre:
>
> Sie setzt
> Wundgelesenes über.
>
> [The in the vert-
> ical, narrow
> daygorge, the upward
> poling ferry:
>
> it carries
> sore readings over.[31]]

This poem recalls the 'transfer'[32] of a writing-wound, as if the text were engraved on the body of the prisoner in Kafka's 'Penal Colony'. There is a movement upstream through a gorge, readable as the part of the body through which voicing passes.

The relationship between time, writing and reading, between merged speech acts[33] and body, recurs in another important text published in 1963. The poem 'Es ist alles anders' ['Everything is Different'[34]] expresses this relationship through hybridization occurring over time – between Celan and his 'brother Ossip'[35] (Mandelstam):

---

30 GWIII, p. 197. 'Immer noch'; Celan, *Selected Poems and Prose*, p. 409.

31 Celan, *Breathturn into Timestead*, p. 12.

32 See John Felstiner, 'Translating as Transference. Paul Celan's Versions of Shakespeare, Dickinson, Mandelshtam, Apollinaire', in *Translating Literatures, Translating Cultures. New Vistas and Approaches in Literary Studies*, ed. by Kurt Müller-Vollmer and Michael Irmscher (Berlin: Erich Schmidt, 1998), p. 168. See also Felstiner's 'Freudian' *lectio* of 'Übertragung' as 'transference'.

33 See about Bakhtinian *Redeverschmelzung* by Celan: Jürgen Lehmann, 'Karnevaleske Dialogisierung', in *Germanistik und Komparatistik. Germanistische Symposien Berichtsbände*, ed. by Hendrik Birus (Stuttgart: Metzler, 1995), pp. 541–55.

34 Paul Celan, *Poems (Revised and Expanded)*, trans. by Michael Hamburger (New York: Persea Books, 2002), p. 195.

35 Gellhaus et al. (eds), *'Fremde Nähe'*, p. 353. 'Bruder Ossip'.

der Name Ossip kommt auf dich zu, du erzählst ihm,
was er schon weiß, er nimmt es, er nimmt es dir ab, mit Händen,
du löst ihm den Arm von der Schulter, den rechten, den linken,
du heftest die deinen an ihre Stelle, mit Händen, mit Fingern, mit Linien,
— was abriß, wächst wieder zusammen —
da hast du sie, da nimm sie dir, da hast du alle beide,
den Namen, den Namen, die Hand, die Hand,
da nimm sie dir zum Unterpfand,
er nimmt auch das, und du hast
wieder, was dein ist, was sein war,[36]

[the name Ossip walks up to you, and you tell him
what he knows already, he takes, he accepts it from you, with hands,
you detach an arm from his shoulder, the right, the left,
you attach your own in its place, with hands, with fingers, with lines,
— what was severed joins up again —
there you have it, so take it, there you have them both,
the name, the name, the hand, the hand,
so take them, keep them as a pledge
he takes it too, and you have
again what is yours, what was his,]

The dialogue between the two poets takes place through and in translation by incorporating poetic themes and discursive devices. Celan's existential self-identification is taken to such a point as to define his own authorial identity in Russian terms, also expressing a tension between the Russian and German cultures (see one of the early subtitles of the poem 'Eine Gauner- und Ganovenweise'[37] ['A Rogues and Ganif's Ditty'[38]]: 'gesungen von Pawel Lwowitsch Tselan, Russkij poët in partibus nemetskich infidelium'[39] [sung by Pawel Lwowitsch Tselan, Russkij poët in partibus nemetskich infidelium]).

Mandelstam's poetic voice is perceived in the inalienable singularity of the proper name 'Ossip'. Passing over time in translation, permeated by a shared presence in different places of language, culture and internal geography, it reawakens the innermost identity of his 'reader' Celan.

Celan's identity, as expressed in the term 'Nähe' [proximity], is located in that great metonymy that 'le mot Russie'[40] represented for him. But closeness

36 GWI, p. 284.

37 GWI, pp. 229–30.

38 Celan, *Selected Poems and Prose*, pp. 160–63.

39 In Paul Celan, *Die Niemandsrose. Vorstufen – Textgenese – Endfassung. Tübinger Ausgabe*, ed. by Jürgen Wertheimer, Heino Schmull and Michael Schwarzkopf (Frankfurt a. M.: Suhrkamp, 1996), pp. 42–45: different variations of the titles.

40 See Philippe Jaccottet, *A partir du mot Russie* (Montpellier: Fata Morgana, 2002).

also finds its home in the 'Fremde' [foreign land] among the German *infideles*, in a *krasis* between the word 'nemetski-' and the German adjectival desinence '-ch'. In Russian, 'nemoi' means 'mute, unable to speak', and in Old Russian, 'niem', 'niemyi' means 'ununderstandable'. 'Nemeckij' designates the Germans.[41] In another poem, 'Und mit dem Buch aus Tarussa' ['And with the Book from Tarussa'][42] the area occupied by the German peoples is defined with a similar circumlocution: 'Stummvölkerzone' [zone of the mute peoples]. Seen from a Russian etymological perspective, German is a language which has lost its voice. Celan's German is written, not spoken, in a francophone land. Thus, in his preparatory notes for the *Meridian* speech (1960), Celan wrote:

> Hättest du in der eigenen Sprache: das ~~Fremdnahe~~ Nah-Gefremdete – ein AltJudenDeutsch aus Mitthimmelsüden, aus der Atem-Provence – : so –:
> Zitieren, L i t t r è – Übersetzung ins Altfranzösische[43]

> [If you had in your own language: the ~~foreignnear~~ the near-unfamiliar – an AltJuden-Deutsch from Middlesouthheaven, from Breath-Provence – : so – :
> Quote, L i t t r è – Translation into Old French].

The deterritorialization of Celan's language at the end of the 1950s acquired its own form, bringing together Slavonic, German and Romance spaces: 'AltJuden-Deutsch' from Middlesouthheaven, from Breath-Provence'.

Gellhaus has documented from a textual-genetic point of view this interdiscursive exchange between Romance and Slavonic languages. Celan wrote in 'Notebook 6' (17 December 1961) a quote from the mediaeval poet Arnaut Daniel. In the 'Divine Comedy' (*Purg.* XXVI, l. 147) Dante has Daniel say: 'sovenha vos a temps de ma dolor' [remember my suffering, in the right time]. Celan singled this out as a possible motto for 'Eine Gauner- und Ganovenweise' and at the same time considered it for the writing of his never published 'Walliser Elegie' ['Valaisan Elegy'].[44]

Gellhaus refers to a further 'petite chose méridienne' [little meridian thing] annotated in 'Notebook 7. 1961–62':

41 Pavel Chernykh, *Istoriko-etimologicheskii slovar' sovremennogo russkogo iazyka*, 2 vols (Moscow: Ruskij jazyk, 1994), II, p. 568.

42 GWI, p. 288; Celan, *Speech-Grille*, pp. 207–9.

43 Gellhaus et al. (eds), *'Fremde Nähe'*, p. 395.

44 Axel Gellhaus, 'Wortlandschaften. Konzeption und Textprozesse', in *'Qualitativer Wechsel'. Textgenese bei Paul Celan*, ed. by Axel Gellhaus and Karin Herrmann (Würzburg: Königshausen & Neumann, 2010), pp. 38–39.

> Après avoir écrit, le 19 décembre, la partie finale de la 'Valiser [*sic*] Elegie', avec, pour la terminer, ce vers du Purgatoire: sovenha vos a temps de ma dolor (qui doit clore tout le recueil), je m'aperçois, aujourd'hui, que la 'Divine Comédie' a eté commencée un vendredi saint. C'est le vendredi saint 1961 que j'ai commencé, a Montana, la 'Valiser [*sic*] Elegie'.
> [...] tout revient, secrètement, tout se retrouve, 'Come... le stèlle' – 'Wer nicht sucht, wird gefunden'.[45]
>
> [After having written, on December 19, the final part of the 'Valaisan Elegy', finishing with this verse from Purgatory: sovenha vos a temps de ma dolor (which must close the whole collection), I realize, today, that the 'Divine Comedy' was started on a Good Friday. It was Good Friday 1961 that I started, in Montana, the 'Valaisan Elegy'.
> [...] everything comes back, secretly, everything is found, 'Come... le stelle' [like... the stars]. – 'Wer nicht sucht, wird gefunden' (Whoever does not search, will be found)].

The annotation quotes the Old Occitan used by Arnaut's proverbial *trobar clus*. An obscure and apparently inaccessible style of poetry was the voice of a deep sorrow, inexpressible in any other form. Using a 'wholly other' language, Dante acquires the ability to recall an indescribable pain. This distant, strange language was thus closely linked to an Italian language yet to come, an Italian which Dante in his writings was creating out of a multi-linguistic fabric strongly marked by memory, as well as by political, religious and aesthetic engagement. In the process of going back over time, language, oeuvres and history, every encounter translates and retraces the lines of pain, putting 'wound-readings | across': Dante-Arnaut, accompanied by Virgil; Celan-Dante, accompanied by Mandelstam, the translator of two great exiled poets, Dante and Ovid. Mandelstam indeed translated Dante's *Commedia* (and wrote an essay about him, which was subsequently interpreted and translated by Celan) and Ovid's *Tristia*, written by the Latin poet while in exile near the Black Sea. The idea of a poetical composition featuring a returning date (the 'Good Friday', the *tenebrae* before a possible rebirth) marks the reciprocity and responsiveness, the 'mutual occupiability'[46] between and among poets over time[47] and space. In this oscillation between space-time and languages, which also meant tracing the path back to exile and re-opening a wound (for Dante and for Celan), the openness towards language and the voice of the Other also provided an opportunity of liberation, 'a

45 Deutsches Literaturarchiv Marbach, Nachlass Paul Celan, Signatur D. 90.1.3294, quoted in Gellhaus, *Wortlandschaften*, p. 40.

46 Celan, *Der Meridian*, *Tübinger Ausgabe*, p. 135; Celan, *Mikrolithen*, p. 147. 'Reziproke Besetzbarkeit'.

47 For a discussion on diachronicity, individuation and dialogism see Sandro Zanetti, *'Zeitoffen'. Zur Chronographie Paul Celans* (Munich: Fink, 2006); on *cesurae* and temporality, see Eskin, *Ethics*, p. 195.

riveder le stelle' ['to see the stars again', which marked the exodus from Hell in the 'Divine Comedy'].

Once again, we must note the surprising parallel between Dante's relationship with Old Occitan and Celan's relationship with his own Yiddish internal dialogue ('AltJudenDeutsch'). This can be seen in the multiple rewritings of titles and mottoes in the previously mentioned self-portrait 'Eine Gauner- und Ganovenweise'. The different versions call to mind a medieval palimpsest, a goatskin with numerous scratchings and rewritings. The provisional subtitle implying imaginary 'Russian' origins ('gesungen von Pawel Lwowitsch Tselan, Russkij poët...')[48] acquires a further layer of meaning: the Old Occitan quote 'sovenha vos a temps de ma dolor'. Last but not least, Celan's declaration of belonging, in the final version of the poem, marks an important geopoetical shift: 'gesungen in Paris emprès Pontoise von Paul Celan aus Czernowitz bei Sadagora'. This subtitle echoes the verses of Villon – 'je suis François, dont il me poise | Né de Paris emprès Pontoise' [I am François which is my cross | born in Paris near Pontoise][49] – but also indicates eastward, towards the 'Holy City' of Chassidism: Sadagora.

Estrangement and proximity run alongside Celan's Slavonic-Romance translational path: 'Fremde Nähe' was the title of an anthology planned by Celan around 1960, to gather his translations from the Russian and from the French, triggered 'aus Neigung' [by his own inclination]. Among these, beside Blok and Rimbaud, in 1960 he listed the Mandelstam and Valéry translations.[50]

Celan's brother poet was a multifaceted alter-ego: he was charged with plagiarism, died in a Gulag, translated both Latin and Italian and was the bearer of a 'message in a bottle' coming from a lost 'East'[51] – picked up over time by Celan himself in his fortieth year. Celan's notes, radio programmes and introductions to the Russian poets, especially Mandelstam, brought about a recovery of the 'wasted generation'[52] of writers who disappeared under Stalin's purges in the 1930s, forgotten both in the Soviet world and in the West. Thanks to Celan, these poets entered the Western cultural field.

---

48 Also written in Montana on 21 December 1961; see Celan, *Mikrolithen*, p. 37.

49 *The Poems of François Villon*, ed. by Galway Kinnel (Hanover: University Press of New England, 1965), p. 207.

50 Gellhaus et al. (eds), *'Fremde Nähe'*, p. 285.

51 GWIII, p. 186; Celan, *Selected Poems and Prose*, p. 396; see Christine Ivanovic, *Das Gedicht im Geheimnis der Begegnung. Dichtung und Poetik Celans im Kontext seiner russischen Lektüren* (Tübingen: Niemeyer, 1996).

52 Ivanovic, *Das Gedicht im Geheimnis*, pp. 89–91, 165.

Valéry's 'Jeune Parque' was transferred as 'Junge Parze' into a discourse on the relationship between form and pain, destruction and construction. In numerous drafts, Celan closely examines philosophical, historical and aesthetic issues connected with Valéry's poetry and with the concept of darkness in poetic writing, in a way responding to the theoretical debate initiated by Hugo Friedrich,[53] by developing an anti-lyrical poetics, which claims darkness, neither in the name of hermetic esotericism nor in the wake of symbolism, but in the search for an ethical statute of poetic language that could respond to Adorno's question about writing after Auschwitz.[54] More generally, Celan's motivations for translating a large number of French poets in the late 1950s lay in the poetological issues set out in *Sprachgitter* [*Speech-Grille*], in a recognizable quest for the 'Schroffheit' [abruptness] of language, 'Engpässe' [tight passes] of earlier and other-language forms, for a scrutiny of his own poetry as well as that of the poets who lived before the war.[55]Celan's search for his own voice and position within the poetic tradition is also intralinguistic. His translation of Valéry also illustrates his coming to terms with the former translators and the traditions they represent.[56]

The *Gestalt* of the speaker

In a letter to Gleb Struve concerning the Mandelstam translations dated 20 January 1959, Celan stated his intention

> bei größter Textnähe das Dichterische am Gedicht zu übersetzen, die Gestalt wiederzugeben, das 'Timbre' des Sprechenden.[57]
>
> [not only of staying as close to the original text as possible, but also of translating the poetry in the poem, rendering form and timbre of the voice speaking in the poem.[58]]

53 Hugo Friedrich, *Die Struktur der modernen Lyrik* (Hamburg: Rowohlt, 1956). See Ute Harbusch, *Gegenübersetzungen. Paul Celans Übertragungen französischer Symbolisten* (Göttingen: Wallstein, 2005), pp. 18, 37–46, 55.
54 Theodor W. Adorno, 'Kulturkritik und Gesellschaft', in Adorno, *Prismen* (Frankfurt a.M.: Suhrkamp, 1955), pp. 302–42.
55 Celan, *Der Meridian, Tübinger Ausgabe*, p. 161. See May, *Ein Klaffen*, p. 65.
56 E.g. Rilke, See Gellhaus et al. (eds), *'Fremde Nähe'*, pp. 269–72; Harbusch, *Gegenübersetzungen*, pp. 51, 378, 381; Florence Pennone, *Paul Celans Übersetzungspoetik* (Tübingen: Niemeyer, 2007).
57 In Victor Terras and Karl S. Weimar, 'Mandelstamm and Celan. A Postscript', *Germano-Slavica*, 2 (1978), 353–70 (p. 362). On 'Timbre' see also Celan, *Der Meridian, Tübinger Ausgabe*, p. 109.
58 Transl. in Olschner, *Anamnesis*, p. 69.

Speaking of timbre means that the textual and existential components in a poem cannot be separated. The text is a *phenomenon*, linked to the perception of a form in which the whole is greater than the sum of its parts. The author being translated is 'the speaker', someone who over time repeats a performance, giving expression to a voice which is the mark of his creatural condition. The desire to capture the voice of the speaker is linked to timbre.

The timbre of any sound, even a thump on the table, is the sum of different simultaneous vibrations: the tabletop, the legs of the table, the objects placed on top of the table and the floor. The sound that we hear is therefore the sum, what we could call the 'Gestalt' [form], of all the sounds of the different vibrations emitted at the same time. The timbre of a musical instrument is made up of the sound, the colour unique to every instrument. Similarly, like a fingerprint, the timbre of the voice identifies every individual. The human body is a resonator; every cavity and piece of soft tissue influences phonation.

Celan's translations tried indeed to capture the timbre, the *Gestalt* of the voice, which is lost and must be retrieved from the past – that is to say: the feature of being non-reproducible can, paradoxically, only be 'repeated' by another, different and non-reproducible subjectivity speaking 'in the cause of the Other'. This non-reproducibility is the poem itself, to which Celan ascribes sentiments, such as hope and expectation:

> Aber das Gedicht spricht ja! Es bleibt seiner Daten eingedenk, aber – es spricht. Gewiß, es spricht immer nur in seiner eigenen, allereigenster Sache. [...] Aber ich denke [...] daß es zu den Hoffnungen des Gedichts gehört, gerade auf diese Weise auch in *fremder* – nein, dieses Wort kann ich jetzt nicht mehr gebrauchen –, gerade auf diese Weise *in eines Anderen Sache* zu sprechen – wer weiß, vielleicht in eines *ganz Anderen* Sache.[59]
>
> [Yet the poem does speak! It remains mindful of its dates, yet – it speaks. Indeed it speaks only in its very selfmost cause. [...] But [...] I think a hope of poems has always been to speak in just this way in the cause of the *strange* – no, I can't use this word anymore – in just this way to speak *in the cause of an Other* – who knows, perhaps in the cause of a *wholly Other.*[60]]

The translator speaks in the cause of the Other, braving the times. As Celan wrote to Werner Weber, speaking 'in the cause of a wholly Other' – as Valéry was for Celan – translation was: '*Übung*, exercise, *Exercitium*, *Exerzitien*'.[61] In this sequence he lists the word in German both from a Germanic and a Latin root.

59 GWIII, p. 196.

60 Celan, *Selected Poems and Prose*, p. 408.

61 In Gellhaus et al., *'Fremde Nähe'*, p. 398.

To translate means to accept with a reckless and apparently paradoxical gesture a gift given by a hand separated from us by an 'abyss'. Poetry in the 'language of the Other' must keep in mind this incongruous position. The *energeia* of the word is released by the dynamic sequence of the same word in different languages.

The next phase across languages, space and time leads to a 'regeneration' in another language ('actualize[d] once again') of its poetic literalness, that is, the words that make the *Gestalt* of the poem, which is all the more authentic for its distance and difference from the original:

> Ja, das Gedicht, das übertragene Gedicht muß, wenn es in der zweiten Sprache noch einmal dasein will, dieses Anders- und Verschiedenseins, dieses Geschiedenseins eingedenk bleiben. [...] Das im französischen Wort Gewordene noch einmal in seiner – dichterischen – Wörtlichkeit zu aktualisieren.[62]

> [Yes, the poem, the transposed poem, if it wants to be there again in the second language, this being other and different, this being distinct must be kept in mind. (...) To actualize once again in its – poetic – literalness what it has become in the French word].

An example of this process of regeneration of literalness preserving the 'Verschiedensein' and the 'Geschiedensein' between the two 'Gestalten' of the same poem, can be observed in the first stanza of Celan's translation of Valéry's 'Jeune Parque'. Comparing the harmonious melody of 'Et quel frémissement d'une feuille effacée' [And what shivering of an effaced leaf is it] with the discontinuous rhythm of 'Welch Beben ists – vom Blatt dort, das da war und das schwand?' [What pulsing is – from that leaf, that was there and then effaced?] in the 'Junge Parze', we notice the dynamic translation of the adjectival participle ('effacée') in an open situation of temporality and action ('das da war und das schwand?'), expressing the constantly changing nature of the word. The translation of 'frémissement' into 'Beben' shows Celan's strategy of translating the latency of the text. This leads us to a second crucial aspect of Celan's translational strategy of repetition, one that is more clearly concerned with the lexical depths of the translated texts, that is, their textual history. 'Frémissement' belongs, in the context of the poem, to the metaphoric field of vegetal life; the 'translating repetition' ('Beben', 'to pulsate', 'tremble') wanders towards the semantic field of 'heart', of 'human life' and 'body'. 'Beben' is the result of Celan's textual analysis of the first drafts of the poem, which he studied and annotated meticulously. In the *manuscrit autographe* of Valéry's 'Jeune Parque', Celan read and underlined the first draft, in which instead of 'frémissement' there was the word 'pal-

62 In Gellhaus et al. (eds), *'Fremde Nähe'*, pp. 397–98.

piter'.[63] The choice of the word 'Beben' is thus based on the genetic history of the French text – it originates from its 'state of nascency' (*statu* [*sic*] *nascendi*).[64] Here we have a clear example of translation as a manifestation of latent meanings, as observed, e.g. by Antoine Berman in Hölderlin's 'Antigone'.[65]

The (re-)nascent state of poetic writing and translation (which share the same essence) gives language the possibility of 'jumping across' the abysses of time and unspeakable traumas. The idea of a 'Sprung' [jump], also mentioned in the letter to Weber, occurs in Celan's drafts for the *Meridian* speech.[66] The works written before the temporal-spatial 'abyss' of Auschwitz, can henceforth only be repeated in a hard, disrupted and 'grey'[67] form. This very broken form releases the energy of the Unsayable. In this context, we may adopt Barbara Cassin's concept of the 'untranslatable' as an everlasting remnant. This unmoveable remnant is the *energeia*, the potentiality that can be liberated only through a translational dynamic, not only once, but again and again.[68]

Retrieving the 'form of the speaker' means the 'presentification'[69] of someone/something lost. Celan's idea of translation as a manifestation of a latency or absence has to do with interpretation and intellectual encounters during the late 1950s and the early 1960s, among which Mandelstam and Valéry are crucial examples. Buber and Rosenzweig[70] must now be added, both implicitly and explicitly quoted in Celan's Bremen and *Meridian* speeches. As May illustrates in his study, Buber claimed that the act of translation could re-enact the Revelation both for the translator and for the reader. Buber and Rosenzweig both took great pains to recover the lost dialogical power of the biblical text, which lay in its 'spoken' nature, in its lexicon, syntax, rhythm. Each translation had its own lin-

---

63 Paul Valéry, *La jeune Parque. Manuscrit autographe, texte de l'édition de 1942, états successifs des brouillons inédits du poème* (Paris: Librairie Gallimard, Foundation Bollingen, 1956), pp. 310–11 [underlined by Celan]. See Camilla Miglio, *Celan e Valéry. Poesia, traduzione di una distanza* (Naples: Edizioni Scientifiche Italiane, 1997), pp. 84–86; Camilla Miglio, *Vita a fronte. Saggio su Paul Celan* (Macerata: Quodlibet, 2005), p. 159.

64 Gellhaus et al. (eds), *'Fremde Nähe'*, p. 398.

65 Antoine Berman, *La traduction et la lettre ou l'auberge du lointain* (Paris: Seuil, 1999), pp. 79–95.

66 Celan, *Der Meridian, Tübinger Ausgabe*, p. 125.

67 Paul Celan, 'Reply to a Questionnaire from the Flinker Bookstore, Paris, 1961', in Paul Celan: *Collected Prose*, trans. by Rosemary Waldrop (Manchester: Carcanet, 1986), p. 23.

68 Barbara Cassin (ed.), *Vocabulaire européen des philosophies. Dictionnaire des intraduisibles.* Présentation (Paris: Seuil, 2004), pp. XVII–XXII.

69 See Anna Glazova, 'Poetry of Bringing about Presence', *MLN*, 123.5: *Comparative Literature Issue* (2008), pp. 1108–26.

70 See May, *Ein Klaffen*, p. 91.

guistic body, permeated by the personal nature and history of the speaker. The new translation aimed to convey each individual layer of the history of Judaism interwoven with German language, culture and history. 'Realized Revelation' is then always

> [h]uman body and human voice [Menschenleib und Menschenstimme], and that always means: *this* body and *this* voice in the mystery of their uniqueness [im Geheimnis ihrer Einmaligkeit].[71]

'Menschenleib' and 'Menschenstimme': here we recall, in the previously cited verses of 'Es ist alles anders', the movement that embraces a name, an arm, a shoulder, a hand – one's own and another's. The body, like language, is present and dismembered, absent and recomposed. It is like the interlocutor who comes towards the poet, repeating ('you tell him | what he knows already'), rewriting, travelling through time ('walks up to you', 'he accepts it from you'), from the past to the 'now' and 'there' of the encounter, which repeats itself every time that the reader or the poet-translator tackles a poem ('there you have it, so take it, there you have them both'); in German: 'da hast du sie, da nimm sie dir, da hast du alle beide' [my underlining]. But given Celan's interlinguistic awareness, the German 'da' can be identified with 'yes' in Russian – and now signifies a return of life. Thus, a double voice is performed, between the 'I' of the translator and the translated 'Thou', to which the 'I' establishes itself in relation. Furthermore, the 'form [Gestalt] of the speaker' is created as individual poetic utterance. The reader discovers the game of question-and-answer in the text. In this way, the fundamental principles of Talmudic and Rabbinic studies are taken up again. To understand the meaning of a poem, it is necessary to find the right question for the answer.[72]

The influence of Buber towards the end of the 1950s thus incorporated and shared in a renewed encounter, an experience from another time and place: the surrealist *question-réponse* game previously played in the poetic circles in Bucharest.[73] Charlotte Ryland indeed, based on Celan's 'encounters with Surreal-

---

71 Martin Buber, *Werke*, II, *Schriften zur Bibel* (Munich: Heidelberg, 1964) discussed in May, *Ein Klaffen*, p. 96; trans. in Martin Buber, 'Toward a New German Translation of the Scriptures', in *The Return to Scripture in Judaism and Christianity. Essays in Post-Critical Scriptural Interpretation*, ed. by Peter Ochs (Eugene, OR: Wipf & Stock, 1993), p. 337.

72 May, *Ein Klaffen*, p. 93.

73 See Camilla Miglio, *Le città dell'artista* da giovane, in *Paul Celan. La poesia come frontiera filosofica*, ed. by Massimo Baldi and Fabrizio Desideri (Firenze: Firenze University Press, 2008), p. 172.

ism', illustrates what Celan intended by a dynamic 'shared space':[74] 'a poem always contains the potential for its future meanings, and so situates this latent potential within the poem itself'.[75] The translator is at one and the same time both reader and writer.[76] The traumatic past intrudes in unpredictable, secret, uncertain and obscure ways into the present reality of the writer, the translator and also the reader, in a 'shifting relationship between poetic language and the poet's and the readers' realities'.[77] Thus, the shared space of the 'communicating vessels' Celan experienced by translating Breton oscillates between the past and present reality and vice versa, opening up an available space to be 'occupied' in the future.[78]

A preparatory note to his planned essay on obscure poetry says:

> Das Gedicht will [...] verstanden sein, es bietet sich zur Interlinearversion dar [...] Vielmehr bringt das Gedicht, als Gedicht, die Möglichkeit der Interlinearversion mit, realiter und virtualiter; mit anderen Worten: das Gedicht ist, auf eine ihm eigene Weise, besetzbar. [...] Ich bitte Sie, sich die Leerzeilen räumlich vorzustellen, räumlich und – zeitlich.[79]
>
> [The poem wants (...) to be understood, it offers itself to the interlinear version (...) Rather, the poem, as a poem, brings with it the possibility of the interlinear version, realiter and virtualiter; in other words: the poem can be occupied in its own way. (...) I ask you to imagine the empty lines spatially, spatially and temporally].

Verse, like blank spaces, can be 'occupied'. Celan's concept of poetry as an interlinear translation derives from this possibility of occupying the blank spaces regenerating the text (over time). Celan often went back to 'occupy' his own actual words. Repetition and re-contextualization, moving words forward, opens them up to other discourses and time frames.[80]

Unlike what occurs unconsciously and spontaneously between languages, in the artistic structuring of a literary work this hybridization always occurs consciously, and the blending of the discourses remains recognizable. Any translation by Celan has multiple voices. The text becomes a palimpsest but also a hy-

---

74 Charlotte Ryland, *Paul Celan's Encounters with Surrealism. Trauma, Translation and Shared Poetic Space* (London: MHRA, 2010).

75 Ibid., p. 183. On the provisional, non-definitive character of poetry, see Leonard Olschner, *Im Abgrund Zeit. Paul Celans Poetiksplitter* (Göttingen: Vandenhoeck & Ruprecht, 2007), pp. 9–56.

76 Ryland, *Paul Celan's Encounters*, p. 184.

77 Ibid., p. 6.

78 Ibid., p. 21.

79 Celan, *Mikrolithen*, p. 132.

80 Arno Barnert, *Mit dem fremden Wort. Poetisches Zitieren bei Paul Celan* (Frankfurt a.M.: Stroemfeld, 2007), p. 63.

brid,[81] manifest in the language into which the text is being translated. The translator's voice answers the translated author's voice.

The shared space also exists as a polylogue: translated poetry, philosophical, scientific and political readings, and contingencies of life all converge and reverberate, modifying each other and the original text at the same time. For Celan, maintaining the 'Geschiedenheit' of two texts while paradoxically hybridizing them into a single shared space meant to focus on the timbre of the rhythm and syntax, the semantics, the etymology and pseudo-etymology, all of which have a bearing on meaning. The issue of shared poetic space stems from an important political root, mentioned in his *Meridian* speech and implied in his explicit references to the theories of Landauer (the idea of reversibility between past and 'presentification', generated by the push for 'utopia' in 'topia')[82] and Kropotkin's idea of hybridization (from biology to solidarity in society).[83] This libertarian, communitarian root may be revisited today in relation to the significance of 'communitas' developed by Roberto Esposito:[84] the dialogical exchange is poetically and politically relevant as a 'munus', etymologically the giving to one another something that does not belong to oneself. The term 'immunitas', also stemming from the same etymological root and related to all politics of exclusion and destruction of the Other, 'has to be contrasted directly with that of *communitas*'.[85] Also in this respect, as Celan writes to Weber, poems and the experience of translating them, jumping across abysses of estrangement, are 'Geschenke' [gifts]. They are, in Esposito's terms, *munera* testifying to a political act of resistance inscribed in the possibility of reversing [Umkehr] the significance of words.

---

81 See the wide-ranging discussion of Bakhtin's theories in the context of Celan's poetics of translation in May, *Ein Klaffen*, pp. 110 – 12.

82 Gustav Landauer, *Revolution and Other Writings. A Political Reader*, ed. by Gabriel Kuhn (Oakland, CA: PM Press, 2010), p. 113.

83 Piotr Kropotkin, *Mutual Aid. A Factor of Evolution* (London: Freedom Press, 1987); see Camilla Miglio, 'Paul Celan, *Il meridiano*', in *Il saggio tedesco del Novecento*, ed. by Massimo Bonifazio et al. (Firenze: Le Lettere, 2009), pp. 279 – 92.

84 Roberto Esposito, *Community, Immunity, Biopolitics*, trans. by Riannon Noel Welch (New York: Fordham University Press, 2013).

85 Ibid., p. 127.

Ricercar and 'genuine repetition'

The issue of repetition is at the core of Peter Szondi's seminal study[86] on Celan's translation of Shakespeare's Sonnet 105.[87] In Celan's translation, Szondi recognizes a transformation of Benjamin's 'intended effect [Intention] upon the language':[88] the eschatological theological structure is lost, compensated for by a conception of language that owes much to Jakobson. The transformation of the style and syntactic structures, adopted consciously with self-reflective and meta-discursive intent, is a form of immanent criticism of the original poem, in which the form and the theme of the poem are the same. The 'translation of distance'[89] between the original and the translation involves all levels of the text. The texts remain 'singular' and yet connected to each other, illuminating each other in turn. The 'Dasein' of the translation – separate, strange, intrinsically other – is conceivable only in relation to the parallel text.

The mother tongue itself may function as a 'parallel text'. Celan's translational writing has a strong intralinguistic aspect. A word – across different temporal thresholds when relocated in new semantic, syntactic, phonic and linguistic fields – creates new areas of meaning, blending memory and future in the 'same' recontextualized, repeated word. In this respect, he mentions the form of 'ricercar'[90] in a letter to Walter Jens (Paris, 9 May 1961) in the context of the charge of plagiarism brought against him by Claire Goll:

> 'Aschenblume' (Mohn und Gedächtnis, S. 53) ist eine Wiederholung von Aschen- kraut' (Der Sand aus den Urnen, S. 37, Mohn und Gedächtnis, S. 16). (Sie nennen das das 'Leitmotivische', lieber Walter Jens, ich würde es, im Musikalischen, vielleicht als ein 'Ricercar' bezeichnen – womit auch die Anamnesis in Ihrem Sinne stärker zum Ausdruck käme.)

86 Peter Szondi, *Celan Studies*, ed. by Harvey Mendelsohn, Jean Bollack et al. (Stanford: Stanford University Press, 2003), pp. 1–26.
87 See Celan, *'Fremde Nähe'*, pp. 417–59.
88 Walter Benjamin, 'The Task of the Translator', in Walter Benjamin, *Illuminations. Essays and Reflections*, ed. by Hannah Arendt (New York: Schocken, 1968), p. 76.
89 See Miglio, *Celan e Valéry*; May, *Ein Klaffen*, p. 63.
90 But see also the posthumously published poem *Ricercar* written in Paris on 21 May 1961. The poem appears in the lists for *Die Niemandsrose* and then remains unpublished. See Celan, *Die Gedichte*, p. 426 and Wiedemann's Commentary, p. 1079. For more on this poem and its relevance see Camilla Miglio, *Nesselschrift, Hauchschrift, Handschrift. Celan's Counter-Counterpoint*, in Christian Emden, Christine Ivanovic, Klaus Weissenberge, (eds.), *Lifelines. Paul Celan's Reconstruction of the World*, Frankfurt a.M.: Peter Lang, 2021, in print.

> UND –: Aschenkraut ist keine Metapher, es ist der Name der Cineraria, also etwas durchaus Konkretes.[91]
>
> ['Ash-flower' (Poppy and Memory, p. 53) is a repetition of 'ash-herb' (The Sand form the Urns, p. 37, Poppy and Memory, p. 16). (You call it 'the leitmotivical aspect', dear Walter Jens, I would rather call it, in a musical language, a form of 'ricercar') – because this expression would express more explicitly what you mean with anamnesis). / AND -: Ash-herb is not a metaphor, it is the real name of the cineraria, i.e. something very concrete.]

Looking around in historical and etymological dictionaries of European languages, as Celan did so obsessively, one comes across interesting information. The term 'ricercar' – from the Provençal 'cercar', 'cercà' in Rumanian, 'chercher' in French, 'kragu' in Slavonic [ring], 'kar'/'car' in Vedic, 'c'akra' in Sanscrit, 'kirkos' in Greek, 'circum' in Latin (adverb meaning 'around'), 'circare' in post-Classical Latin (meaning 'going around', almost in a circle, like someone who is looking for something) – embraces the idea of searching around for something and therefore involves the concept of repetition. Rumanian, a conservative language of the 'Latin periphery', gives evidence of the meaning 'striving to find that which is required, that which is desired, that which is lost' in the similar word 'cercetà' (from post-Classical Latin 'circitare'). This meaning is also present in the musical (Italian-Romance) term 'ricercar', dating back to the sixteenth/seventeenth centuries, similar in form to the *toccata e fuga* and linked to the retrieval of melodies embedded in one's memory.

There thus exists a strong link between 'ricercar', 'repetere' and 'wiederholen'. The meaning of 'reclaiming', from the French-Latin word 'répétition', may have inspired Celan's perception of the German linguistic space introduced by the word 'Wiederholung':

> WIEDER-HOLEN; HOLEN, from *halon*, related to the Greek *Kalos* (rope), or the indo-Germanic **kal-* (to pull); to *Kal, kla* (to lead, to bring); or, furthermore, to the indo-Germanic verb **kel*, (to call). It is associated with the family of hall, hence *Hall, hallen* (to resound, to call in a closed space).[92]

Celan's intrinsically interlinguistic and polyphonic knowledge allows for both etymological meanings of the word. Originally,[93] 'repetere' means 'to demand',

91 Akademie der Künste, Berlin, Walter Jens Archiv, no. 168, quoted in Barnert, *Mit dem fremden Wort*, p. 63.
92 Günther Dosdrowski, *Das Herkunftswörterbuch der deutschen Sprache* (Leipzig: Duden, 1989).
93 *Dizionario etimologico della lingua italiana*, ed. by Manlio Cortelazzo and Paolo Zolli (Bologna: Zanichelli, 1992), pp. 1085–86.

'to ask again', with regard to different contexts; it means 'to say again' and 'to demand the return of'. Repetition in this sense enters a zone also inhabited by the impulses of relationships, reactions, repetitions and hybridizations. Indeed, 'in a musical language': far from being 'leitmotivical', Celan's 'repetition' is as a transformational 'ricercar'. In a philosophical language: it is not tautology, but near to Kierkegaard's 'genuine repetition'. It shares the impulse of 'recollection' but in a forward-propelling movement, 're-collecting forward', thus miming the effect of the translation. It is possible to read the above quoted passage in the light of Kierkegaard's *Répétition*, a French copy of which is stored in the Marbach Archive, annotated by Celan himself. This very passage is underlined in pen and a vertical mark in the margin stresses its importance:

> Répétition et ressouvenir sont le même mouvement, mais en sens opposé; ce dont on se ressouvient, a été; c'est une répétition en arrière; la répétition proprement dite, au contraire, est un ressouvenir en avant.[94]
>
> [Repetition and recollection are the same movement, but in opposite directions; for what is recollected has already been, is repeated backwards, whereas genuine repetition, on the other hand, is recollected forward.[95]]

The pseudonym under which Kierkegaard wrote his essay speaks volumes: Constantin Constantius. His problem was that he expected and seemed to be looking for an identical core experience like the one he remembered. His failure lay in his inability to bring about the 'répétition proprement dite', which is, in fact, a transformation over time. This very aspect awakened the interest of utopian, anarchic writers such as Shestov and Kropotkin. It is no coincidence that Shestov translated Kierkegaard into Russian.[96]

Bearing in mind the idea of a Celanian-Kierkegaardian 'genuine repetition' as a 'translation of pain',[97] let's go back to his particular use of the form of 'ricercar'. He annotates:

---

94 Søren Kierkegaard, *La Répétition. Essai d'expérience psychologique par Constantin Constantius*, trans. by Paul Henry Tisseau (Bazoges-en-Pareds: Tisseau, 1948), p. 9.

95 Søren Kierkegaard, *Repetition and Philosophical Crumbs*, ed. by Edward F. Mooney (Oxford: Oxford University Press, 2009), pp. 11–131. See Camilla Miglio, *'Wiederholung ist eine Erinnerung in Richtung nach vorn'. Ein Kierkegaardsches Muster in Celans Poetik der Übersetzung*, in *Fremdes wahrnehmen, aufnehmen, annehmen. Studien zur deutschen Sprache und Kultur in Kontaktsituationen*, ed. by Barbara Hans-Bianchi, Camilla Miglio et al. (Frankfurt a.M.: Peter Lang, 2013), pp. 97–108.

96 See *Kierkegaard's International Reception*, I, ed. by Jon Stewart (Ashgate: Aldershot, 2009), pp. 421–73.

97 See Miglio, *Vita*, pp. 247–52.

> Ricercar–
> Deine Umkehr [...] Erst wenn du mit deinem allereigensten Schmerz bei den krummnasig und mauschelnden und kielkröpfigen Toten von Auschwitz und Treblinka und anderswo gewesen bist, dann begegnest du auch dem Aug und seiner Mandel. Und dann stehst du mit deinem verstummenden Denken in der Pause, die dich an dein Herz erinnert, und sprichst nicht davon. Und sprichst [...] später, von dir. [...] In diesem später, in den dort erinnerten Pausen, in den Kolen und Moren, gipfelt dein Wort. [...] Das Gedicht heute – es ist eine Atemwende [...], daran erkennst du's – nimm es wahr.[98]

> [Ricercar–
> Your turning back (...) Only when you have been with your very own pain to the crooked-nosed and mumbling and keel-crowned dead of Auschwitz and Treblinka and elsewhere, you will also meet the eye and its almond. And then you stand with your silent thinking in the pause that reminds you of your heart, and you do not speak of it. And you speak (...) about yourself later. (...) In this later, in the pauses remembered there, in the Kolen and Moren, your word culminates. (...) The poem today – it is a breathturn (...), that is how you recognize it – perceive it.]

'Ricercar' is thus a sort of particularly painful *nota di volta*, a contrapuntal 'breathturn' (ascending-descending, consonant dissonant and 'later' consonant) movement. 'Ricercar' is for Celan another name for 'Umkehr', of anamnetic going/coming back to/from traumatic memories and giving them a form. 'Ricercar' describes the anamnetic movement of 'today's poetry' as well as the movement of all translations raised from a particular inclination ('Neigung') and 'poethical' involvement.

Celan's translational poetics, seen as an aspect of a 'genuine repetition', stems from the *repetitio* in poetry of the mnemonic *loci* of his lost land and the destruction caused by 'that which happened',[99] which became in fact his first parallel text. It expands – as a result of Celan's polyphonic art of memory – between the poles of Czernowitz and Paris, Pontoise and Sadagora, Normandy and Prague, the Seine and the River Bug and Russia – but at the same time, it is reduced to a handful of carved names and places 'sewn under the skin' of his hand.[100] In a quasi-cosmogonical complex system of relationships, the dialogue between translator and translated text always forms part of a network of historical reality as well as individual and collective memory. Within these unexpected connections, mnestic territories emerge[101] and open.[102]

---

98 Celan, *Der Meridian, Tübinger Ausgabe*, p. 127.

99 GWII p. 186; Celan, *Selected Poems and Prose*, p. 395. 'Das was geschah'.

100 GWII, p. 49. 'Unter die Haut meiner Hände genäht'.

101 Raymond Tallis, *Enemies of Hope* (London: Palgrave Macmillan, 1997), p. 273.

102 Leonard Olschner, 'Anamnesis. Paul Celan's Translations of Poetry', *Studies in 20th Century Literature*, 12.2 (1988), pp. 163–97.

'Remembering' translation

We started by observing the translational roots of Paul Antschel's works and life: from his origins in a distant and obliterated land where cultural translation and the management of conflicts were part of the individual and collective experience. A 'minor' and hybrid language was endowed with a political, identity-defining value that differed completely from the 'Gesamtdeutsch' which was also part of the public and cultural sphere of his exile. From his 'parallel' position, through his translations and also through most of his poetry (which often dealt with translation, either implicitly or explicitly), Celan configured an interior space linking the Russian, Slavic, Yiddish, Rumanian, Oriental and Cyrillic worlds together with the Western-Romance, Germanic, Anglophone, Hebrew worlds. He created a linguistic space for everyday French together with the French of contemporary poets whom he translated (Char, Dupin, Michaux, Desnos); Italian, introduced to him by Mandelstam and by Bachmann (Ungaretti); the Portuguese of Pessoa; the Hebrew of Rokeah and Amichai; the English of Shakespeare; and the Anglo-American of Frost and Dickinson; and, finally, his deterritorialized German, 'wholly other' from 'Gesamtdeutsch'.

Thus, Celan places the reader in the position of being attentive, of 'écouter ce qu'un texte *fait* à sa langue'[103] [listening to what a text *does* to his language]. Celan took on the uncomfortable role as a speaker of German as a 'minor' language, forged in the translational zone (Cernowitz-Cernăuţi-Černivci) and put across, transferred and 'enriched' across the Seine. His translational oeuvre, though very different in its phases and irreducible to a coherent 'poetics of translation', discloses a greater echoing space in which a net of voices, times and places may resonate. The translations with their parallel text(s) and author(s) extend towards future readers, translators and voices. Thus, in a 'ricercar' of words and discourses, Celan's translations 'do' the following 'to' their language: they 're-member' (in Assmann's sense of putting the *disiecta membra* of the dead together)[104] a different, porous German, again and again reverberant in the dialogic spaces opened up in exchange with their readers, in different places, time frames and languages.

103 Henri Meschonnic, *Ethique et politique du traduire* (Lagrasse: Verdier, 2007), p. 78.
104 Jan Assmann, *Death and Salvation in Ancient Egypt* (Ithaca: Cornell University Press, 2005), p. 95.

Charlie Louth

Celan in English

Celan's poetics can be understood as a poetics of translation, so that to translate him is to participate in his mode, to enter into what the poems themselves imply and intend. There is also the compelling example of Celan's extensive work as a translator, a practical instance of the intimate connection his work knits between poetry and translation.[1] Many aspects of his poetics can be associated with, and clarified by, the idea and practice of translation, and one of the best ways of following the relationship is by reading *Der Meridian* alongside the radio-essay 'Die Dichtung Ossip Mandelstamms'.[2] But, as no more than an allusion to a context which can merely be hinted at here, consider the idea of the meridian itself: a line which joins what may lie far apart, which puts things into relation and permits orientation, which like one language over another traces a path whose connection to the terrain it covers is a matter of faith and consensus. It is, in the closing words of *Der Meridian*, 'etwas – wie die Sprache – Immaterielles, aber Irdisches, Terrestrisches' [something – like language – immaterial, but earthly, terrestrial].[3] The language of translation maintains a comparable relation to the original it retraces, while making its own habitation in the idiomatic structures at its disposal.

Celan first came into English, at least in book form, in America, in a remarkable anthology of *New Young German Poets* published in 1959 in the famous Pocket Poets series issued by Lawrence Ferlinghetti's City Lights bookshop in San Francisco. The editor and translator, Jerome Rothenberg, gave Celan a good deal more space than anyone else, and apart from Karl Krolow, he is already the senior of the ten 'young poets' in the book. There are eight of his poems, including 'Todesfuge', 'Corona' and 'Schibboleth', and also 'Schneebett', a *Sprachgitter* [*Speech-Grille*] poem Rothenberg presumably translated from its original printing in the journal *Akzente* in 1958, since *Sprachgitter* appeared in March 1959. Rothenberg presents his poets as 'a new avant-garde (opposing the inherited dead world with a modern, visionary language)', and his Celan translations bring the more unconventional aspects of his language across literally, as well as maintaining a proximity to Celan's rhythm. He tends to translate

1 On these matters, Leonard Olschner's *Der feste Buchstab. Erläuterungen zu Paul Celans Gedicht-Übertragungen* (Göttingen: Vandenhoeck & Ruprecht, 1985) is essential.
2 For the latter, see Paul Celan, *'Mikrolithen sinds, Steinchen'. Die Prosa aus dem Nachlaß*, ed. by Barbara Wiedemann and Bertrand Badiou (Frankfurt a.M.: Suhrkamp, 2005), pp. 196–206.
3 'Der Meridian', in *Gesammelte Werke*, III, pp. 187–202 (p. 202).

https://doi.org/10.1515/9783110658330-007

syllable for syllable, so that in 'Schneebett' ['Snowbed'] the line 'Zehnfingerschatten – verklammert' is given as 'Tenfingershadows – clamped shutfast', where the double translation of 'verklammert' must stem from the desire to copy its metrical pattern, and 'shutfast' is an incidence of a Celan-like idiom unprovoked by the lexical make-up of the word being translated ('clamped' would have sufficed for that).[4] This extends – further instances from 'Schneebett' – to 'heartsplace' for 'Herzen' [heart], and we also find 'Breathspecklespattered' for 'Atemgeflecktes'. Even where no doubling is required to make the metre – 'Moonmirror steepwall' for 'Mondspiegel Steilwand' – we might doubt whether this attempt to mimic Celan's practice in English always comes off. It is a fundamental problem to which we shall return, but these examples already suggest the difficulties of trying to make English behave like German, as well as the necessity of making the attempt. 'Mondspiegel' may not exist in German (though one should always be wary of assuming that Celan's words are invented), but there are enough compounds close to it in formation and implication – 'Mondscheibe', 'Mondsichel', 'Mondsilber' – to make it an organic development, a word waiting to be found; and 'Steilwand', unlike 'steepwall', is a perfectly good word. So what seems to be happening is that the imitation of Celan's idiom results in a much stranger-feeling text, giving the impression that his way with German is more wilful than it is.

Rothenberg's readiness to break the bounds of English stands out in what one might call the first phase of translating Celan into English. The earliest translations to appear in Britain are more cautious in idiom and also in the poems they venture on: the 1962 anthology *Modern German Poetry 1910–1960*, edited by Michael Hamburger and Christopher Middleton, contains versions of 'Todesfuge' and 'Die Krüge' by Middleton and of 'Schibboleth' and 'In Memoriam Paul Eluard' by Hamburger, that is, two poems from each of the first two 'official' collections.[5] The third, *Sprachgitter* (1959), in which Celan's style shifts quite markedly, had appeared by then, but is not represented in the volume, an indication of the time needed to digest Celan before his poems could be accommodated.[6]

4 *New Young German Poets*, ed. and trans. by Jerome Rothenberg (San Francisco: City Lights, 1959), p. 24; Paul Celan, *Die Gedichte*, Kommentierte Gesamtausgabe, ed. by Barbara Wiedemann (Frankfurt a.M.: Suhrkamp, 2003), p. 100.

5 (London: MacGibbon & Kee, 1962), pp. 318–27.

6 The *Celan-Handbuch* has sections on Celan's reception in France, in Italy and (very briefly) in Romania, but nothing on the Anglo-American. This despite the fact that substantial translation of Celan was underway early on in English, and his influence on English-language poetry has been extensive. The very first book-length publication devoted wholly to Celan in translation ap-

Celan's most direct appearance in English can be said to be John Felstiner's translation of 'Todesfuge' in 1984, which brilliantly allows the German poem to seep into the English in the form of its actual words, so that by the end – 'dein goldenes Haar Margarete|dein aschenes Haar Sulamith' – original and translation have attained a parity translators usually only dream of.[7] This is brilliant because the English participates in the fugal structure of the German, not just mimicking it as, as a translation, it is in any case condemned to do, but inventing a counterpoint between languages of its own, so that the repetition in the German becomes a way of introducing elements from the original in less and less mediated form. As words which have already been translated recur, the need for them to be in English falls away, and the effect is of a gradual and inevitable arrival of the poem and its terrible truth into the host language, which has, by the end, actually been pushed aside or rendered superfluous.

The achievement of this, Felstiner's extension of what we think of translation as doing, sets a standard but is unfortunately also unrepeatable, since it depends so completely on the composition of the original. (Possibly it also presupposes a certain presence of the poem in English – numerous translations had by then been published, including at least those by Middleton, Rothenberg, Hamburger and Joachim Neugroschel.)[8] Nevertheless, it points to the way Celan's German seems to demand and encourage a rethinking of what translation is and is capable of, to the delicacy and significance of the operation that his translators consider themselves involved in. The critical nature of the transaction can only really be compared to the translation of a religious text, where the consequences of failure – omission, alteration, generally falling short – are so momentous that the undertaking is almost impossibly fraught. From the beginning, Celan's status as a poet unlike any other became part of the drama of translating him – making it crucial and impossible to do so. *Not* to translate (to use the German) is a way around this, but not of course one that in practice can be taken very often.

---

pears to have been in Slovak, by Ivan Kupec in 1966. See Jerry Glenn, *Paul Celan. Eine Bibliographie* (Wiesbaden: Harrassowitz, 1989).

7 *Selected Poems and Prose of Paul Celan*, trans. by John Felstiner (New York and London: Norton, 2001), pp. 30–34. The translation of 'Todesfuge' first appeared in *The New Republic*, 2 April 1984, in a slightly different version. Felstiner was, however, anticipated (by some twenty-five years) by Rothenberg, who keeps 'nach Deutschland' and 'aus Deutschland' in his version in *New Young German Poets* (pp. 16–17), but doesn't attempt the incremental arrival of the original into the translation.

8 In Paul Celan, *Poems*, trans. by Michael Hamburger (Manchester: Carcanet, 1980); and in Paul Celan, *'Speech-Grille' and Selected Poems*, trans. by Joachim Neugroschel (New York: Dutton, 1971).

Something of the process of acclimatization that was necessary for Celan to come into English can be seen in the early issues of the magazine *Modern Poetry in Translation*, founded by Ted Hughes and Daniel Weissbort in 1965. Poems by Celan first appeared in the third issue (Spring 1967). This contains a very large selection of Ingeborg Bachmann (about forty poems) and two poems from *Mohn und Gedächtnis* translated by Michael Bullock: 'Corona' and 'Chanson einer Dame im Schatten'. The headnote calls Celan 'the foremost German surrealist poet of his generation and by many considered the greatest post-war German poet'. The editorial to the same issue repeats the reference to Celan's 'surrealism', which 'seems altogether more convincing than that of so many of his contemporaries', and announces the desire to publish a fuller selection of this 'major figure in modern German poetry' in a future issue.[9] In fact, this did not happen until after his death. *MPT* 7 (June 1970) contains five poems translated by Hamburger, the headnote being 'extracted' from his 'broadcast tribute' which would have been aired on BBC Radio 3. Hamburger's words, which precede versions of 'Tenebrae', 'Es war Erde in ihnen', 'Zürich, Zum Storchen', 'Psalm' and 'Du warst', list some of the difficulties involved in bringing Celan across:

> Much of the later poetry is virtually untranslatable because the increasingly personal vocabulary tests and dislocates linguistic conventions. The syntax is abrupt, halting and tentative, the diction full of ambiguities, new word formations, semantic leaps and twists. The five poems printed below, which did prove translatable, tell us something we want to know, but often cannot be sure of understanding, about the extremism of Celan's work, its groping towards religious and social communion, in the teeth of acute isolation, scepticism and pain.[10]

The 'extremism' of Celan's work, like his 'surrealism', suggests how hard it was to adjust to the strangeness of his utterance as it appeared at about the point of his death. It is of course his death itself which contributed to the sense of his poetry as something absolute, which translation could hardly hope to approach, but the fascination his work invites means that there has been no shortage of translators, sometimes aided by the knowledge that criticism has brought to light, willing to tackle the problems Hamburger identified. Like Hamburger, they have often devoted a lifetime's work to the task, gradually extending the domain of the translatable: just as Celan's own poems have years of reading and word-research behind them and often seem to depend on linguistic finds from all man-

9 *Modern Poetry in Translation* 3 (Spring 1967), pp. 1 and 20–21.
10 *Modern Poetry in Translation* 7 (June 1970), p. 27.

ner of sources, so his translators have also needed years of patience, of similarly varied reading and chance encounters, for things to slot into place. The particular difficulties presented by Celan's later poetry (after *Die Niemandsrose* [*No One's Rose*]), especially early on when the idiom was unfamiliar and had not yet begun to alter poetic practice in the way it later did, can be seen from Hamburger's first book of Celan translations, *Nineteen Poems* (Carcanet, 1972). This volume, which an advertisement in *MPT* announces as a collaboration between Carcanet and *MPT*, contains no poems later than those printed in *MPT* 7, and by not including 'Du warst' (one of the poems in that issue) confines itself to poems from *Die Niemandsrose* and before (over half are from *Mohn und Gedächtnis*). It seems likely that the book was intended to appear earlier, since in the same year Celan was published in the Penguin Modern European Poets series in translations by Hamburger (and a small handful by Middleton), including selections from all the collections up to and including *Schneepart*. In his introduction to this Penguin volume, Hamburger emphasizes the 'difficulty and paradox' of Celan's poetry, 'the anomaly and extremity of his position as a poet': 'Such poetry demands a special kind of attention and perhaps a special kind of faith in the authenticity of what it enacts', an attention and faith akin to that required to write the poems in the first place.[11] It is this ability to convince of its authenticity that paradoxically makes the poems translatable: Hamburger notes that what renders translation possible is 'whether I could respond to the gesture of a poem as a whole. If the gesture of the poem made sense, the oddities of diction and usage, including the ambiguities, could usually be reproduced in English' (pp. 14–15), even in full consciousness that not all allusions were being caught. Hamburger's pioneering and slow-burning work, which continued until 2007, incorporated continuous revisions as obscure details clarified over time.[12]

Part of the process of Celan's coming into English was the recognition of his work in writing by contemporary poets in English and also the development of English poetic idiom into a mode which is perhaps more accommodating of Celan. One notable instance of Celan's work being taken up in English is Geoffrey Hill's *Tenebrae* (1978), a collection whose title has Celanian resonances, though they are not the dominant ones. *Tenebrae* contains 'Two Chorale-Preludes on melodies

11 Paul Celan, *Selected Poems*, trans. by Michael Hamburger and Christopher Middleton (Harmondsworth: Penguin, 1972), pp. 10, 11, 19.

12 See *Poems of Paul Celan*, trans. by Michael Hamburger (London: Anvil, 2007). For an assessment of Hamburger as translator of Celan, see Charlotte Ryland, 'Keeping Faith: Michael Hamburger's Translations of Paul Celan's Poetry', *Jahrbuch für Internationale Germanistik*, 43 (2011), 63–76.

by Paul Celan', the melodies being, as Hill's note informs us, two poems from *Die Niemandsrose*, 'Eis, Eden' and 'Kermorvan' (neither, be it noted, was included in the 1972 *Selected*, so Hill's poems are their first English manifestations at least in the British domain). The 'Chorale-Preludes' have Latin titles and German epigraphs, the Latin being the opening words (or titles) of, in the first case, a Marian antiphon for the close of compline ('Ave Regina Coelorum') and, in the second, of an even older hymn for compline ('Te Lucis Ante Terminum'); and the German being the first line of 'Eis, Eden' ('Es ist ein Land Verloren…') and the fourth line of 'Kermorvan' ('Wir gehen dir, Heimat, ins Garn…').[13] Each of Hill's poems has approximately the same form as its German template. The Latin hymns are also in quatrains, but otherwise their relation is formally more distant, and 'Ave regina coelorum' has only two verses to Hill's and Celan's three. In the first poem, Hill begins with straightforward and indeed close translation: 'There is a land called Lost', but thereafter the relationship to 'Eis, Eden' is more glancing. We find the moon and the frost ('ein Mond im Ried', 'erfroren'), but otherwise the first verse distances itself from the German not just in its decision not to translate but in its troubling of the 'melody' of the Celan poem. Where 'Eis, Eden' is perfectly regular, with full rhymes, Hill's rhyming repetition of 'heads' and the inverted foot of 'vivifies' seem to want to disrupt the balance of the base as soon as it is established:

> There is a land called Lost
> at peace inside our heads.
> The moon, full on the frost,
> vivifies these stone heads.[14]

The rest of the poem takes cues from the German but cannot be considered a translation or even a version in anything like the usual sense. Celan's poem provides at most a 'point of departure'.[15] The play with forms of *sehen* ('Es sieht, es sieht, wir sehen, | ich sehe dich, du siehst') is taken up in 'Moods of the verb "to stare", | split selfhoods, conjugate | ice-facets from the air', which also borrows from 'Das Eis wird auferstehen' (line 11 of Celan's poem), but the poem is now closer to the Latin antiphon whose title it bears. The last verse addresses Mary ('Look at us, Queen of Heaven'), and line 8 ('the light glazing the light') seems to owe something to 'lux est orta' [light is risen]. On the other hand, the last

---

13 For the German poems, see *Die Gedichte*, pp. 132 and 151.
14 Geoffrey Hill, *Collected Poems* (Harmondsworth: Penguin, 1987), p. 165.
15 See Hill's note on *Tenebrae:* 'Spanish and German poems have provided points of departure for several poems in this book': *Collected Poems*, p. 204.

verse is metrically the closest to Celan and combines full feminine and masculine rhyme in the same way, so it might be thought to return to Celan's 'melody', though what Hill means by melody is far from clear.

Hill's own description of what he is doing is this: 'I have combined a few phrases of free translation with phrases of my own invention'.[16] He makes no mention of the Latin poems despite displaying them in his titles. The second poem takes almost nothing identifiable from its Latin antecedent other than the title, but a bit more from 'Kermorvan'. This poem begins:

> Du Tausendgüldenkraut-Sternchen,
> du Erle, du Buche, du Farn:
> mit euch Nahen geh ich ins Ferne, –
> Wir gehen dir, Heimat, ins Garn.

Hill begins with botanical accuracy, in what can be construed as a kind of love-song to the original:

> Centaury with your staunch bloom
> you there alder beech you fern,
> midsummer closeness my far home,
> fresh traces of lost origin.[17]

The word 'staunch' seems to be suggested by the sounds/appearance of 'Sternchen'; line two retains the trees but is unusually (un)punctuated for Hill and, as perhaps with 'ice-facets' earlier, possibly borrows Celan's idiom against the specific context of the line it is translating. Lines 3 and 4 can be read as variations on the equivalent German lines, but they become at the same time a reflection on the act of translation in which they are engaged, a further dwelling on the dynamics of nearness and distance and of finding and losing from which the negative connotations of 'Garn' are notably absent. Hill's poem then seems to diverge quite explicitly in the following line, which keeps the structure of the German, but reads *like* mistranslation:

> Silvery the black cherries hang
>
> Schwarz hängt die Kirschlorbeertraube

---

16 *Collected Poems*, p. 204.
17 *Collected Poems*, p. 166.

Silvery rather than black, black cherries rather than cherry laurel – Hill is deliberately marking his difference now (perhaps playing with the idea of falling into a trap) and largely leaves the German behind at a point where, as Michael Hamburger notes, we might have expected him to be drawn to the Christian themes of faith, hope and charity.[18] 'BE FAITHFUL' in line 11 is a displaced remnant of '*Ich liebe, ich hoffe, ich glaube*', but the phrase '*Servir Dieu est régner*' in line 10 of 'Kermorvan' – the heraldic motto of the knights of Kermorvan in Brittany, where the Celans had a house – is replaced by words from another Christian source, Walter J. Ong's essay 'Voice as Summons for Belief': 'a "kind | of otherness"'.[19] They are in the same position (lines 9–10), and 'self-understood', the words that complete line 10, are a condensation of Celan's line 9: 'Ein Spruch spricht – zu wem? Zu sich selber'. So altogether the relations running between 'Kermorvan' and 'Te Lucis Ante Terminum' are many and intimate, even though they are quite different poems. Celan comes into English here by becoming something else, an accented version of what is always also the case in more straightforward translation. We can also understand Hill's method in these poems as a more involved form of Celan's interweaving of texts. And not just texts: chorale preludes are organ pieces which take a hymn-tune ('melody') as the basis for contrapuntal elaboration. There is thus a possible memory of or even allusion to 'Todesfuge' lurking in Hill's two poems.[20]

It is also possible that 'Te Lucis Ante Terminum' remembers one of the first English-language responses to Celan, the poem 'Es Lebe der König' by J. H. Prynne, which was first published in 1970 and carries the dedication '*(for Paul Celan, 1920–1970)*'.[21] This poem has several words and phrases whose presence in Hill it is difficult to be sure is coincidence, even though some of them may go back to the common root of 'Kermorvan'. In the following pairs, the first term is from Prynne's poem, the second from Hill's: 'oozes'/'oozes', 'cracks'/'cleft', 'the plum exudes its | fanatic resin'/'the plum-tree oozes through each cleft', 'alder'/'alder'. 'Kermorvan' supplies alder ('Erle'), crack/cleft ('klafft'), and perhaps plum in that the cherry laurel's Latin name is *Prunus laurocerasus*. Even if these *are* mere coincidences, 'Es Lebe der König' – which takes for its title Lucile's cry at the end of Büchner's *Dantons Tod*, characterized by Celan in *The*

---

18 Michael Hamburger, 'On Translating Celan', in *Poems of Paul Celan*, pp. 405–22 (p. 419).
19 See *Die Gedichte*, p. 699; and *Collected Poems*, p. 204.
20 See further: Leonard Olschner, 'Von der Kontrafaktur. Paradigmatisch-poetologische Resonanzräume zu Paul Celan: John Banville (2006/2008), Lawrence Norfolk (2000), Geoffrey Hill (1974/1978)', in *Celan-Referenzen. Prozesse einer Traditionsbildung in der Moderne*, ed. by Natalia Blum-Barth and Christine Waldschmidt (Munich: V&R unipress, 2016), pp. 159–82.
21 J. H. Prynne, *Poems* (Newcastle upon Tyne: Bloodaxe, 1999), pp. 169–70.

Meridian as the 'Gegenwort' [counter-word] of poetry[22] – is an early instance of the dangerously high regard in which Celan is held, a fact which adds to the delicacy of translating him. It is also an early example of Celan's making his way into English via other poets, a passage closely connected to the history of his translation and to the shifting of what is possible in it. Both tendencies might be summed up in Douglas Oliver's lines on Celan as 'the only poet I have to struggle against | because none wrote more beautifully post-war | of the perfection and terror of crystal'.[23]

On 27 December 1966 Celan said in a letter to his wife, Gisèle Celan-Lestrange, that he had just written a poem 'dur, difficile à traduire' [hard, difficult to translate]. The poem, 'Wenn ich nicht weiß, nicht weiß', later appeared in *Fadensonnen* [*Threadsuns*].[24] Celan doesn't explain which aspects of the poem are particularly resistant to translation, but versions of the difficulties it presents occur in most of the poems, especially the later ones: involved and precarious syntax (the twenty-five lines of the poem form a single sentence), neologisms, polysemous words whose meanings are all in play, a memory of a Hölderlin poem (or possibly more than one), words from Hebrew and French, and then the elusiveness of the poem as a whole, which invites and repulses understanding at the same time, seems very specific while not quite revealing what it is being specific about. That these things render the poem difficult to translate is not as obviously true as it might seem, and there is even a sense in which Celan can seem quite amenable to translation. Most of his poems offer no particular metrical difficulties, and because the words give the translator so little leeway, above all when set out in the predominantly short lines of the later poems, they can, and must, be simply transposed: what makes them exacting also narrows a translator's choices in ways which may actually facilitate the arrival at a convincing version. Four translations of this poem appeared within about a year: by Pierre Joris and then Nikolai Popov and Heather McHugh in 2000, and by John Felstiner and also Ian Fairley in 2001.[25] The divergences between them are not great, and

22 *Gesammelte Werke*, III, pp. 189, 194.

23 'A Little Night', from *Penguin Modern Poets 10. Douglas Oliver, Denise Riley, Iain Sinclair* (London: Penguin, 1996), p. 41. Many other of Oliver's poems in this selection contain references to Celan. See especially 'Crystal Eagle 1 (*In memoriam* Paul Celan)' (pp. 48–49). They originally belong to a sequence called *Shattered Crystal.*

24 *Die Gedichte*, pp. 237–38.

25 *Fathomsuns* and *Benighted*, trans. by Ian Fairley (Manchester: Carcanet, 2001), p. 111; *Selected Poems*, p. 295; *Breathturn into Timestead. The Collected Later Poetry*, trans. by Pierre Joris (New York: Farrar, Straus & Giroux: 2014), pp. 157/9 (Joris originally published his version of *Fa-*

where the English has been more venturous it has often ended up somewhere questionable or even in error. Here are some of the kinds of differences to be found:

in line 2: for 'ohne Du', Joris and Popov/McHugh have 'without a You', Fairley 'without You', Felstiner 'with no Thou';

in lines 4–5: for 'die | Freigeköpften', Joris has, 'the | freebeheaded', Felstiner 'those | free beheaded', Popov/McHugh 'acephalic by choice', Fairley 'the elective beheaded';

in line 16: for 'gespritzt', Joris has 'injected', Felstiner 'squirted', Popov/McHugh 'ejaculated', Fairley 'shot';

in line 20: for 'karpatisches Nichtnicht beharft' (l. 20), Joris has 'harps Carpathian nono', Felstiner 'harps Carpathian Notnot', Popov/McHugh 'strums a Carpathian not-not', Fairley 'plucks the Carpathian Nichtnicht'.

One might observe the following. With 'die | Freigeköpften' the sense has clearly to do with people whose heads have been removed. If they are 'free', they are at least as much free of their heads as they are free in any more positive sense, and the meaning of freedom has in any case been put in question. To use 'acephalic' seems wrong as it points to creatures who never had heads rather than to those that have lost them. And 'by choice', translating 'frei-' by analogy with *Freitod* [suicide], compounds the inappropriateness of suggesting that these people (who seem to be the Jews) have not suffered a terrible fate. Fairley's 'elective' has similar problems, so that although they sound less inventive and more beholden to the German, the versions by Joris and Felstiner are probably to be preferred. In the case of 'karpatisches Nichtnicht beharft', 'nono' seems best avoided as it has an existing sense in English that isn't quite right (the double 'Nichtnicht', Barbara Wiedemann suggests in her commentary, refers to the way Bukovina has been annulled by the resettlement of its Germans and by the extermination of its Jews);[26] to keep 'Nichtnicht', apart from the obvious problem, might lead one to think that it has a specific untranslatable meaning, so that the straightforward 'not-not' or 'Notnot' (but why the capital?) seem unimaginatively best. It is interesting that none of the translators tries 'harps on' for 'beharft'.

To allow in a little more context, we can look at the closing lines of the poem:

---

densonnen as *Threadsuns* in 2000); *Glottal Stop. 101 Poems*, trans. by Nikolai Popov and Heather McHugh (Middletown: Wesleyan University Press, 2000), p. 56.

26 *Die Gedichte*, p. 765.

dann spitzenklöppelt die
Allemande

das sich übergebende un-
sterbliche
Lied.[27]

Popov/McHugh:

then the
Allemande
starts tatting
her im-
mortal self-sick
song.

Felstiner:

then the Allemande
knits lace out of
thrown-up im-
mortal
song.

Joris:

then the Allemande
bobbins her lace for
the vomiting im-
mortal
song.

Fairley:

the Allemande drills
to

the evacuate im-
mortal
song.

---

27 The stanza-break is correct but easily overlooked on the page-turn in *Gesammelte Werke* (II, pp. 154–55), hence its elision by most of the translators.

All the translators end in consonance with the original, taking the opportunity to split 'im- | mortal' as in the German, though Popov/McHugh interpolate 'self-sick' for reasons that are not clear. All the translators also keep 'Allemande' (which may make us think of Celan's mother, or of his wife, but also names a dance or a movement in a suite).[28] The two 'difficulties', or parts that offer or require more knowledge and ingenuity, are 'spitzenklöppelt', a reference to lace-making, and 'sich übergebende', an adjectival form of a verb usually meaning 'to be sick' but literally 'to give oneself over'. Fairley seems not to pick up, or in any case not to transmit, the lace-making: it is hard to see how 'drills | to' is arrived at. And then the Miltonic 'evacuate' (not found in the *OED* as an adjective) seems over-abstruse and not an obvious solution to any of the trickiness of the original. Popov/McHugh's 'tatting' is a real find in that it refers to the right thing, gets some of the hard-edgedness of 'spitzenklöppelt' and avoids the awkwardness of 'knitting' lace (Felstiner) or the inexactness of 'bobbins' (Joris). Crucially, it can also be used transitively: Felstiner and Joris have to introduce prepositions ('out of', 'for') which both impede and over-explicate the sense.

The problem of 'sich übergebende' is also dealt with differently by each translator: Joris goes for the dictionary-sense 'vomiting', which seems to lack the openness of the German and neglects the make-up of the German word. He is of course correct that in an ordinary context this would be the word's main tilt, but here the ordinary meaning, as the line and stanza breaks slow the poem down, is tempered by what the words more literally convey and indeed by what is happening, as the poem hands itself over to us and the possible consonance between the 'Lied' we are reading about and the poem we are reading, into which the prevarication as to whether it is 'im-mortal' or not plays (the word 'unsterblich' has in a sense been beheaded), is held in its final word. There may be no way of conveying this, but Felstiner's 'thrown-up' perhaps has the advantage of allowing a wide range of sense (a problem, a heap, hands, a game and many other things can be thrown up besides the contents of a stomach). Popov/McHugh's 'self-sick' is harder to assess: clearly it tunes into the reflexive element in 'sich übergebende' and so permits us to catch at its complexity, alluding perhaps to the notion that the poem and the 'song' may be one and the same. It also possibly brings in an allusion to Blake ('O Rose, thou art sick'), which would not be out of place. It tones down the normal sense, in a way the German arguably also does. On the other hand, it forfeits some of the movement. But in the end it seems to work as part of an attempt to make the translation unfold as a

28 Wiedemann tells us that the poem was written on Celan's fourteenth wedding anniversary (*Die Gedichte*, p. 764).

poem. Of all the versions, there is no doubt that Popov/McHugh achieve the best cadence, and the out-of-position 'self-sick' comes off in part because the sounds of '-liche | Lied' find an equivalent in 'self-sick | song'. They are the only ones to diverge from the disposition of the original's lines, taking six lines to translate the final five (having used one less for the second stanza). This seems to be a way of indicating and asserting a little more freedom from the German. It's worth noting that Popov/McHugh are the only translators of those being discussed not to supply a parallel German text.

These comments are intended to point to some of what is at issue in translating Celan. What in the end makes the task difficult is his precision in the use of language and in the placing of words in the line, in his notation of realities physical and mental, and in his exploration of the language web. It is this precision that is so hard for any translator to match: the poems are the result of, part of, a life lived with a precision that made it unbearable. Popov and McHugh, in their interesting preface, note that 'only a wide *range* of translatorial approaches can do justice to a poetry as complex as Celan's'.[29] They see their own work as seeking 'to create poems that follow Celan's intentional mode (Benjamin's *Art des Meinens*), and the intensity of his listening to language itself'. What they are trying to translate is a practice, and they even claim to be after 'higher levels of fidelity than those of the word, the line, or the individual poem'.[30]

To translate, then, is not (only) to attend to the meaning of a particular poem, but to enter into Celan's language-work *by* performing a comparable tapping and fitting of English. The translations are of course in close dialogue with the shape and import of the individual poems, just as translations by others which think of themselves as more concerned with following the original's trace word by word also necessarily engage in the probing of language and work an equivalent of it in English. Similarly, when Popov and McHugh say they have restricted themselves to 'poems for which we could find, in English, sufficiently rich or opportune poetic resources to justify publication', that will not be any different from Hamburger or Felstiner's practice, though it is different from Joris and Fairley, who have committed themselves to whole collections. Even for translators picking their poems, the question of how much and what kind of understanding is necessary for a poem to be translated will always remain. Celan's poetics involved an idea of 'Dunkelheit' [darkness], quite possibly arrived at in conscious opposition to Heidegger's concept of the 'Lichtung'. If his poetry carries or conceals an intrinsic darkness, something that inhabits it that

29 *Glottal Stop*, p. xi.
30 *Glottal Stop*, p. xii.

cannot be elucidated or dispersed and without which it would not be what it is, then the translator necessarily has to convey that darkness, possibly even as its most essential element. Hamburger, a translator of great integrity, has spoken of how an elusive detail in a poem prevented him from translating it.[31] Felstiner admits that though translation can bring understanding, 'with inscrutable poems or lines, I gladly pass them along to the reader within the full stream of Celan's writing'.[32] This does match the experience of reading much of Celan, where the overall movement of a poem allows us to receive and respond to it without being able to account for every element of its composition, and where it is the wider context of Celan's work which permits the intuitive grasping of the details. A significant component of the original poems, of the darkness they bear with them, cannot in any case form part of a translation (except partially in the case of Felstiner's 'Todesfuge'): the very fact of their being written in German.

As Popov/McHugh point out, 'No one can reproduce in a language other than German Celan's tragic relation to a language which was his instrument and life'.[33] But perhaps the sense that the enterprise of translating Celan is flawed from the start introduces a fraughtness which actually becomes part of the tension of the translation and enables it to operate as a distinct but related poem. The necessity and difficulty of being written in German, which inheres in the original, shifts into the necessity and difficulty of appearing in another language (here, English). What could be called the drama of translation is already present in the originals and is brought out in the translations.

To close, we can look in more detail at a particular poem and its various versions in English. It is notable that later translators, who have benefited from the groundwork done by people like Hamburger and Felstiner, gravitate towards the later poems, which is to say that the slow process of coming to terms with Celan has made the approach possible. Popov and McHugh explicitly concentrate on poems not yet available in English at the time they were working on their book, and as a consequence there are not that many poems that have been attempted by a wide chronological span of translators. 'Erzflitter', from the volume *Schneepart* [*Snow Part*], exists in versions by Popov/McHugh (2000), Fairley (2007) and Joris (2014):

> ERZFLITTER, tief im
> Aufruhr, Erzväter.

---

31 See his remarks on the word 'Kolben' in 'Coagula': 'On Translating Celan', pp. 414–16.

32 *Selected Poems*, p. xxxi.

33 *Glottal Stop*, p. xi.

Du behilfst dir
damit,
als sprächen, mit ihnen,
Angiospermen
ein offenes
Wort.

Kalkspur Posaune.

Verlorenes findet
in den Karstwannen
Kargheit, Klarheit.[34]

Popov/McHugh (no parallel text, brief notes):

Particles, patriarchs, buried
in the upheaval, spangles
of ore.

You make the most of things
with them,
as if angiosperms
were having a
forthright
word
with you.

Shofar traced in limestone.

In karst caverns
what is lost gains
rarity, clarity.[35]

Fairley (with German *en face*, no notes):

OREFLASHES, orefathers,
deep in the uproar.

You make of it
what you can,
as if angiosperms were
to speak with them
an open
word.

---

34 *Die Gedichte*, p. 336.
35 *Glottal Stop*, p. 99.

Chalkmark clarion.

In karst basins
what's lost finds
poverty, clarity.[36]

Joris (with German *en face* and notes):

OREGLITTER, deep in
turmoil, urfathers.

You help yourself
thus,
as if
angiosperms spoke
a clear word,
with them.

Chalktrace trombone.

In the karst depression
the lost finds
sparseness, clarity.[37]

First, we can observe that only Popov/McHugh, as we have already seen, do not feel bound by Celan's arrangement of lines. Unlike Fairley and Joris, they add a line to each of the first two stanzas, and again this goes with a more relaxed approach to the poem. There is a spoken, even demotic feel to their lines not found in the other versions. But they return faithfully to the poem at the end, and all three versions end on the same word and with a similar gait. Popov and McHugh are also the only translators to sidestep the compound with which the poem begins. One of the chief problems facing translators of Celan is how to deal with composite words, especially if they are also, or have the appearance of, neologisms. German is naturally rich in such words – many common words are made up of two elements that have clear and separate existences on their own. So 'Flugzeug' means aeroplane, but literally 'flight-thing'; 'Herzkammer' means ventricle, but literally 'heart-chamber'. German's etymological roots are much closer to the surface than those of most languages: many medical and scientific terms are made out of common elements where in English we tend to use a term from Latin or Greek. So when Celan invents a word such as 'Erzflitter' (if indeed it is an invention), he is doing something very much within the domain of

36 Paul Celan, *Snow Part/Schneepart*, trans. by Ian Fairley (Manchester: Carcanet, 2007), p. 109.
37 *Breathturn into Timestead*, p. 375.

how German operates. To imitate him by making 'oreflashes' or 'oreglitter' seems unobjectionable, even unavoidable, but the effect, especially cumulatively, is to make Celan appear much odder than he is. Celan is often thought of as working against the grain of the German language, dismantling it, but it is at least as accurate to say that he worked with and in it. All translators recognize this to an extent, but one can still see that Popov/McHugh and Fairley carry the recognition over into their practice more deliberately and (especially in Fairley's case) overtly, with the difference that Popov/McHugh are more wary of transposing German methods directly and more inclined to keep to the idiom of a contemporary poem in (American) English. Joris tends to lie somewhere between the two, but in this poem is closer to Fairley in his desire to mirror the German.

Fairley focusses on the modulation of 'Erzflitter' into 'Erzväter' without feeling bound by the word order, so foregrounding the wordplay. His 'Oreflashes, orefathers' in one line neatly brings out the dual sense in 'Erz-' of ore and arch, with 'orefathers' summoning and withholding 'forefathers'. '[D]eep in the uproar' then doubles down, outdoing the German in its repetition of the key sound and running a risk, perhaps, of approaching babble in a way that is justifiable given the context of primal stirring. Joris follows the German much more closely (word for word) and finds his own way of dealing with the repetition of 'Erz-', though 'urfathers' is less likely to summon 'forefathers' and reads like an attempt to avoid a previous solution. Against this background, Popov/McHugh seem to be operating very differently, but they are also working to reproduce some of the original's effects. It is notable that they translate 'Erzväter' by its true dictionary equivalent, 'patriarchs', and introduce 'particles' apparently for the sound, in response to 'Erz-'. They thus gesture towards beginnings, to the elemental (suggested also in 'tief' which they give as 'buried'), but lose some of Celan's concision. Notably also, they avoid trying to imitate the compound and come up with something more idiomatic: 'spangles | of ore'. Their version of the next stanza is also easily the most idiomatic, but seems to have misplaced 'mit ihnen', so that the angiosperms are made to speak 'with you' instead of with the 'Erzflitter [...] Erzväter'. It also seems odd not to let the stanza close on 'word', but Joris avoids this too, and only Fairley lets the sentence settle in this way, without quite convincing with 'an open | word', where the problems of tracking the German too closely are evident: 'ein offenes Wort [reden]' is normal German, whereas 'to speak an open word' sounds out of tune. This is a good example of Celan's way with language – an everyday phrase, and yet one which the context pulls into a new sense, since 'offen' here works in opposition to the meaning of angiosperms, which are a class of plants with enclosed seeds (as Joris and Popov/McHugh tell us in their notes).[38]

The solitary next line, 'Kalkspur Posaune', also provides the occasion for some interesting divergences. Joris and Fairley both cleave close, probably too close. 'Kalk' is limestone (or lime) rather than chalk, and neither 'chalkmark' nor 'chalktrace' really make much sense of the juxtaposition with 'Posaune', since the kind of trace intended and confirmed by 'Karstwannen', is not a line drawn on something, but a hollowing, an opening. 'Trombone', for 'Posaune', also strays towards the literal, since as Michael Hamburger pointed out long ago with reference to the later poem 'Die Posaunenstelle', the use of 'Posaune' in Luther's Bible corresponds to 'trumpet' in the Authorized Version and later English Bibles.[39] Fairley's 'clarion' does not rule that out, but Popov/McHugh's 'shofar' more surely fills in the right context, and their 'traced *in* limestone' much more readily leads into the karst landscape evoked at the end, which focusses on the empty forms left by the passage of water (a negative of what is lost, a possible definition of or allusion to the poem). 'Karstwannen' are better as 'basins' or perhaps 'depression' than 'caverns', since the traces need to be visible. And 'rarity' is odd for 'Kargheit', which in context denotes a denuded landscape.

Again, these remarks are intended to draw attention to some of the difficulties and to give an idea of the range of possibilities and solutions that have been found. Hamburger's method of translation, which forms a kind of substratum over which later translators have moved, has been called by Christopher Middleton 'documental' (in reference to his Hölderlin translations). The translations build on one another over time, and so the originals work their way into English almost organically, unfolding in a series of life-forms. But it is worth pointing out that though a vast amount of inventiveness has been devoted to translating Celan, none of his translators can be said to be aiming at 'versions' of Celan in the recent sense which distinguishes 'versioning' from translating.[40] Allegiance always seems to be squarely towards the original and towards the absolute status Celan continues to enjoy. There are poems for and about him, or strong allusions of the kind we saw in Hill's 'Chorale-Preludes', but the translations seem always to be attempts to tap the depths of the German, not exercises in variation. This is true even of Popov/McHugh, who perhaps do the most to

---

38 *Breathturn into Timestead*, p. 600: 'a plant that produces seeds within an enclosure'.

39 Hamburger, 'Introduction', in *Poems of Paul Celan*, pp. 36–37.

40 On which see Don Paterson, 'Fourteen Notes on the Version', in *Orpheus. A Version of Rilke's* Die Sonette an Orpheus (London: Faber, 2006), pp. 73–84, but take it with a pinch of salt.

make something with its '*own* pattern of error and lyric felicity'.[41] This is connected to a function which translations of Celan, particularly of the later work, fulfil more than is usually the case: they are themselves readings, interpretations, elucidations, serving the originals and our understanding of them.

41 Paterson, 'Fourteen Notes', p. 73.

Áine McMurty

'Ruf's, das Schibboleth, hinaus | in die Fremde der Heimat'. *gebietscelan* in the Poetry of José F. A. Oliver

> Das Nicht-Verstehen zulassen, immer tiefer hineinhören in die w:orte, um gehört zu werden angesichts all der Erklärungsmuster, die immer auch Ausgrenzung bedeuten... Sprachwirksamkeit und Wortwirksamkeit, die zerstören: vernichten. Wie diese – nur so kann ich mir Celans Sprache gegen das Verstummen nach Auschwitz ahnbar machen – zur Shoa geführt haben. Nicht 'führten'. Kein Präteritum des Wortes 'führen', denn die Tat ist vergangen, nicht die Zeit mit ihr zu leben.[1]

> [Permit non-understanding, listen ever deeper into the wor(l)ds[2] to be heard in the face of all those patterns of explanation, which always also imply exclusion... Destroy damaging calls for efficacy of language and word. How such things – only in this way can I begin to grasp Celan's language against the silencing after Auschwitz – have led to the Shoah. Not 'led'. We cannot employ the simple past form of the word 'to lead', since the deed is done, not the time for living with it.]

The above reflections on the enduring resonance of Paul Celan's literary project appear in a textbook on teaching lyric writing that was published in association with the Stuttgart Literature House and the Robert Bosch Foundation in 2013. As part of a section that conceives poetry as dialogue, Celan is identified alongside Bertolt Brecht and Gottfried Benn as a paradigmatic German-language poet of the twentieth century, whose dialogic writings set out to find words for the unsayable, an unending task in the post-Auschwitz era when the possibility of recurrent catastrophe can never be ruled out. The author of the book – José F. A. Oliver – is one of the most significant and prolific poets writing in German today and whose own experimental poetry has been frequently compared to the fragmented and discontinuous forms of Celan's later work.[3]

Note: I am grateful to José F. A. Oliver and Suhrkamp for permission to reproduce his work. Unless otherwise indicated, translations of Oliver's texts are my own.

1 José F. A. Oliver, *Lyrisches Schreiben im Unterricht* (Seelze: Klett/Kallmeyer, 2013), p. 212.
2 I follow Marc James Mueller's translation of 'w:orte' as 'wor(l)ds' in Oliver's oeuvre for its effective English-language rendering of the German wordplay. Cf. José F. A. Oliver, *Sandscript: Selected Poetry 1987–2018*, trans. by Marc James Mueller (Buffalo, NY: White Pine Press, 2018).
3 Cf. Harald Weinrich, 'Rede zur Verleihung des Adelbert-von-Chamisso-Preises 1997', pp. 1–7 (p. 6) (http://oliverjose.com/wp-content/uploads/2016/12/Harald-Weinrich-Rede-zur-Verleihung-des-Chamisso-Preises-an-Jose%CC%81-F.A.-Oliver-1997.pdf).

https://doi.org/10.1515/9783110658330-008

Born in 1961 to Andalusian parents who had come to the Black Forest just after the first foreign recruitment agreement between German and Spain, Oliver has frequently suggested that negotiating multiple languages and dialects is what drives his literary practice and its critical concern to take issue with monolingual assumptions and forms of essentialism. In his textbook, which grew out of workshops held in schools, Oliver underlines his pedagogic commitment to promoting linguistic experimentation and provides practical exercises, as well as student responses, focused on the formal features of lyric writing. Oliver stresses Celan's status as one of the writers who have most influenced and inspired his own lyric development, highlighting the radical, political character of his predecessor's formal experimentation. For Oliver, the material dimensions of aural forms of language are attributed a significant role in processes of lyric resistance, since they disrupt communicative forms of language that purport to convey meaning and, instead, permit instances of incomprehension, tension, and active non-understanding. In order, then, to consider the contemporary aesthetic and political resonance of Celan's oeuvre for German-language poetry today, this chapter will focus on ways in which José F. A. Oliver establishes his own original dialogue with his lyric predecessor's disruptive and resistant poetics. To do so, I take as my starting point the well-known lyric appeal in Celan's poem 'Schibboleth' ['Shibboleth'] (1955) to '[c]all the shibboleth, call it out | into your alien homeland'.[4] Drawing on Jacques Derrida's understanding of the shibboleth as 'a rallying cipher, a sign of membership and a political watchword' in his seminal Celan essay,[5] I will explore how this call is taken up throughout Oliver's lyric oeuvre to issue a multilingual challenge to majoritarian forms of language and politics through the accented lyric word or 'w:ort'. The quintessentially German conception of 'Heimat', originally a legal term for permission to reside that came to stand for an emotionalized notion of homeland notoriously feted under National Socialism – will be understood to reference the political instrumentalization of national belonging throughout this essay.[6] The older poet's significance will be traced in the deconstructive experimentation that inscribes historical dates, places and events into the disruptive body of the multilingual lyric text. In the essay's closing section, I will consider how a visit to Celan's home-

4 Paul Celan, *Poems of Paul Celan*, trans. by Michael Hamburger (New York: Persea Books, 2002), p. 67.
5 Jacques Derrida, 'For Paul Celan. A Shibboleth', in *Sovereignties in Question. The Poetics of Paul Celan*, ed. by Thomas Dutoit and Outi Pasanen (New York: Fordham University Press, 2005), pp. 1–64 (p. 23).
6 'Heimat', *Online-Lexikon zur Kultur und Geschichte der Deutschen im östlichen Europa* (https://ome-lexikon.uni-oldenburg.de/begriffe/heimat/).

town of Czernowitz enables an encounter with a long-imagined geographical terrain and 'w:orte' that Oliver comes to term 'gebietscelan',[7] which will be understood as offering a deterritorialized form of *Heimat*, closely connected with the writing process itself.

As Celan points out in a letter of October 1954 to Isac Chiva, a fellow Jewish Romanian émigré in Paris, 'Schibboleth' derives from a Hebrew word from the Old Testament that – in German – roughly equates to 'Erkennungszeichen' [distinguishing feature].[8] This meaning originates with a biblical story in which forms of spoken language function as a pretext to massacre. In the Book of Judges (Jdg 12: 5–6), the Gileadite army defeats the Ephraimites and captures the fords across the River Jordan. Since the Gileadites know that the Ephraimites cannot pronounce the phoneme 'sh', they demand that anyone seeking safe passage across the river first say 'shibbólet', a word for the part of the plant containing grain, in order to kill anyone who failed to pronounce the word correctly.[9] For Derrida, the shibboleth comes to denote the existential implications – life-saving or death-bringing – of apparently insignificant language difference:

> Multiplicity and migration of languages, certainly, and within language itself, Babel within a *single* language. *Shibboleth* marks the multiplicity within language, insignificant difference as the condition of meaning. But by the same token, the insignificance of language, of the properly linguistic body: it can take on meaning only in relation to a *place*. By place, I mean just as much the relation to a border, country, house, or threshold as any site, any *situation* in general from within which, practically, pragmatically, alliances are formed, contracts, codes, and conventions established that give meaning to the insignificant [...].[10]

Within Celan's oeuvre, reference is made to the shibboleth in two obviously political poems, 'Schibboleth' in *Von Schwelle zu Schwelle* [*From Threshold to Threshold*] (1955) and 'In eins' ['In one'] from *Die Niemandsrose* [*No One's Rose*] (1962), the poem that forms the central subject of Derrida's reading. In both texts, places and their dates are centrally inscribed through the lyric association of the shibboleth with the Spanish revolutionary cry 'No pasarán' [they shall not pass], used by anti-fascist troops fighting Franco as a rallying call in defence of Madrid. As Celan underlines in his letter to Chiva, the word is accorded title significance in the 1955 poem where it is brought into explicit relation with the socialist uprisings that took place in Austria and Spain in the 1930s:

---

7 José F.A. Oliver, 'Czernowitz, 5 km', in *fahrtenschreiber* (Berlin: Suhrkamp, 2010), p. 68.
8 *Celan Handbuch. Leben – Werk – Wirkung.* ed. by Markus May, Peter Goßens and Jürgen Lehmann (Stuttgart: J.B. Metzler, 2012), p. 69.
9 (https://www.biblica.com/bible/niv/judges/12/).
10 Derrida, *Sovereignities in Question*, pp. 28–29.

'denke der dunklen | Zwillingsröte | in Wien und Madrid [...] Ruf's, das Schibboleth, hinaus | in die Fremde der Heimat: | Februar. No pasaran'[11] [remember the dark | twin redness | of Vienna and Madrid [...] Call the shibboleth, call it out | into your alien homeland: | February. *No pasarán*'[12]]. The suggestion of a personal and historical burden sketched in the opening lines of the poem is quickly related to a condition of antipathy towards a nascent political regime to which the first-person speaker feels no loyalty. The poem indicates its dates in the references to February and mention of Vienna and Madrid, pointing to the ultimately unsuccessful workers' uprising against the Austro-fascist Dollfuß regime in Vienna on 13 and 14 February 1934,[13] and to the short-lived success of the left-wing Popular Front in the Spanish General Election of 16 February 1936. As the lyric speaker surveys their isolated situation in the middle of the marketplace, the slogan 'No pasaran' is used to declare resistance in the face of present-tense extremis.

Similarly, in the 1962 poem 'In eins', references to a further February date and European capital call up a contemporary moment of political dissent by invoking the Spanish-language shibboleth: 'Dreizehnter Feber. Im Herzmund | erwachtes Schibboleth. Mit dir, | Peuple | de Paris. *No pasarán*'[14] [Thirteenth February. In the heart's mouth | an awakened shibboleth. With you, | Peuple | de Paris. *No pasarán*].[15] Here, the fourfold multilingual address that moves through Austrian-inflected German, Hebrew, French and Spanish creates a layering that recalls both the earlier historical uprisings and – as John Felstiner has pointed out – 'dat[es] its own emergence' to a mass-demonstration of 13 February 1962.[16] With the French-language reference to the Parisian people, the poem explicitly points to the hundreds of thousands who took to the streets to protest against the police killings of nine left-wing activists opposing the ongoing involvement of France in the Algerian War.[17] In formal terms, the cultural-political implications of language difference in Celan's work have been drawn out by Till Dembeck, who points to the shibboleth as a word that withholds access from

---

11 Paul Celan, *Gesammelte Werke*, ed. by Beda Allemann and Stefan Reichart, 7 vols (Frankfurt a.M.: Suhrkamp, 2000), I, p. 131.
12 Celan, *Poems of Paul Celan*, p. 67.
13 (https://www.wien.gv.at/english/history/overview/february-1934.html).
14 Celan, *Gesammelte Werke*, I, p. 270.
15 Paul Celan, *Selected Poems and Prose of Paul Celan*, trans. by John Felstiner (New York, NY and London: W.W. Norton, 2001), p. 189.
16 John Felstiner, *Paul Celan. Poet, Survivor, Jew* (New Haven and London: Yale University Press, 1995), p. 187.
17 (https://www.france24.com/en/20120208-algeria-war-charonne-paris-metro-police-shooting-protester).

those unreceptive to its significance. In considering the function of the foreign sound in the multilingual poem, Dembeck notes the missing accent on 'pasarán' in the first and subsequent publications of 'Schibboleth', as well as in all extant handwritten drafts, which would indicate that the stress in pronunciation should fall on the final syllable. His reading underscores the political stakes of this unpronounceable sound, which may or may not be deliberate on the part of the poet, in refusing legibility and frustrating unambiguous meaning-making.[18] Dembeck's analysis of the formal complexity of the multilingual project and of the cultural-political significance of lyric poetry as 'a genre of genuine cultural politics'[19] might be seen to offer a nuanced alternative to what has been identified in recent criticism as a propensity within Celan reception to prioritize abstract philosophical questions over issues of lyric form. Marjorie Perloff, in particular, has objected to tendencies to 'place Celan in a kind of solitary confinement, a private cell where his every "circumcised word" (Jacques Derrida's term) can be examined for its allegorical weight and theological import', relating this tendency to a 'crippling exceptionalism' in Celan's broader reception that – as Charles Bernstein suggests – 'has made his work a symbol of his fate rather than an active matrix for an ongoing poetic practice'.[20] Perloff further references comments by Pierre Joris, Celan's leading contemporary English-language translator, who has also insisted on the necessary refusal of comprehensibility throughout Celan's work.[21] By focusing this chapter on the continuing dialogue with Celan's poetics in the work of the poet José F. A. Oliver, my concern is to illuminate the particular cultural politics engendered by the contemporary multilingual lyric project.[22] To do so, I will explore how Oliver's textual practice harnesses instances of language difference through the accented lyric 'w:ort' in taking up Celan's appeal to '[c]all the shibboleth, call it out | into your alien homeland'. Ultimately, I situate Oliver's polyphonic poetics within a modern German-language tradition crucially concerned to challenge majoritarian forms of language and politics through multilingual linguistic experimentation.

---

18 Till Dembeck, '"No pasaran" – Lyrik, Kulturpolitik und Sprachdifferenz bei T.S. Eliot, Paul Celan und Rolf Dieter Brinkmann', *arcadia*, 48.1 (2013), 1–41 (p. 24).

19 Dembeck, '"No pasaran"', p. 1.

20 Charles Bernstein, 'Celan's Folds and Veils', *Textual Practice*, 18.2 (2004), 199–205 (p. 201).

21 Pierre Joris, 'Introduction. "Polysemy without mask"', in Paul Celan, *Selections*, ed. and trans. by Pierre Joris (Berkeley: University of California Press, 2005), pp. 3–35 (p. 35).

22 For a wider account of Celan's reception in modern German-language poetry, see: Helmut Korte, 'Säulenheilige und Portalfiguren? Benn und Celan im Poetik-Dialog mit der jüngeren deutschsprachigen Lyrik seit den 1990er Jahren', in *Schaltstelle. Neue deutsche Lyrik im Dialog*, , ed. by Karen Leeder (Amsterdam and Atlanta, GA: Rodopi, 2007), pp. 111–37.

A preoccupation with the complex, often ambivalent and always linguistically mediated relationship with homeland marks much of José F. A. Oliver's literary oeuvre. Born and raised in Hausach, Baden-Württemberg, by Málagan parents in a household where Andalusian was spoken alongside German and the regional dialect of Alemmanic, Oliver frequently thematizes the inextricable relationship between place and language in his work. In the title piece of his first essay collection *Mein andalusisches Schwarzwalddorf* [*My Andalusian Black Forest Village*] (2007), the mature writer reflects on his necessarily multiple ties to the village where he grew up:

> 'My Andalusian Black Forest village' is my name for this place. Not out of presumption or coquetry, rather at one with my own contradictions. Affection towards my own foreignness caught in the balancing act between adopted biographies. Foreign people who gradually settled and became the land. [...] Some call this necessary refuge 'adopted homeland', others assume it involves a state of inner conflict. In contrast, I simply feel at home and cast free in this green moor, that smells of forest and shady hollows. Of air that tastes of air, and of thoughts that flow into feelings; that come into consciousness, travel on and make up a MORE in terms of identities. By no means a loss.[23]

The speaker's highly personal claim on the Black Forest village of his upbringing forms a playful challenge to the exclusions of linguistically constituted conceptions of belonging by highlighting the complementary co-existence of multiple cultural identities. In the course of the text, the abstract linguistic categories give way to an evocation of affinity with the natural world, where the sights and smells of forest landscapes are associated with a synesthetic sensory state in which thought and feeling are said to exist in close relation. It is in lyric language – encapsulated in the homonymic 'Meer' [sea] and 'MEHR' [more] – that an alternative expressive mode is forged for this necessarily multiple condition, which through reference to a waterscape relinquishes exclusive claims on the homeland and refuses any notion of loss. In the collection's essayistic recollections, childhood, language and place – encapsulated in the archetypal settings of the natural world and familial home – can be seen to co-exist in harmonious relation. In Oliver's wider oeuvre, however, this positive early experience of mutuality between languages and cultures is tempered by acute awareness of the socio-political reality of immigrant lives within a system that treats minority groups as second-class citizens.

It is particularly in Oliver's early published work that antipathy and ambivalence towards the notion of homeland determine both the tone and subject mat-

---

23 José F.A. Oliver, 'Mein Hausach', in *Mein andalusisches Schwarzwalddorf* (Frankfurt a.M.: Suhrkamp, 2007), pp. 9–15 (p. 11).

ter of many of his lyric interventions. Oliver became involved in political activism when he moved to Freiburg to study Romance Languages, German literature and Philosophy.[24] As part of a group of international writers that included the prominent Italian-German poet Franco Biondi and Syrian German author Rafik Schami, Oliver was involved in co-founding the PoLi-Kunstverein [Poly-National Literature and Art Association], a group that sought socio-political change by promoting poly-national culture and understanding.[25] This work led to collaborations with writing and publishing collectives such as Südwind [Southwind], a literary and political platform for migrant groups, and the publication of a number of anthologies that sought to raise the profile of migrant authors in the Federal Republic. The impact of these years can be seen in Oliver's first lyric collections *Auf-Bruch* [*Parting Tears*] (1987), *Heimatt und andere fossile Träume* [*Homelan(d)guid and other Fossil Dreams*] (1989) and *Weil ich dieses Land ... liebe* [*Because I love this Land*] (1991),[26] whose titles are marked by a subtle questioning of terms and categories around homeland through linguistic experimentation. Selected poems from these three volumes were reissued in 2015 in a collection of early verse entitled *Heimatt*, which further contains an interview with the writer Ilija Trojanow in which Oliver comments explicitly on his chosen titles and political motivation for writing: 'Ich breche also auf, bin auf Bruch mit etwas Altem, sehe mich einem Heimatbegriff gegenüber, der nicht meiner ist, aber der tradiert schien in diesem Land, den setze ich für mich schachmatt. Ein Land, das ich ... liebte. Deshalb mischte ich mich ein.'[27] [So I'm breaking out, breaking with something old, consider myself opposed to a concept of homeland that isn't my own but seems well-established in this country and that I will put into checkmate. A country that I ... loved. That's why I decided to get involved]. By integrating the adjective 'matt' [dull/languid] into the conception of homeland, Oliver's neologism 'Heimatt' can be seen to signal the oppressive and exclusionary character of worn tropes around nation and belonging.

The word also features in the titles of three poems from Oliver's second collection which offer matter-of-fact vignettes of life in the Black Forest. The poem 'heimatt' (1989) – neatly translated by Marc James Mueller as 'homelan(d)guid'[28]

---

24 Oliver, *Sandscript*, p. 17.

25 José F. A. Oliver, *HEIMATT. Frühe Gedichte*, ed. by Ilija Trojanow (Berlin and Tübingen: Hans Schiller, 2015), p. 105.

26 In this chapter, the translations of the titles of Oliver's lyric collections are taken from Marc James Mueller's *Sandscript* volume.

27 Oliver, *Heimatt*, p. 87.

28 Oliver, *Sandscript*, p. 53.

– sketches a portrait of the poet's mother late in life. Accumulating details of objects and habits acquired over the course of a lifetime, the three-part text gives contours to a woman worn down by domestic routines within a culture that has no place for her during old age: 'übriggeblieben sind | die gebügelten hemden falten | im gedächtnis eingelegte geschichten | und die augen die stechenden | der herren | die sie leichtzüngig doña nannten | manchmal señorita'[29] [she's left with | ironed shirt creases | stories preserved in memory | and the glaring eyes | of men | who light-tongued called her doña | sometimes señorita]. Seen in the references to household appliances, which gesture towards the waves of migration to West Germany during the Economic Miracle of the 1960s, the text provides enough temporal markers to indicate its historical moment, yet maintains an openness that allows its central figure to stand for an entire generation of Spanish women who left their homeland in search of work and a better future: 'übriggeblieben sind | staubsauger geschirrspüler toaster | und ein mea culpa mea maxima culpa' [she's left with | vacuum cleaners dishwashers toasters | and a mea culpa mea maxima culpa]. The free verse form and absence of punctuation ensure a gentle rhythm marked by care for the mother, whilst the text of the poem includes clear testimony to the damaging long-term impact of such labour in its stress on her intense tiredness and cardiac condition. In its pointed reference to election leaflets from the National Democratic Party (NPD), a far-right party that made electoral gains with an anti-immigration agenda in the late 1980s, the poem further provides explicit political coordinates for the ultra-nationalist climate of the time that denies the lived reality of Germany's ageing migrant populace, who – with their German-born families – have come to stay in their adopted homeland, albeit without any of the protections enjoyed by its citizens: 'übriggeblieben sind ihr | die haare ausgefranste fächer | die lust zu schlafen schlafen | und ein herzklappenfehler | wiegenlieder | manch spanischer trauerflor | und NPDwahlanzeigen' [she's left with | her hair tattered fans | the desire to sleep sleep | and a valvular defect | lullabies | NPD election pamphlets]. Instead, the repetitions that open each section highlight the disparate remnants of domestic routines and religious rituals which now make up the older woman's experience. By highlighting that which remains, these repetitions also gesture towards the unspoken losses – further signalled in the reference to black mourning attire – that inevitably mark an existence lived in exile.

The stress throughout the poem on a highly ambivalent relation with the country of settlement thus invites the reader to consider what kind of *Heimat* might ever be possible for the migrant subject denied basic legal recognition

29 José F. A. Oliver, *Heimatt und andere fossile Träume* (Berlin: Das Arabische Buch, 1989), p. 23.

and rights. Remembering Celan's lyric appeal in 'Schibboleth', I would suggest that – in this light – Oliver's chosen title for his poem might itself be read as a form of shibboleth whose orthographic deviation serves to call out the impossible long-term position of those 'guest workers' treated as disposable labour by a host country in denial about its own reliance on a workforce from abroad. Constantly targeted as the others of an exclusive nationality law that – until the year 2000 – determined its citizens according to the ethnic principle of *jus sanguinis*, long-term foreign residents and their descendants were effectively denied a homeland, even if they had been born on German soil.[30] Not so much a political watchword as a subversive undermining of the populist rallying cry, Oliver's shibboleth calls out the hypocrisies and double-standards of the dominant order. By semantically inscribing the deadening human impact of its exclusions onto the word itself, Oliver's vision of *Heimatt* exposes the artificiality of an idealized discursive construct that exists at a remove from those lived experiences through which it purports to be constituted.

The poem was first published in an edition that, alongside its political lyric interventions, includes essayistic notes with commentary and context on the circumstances of writing. In one of these entries, Oliver remarks on the political motivation for his poetological project to uncover the foreign within:

> My language is a rejection of the official language of a country that did not and is not able to accept us. Through this act of refusal, our speechlessness will be overcome, and questions will be uncovered. Yet the language of our fathers is also being challenged and their way of life mistrusted. [...] Knowledge of language is the prerequisite for recognizing the foreign 'inside' that is bound up with the foreign 'outside', like life and death, and this is only graspable if you have lived experience of being a foreigner and a native simultaneously.[31]

The experience of living as both insider and outsider in relation to the dominant social order is said to have provoked Oliver's awareness of the discursive character of distinctions between native and foreigner, as well as his conviction of the need to resist such binaries through deconstructive linguistic practice. As Marc James Mueller, translator of the most substantial published collection of Oliver's work in English, has suggested: 'In Oliver's work, foreignness is not associated with negativity, exclusion, or the need to be overcome [...], foreignness and familiarity enter into a dynamic, temporary, and thus unstable dialogue, deconstruct-

30 (http://eudo-citizenship.eu/NationalDB/docs/GER%20Nationality%20Act%20(1913,%20as%20amended%201999,%20English.pdf).
31 Oliver, *Heimatt und andere fossile Träume*, p. 11.

ing fixed expectations and stereotypes.'[32] The early poem 'Fremd' ['Foreign'] (1987) from Oliver's first collection forms a clear example of his longstanding project to acknowledge the unfamiliar within:

Fremd

von außen
suche ich Verständnis
für das Fremde

ohne
mich zu erinnern
an das Fremde
im Innern[33]

[Foreign

from outside
I look for understanding
of the Other

without
remembering
the Other
inside me]

In other texts, the relatively abstract contemplation of subjecthood gives way to a pointed deconstruction of such discursive categorizations as 'self' and 'other'. Many of Oliver's early poems, for example, engage with the bureaucratic language of migration, grappling with the oddities and contradictions of legal terms, conventions and abbreviations particular to the German context. The 1989 poem 'zeitgeist', for example, considers invisible forms of bureaucracy and their manifold incursions into basic human freedoms: 'die wahren feinde | riecht ihr sie nicht | grün grau modisch verkleidet || die epoche der abkürzungen dient auch der täuschung [...] die wahren feinde | hört ihr sie nicht | lautloses aktenblättern mit computerchips || die sprache der abkürzungen ist die neue esoterische poesie'[34] [real enemies | won't be sniffed out | green grey fashionably dressed || the era of abbreviations is also in the service of subterfuge [...] real enemies | won't be heard | soundless file browsing on computer chips [...] the language of abbreviations is the new esoteric poetry].

32 Marc James Mueller, 'Translator's Introduction', in Oliver, *Sandscript*, pp. 9–35 (pp. 22–23).
33 José F.A. Oliver, *Auf-Bruch* (Berlin: Das Arabische Buch, 1987), p. 13.
34 Oliver, *Heimatt und andere fossile Träume*, p. 78.

To deliver its damning critique of the linguistic dimensions of insidious modes of surveillance, the text takes its starting point with two quotations by Horst Herold, President of the Federal Criminal Police from 1971–1981 and a leading figure in the campaign against the Red Army Faction, which predict possibilities for total societal monitoring through technological surveillance and data mining. The author of numerous essays on policing in an era of counter-terrorism, Herold was famously responsible for introducing the 'Rasterfahndung' method, a mode of computer searching that uses generalized criteria to scan a database.[35] Oliver's poem raises ethical questions about a system that operates through ciphered forms of linguistic short-hand and seeks state security through the mechanized indexing of difference: 'wer zu spät ins bett geht | wird registriert | wer zu spät aufsteht | wird registriert | wer überhaupt nicht schläft | wird registriert | wer zu viel spazieren geht | wird registriert'[36] [whoever goes to bed too late | will be registered | whoever gets up too late | will be registered | whoever doesn't sleep at all | will be registered | whoever goes for too many walks | will be registered]. In its apparently endless listing of sub-categories of behaviours and identities, the lyric text suggests the all-pervasive monitoring and suspicion that fall on anyone perceived as an outsider.

Subtitled 'ein auf-führ-bares ge-dicht', literally a poem that can be performed, Oliver's text manifests sustained preoccupation with oral and aural aspects of language and their human impact. In formal terms, the poem is built around repeated words, phrases and lyric structures that convey the impersonal onslaught of mechanically reproduced forms of language: 'die sprache der abkürzungen | mad mad mad mad mad mad mad mad | [...] bfv bfv bfv bfv bfv bfv bfv bfv | [...] bnd bnd bnd bnd bnd bnd bnd bnd || zack ein neues wort | wie aus dem heiteren Himmel[37] [the language of abbreviations | mad mad mad mad mad mad mad mad | [...] bfv bfv bfv bfv bfv bfv bfv bfv | [...] bnd bnd bnd bnd bnd bnd bnd bnd || whack a new word | as if out of nowhere]. Immediately, the barrage of acronyms works with disarming effect, leaving readers faced with the dilemma of how to interpret signs they may or may not recognize. Indeed, the multilingual and fairly universally recognizable 'mad' seems to invite understanding of a lyric critique of pathological forms of language. As gradually emerges, the acronyms refer quite concretely to Germany's three federal intelligence agencies: *mad* – Bundesamt für den militärischen Abwehrdienst' [Military Counterintelligence Service]; *bfv* – Bundesamt für Verfassungsschutz

35 (https://www.spiegel.de/panorama/justiz/horst-herold-und-rasterfahndung-vereinzelt-optimiert-beschleunigt-a-1245011.html).

36 Oliver, *Heimatt und andere fossile Träume*, p. 81.

37 Oliver, *Heimatt und andere fossile Träume*, p. 79.

[Federal Office for the Protection of the Constitution]; and *bnd* – Bundesnachrichtendienst [Federal Intelligence Service]. Yet the staccato accumulation of the ciphered words simultaneously undermines any effort to uncover the semantic signifiers behind the abbreviations, stressing instead the inherent violence of impenetrable legalistic and bureaucratic forms of language. The onomatopoeic repetitions of the subsequent stanza further compound a quite literal scene of linguistic assault as words themselves are styled as missiles. The dense materiality of the play with signs in Oliver's poem thus works to stage the linguistic terrain on which the politics of exclusion play out, performing the opacity of state-sanctioned forms of language and baffling array of ever-new terms and acronyms that camouflage invisible power structures. As in 'Heimatt', the deconstructive lyric project issues a material challenge to majoritarian forms of language and politics through the disruptive displacement of its signs. By inserting breaks within words which refer to the anonymous agents and instruments of surveillance, the syllabic oral account generates a mechanical listing that exposes the mindlessness of their machinic implementation within disembodied political systems.

Throughout Oliver's oeuvre, sustained efforts can be discerned to dissect forms of language and discourse implicated in the oppressions and silences of the dominant order through experimental techniques that have much in common with Celan's later writings. In Oliver's view, '[e]s gibt angesichts der *Banalität des Bösen* kein Sprach-Los, das in seiner Entschiedenheit und Radikalität wort- und sprachschöpfendbedingungsloser wäre als Paul Celans lyrisches Werk'[38] [in the face of the *banality of evil*, there is no speech-lessness[39] that, in its resolute radicality, would be more unconditional in creating words and language than Paul Celan's lyric work]. And this radical resolve to address acts of language-defying atrocity is also found throughout Oliver's own lyric production. In particular, the collection *Gastling* [*Guestling*] (1993) ranks amongst Oliver's most political works; it engages explicitly with post-reunification Germany and the hostile environment for minorities and migrant communities there during the early nineties.[40] The right-wing riots and notorious terror attacks against minority groups and asylum seekers at Hoyerswerda, Mölln and Solingen feature especially prominently throughout the volume, as Oliver inscribes these historical places into his lyric texts: 'Es gibt kein Wort ohne Vergangenheit, und es gibt

38 Oliver, *Lyrisches Schreiben im Unterricht*, p. 130.

39 The wordplay contained in Oliver's ambivalent coinage 'kein Sprach-los' is not captured in the translation 'speechlessness'. Whilst the adjective 'sprachlos' does mean 'speechless', the noun 'ein Los' can be used to denote the more positively connoted 'fortune', 'lot' or 'batch'.

40 José F. A. Oliver, *Gastling* (Berlin: Hans Schiller, 2015).

kein Gedicht ohne *w:orte*. Orte der *w:orte*, die aus dieser Vergangenheit Erlebtes sind [There can be no word without a past, and there can be no poem without wor(l)ds. Places within wor(l)ds, which constitute that experienced from this past].'[41] The three-part cycle 'dreifacher Tod zu Mölln' ['threefold death at Mölln'] remembers the neo-Nazi arson attack on 23 November 1992 that targeted two Turkish families in the rural north German town, killing three people – including two children – and seriously injuring nine others.[42] The text thematises the all-prevailing silence in the small community, questioning local authorities' response to the hate crime. Elsewhere, Oliver makes explicit the continuities between the atrocities of his contemporary era and those being confronted in the immediate post-war situation. With its title dedication to Celan's close friend and contemporary, the six-line poem 'für Ingeborg Bachmann' ['for Ingeborg Bachmann'] calls attention to the older poet's significance for contemporary testimony: 'die gestundete zeit auch hier | für einen augenblick erfüllt | die flammenhaut spannt tod mir ein | dein bett verwaist die betten | wie kinder die ermordet werden | ohne nachruf fernab tod'[43] [borrowed time here too | replete for a moment | flaming skin harnessing death to me | your bed orphans the beds | like children being murdered | without epitaph beyond death]. Alluding simultaneously to Bachmann's early poetry with its central focus on the perpetuation of fascism in the post-war everyday and to her notorious death following a housefire that started when she dropped a cigarette in bed, Oliver's short poem suggests not only historical continuities with the iconic lyric poet but also signals differences within a society that affords no space for mourning the Turkish-German children burned alive by fascists as they slept.

In other lyric texts of the collection, linguistic echoes and connections are explored between the crimes that took place during the Third Reich and those happening in post-reunification Germany through a close focus on individual letters, as seen in the titles of the three poems 'buchstabe H' ['letter H'], 'buchstabe T' ['letter T'] and 'buchstabe S' ['letter S']. Celan's famous comments in the *Bremer Rede* [*Bremen Speech*] (1958) on the indelible traces of historical atrocity on forms of language might be used to illuminate the forensic character of Oliver's lyric project:

> Sie, die Sprache, blieb unverloren, ja, trotz allem. Aber sie mußte nun hindurchgehen durch ihre eigenen Antwortlosigkeiten, hindurchgehen durch furchtbares Verstummen, hindurch-

41 Oliver, *Lyrisches Schreiben im Unterricht*, p. 128.

42 Oliver, *Gastling*, pp. 57–59.

43 Oliver, *Gastling*, p. 47.

gehen durch die tausend Finsternisse todbringender Rede. [...] Ging hindurch und durfte wieder zutage treten, 'angereichert' von all dem.[44]

[It, the language, remained, not lost, yes in spite of everything. But it had to pass through its own answerlessness, pass through frightful muting, pass through the thousand darknesses of deathbringing speech. [...] Passed through and could come to light again, 'enriched' by all this.[45]]

The act of lyric composition as a means of self-orientation in the reunification moment emerges particularly clearly in the poem 'buchstabe S', which engages with one of the most extreme acts of xenophobic violence in modern Germany, an arson attack by far-right youth on the home of a Turkish family in the town of Solingen, North Rhine Westphalia, on 29 May 1993. The attackers killed five people, including three children, and injured fourteen others. The palimpsestic character of the letter S can be seen throughout the poem, where it functions as a cipher signalling and connecting diverse referents and historical contexts. Immediately, Solingen's status at the centre of the German knife industry is foregrounded, as the crafting of blades is presented as both a regional and national preoccupation that implicates the entire populace in acts of violence. Officially known as 'Klingenstadt Solingen' [Solingen, City of Blades], the town has been the site of sword-making since medieval times, and Oliver's poem suggests the fatal repercussions of this long, bloody legacy on the town's self-image and -understanding: 'Solingens messer sind rot | sorot/ diesrot | beschliffen [...] Solingens messer sind deutsch | gedörfelt / gestädtet | zu meucheln [...] Solingens särge sind rot [...] Solingens särge sind deutsch'[46] [Solingen's knives are red | sored/ thisred | sharpened [...] Solingens knives are german | villaged and towned | to assassinate [...] Solingens coffins are red [...] Solingens coffins are german]. The dubious mythologizing dimensions of this heritage are further conveyed through reference to Siegfried, the legendary Germanic hero feted under National Socialism, as the text exposes the town's status as an early scene of National Socialism that – in May 1933 – conferred honorary citizenship on Adolf Hitler.[47]

As is true of Celan's later work, Oliver's lyric language resists definitive interpretation, yet it manifests consistent efforts to indicate its own specific dates and historical contexts. As the long fourth section of the text establishes, while sig-

44 Celan, *Gesammelte Werke*, III, pp. 185–86.

45 Celan, 'Speech on the Occasion of Receiving the Literature Prize of the Free Hanseatic City of Bremen', *Selected Poems and Prose of Paul Celan*, pp. 395–96.

46 Oliver, *Gastling*, p. 67.

47 https://de.wikipedia.org/wiki/Geschichte_der_Stadt_Solingen.

nalling the geographical place name, the letter S is irrevocably associated with the NS-regime. In this light, the reference to 'meucheln' [assassinate] seems likely to point to the latent presence of the SS or 'Schutzstaffel' [Protection Squadron] as the major paramilitary force for security, surveillance and terror in Nazi Germany, and – given the text's thematic focus – to the notorious Night of the Long Knives in early July 1934, when members of the SS and Gestapo carried out extrajudicial executions to consolidate Hitler's power. Verbs denoting acts of physical violence dominate the structure of the lyric text, resonating at the end of consecutive sections. With the mention of 'damalsruf' [backthencry] and 'Gelbstern' [yellow star], a small yellow woodland flower common to the German context, the text alludes to the national dimensions of the fascist marking and persecution of Jews during the Third Reich and continuing, present-day hate crimes against minorities. Consistent throughout the text is the effort to implicate the German nation in the cultivation of a hostile environment for its various migrant communities who are constantly othered as non-citizens: 'in den stuben der republik | wird gegen die trauer ermittelt' [in the sitting rooms of the Republic | mourning is under investigation]. Here, reference can be identified to Chancellor Helmut Kohl's refusal to visit Solingen or attend any of the victims' memorial or funeral services, preferring instead to issue a second-hand statement condemning other politicians for indulging in 'condolence tourism'.[48] The poem closes in powerful evocation of the famous photograph of the coffins of the five arson victims wrapped in Turkish flags, laid out front of the burned out Solingen home that was itself hung with four national and regional flags: 'Solingens särge sind rot | mondbesichelte heimkehr | türkisch |nicht nur || Solingens särge sind deutsch | auch / besonders / und' [Solingen's coffins are red | moon-sickled homecoming | turkish | not only || Solingen's coffins are german | also / especially / and].[49] The lexical juxtapositions and orthographic alternatives call on readers to question the discrete cultural identities constructed in the iconic image, as well as through exclusive linguistic and legal categories of cultural belonging, implying the more complex simultaneities at work. Interview remarks by Oliver elucidate the reflexive project that drives this contrastive technique:

48 Ferda Ataman, 'Miteinander in der Stunde des Schmerzes', *Spiegel*, 27 May 2008 (https://www.spiegel.de/politik/deutschland/solingen-jahrestag-miteinander-in-der-stunde-des-schmerzes-a-555553.html).

49 http://www.general-anzeiger-bonn.de/news/politik/deutschland/Solingen-Das-Foto-zeigt-die-S%C3%A4rge-von-f%C3%BCnf-T%C3%BCrkinnen-vor-dem-ausgebrannten-Haus-in-Solingen.-article3864337.html.

> For me, breaks, colons, the splitting of words means that I free up these words in their meanings, free them in lexical terms, but on the other hand also gain a poetic dimension and so create linguistic consciousness both for myself and – in so doing – for those reading the poem. [...] That means that, for me, it's a way to create consciousness in language.[50]

In this light, the closing lines of the poem can be seen to expose the fallacy of the construction of the Solingen attack as exclusively pertaining to its Turkish community by stressing the indisputably German character of this latest hate crime. Once again, the self-conscious experimentation with forms of language and language difference found throughout Oliver's oeuvre, which follows Celan in exploring material dimensions of language in order to challenge the status quo, is preoccupied with the presence of the foreign and the strange within the familiar. The trenchant critique of exclusionary forms of language and discourse in Oliver's poetry of the 1980s and early 1990s unfailingly addresses the antiquated laws that, until 2000, tied German citizenship to ethnicity and, until 2007, further denied dual citizenship to adult members of the European Union. Consistently, then, Oliver's poems target the political instrumentalization of *Heimat* discourses to marginalize and other Germany's various minority communities through their radical linguistic experimentation that exposes the destructive impact of identitarian politics and ethno-nationalist movements.

In order to conclude this consideration of Celan's contemporary legacy as manifested throughout José Oliver's lyric oeuvre, this chapter will close with brief discussion of selected poems from a more recent collection, *fahrtenschreiber* [*tripwriter*] (2010), which reflect on Oliver's journey to Czernowitz, and the alternative *Heimat* found through visiting the older poet's birthplace in a region where different languages and cultures once came together. Critics have frequently drawn attention to the 'transit' condition of many of Oliver's texts[51] and the title of the collection alludes to the poet's status as someone who documents life's journey. Its texts present a series of further destinations including Bratislava, London, Tunis and Vienna, which offer alternative visions of linguistic and sensory belonging beyond the conventionally imagined *Heimat*. With the poem 'Czernowitz' as the very first in the volume, however, it is the city now known as Chernivtsi in the contemporary Ukraine that once formed part of the famously multicultural Bukovina, which is accorded structural prominence in the collection. Described by Oliver as 'ein erkennendes und orientierungsbe-

---

50 Hannelore van Ryneveld, 'Im Gespräch mit José F. A. Oliver – "viel stimmig und *meer*sprachig"', *Acta Germanica*, 36 (2008), 119–40 (p. 134).

51 Cf. Michael Braun, 'Transit ins Ungewisse', *Badische Zeitung*, 20 June 2018 (https://www.badische-zeitung.de/transit-ins-ungewisse-153754079.html).

wusstes Gedicht' [a prescient and consciously oriented poem], which he chose as his prelude,[52] the text gives precise contours to a place that proves at once familiar and foreign to the lyric speaker:

> Czernowitz
>
> vom silber der dächer
> kraucht lärm / ein laut-
>
> fall der spatzen & verse
> die sind
>
> biographische lotsen
> mediterrane matrosen
>
> mein vogelaug streift
> I meer übers land & fasst
>
> einen lufttisch dem gast
> mit heimweh gedeckt / das
>
> sammelt sich fort
> & trägt
>
> ein paar schuhe
> im hals / mein geburtsort
>
> ein atlas
> der bleibendes ist
>
> & flickwerk der straßen &
> heimatlos nah / ein
>
> paar Tage C.
> verschluckt meine haut
>
> buchenverbrämt
> julidaheim[53]
>
> [Czernowitz
>
> from the silver of the roofs
> crackles noise/ a sound-
>
> tumble of sparrows and verses
> that are
>
> biographical pilots
> mediterranean seafarers

52 Oliver, *Lyrisches Schreiben im Unterricht*, p. 146.
53 Oliver, *fahrtenschreiber*, pp. 13–14.

my bird's eye glimpses
1 sea over land & grasps

an airtable for the guest
set with longing for home / that

builds and sets forth
& carries

a pair of shoes
in the throat / my birthplace

an atlas
that is enduring

& patchwork of streets &
close without home / a

few days C.
swallows my skin

beechembellished
julybackhome]

These opening lines sketch visual and aural impressions of Czernowitz that are implied to possess simultaneous literary status through their association with verses that have long accompanied the lyric speaker. Whilst other poems in the collection are explicit in associating Celan with this historical place, the opening text does not confer authorship onto the verses that are said to serve as biographical pilots for the speaker. Instead, readers are left to make their own connections with the many German-Jewish poets of the Bukovina such as Alfred Margul-Sperber, Rose Ausländer and Manfred Winkler, who – alongside Celan – grew up in this multilingual city of the Habsburg Empire. Known as the 'Vienna of the East', Czernowitz was – according to Celan's famous formulation – 'eine Gegend, wo Menschen und Bücher lebten' [a region where human beings and books used to live].[54] As Marianne Hirsch has pointed out, long after the city ceased to exist as a political entity, for many 'the place forever remained Czernowitz, capital of the outlying Austrian-Habsburg imperial province of the Bukowina',[55] where 'even when political reality indicated otherwise, Jews [...] kept alive an *idea* of a pre-First World War multicultural and multilingual tolerant city and a modern, cosmopolitan culture in which German literature, music, art, and philosophy flourished among a significant majority of their num-

54 Celan, *Gesammelte Werke*, III, p. 185.

55 Marianne Hirsch, *Ghosts of Home* (Berkeley and Los Angeles: University of California Press, 2010), p. xiii.

bers.'[56] Oliver's poem engages with the historical city's imaginative status as a projected homeland, consistently deferring precise topographical coordinates. Indeed, the lyric figuration of the verses as sparrows guiding the lyric speaker's biography takes on further metamorphic character as the speaker claims their own bird's-eye view of a merging land- and sea-scape that – as in Oliver's earlier essay on his Andalusian Black Forest – relinquishes exclusive claims on any defined territorial space. Instead, the experience of visiting new domains heightens the nomadic speaker's physical awareness of their own longing for home, a sentiment captured in the striking corporeal image of shoes caught in the throat. The line-breaks that disrupt the syntactical cohesion of clauses throughout the poem confer a sense of structural dislocation on the text, whilst the sustained employment of forward slashes compounds this impression by introducing further breaks that range different thought-images alongside one another. These juxtapositions assist the reader by marking out the principal sections of the text, which signal subtle moments of development. As suggested by the oddly contradictory 'heimatlos nah', consistently evident is a lyric preoccupation with displacement that is marked by awareness of simultaneous distance and proximity, which implies a form of literary belonging that might be found in exile. Elsewhere, Oliver has commented on this apparent contradiction in considering his inevitable place on the periphery: 'Ich bin dem Fremdwerden nah und dem Nächsten kontinuierlich fremd. Ein staunender Schreibnomade. Dies Staunen hält mich wach. Und Wachheit ist mein Zentrum: Segen und Fluch der Migration' [I am close to becoming foreign and continuously foreign to that which is close. A marvelling writer-nomad. This state of marvel keeps me alert. And alertness is my centre: the blessing and curse of migration].[57] Consistently in 'Czernowitz', the lyric speaker neglects to provide precise geographical or biographical coordinates, yet – as implied in the affirmative closing lines – the poem nonetheless communicates a material recognition of the lost land- and sound-scape of the Bukovina or 'Buchenland' [land of beech trees] that has been transmitted through the writings of older German-language poets. The close of another short poem of the collection – 'Czernowitz, 5 km' – explicitly references Celan in its own tentative assertion of literary possibility upon entering a familiar landscape: '[dämmerhunde, dunkel- | licht & wortankunft, gebietscelan]'[58] [duskyhounds, dark- | light & word advent, realm celan]. These lines fig-

56 Hirsch, *Ghosts of Home*, p. xv.

57 José F. A. Oliver and Marie T. Martin, 'José F. A. Oliver im Gespräch mit Marie T. Martin: "Alles Leben ist Peripherie und Zentrum zugleich"', *poet*, 15 (2013), 164–69 (p. 164) (http://www.poetenladen.de/marie-martin-jose-oliver.htm).

58 Oliver, *fahrtenschreiber*, p. 68.

ure 'gebietscelan' as a liminal space, intuitively known by the lyric speaker, in which a form of ambivalent epiphany suggested in the declaration of simultaneous light and darkness enables the arrival of words. The lyric dialogue with the older poet can therefore be seen to underpin the present-day encounter with a long-imagined space and its '*w:orte*' which offer a deterritorialized form of *Heimat*, closely connected with the writing process itself.

It is, of course, significant that the allusive lyric engagement with Celan and his oeuvre through the poems of *fahrtenschreiber* consistently frustrates interpretative attempts to recuperate the post-war poet into any easily readable contemporary project. Nowhere is this made clearer than in the poem 'Celans geburtshaus, kein irrtum' [Celan's birthplace, no mistake] which reworks a biographical incident from Oliver's visit to Czernowitz into a lyric reflection on unknowability:

> Celans geburtshaus, kein irrtum
>
> hier sei er aus dem fenster gesprungen
> vom falschen
> ins richtige haus
> in den hinterhof sei
> er später gesprungen ins wasser
> aus dem fenster
> geklettert aus den kinderspielen
>
> in die toten
> fenster des Libanon
>
> wo liegt Czernowitz? Wo
>
> in ukrainischen briefkästen
> die antwort die frage
>
> man hat das falsche haus renoviert[59]
>
> [Celan's birthplace, no mistake
> here they say he jumped out the window
> from the wrong
> into the right house
> in the back yard they say
> he later jumped into the water
> out of the window
> climbing out of children's games
> into the dead
> windows of Lebanon

59 Oliver, *fahrtenschreiber*, p. 69.

where does Czernowitz lie? Where

in Ukrainian letterboxes
the answer the question

they renovated the wrong house]

Despite the poem's titular assertion of a singular location and a number of pointed biographical and historical referents, its allusive text offers a second-hand account of reported movement that ultimately proves resistant to tracking and legibility. Oliver has suggested that the poem's composition began after a guided tour of Czernowitz which stopped outside a house with a commemorative plaque identifying it as Celan's birthplace. As Oliver was imagining the poet sitting at its windows, his thoughts were interrupted by the voice of the tour guide who informed the group that all was not as it seemed. During the official opening ceremony, a visiting cousin of Celan's had declared that the wrong house had been renovated, since as children they used to climb, not into the front, but the backyard to play under a chestnut tree. Oliver describes his pleasure at this anecdote, describing it as 'eine Metapher gegen die Eindeutigkeit' [a metaphor against unambiguousness].[60] His poem can be seen to give lyric utterance to the frustrated pursuit of biographical truth by staging a deferred encounter with the historical Celan which raises – just as much as answers – questions and reflects the wider resistance in the poets' mutual lyric oeuvres to biographical recuperation or semantic fixity. As suggested in the quotation with which this chapter begins, throughout Oliver's oeuvre Celan's work provides a consistent point of reference for the contemporary literary project to permit incomprehension and active non-understanding through forms of language that resist patterns of explanation and meaning-making. Instead, the disruptive texts of the older poet offer a model for processes of lyric resistance which issue a challenge to majoritarian forms of language and politics through the accented lyric word. By following Celan's call to explore material dimensions of language-sounded, Oliver's meticulous lyric practice draws particular attention to the presence of the foreign and the strange within the familiar. And, in this light, the ongoing dialogue with the lyric predecessor can be seen to generate a deterritorialized form of *Heimat* that offers both a medium for lyric remembrance and a mode of virtual belonging that opens up lyric lines of flight towards other times and eras.

60 Oliver, *Lyrisches Schreiben im Unterricht*, pp. 155–56.

Denis Thouard

Philosophical readings of Paul Celan in France. Three Steps

A language that no one *speaks* is anti-poetic.[1]

Paul Celan published his first collection of poems, *Der Sand aus den Urnen* [*The Sand from the Urns*], in Vienna in 1948. That same year, he arrived in Paris, where he lived until his death in 1970. Celan wrote most of his work in France, but in German. He never tried to adapt to French as a writing language, as Ionesco and Cioran did, or even experimentally, as Rilke had done. What welcome could he expect for his poetry in this country?

Celan's poems were primarily addressed to a German audience, as they were written in the German idiom. The German language, which he had loved since childhood, had also been the language of the killers. Everything had to be redone. He could have turned away completely from German. Instead, he chose to concentrate on building a relationship with the language. It became his own challenge.

Living in Germany or even Austria would have been perhaps too much to bear and was probably something Celan could not imagine doing. Paris, by contrast, seemed like an option, a city of voluntary and assumed exile. However, the challenge for his poetry lay elsewhere: to have his poetry recognized, through the unprecedented force of his language, as equal to that of the greatest poets. It was thus important for him to introduce a critical vigilance into his poetry: in a way, to reconcile the language of Heine with the lyricism of Hölderlin.

After 1945, many writers shared the view that the world and language had been exposed to an untold destruction. For many, this consciousness came with the desire to forget, to start afresh. As Swiss author Charles-Albert Cingria, who returned to Paris in 1944 after having left it during the war, writes:

> I asked the world in vain for details about the [German] occupation. People don't answer, they want to talk about something else. I would have liked to see ruins: there are none, there are none. I know, however, that terrible things have happened – I read about it in the newspapers. [...]

1 A quotation attributed to Celan by Hugo Huppert after he visited him on 26 December 1964: 'The notes I took from this conversation with Celan, which I later expanded into stenographic records in my hotel room [...]', Hugo Huppert, 'A Visit to Paul Celan', in *Translating Tradition. Paul Celan in France*, ed. by Benjamin Hollander, *Acts*, 8/9 (1988), p. 158.

https://doi.org/10.1515/9783110658330-009

> Others, certainly more numerous, were forcibly sent to Germany. Have they come back? Alas not all of them, but a number of them. Can we question them? It's a lost cause. Some of them have faced death in the dreariest camps. They are the most hermetic. All they can tell us is that they've come back. Escapees? Maybe... and not even. Big words – especially a feverish questioning from those who have no rights or can't put any objective meaning into them – have the ability to make them inert. We understand that our whole vocabulary has to be remade.[2]

The situation in post-war Paris that Cingria describes is that recalled by someone who was at a safe distance from events, who only read about them in the newspapers. Yet even he concludes very clearly that 'our whole vocabulary has to be remade – an imperative that was much more urgently felt by Paul Celan, who had experienced the labour camps and the dehumanization, whose parents had been murdered, who knew the fate of the Jews in the German camps. The challenge of writing in German was, then, to continue the struggle *in that language*, to recall the events that were so quickly forgotten and to question what had made them possible *in that language*. Poetry became the site of a constant battle with the German language. More than just inventing a new vocabulary, it was necessary to *remake* words themselves, the syllables, letters and primitive sounds that make them up.

How would this project have been understood in Paris? Language was probably not the main obstacle, because Celan's poetry was also challenging for German speakers. It had a precision and difficulty that went beyond the skills of ordinary German readers. However, this demanding poetry managed to convince the German public of its greatness. It soon interested philosophers in Germany, who appreciated the speculative dimension of poetry, following Heidegger's enthusiastic readings of Hölderlin's work from the 1930s onwards, which were closely linked to his political and philosophical project. After 1945, Heidegger nevertheless managed to propose, with 'Wozu Dichter?' ['What are Poets For?'] (1946), a way of reading poetry that was to meet with surprising success, even

---

2 'J'ai en vain questionné le monde pour avoir des détails sur l'occupation. Les gens ne répondent pas, veulent parler d'autre chose. J'aurais voulu voir des vestiges: il n'y en a point, il n'y en a aucuns. Je sais pourtant qu'il s'est passé des choses terribles – je lisais cela dans les journaux. [...] D'autres, certes plus nombreux, ont été envoyés de force en Allemagne. Sont-ils revenus? Hélas pas tous, un certain nombre quand même. Ceux-là, on peut les questionner? C'est peine perdue. Certains ont côtoyé la mort dans les plus sinistres camps. Ce sont les plus hermétiques. Ils ne savent que nous dire qu'ils en sont revenus. Évadés? Peut-être... et même pas. Les grands mots – surtout un questionnaire fébrile de la part de celui qui n'y a aucun droit ni qui ne peut y mettre aucun sens objectif – ont le don de les rendre inertes. On comprend que tout le vocabulaire est à refaire.' Charles-Albert Cingria, *Bois sec, bois vert*, (Paris: Gallimard, 1948), pp. 100 – 1.

though it was no longer part of a larger political and ontological project.[3] Poetry now offered only traces of the origin and no longer a new mythology of the German people. By extending the reach of his readings of Hölderlin's work, Heidegger's disciples helped establish this new philosophical approach to poetry on the intellectual scene of the time.[4]

This approach to poetry had an important impact after the war, particularly in France. Modern poetry, from Char to Saint-John Perse, tended to be read in reverent philosophical terms. This was also the case with Celan's poetry, even though he was deeply apprehensive of the ideological framework that characterized such praise for poetry. The conditions of Celan's poetry in particular, namely his relationship to the events of extermination, were in fact the opposite of the Heideggerian glorification of the 'Heimat' [homeland]. The recent publication of Heidegger's *Black Notebooks*,[5] which contain his reflections from the 1930s on the links between poetry and politics in the Nazi years, has helped to put into perspective this philosophical reverence for poetry that has characterized the intellectual landscape of the last half-century, particularly in France. The encounter between Celan's poetry and interpretative approaches inspired by Heideggerian philosophy in France is a vast topic. In this chapter, I will discuss three particularly significant moments in this encounter, from 1972, 1986 and 2016 respectively.

Blanchot: Praising and rewriting Celan

Maurice Blanchot (1907–2003) only wrote one essay on Paul Celan – 'The Last One to Speak' – but his analysis is extremely significant. Published in the tribute issue of the *Revue des Belles Lettres* in 1972 after Celan's suicide, it was reprinted in a separate volume in 1986, then integrated in 2002 into the volume *Une voix venue d'ailleurs.*[6]

---

3 For a short account of this evolution, see Denis Thouard, 'The Dark Poetry of the "Black Notebooks". On the Use of Poetry by Heidegger During the 30s and After', in *What should we do with Heidegger?*, ed. by André Laks, in *Tópicos* (2018), 147–66.

4 They move quite naturally from Hölderlin to Celan, like Hans-Georg Gadamer, Otto Pöggeler, Beda Allemann. For a framing of this phenomenon, see my book, Denis Thouard, *Pourquoi ce poète? Le Celan des philosophes* (Paris: Seuil, 2016).

5 Martin Heidegger, *Gesamtausgabe* 94–96, ed. by Peter Trawny (Frankfurt a. M.: Klostermann, 2014).

6 Maurice Blanchot, 'Le dernier à parler' [1972], in *Une voix venue d'ailleurs* (Paris: Gallimard, 2002); 'The Last One to Speak', translated by Joseph Simas, in *Translating Tradition. Paul Celan in France, Acts* 8/9, 228–39.

Blanchot proposed an extremely high, elitist and exclusive concept of literature after World War II. He separated writing from its social and historical context and placed it within a separate sphere that he called 'l'espace littéraire' [literary space]. He argued, first and foremost, for the eminent value of literary experience, which he viewed in the light of his ambition for a literary absolute, as imagined by Mallarmé or Kafka. Such an abstraction of literature made sense in the context of the post-war generations' desire to turn the page and start afresh: there are similar abstractions to be found in structuralism and the 'theatre of the absurd'.[7] The philosophical importance that Blanchot ascribed to literature also made sense in the context of his own philosophy: he was indeed the one to introduce many Heidegger-inspired topics into literary criticism, such as death, nothingness and space. The insistence on space instead of time extends the relationship to death, which becomes pervasive.[8] This process of abstraction is particularly visible in his essay on Celan.

'The Last One to Speak': the title of the essay can be understood in many ways.[9] The reader may interpret it as suggesting that Celan would be the last (poet) who could speak, the culmination of poetry in a sense. But we could also understand the 'last one' as a figure who bears witness to an annihilation he narrowly escapes. The verse that guides the latter reading, 'Niemand zeugt für den Zeugen', is translated by Blanchot as 'Nul ne témoigne pour le témoin' [No one witnesses for the witness]. The quotation from Plato that Blanchot jux-

7 This expectation was already present in the previous quotation of Cingria. Blanchot wrote in the Review *Paysage Dimanche*, 2 December 1945: 'Real books are absolute, they merge with their law and do not change any more than it does, escaping the flow of things, always being whatever the circumstances, their own explanation, their eternal light. Language saves us time, literature saves the language of history', 'Charles Du Bos' criticism', in *La condition critique. Articles 1945–1998*, ed. by Christophe Bident, (Paris: Gallimard, 2010), pp. 39–40. I have sought to interpret the link between the absolutization of the literary and the erasure of history in Blanchot's work in 'Orphée politique. De Ballanche à Blanchot' (forthcoming publication, in *Götter in Exil*, ed. by Ralph Häfner and Markus Winkler [Heidelberg: Winter, forthcoming]).

8 I know that Blanchot has been seen as an opponent of philosophy, for example, in Gerald L. Bruns, *Maurice Blanchot. The Refusal of Philosophy* (Baltimore: The Johns Hopkins University Press, 1997). However, this is not very convincing. By 1950 at the latest, Blanchot insisted on Heidegger and his readings of Rilke and Hölderlin, which largely determined the physiognomy of the literature given in *L'Espace littéraire* (Paris: Gallimard, 1955). See in particular M. Blanchot, *La condition critique*, p. 172–84. Blanchot's critical work is part of the structure of Heideggerian ontological difference, which he thinks is neutral, unspeakable origin, inspired by Levinas' 'There is'; see Emmanuel Levinas, *De l'existence à l'existant* [1947] (Paris: Vrin, 1984).

9 Borrowed from the poem 'Sprich auch Du', from *Von Schwelle zu Schwelle*, GW I, p. 135.

taposes with this verse, 'For of death, no one has knowledge',[10] gives the Celan verse the status of a philosophical saying.

Blanchot seized this 'no one' to apprehend a voice from beyond, letting the event speak without a witness to the extermination. He aimed to capture the impersonal implications of the 'Niemand', of the formulation 'it speaks': at one point he writes of 'that which speaks to us here', at another of 'that which speaks to us'. The 'Niemand', the 'no one', entails the author's removal as a subject endowed with an intention. In his place there is only a word or language that 'does not strike the other, is animated by no aggressive or destructive intention'.[11] From the start, he sought to communicate his conception of Celan's poetic speech as a language liberated from subjectivity, in which it was 'as if the destruction of the self had already taken place to preserve the other, or, *to maintain a sign carried through darkness*'.[12]

The Other must be preserved, not reduced to the self, yet the self must undergo destruction. The reciprocity of pronouns – a constitutive element of Celan's poetics – is abandoned as the subject is removed. Depersonalization implies an ontologization of language. Depersonalized language speaks for itself alone, resisting all speech, intention, altercation. *Die Sprache spricht.* Towards the end of the essay Blanchot explains this euphemistic characterisation of German in Celan as a language that speaks for itself and on its own by describing it as 'the language through which death came to him [Celan], to those close to him, to millions of Jews and non-Jews, an event without response'.[13] Blanchot does not see Celan's choice to write in German as a struggle with the language, but as 'possibility which was not taken from him'[14] – as if it were a blessing to be able to participate in this language. The eviction of the subject reinforces the language in its 'aura' and eminent destiny and removes the responsibility of the perpetrators from it.

Finally, in the paragraph ending '*to maintain a sign carried through darkness*', Blanchot is quoting the following, albeit without qualifying it (we will return to this later on): 'Daß bewahrt sei | ein durchs Dunkel | getragenes Zeichen.'[15] This quotation calls for some remarks. Blanchot understands the 'durch' [by means of, through] as an instrumental, 'with'. Darkness thus materializes, it is substantiated. There is good reason to believe that, for Celan, the

---

10 Plato, *Apology* 29a (quoted p. 228).

11 'The Last One to Speak', p. 228.

12 Ibid.

13 Ibid., p. 238.

14 Ibid.

15 *Schliere*, GW I, p. 159 (in the original in two lines, not three).

'durch' refers to a crossing of the abyss, a process that carries in it the poetic truth [bewahrt]. There is no poetry without confronting extermination. The dead confer on the poem a 'Mitlaut', a kind of mute consonant that is nonetheless attuned to the soundness of speech. Thinking through the negativity that is the central concern of Celan's poetry and explains its relationship to Dante's *Divine Comedy* allows us to return to the verse quoted by Blanchot at the beginning of his text: 'No one witnesses for the witness.'

This quotation is often understood in a flat way, believed to indicate the non-transitivity of the testimony. We also know that testimony needs to be corroborated to be legally valid. The testimony of 'the last one to speak' cannot be heard; this is already implied in the phrase 'the last one to speak' itself. That is the survivor's tragedy. There seems to be no doubt that Blanchot, without stopping at the paradoxical structure of the testimony, is addressing the relationship between speech and death. Celan's poetry, marked by death and commemorating the dead, is constantly facing the possibility of its own disappearance. It inhabits the closure of literature, which is structurally linked to death.[16]

Is that the meaning that Celan himself gives the verse 'Niemand zeugt für den Zeugen'? Poetry comes from the negative: there is 'niemand', no subject, behind it, yet there is also a subject that brings the negative into the language of the poem. Against grammar, injuring it, Celan makes 'niemand' – 'no one' – a grammatical subject. The activity of the negative subject (as in the French 'personne') extends into the creativity of a poetry whose testimony is one of the forms of invention. 'Zeugen', witnessing, also means creating, producing, generating. 'No one', especially in French, is suspended between the negative and the personal, the concrete and the existential, and yet Blanchot departs from it to propose a straightforwardly metaphysical reading of the relationship between writing and death. If he had only paid attention to the internal tensions in Celan's *Niemandsrose* [*No One's Rose*], then he would have recognized this dimension of the pronoun 'niemand'.

That Blanchot pays homage to Celan by rewriting his poetry indicates just how little attention he paid to the singular form of Celan's poetry: Blanchot composed a medley (or, to use the more traditional term for it, a *cento*) of Celan's poetry, effectively using poems that never existed as a basis for his analysis. Let us consider some evidence of this form of quotation:

---

16 This paradoxicality has been replayed by Jacques Derrida: 'Le témoignage semble supposer une instance de l'instant qu'à l'instant pourtant il détruit. Il le détruit comme s'il détruisait sa propre condition de possibilité.' Derrida, *Demeure Maurice Blanchot* (Paris: Galilée, 1998), p. 33.

Das Schneebett unter uns beiden, das Schneebett.
Kristall um Kristall,
zeittief gegittert, wir fallen,
wir fallen und liegen und fallen.

Und fallen:
Wir waren. Wir sind.
Wir sind ein Fleisch mit der Nacht.
In den Gängen, den Gängen.
Du darfst mich getrost mit Schnee bewirten.

[The snowbed beneath us both, the snowbed.
Crystal by crystal,
Latticed time-deep, we fall,
we fall and lie and fall.

And fall:
We were. We are.
We are one flesh with the night.
In the passages, passages.
You may confidently treat me to snow.][17]

He dismembers and reassembles the text according to his own understanding of the work, but to the detriment of the integrity of the poems that it make up. He thus joins, as if the verses composed a single poem, the last verse of 'Schneebett' ['Snow Bed'], from *Sprachgitter* [*Speech-Grille*] (1959), with the first verses of the *Atemwende* [*Breathturn*] cycle placed together, 'Du Darfst' ['You may'], from 1965. Another example:

O diese wandernde leere
gastliche Mitte. Getrennnt,
fall ich dir zu
Ein Nichts
waren wir, sind wir, werden
wir bleiben, blühend:
die Nichts-, die
Niemandsrose.

[O this erring centre empty and
hospitable. Separate,
I fall into you
We were, we shall remain
A Nothing.
Blooming:

17 Blanchot, 'The Last One to Speak', op. cit. p. 233 ('Le dernier à parler', p. 87).

the Nothing, the
No-one's-Rose.]

This piece comprises a verse from 'Zu beiden Händen' [Of both hands] (GW I, 219) followed by a stanza from 'Psalm' (GW I, 225), both belonging to *Niemandsrose* (1963). The transition from one poem to another is merely suggested by the ellipsis that interrupts the quotation, but is not explained further. Blanchot effectively treats Celan's poetry like raw matter pliable to the interpreter's will, at the expense of the poems themselves. He makes a new text out of two existing poems without any regard for internal coherence.

In both cases cited above, Blanchot takes on the role of a speculative commentator who arranges the primary text to serve his own argument, indifferent to the logic of the poems themselves. To rearrange a text to fit one's own interpretation, however, one must be firmly convinced of its merits. Disdain for philology, which is admittedly often very down-to-earth, leads the brilliant critic to reinvent the work he claims to serve. By rearranging Celan's poetry in such an authoritative and nonchalant way, Blanchot legitimized a certain speculative use of Celan's poetry that would become common in France. Selective reading assembles a corpus in accordance with a pre-existing idea that one wants to illustrate. By using this method, the literary critic Blanchot paved the way for philosophical appropriations of literary texts in the vein of Heidegger's readings of Hölderlin and Rilke.

Making continuous text by taking disparate verses written at different times and mixing them without regard for differing registers is effectively a kind collage. This may be acceptable in the context of a tribute paid shortly after the poet's death, long before his poems can be properly understood. But it is significant that this textual practice, which gives priority to language over meaning, to the utterance over the statement, has become a tradition in some circles of the philosophical avant-garde. The speculative discourse on literature and death unfolds autonomously from the great body of literary work in reference to which it legitimizes itself.

Lacoue-Labarthe: Poetical experience and its philosophical reading

In *La poésie comme expérience* [*Poetry as Experience*],[18] Philippe Lacoue-Labarthe (1940–2007) approaches Celan's work on the basis of two selected poems: 'Tübingen, Jänner', from *Die Niemandsrose*, and 'Todtnauberg', from *Lichtzwang* [*Lightduress*]. Why this choice? The title of the second poem refers to Heidegger's cabin in the Black Forest, which Celan had visited; the first to Hölderlin, the poet from Tübingen, upon whose work Heidegger had commented. For the philosopher Lacoue-Labarthe, Heidegger was an obvious point of access to Celan's poetry.

Lacoue-Labarthe's reader is carried away in a meditation on the poetic experience as an experience that originated beyond the technical world of reason and subjectivity. Poetry allows us to depart stealthily from being as presence, being in what Heidegger calls an 'ontic' sense.[19] By playing with combinations of words, it evokes the void of nothingness, the event of nothing, that leads towards 'being' in an ontological sense. Because of this, 'the poetic act is ecstatic'.[20] The whole game of 'ontic' comparisons only produces movements: the *being* escapes it. It is incomparable. It is, Lacoue-Labarthe paraphrases Heidegger, '[t]he unrepresentable pure and simple'.[21] Poetry as an experience is therefore not about wordplay or being creative with words, but about preparing for what goes beyond words. It is about the nothingness or interruption that negatively refers to the ineffable being. Poetry, as Heidegger suggested, must bring about Rilke's *Offene* [Open].

Lacoue-Labarthe reads Celan's poetry within this ontological framework. His reading is based on a rejection of interpretation. In fact, he suggests, a hermeneutical approach is a symptom of the desire to rationalize contingency, to reduce it to reason. Interpretation risks falling from the ontological level of poetry onto the ontic level of objectivity. From the start, he rejects philology as part of his methodology and suspects reason of being an assertion of a desire for power. According to Heidegger, who reconstructs the evolution of the subject from Leibniz and Schelling to Nietzsche, the modern subject culminates in a will towards

18 Philippe Lacoue-Labarthe, *La poésie comme expérience* (Paris: Bourgois, 1986).
19 Heidegger differentiates between being as presence, in an objective sense (in his words in an 'ontic' sense), and being as beyond presence, taken as 'ontological'. See *Was ist Metaphysik?* (Frankfurt a.M.: Klostermann, 1969).
20 Ibid., p. 99.
21 Ibid., p. 100.

will. Poetry allows us to escape precisely this nihilism of technique as a feature of rationality. Work has an intention, a purpose, which must be absent from the poem. Only the 'desire to say nothing' is great. Only this desire makes it possible to escape the 'cancer of the subject'.[22]

Lacoue-Labarthe reduces the roles of both the poet and the interpreter of poetry: the poet's relationship to his language must be devoid of mastery, since the truth of the poem exceeds and even escapes the intention of its author; and the interpreter must be attuned to the ontological experience communicated in the poem without claiming to reconstitute a plausible meaning from it.

The following is a preliminary statement that guides Lacoue Labarthe's reading of the texts in advance:

> I believe these poems to be strictly untranslatable, even within their own language, and for that reason incommensurable. They necessarily avoid interpretation, they forbid it. They are written, ultimately, to prohibit it.[23]

More than a comment on Celan's poetry itself, this preamble seems to be a statement of Lacoue-Labarthe's philosophical intent. Indeed, it can be read as a continuation of Heidegger's meditations in, for example, 'The Origin of the Work of Art' from 1936.[24] It is about creating a sacred space; its focus is language as a place to receive the ontological event, escaping the interested, technical, commercial logic of ontic reason. Yet privileging poetic language in this way necessarily goes against Celan's poetic project. It precludes the possibility of a critical poetry that draws on the German lyrical tradition, denies Celan the rights to the German language and all its linguistic and cultural constituents.

The paradox of Lacoue-Labarthe's reading of Celan is that, while he intends to defend modern poetry as a means of resistance and escape from the hyper-rationalized modern world, doing so inevitably leads him to deny the poet (and Celan more specifically) any conscious intervention in or control of his words. Celan's rather obscure language appears to Lacoue-Labarthe as that of a kind of modern Hölderlin, who was, in his own way, also a prophet of a poetic existence. Yet he necessarily sees this language as a space of a certain passivity. Of course, Lacoue-Labarthe is aware of the political implications of this and occa-

---

22 Ibid., p. 24. Lacoue-Labarthe wants to explain perhaps that the subject reproduces the structure of domination and rationalization wherever he is. But such rhetorical violence remains questionable.

23 Ibid., p. 23.

24 Martin Heidegger, *Der Ursprung des Kunstwerkes* [1936] (Stuttgart: Reclam, 1960). The text is part of the collection *Holzwege* [1949], GA 5.

sionally struggles with Heidegger's Nazism.[25] But the fact remains that he places Celan in the position of a poet who welcomes the German language as an ecstatic experience of the 'Offene'. It is clear that, far from welcoming it in confidence, Celan was grappling with this language: it was both his opponent in a merciless struggle and what was at stake in it.

Lacoue-Labarthe's readings of the two Celan poems associated with Heidegger are rather brief. He wanted to avoid seeing *Todtnauberg* as a hagiography, which he reproached Gadamer for doing.[26] But did he do anything else? He found few enlightening comments on Celan, but cites those by Blanchot and Levinas, although he calls them 'gnomic' and marked by Heidegger's texts on Hölderlin. He was well aware that Peter Szondi went further in his reading of Celan, but Lacoue-Labarthe's premise forbade him from following Szondi, because the latter was moving in the direction of a 'deciphering', a 'translation almost without rest'.[27] His sacralization of Celan's idiom kept him even attempting to test its intelligibility. Though he invokes the extreme singularity of his object, preserving it at all costs, his philosophical discourse remains perfectly universal, unaffected by its object. It is this discrepancy that is problematic.

Much of the essential impetus for discourses on poetry in post-war France came from Heidegger. This undoubtedly played a role in the legitimization of poetry at a time when the formulas of surrealism and the political poetry of the Resistance had run their course – the former because they became caught up in advertising discourses, the latter because circumstances had changed. With more or less caution, poets themselves showed interest in a philosopher who gave them such a satisfying role. This is not, however, to say that they only understood themselves in their relationship to this philosophy, and no one less so than Celan.

Lacoue-Labarthe's claim that 'Celan's poetry is entirely a dialogue with Heidegger's thought, that is, essentially the parts of Heidegger's thought that were in dialogue with Hölderlin's poetry'[28] is certainly exaggerated, and builds a kind of genealogy of eminent thinkers and poets in dialogue with one another. It produces, in another words, a philosophical myth at the expense of the diversity of the

25 Celan's Jewishness makes it possible to reimport the Heideggerian way of reading texts without having to discuss it critically, because the Jewishness absolves the method. It is therefore possible to be leftist and Heideggerian after World War II.

26 Lacoue-Labarthe, *La poésie comme expérience*, pp. 130 – 33.

27 Ibid, p. 26. For more on Szondi, the reader may refer to my essay, Denis Thouard, 'Form and History. From Lukács to Szondi', in *Textual Understanding and Historical Experience. On Peter Szondi*, ed. by Susanne Zepp, (Munich: Fink, 2015), pp. 31 – 42.

28 Lacoue-Labarthe, *La poésie comme expérience*, p. 50.

poetic work, in ignorance of its critical dimension.[29] Roughly thirty years later, we can see that, beneath the changing surface of philosophical positions, the relationship between philosophy and poetry established by Lacoue-Labarthe remains relatively constant.

Badiou: Celan at the end of the 'age of the poets'

Alain Badiou first started working on Celan in the early 1990s, when he proclaimed the end of the 'age of the poets' in a seminar led by Jacques Rancière. These texts were published in the 2016 volume *Que pense le poème?* [*What Does the Poem Think?*], which contains further reflections on Paul Celan's poems.[30]

A distinction must be made between Badiou's reflections on the relationship between poetry and philosophy on the one hand and the proposed 'age of the poets', spanning from Hölderlin to Celan, on the other. Let us first consider Badiou's general point. Although philosophy has a mathematical dimension that detaches it from 'all nativity', it is also pulled in another direction through great poetry, a 'detachment that takes place within the mother tongue'..[31] With this double detachment, philosophy opens up a space beyond objectivity; it cuts loose from the present and heralds something else entirely. Furthermore, Badiou claims in an interview that concludes the book, there is a 'global delay of philosophy over poetry'.[32] In a way, Badiou here endows poetry with an explosive power that enables it to represent the unrepresentable. Here, he follows the Heideggerian opposition of (ontic) presence (*Vorhandensein*) and ontological appearance. But he complements this approach with another definition, asserting that poetry aims 'rather to capture in language the singularity of the presence of

29 The negativity that pervades Celan's poems is not an ontological abstraction but rather recalls the very historical experience of the dead and of extermination in the Nazi camps.

30 Alain Badiou, *Que pense le poème?* (Caen: Nous, 2016), hereafter referred to as 'Badiou'. I have further commented on the former interpretations to which I simply refer in Denis Thouard, 'La politique du poète', *Europe* 1049–1050, *Paul Celan* (2016), 81–91. Both 'What Does the Poem Think' and 'The Age of the Poets' can be found in English translation in Alain Badiou, *The Age of the Poets and Other Writings on Twentieth-Century Poetry and Prose*, trans. by Bruno Bosteels, ed. by Emily Arpels and Bruno Bosteels (London/New York: Verso, 2014), hereafter referred to as 'Badiou (trans.)'.

31 As an 'internal tearing away from the mother tongue', says Badiou, ibid., p. 8.

32 Ibid., p. 168 (interview with Charles Ramond).

the perceptible'.[33] With this view of poetry he moves beyond the initial opposition he has established. The interruption produced by the poem takes place in language: 'It lodges silence in the central framework of language, and from there, skews it towards an unprecedented affirmation.'[34] Such silence marks a halt, 'it stops language in its tracks'.[35] By interrupting communication in this way, 'the poem is the guardian of the decency of the saying',[36] which is more precise than the Heideggerian 'shepherd of being'. Finally, 'the poem is the delicacy of language towards language; it is a delicate *touching* of the resources of language'.[37] These expressions balance the use of the theme of poetry as an experience of the 'Offene' and as access to being, which Badiou also assumes. While I will not go much further into the role of poetry in Badiou's philosophy here, it is worth noting that poetry, for Badiou, introduces an element of excess that provokes and challenges philosophy without becoming knowledge in the traditional sense (which for Badiou is objective and linked to an object). Poetry tries to 'restore singularity'.[38] This brief sketch is only an overview of Badiou's philosophical interest in poetry, an interest that led him to Celan.

Yet from the beginning, Badiou's philosophical assumptions, most notably his thesis of 'the age of the poets', conditioned – and limited – his readings of Celan's poetry. For Badiou, 'the age of the poets' is a philosophical category, as we will see. In 1989, he championed the idea of a poetic continuity from Hölderlin to Celan, a genealogy of poets who grappled with distinctly philosophical problems. As poets, they had a privileged relationship with the truth, but they were also able to 'think this thought'. Poetry dealt with truth and was able to reflect upon it as well. Badiou's idea echoes both Heidegger's characterization of Hölderlin as the 'poet of poets', and Celan's view of Mallarmé as 'thinking things through to the end'.[39] This last statement from *Der Meridian* probably makes Celan, for Badiou, the poet at the close of his 'age of the poets'.

That Badiou places him at the end of his envisaged 'age of poetry' suggests that he viewed Celan's 'philosophical' status as ambiguous. It implies a renunciation of thought, perhaps even of meaning, in philosophical poetry. Badiou thus advances that 'Celan [...] takes the imperative of the weakness of sense all the way to the point of breakdown of song, because in the intimacy of

33 Ibid., p. 169.
34 Ibid., p. 15. Badiou (trans.), p. 24.
35 Badiou (trans.), p. 25.
36 Ibid.
37 Badiou, p. 16; Badiou (trans.), p. 25.
38 Badiou, p. 170.
39 GW III, p. 193.

song there still remains something like an excessive deposit of sense'.[40] To illustrate this idea, he uses a verse from the poem 'Wanderstaude' ['Wandering Bush'], which opens the first posthumous collection, *Zeitgehöft* [*Timestead*]. The poem consists of a single sentence split between three verses, of which Badiou gives only the third, as if it constituted a whole. I translate it here in its entirety:

> Wanderstaude, du fängst dir
> eine der Reden,
>
> die abgeschworene Aster
> stößt hier hinzu,
>
> wenn einer, der
> die Gesänge zerschlug,
> jetzt spräche zum Stab,
> seine und aller
> Blendung
> bliebe aus. [41]
>
> [Wandering bush, you grasp
> one of the speeches,
>
> the aster abjured
> invites itself here,
>
> if someone, who
> broke the songs,
> now were talking to the stick,
> his blinding
> and that of all,
> would be missing.][42]

Without reading this poem more closely, I would like to contrast it with what Badiou is suggesting. For him, 'the breakage of the poem as aesthetic ethos'[43] is the condition for the lucidity of thought. Negativity takes hold of poetic form. The internal negation of the poem frees up a 'clear and unblinded thought', ready to consider the (ontological) event.

However, the rhythm of the poem that Badiou cites here as a whole makes a different interpretation possible. First there is a selection in the wandering matter of the bush (1); then the addition of the negative, under the sign of the star

40 Badiou, *Que pense le poème?*, p. 38 (and all further references). Badiou (trans.), p. 11.
41 GW III, p. 69.
42 My translation.
43 Badiou (trans.), p. 11.

(evoked through the etymology of the word 'Aster'), which here indicates the Judaization of the poetic language, the introduction of the negativity within the poetic tongue (2); the third moment marks the conditions of overcoming blindness: the song is broken, and this break is the condition of a written word, following the letter (the 'Stab'), which marks the stopping of time (3).[44] Lucidity involves the critical work of destruction of all that obliterates lucidity: it is only articulated in terms of a negation, through writing. This third step can also be understood as the production of blindness as a poetical condition, as it was regarded throughout antiquity.

There are two sets of references in this poem that prompt us to reflect on Celan's choice of words and the relevance of his context. On the one hand, as Jean Bollack shows,[45] we find references to Greek singers and rhapsodes, to Homer, Hesiod and Pindar; on the other hand, there is the biblical scene of Moses and Aaron, in particular with the opposition of the broken tables (here they are the songs) and the stick, but also the themes of difficult communication and blindness.[46] Breaking the songs, the poet is fighting against a certain hymnic tradition of magnifying poetry; speaking to the stick, he engages in another mode of poetic saying. The stick (which can be taken from Schadewaldt and Celan's first sketches) brings a specific scansion (the scansion of the 'now') into poetical language.

Badiou sees a renunciation of the poem, or even its annihilation, as a condition for the emergence of a 'new meaning', 'at the heights of the defection from all presence'.[47] He does not take account of the practice of 'talking to the stick' that engages the whole dimension of writing as a condition of lucidity. He also ignores the poet's confrontation with the signs of abjection as trial and choice of the negative, which weighs down Celanian poetry in its singularity. The quotation of 'Wanderstaude' takes on an a merely illustrative function in Badiou's text; it follows the quotations from Mallarmé, Trakl, Pessoa and Mandelstam

---

44 'St' appears in 'Wanderstaude', in 'Aster' and concentrates itself in 'Stab', the instrument of writing and verticality, a promise of life.

45 The genesis of the poem shows that Celan was influenced by his reading of Wolfang Schadewaldt's *Von Homers Welt und Werk* (1944); see Jean Bollack, *Poésie contre poésie* (Paris: PUF, 2001), pp. 183–87; Werner Wögerbauer, 'Textgenese und Interpretation. Zu Paul Celans Gedicht Wanderstaude', in *Dokument/Monument. Textvarianz in den verschiedenen Disziplinen der Germanistik. La variance des textes dans les différentes disciplines de la germanistique*, ed. by F. Lartillot and A. Gellhaus (Bern: Peter Lang, 2007), pp. 327–71.

46 *Exodus* 32, 15; *Numbers* 17–18. Celan also should have been familiar with Schönberg's *Moses and Aaron.* This second set of references is not directly attested but can be introduced with caution.

47 Badiou (trans.), p. 12.

that Badiou uses in a similarly bold way. Poetry provides him only with a set of aphorisms.

We have now looked at three readings in which Celan is taken to exemplify a kind of contemplative poetry that is sufficiently obscure and sublime as to deserve philosophical attention, or even to suggest complicity with philosophy. Unlike German philosophers who have taken an interest in this poetry – such as Otto Pöggeler or Hans-Georg Gadamer, who wrote commentaries on entire poems – the French philosophers discussed here prepared their subject matter in advance. Blanchot selected extracts from Celan and combined them into an original text that suited his interpretation. Lacoue-Labarthe selected the two poems by Celan that he thought most likely to contain a link to Heidegger's thought, and developed a theory of the poetic experience at a good distance from Celan's work. Alain Badiou, finally, explicitly used Celan's poems in a merely illustrative way, thus going against the very project of Celan's poetry. Badiou, too, privileged a philosophical 'universal' over the particularity of Celan's poetry.

All three readings are based on the same paradox of an extreme valorization of poetry and its subordination to a general purpose. They posit that philosophical discourse listens and pays attention to the poetic word, which is a priori virtuous, while their own philosophical discourse disregards the letter of the poems and overlooks their singularity in its effort to articulate a general theory of poetry in the modern world.

The readings above indicate that philosophical approaches to poetry are part of a criticism of the rationalized world. Celan's poetry lent itself particularly well to such approaches, whose conceptual tools originated in the age of Romanticism and matured in Heidegger's thinking. Philologists rarely intervene, letting philosophy take hold of the category 'poetry'. The systematic nature with which this phenomenon occurs in Alain Badiou reveals a pervasive shared attitude.

On the basis of the assumption that poets can and do speak to philosophy, however, one can guess at the possibility of different readings. Celan's poetry is redeemed by its own individuality. It is *his* writing and *his* cause. It requires another form of attention and cannot be reduced to concepts. It questions philosophy in its own way, engaging with temporality and providing a different take on naming. His poems name singularity. They remember a lost presence and are open to the contingency of the occasion on which they were written, which often contributes to their specific ciphering. Coming to Celan with a toolbox of ontological categories more suited to the analysis of hymns than of poetry, it is little surprise that philosophers often overlooked the hidden nuances of Celan's poems.

Kristina Mendicino

Language, Barred. Paul Celan's Poetological Reduction

Erst die Suspendierung der Sicht läßt das Sichtbare hervortreten.
[It is the suspension of vision that first allows the visible to step forth.]
– Werner Hamacher, *Für–die Philologie*

Among Paul Celan's draft materials for the *Meridian*, there is a remark that addresses the phenomenon of (poetic) language with the language of phenomenology: 'Miterscheinen der Sprache im Gedicht oder: die Sprache als miterscheinender (das Gedicht als durchscheinend~~er~~ ⌊Ge⌋) Hintergrund ='. [The co-appearing of language in the poem or: language as co-appearing (the poem as translucent/trans-appearing ⌊po⌋) background =.].[1] With these words Celan modifies a passage from Edmund Husserl's *Logische Untersuchungen* [*Logical Investigations*] as it appears in Georg Lukács's study of 1917, 'Die Subjekt-Objekt Beziehung in der Aesthetik' ['The Subject-Object Relation in Aesthetics'], which Celan cites directly in the notes surrounding this phrase.[2] In his essay, Lukács draws upon Husserl in order to distinguish the object of aesthetic experience, which should be conceived of as 'thought as the sole existing [object]',[3] from the objects of knowledge, which know no such independence. Each is only separable from surrounding, co-appearing phenomena owing to an arbitrary act of imaginative variation, and even then, writes Husserl, 'we inescapably present it in a context, the *content stands out in relief from a co-appearing objective background*, it is inescapably given with many other contents, and is also in a way united to them.'[4] With or without look-

1 Paul Celan, *Der Meridian. Endfassung – Vorstufen – Materialien*, ed. by Bernhard Böschenstein and Heino Schmull (Frankfurt a. M.: Suhrkamp, 1999), pp. 105, 207. Unless otherwise noted, all English translations of this text are provided according to Paul Celan, *The Meridian. Final Version–Drafts–Materials*, trans. by Pierre Joris (Stanford: Stanford University Press, 2011). Since the pagination is the same in the English and the German versions of *The Meridian*, only one page reference will be provided each time Celan's speech is quoted. Joris's translation has also been occasionally modified (KM).

2 Georg Lukács, 'Die Subjekt-Objekt-Beziehung in der Aesthetik', *Logos*, 7.1 (1917/18), 1–39 (pp. 15–16). See Celan, *Der Meridian*, pp. 99–107, 204–13, 234, 248. All translations of passages from this essay are mine (KM).

3 Ibid., p. 15.

4 '[W]ir stellen ihn doch unausweichlich in einem Zusammenhang vor, der *Inhalt hebt sich von einem miterscheinenden gegenständlichen Hintergrund ab*, er ist unausweichlich mit vielfältigen anderen Inhalten zugleich gegeben und mit ihnen in gewisser Weise auch einig' (ibid.,

https://doi.org/10.1515/9783110658330-010

ing further to Lukács's argumentation, Celan's note thus seems to relate poetic language to language along the lines of the nexus that ties each perceptual object inextricably to the others that surround it as described in Husserl's investigation, 'On the Theory of Wholes and Parts'. But nothing about this relationship between language and language becomes even partly transparent, not least because it is unclear whether and how Husserl's phenomenology could translate to a commentary on the phenomenality of (poetic) language.

In *Logischen Untersuchungen*, Husserl addresses language primarily in terms of significative units of meaning whose value hinges upon the possibility of intuitive fulfilment and whose syntax is founded in preverbal categorial acts of intuition.[5] Although Husserl begins his book with investigations into meaning and expression, language – and especially those characteristics of language that do not reflect semantics or proto-logical syntax – could thus be seen as an epiphenomenon within his phenomenological project. Accordingly, Husserl suggests that words appear solely in order to vanish: 'Both are "lived through", the presentation of the word and the sense-giving act: but, while we experience the former, we do not live in such a presentation at all, but solely in enacting its sense, its meaning.'[6] Celan's adoption of phenomenological vocabulary in his notes on (poetic) language does not so much clarify that language, then, as it provokes the question: how would an intentionality towards language look?[7] Before and beyond the intentionality that should shape meaningful words, Celan's writing suggests the need to address what he will call – again recalling the language of Husserl – the 'Auf-die-Sprache-Gerichtetsein des Dichters' [being-directed-towards-language of the poet].[8] This directionality towards language as such differs from the intentionality towards meaning that drives not only Husserl's inves-

---

pp. 15–16, my emphasis). The quoted passages appear in Edmund Husserl, *Logische Untersuchungen. Zweiter Band, Erster Teil*, ed. by Ursula Panzer (New York: Springer, 1984), p. 238. The translation is given in Edmund Husserl, *Logical Investigations*, 2 vols, trans. by J. N. Findlay, ed. by Dermot Moran (London and New York: Routledge, 2001), vol. 2, p. 9, trans. modified (KM).

5 Although Husserl will argue for the meaning of 'absurd' expressions such as a 'round square', the laws of categorial forms are decisive for the truth-value of any proposition. See, for example, Husserl, *Logische Untersuchungen*, pp. 335, 720. These laws are preverbal, since the perception of even a part within a whole is already constituted by what Husserl calls 'artikulierende Akte' (ibid., p. 681).

6 Husserl, *Logical Investigations*, vol. 1, p. 193; cf. Husserl, *Logische Untersuchungen*, p. 46.

7 The phenomenologically inflected 'intentionality towards language' which will be elaborated in the pages that follow differs from the 'Intention auf die Sprache' which Winfried Menninghaus aligned with an intentionality towards the name in *Paul Celan. Magie der Form* (Frankfurt a.M.: Suhrkamp Verlag, 1980).

8 Celan, *Der Meridian*, p. 116.

tigations but also the more differentiated phenomenological-linguistic texts that Celan would later study, such as Roman Jakobson's 'Kindersprache, Aphasie und allgemeine Lautgesetze' ['Child Language, Aphasia and Phonological Universals'], where Jakobson will speak of 'Lautgebung' [donation of the phoneme] rather than Husserl's 'Sinngebung' [donation of sense], but will describe the former nonetheless as an 'intentionsgemässe[n] Bewegung' [movement structured according to intentionality] that aims at the 'distinktive[n] Wert des Lautes' [distinctive value of the phoneme] so as to build the 'phonometische[n] Rahmen' [phonometic frame] for meaningful speech.[9] Yet because an intentionality towards language could not be framed by these or any other possible functions of language – including the function of a subject – there is also no telling how an 'Auf-die-Sprache-Gerichtetsein' might be addressed once the question of phenomenality has shifted from the field of transcendental subjectivity to a field where, as Jacques Derrida would argue, 'every present subject can be absent'.[10] With the exception of Werner Hamacher's readings of Celan, and especially his reading of the poem, 'Klammer auf, Klammer zu' [Bracket Opened, Bracket Closed], this directionality towards language tends not to be addressed in the commentaries on Celan's engagement with Husserl, leaving the implications that Celan develops from phenomenology in his notes and in other poems in need of further commentary.[11] This essay will offer a reading of those passages

---

9 Roman Jakobson, 'Kindersprache, Aphasie und allgemeine Lautgesetze', in *Selected Writings 1. Phonological Studies* (The Hague: Mouton, 1962), pp. 328–401 (pp. 353, 377), my translation. Cf. Roman Jakobson, *Child Language, Aphasia, and Phonological Universals*, trans. by A. R. Keiler (Mouton: The Hague, 1968), p. 42. Jakobson also explicitly cites Husserl in this piece ('Kindersprache', pp. 350, 354). Celan had owned the edition of Jakobson's book that appeared with Suhrkamp Verlag in 1969, on which see Barbara Wiedemann's commentary in Paul Celan, *Die Gedichte*, ed. by Barbara Wiedemann (Berlin: Suhrkamp Verlag, 2018), pp. 1227–28.

10 Jacques Derrida, *Edmund Husserl's* Origin of Geometry. *An Introduction*, trans. by John P. Leavey (Lincoln and London: University of Nebraska Press, 1989), p. 88. With reference to Sigmund Freud's *Das Unbehagen in der Kultur*, Celan will similarly write of the poem: 'Im Gedicht, und das Gedicht ist, als Schrift, "Sprache eines Abwesenden", tritt ein Abwesender an dich, den ⌊noch⌋ Abwesenderen, heran. Der Gedanke, die Begegnung der Abwesenden könnte ausbleiben, liegt nahe' [In the poem, and the poem is, as writing, 'the language of an absent one', someone absent steps up close to you, the ⌊even more⌋ absent one] (Celan, *Der Meridian*, p. 136).

11 Several readings of Celan's engagement with Husserl's *Vorlesungen zur Phänomenologie des inneren Zeitbewußtseins* include Jean Greisch, '*Zeitgehöft et Anwesen*. La dia-chronie du poème', in *Contre-jour. Études sur Paul Celan*, ed. by Martine Broda (Paris: Éditions du Cerf, 1986), pp. 167–83; Marko Pajević, *Zur Poetik Paul Celans. Gedicht und Mensch – die Arbeit am Sinn* (Heidelberg: Universitätsverlag C. Winter, 2000), pp. 200–5; Roland Reuss, *Im Zeithof. Celan-Provokationen* (Frankfurt a.M.: Stroemfeld Verlag, 2001), pp. 103–5; Sandro Zanetti, *'zeitoffen'. Zur Chronographie Paul Celans* (Munich: Fink Verlag, 2006), pp. 143–48. Werner Hamacher's

from Celan's notes on the *Meridian* that indicate the difference between the phenomenon of language and the descriptions of perceptual phenomena and meaning that Husserl provides in his early oeuvre. It will then retrace the even sharper analysis of speech and phenomena which may be seen in the language of Celan's poem 'Sprachgitter' [Speech-Grille].

By speaking of language through its modes of appearing (*Miterscheinen, Durchscheinen*), Celan not only emphasizes its sheer phenomenality over any function it may perform; he also suggests that it is never constituted as a unified appearance (*Erscheinung*) at all. And beyond this, its difference to intentional objects of perception – to say nothing of words or meanings – emerges through the way in which the 'Miterscheinen der Sprache im Gedicht' [co-appearing of language in the poem] can only refer to the language that is *not* spoken in it. Shortly before this note, Celan will write: 'Das Gedicht ensteht durch den Umgang mit einem uns [U]unsichtbar B bleiben[den]: im Umgang mit der Sprache' [The poem comes into being through intercourse with something that remains {i}invisible to us: through intercourse with language], which can only be asserted without contradiction if even the invisibility of language does not appear to us. Celan underscores this in his remark by allowing the 'uns' [us] to echo and blend into the '*Uns*sichtbar[e]' [invisible], which thereby resounds as the 'Uns-Sichtbare' [visible-to-us], as though the 'invisible' were itself blended out by 'us'. Hence, a more impersonal remark follows: 'Begegnung mit der Sprache ist Begegnung mit dem Unsichtbarem' [a meeting with language is a meeting with the invisible] and finally: 'Dem Aufmerksamen fällt etwas vom Vorwissen der Sprache zu: Unsichtbares vom "Kristallisationspunkt"' [To the attentive falls something from / of the pre-knowledge of language: something invisible from / of the 'crystallisation point'].[12] As it unfolds the implications of the 'Miterscheinen der Sprache im Gedicht', this series of remarks makes explicit that the 'co-appearing' of language in the poem constitutes the co-appearing of that which not only *is*, but which also *remains* invisible, structurally escaping subjective certitude and becoming itself utterly uncertain and *unsicher.*

In this regard, Celan's note speaks less to Husserl's horizon of perception than to what Werner Hamacher describes as the 'Atopischen, Aphänomenalen und Averbalen' [atopic, aphenomenal and averbal], from which the phenomena first come into relief and which could be called 'language' if it were not that, as

study, 'Epoché. Gedicht. Celans *Reimklammer* um Husserls Klammern', in *Keinmaleins. Texte zu Celan* (Frankfurt a. M.: Vittorio Klostermann, 2019), pp. 143–79, analyses Celan's 'Verschärfung' of the phenomenological *epoché* in 'Klammer auf, Klammer zu' (Hamacher, 'Epoché. Gedicht', p. 165).

12 Celan, *Der Meridian*, p. 105.

Hamacher also says, the movement which first allows for a word to be given of it (and anything else) could not itself be fixed and encompassed by a word.[13] And because these very arguments also indicate that 'language' does not and could not appear as such, it can only be the poem that first permits this 'Hintergrund' [background] to appear by shining through it: 'die Sprache als miterscheinender (das Gedicht als durchscheinend~~er~~ [Ge]) Hintergrund =' [language as co-appearing (the poem as translucent / trans-appearing / ⌊po⌋) background =].[14] Since this also means, however, that the poem barely differs from the *co*-appearing, that is to say the *non*-appearing language it illuminates, the poem nearly seems to be nothing per se but a sheer perspective that opens within the otherwise aphenomenal background through which it appears. It is in this light that one could read Celan's evocation of the poem as a 'Kristallisationspunkt' [crystallisation point] from which 'etwas vom Vorwissen der Sprache' [something from / of the pre-knowledge of language] may fall to the attentive, without crystallizing into a saturated appearance that could become an object of knowledge (*Wissen*). It is in this light that one might read his surrounding notes on the porosity of the poem, which imply that whatever may be perceived as a poem is also the sieve which takes shape through it but captures nothing. And it is in this light that one could read Celan's repeated returns to the *one* poem and *one* figure for language that is most often cited in the pages of his manuscript, namely, 'Sprachgitter'.[15]

Still, nothing about the relationship of poetic language to language thereby becomes transparent. Precisely because of its thoroughgoing openness to language, there is no getting behind the poem – Celan writes: 'das Gedicht ist schon das Dahinter' [the poem is indeed what is behind] – while every attempt to see through it renders it more opaque: 'vom Durchschautwerden werden die Gedichte undurchsichtig; Opazität –' [from being seen-through the poems become non-transparent; opacity –].[16] But already the sheer fact that Celan's parenthetical remark on the poem 'als durchscheinend~~er~~' [as translucent] may be

---

13 Hamacher, "Epoché. Gedicht', pp. 147, 155, 166. For further commentary on the aphenomenal from which phenomena – linguistic and otherwise – emerge, see also *95 Thesen zur Philologie* (Werner Hamacher, *95 Thesen zur Philologie* [Frankfurt a. M.: Roughbook, 2010], p. 39), and Werner Hamacher, 'What Remains to Be Said. On Twelve and More Ways of Looking at Philology', trans. by Kristina Mendicino, in *Give the Word. Responses to Werner Hamacher's* 95 Theses on Philology, ed. by Gerhard Richter and Ann Smock (Lincoln: University of Nebraska Press, 2019), pp. 217–354 (pp. 330–40).

14 Celan, *Der Meridian*, p. 105.

15 Ibid., p. 105, cf. pp. 103–4.

16 Ibid., pp. 97–98.

grammatically completed only by the 'Hintergrund' [background], which stands outside the closing parenthesis, suggests that the parentheses give no closure with regard to what may or may not appear within their scope. The opacity of these lines is only intensified, moreover, when the parentheses are also read as those diacritical indices that mark the phenomenological reduction of every 'Vollzug irgendeines Seinsglaubens' [execution of any belief in being] to a 'bloße[n] Seinsanspruch' [mere claim to being].[17] For if the parentheses indicate that the language of the poem appears, but merely *claims* to be, while the language beyond it *is*, but does not appear, the indefinition of the parentheses in Celan's note would mark their divergence from their function in phenomenology by exceeding the control of the subject who sets them and by exceeding their proper phenomenality. This detail in Celan's remarks thus unsettles even the belief that one could sufficiently carry out a reduction in order to observe an appearance that could claim to be language, poetic or otherwise.[18] Hence, whereas Husserl's reduction allows for reflection upon transcendent objects of consciousness as mere phenomena, Celan's parentheses render the poem the mere appearance of appearing and, ultimately, the mere appearance of an appearing of that (language) which withdraws from appearance. As Celan says in a note that comes shortly before those which have been cited so far: 'Das Gedicht ist als Figur der ⌊ganzen⌋ Sprache eingeschrieben; aber die Sprache bleibt unsichtbar {.}; das sich Aktualisierende – die Sprache – ~~nimmt~~ tritt, kaum ist das geschehen, in den Bereich des Möglichen zurück' [The poem is inscribed as the figure of the ⌊complete⌋ language; but language remains invisible {.}; that which actualizes itself – language – ~~takes~~ steps, as soon as that has happened, back into the realm of the possible].[19]

This is not to say that nothing remains to be seen – the poem is, after all, 'eingeschrieben' [inscribed] – but only that this inscription would need to be seen as the trace of a movement that will have occurred with and against the speechlessness of language and which therefore approaches its withdrawal pre-

---

17 Edmund Husserl, *Cartesianische Meditationen und Pariser Vorträge*, ed. by S. Strasser (Dordrecht: Springer, 1991), pp. 58, 60, my translation. As Hamacher first emphasized, this passage appears on a page that Celan had marked in his edition of Husserl's text. See Hamacher, 'Epoché. Gedicht', p. 166, as well as *Paul Celan – La bibliothèque philosophique*, ed. by Alexandra Richter, Patrik Alac, and Bertrand Badiou (Paris: Editions Rue d'Ulm, 2004), p. 419.

18 Hamacher observes a similar movement in his reading of 'Klammer auf, Klammer zu'. 'die dichterische Klammer Celans klammert noch die phänomenologische Klammer und damit nicht nur die Weltgegenständlichkeit, sondern die transzendentale *Urthesis* des Subjekts ein, auf die jene Gegenständlichkeit zurückgeführt wird', in Hamacher, 'Epoché. Gedicht', p. 168.

19 Celan, *Der Meridian*, p. 104.

cisely in moving towards its appearance. Hence Celan's lapidary phrase – '⌊X → ins Sprachlose – ⌋ Vom Tode her bestimmt: das Winterliche, Kristallnahe, Anorganische als Bereich der eigentlichsten Zuwendung des ⌊im Gedicht⌋ Sprechenden' [⌊X → into the speechless – ⌋ Determined from the direction of death: the wintery, crystal-like, inorganic as realm of the most essential turning-toward the one speaking ⌊in the poem⌋][20] – which Celan will go on to relate to Sigmund Freud's hypothesis on the death drive (which, like language, withdraws from appearance).[21] From this perspective, all apparent words in the poem would be – beside 'themselves' – what one could call, with Freud, 'Wortreste' [word-remnants][22] left over from a movement towards 'Sprache' [language], which at the same time can only be a movement 'ins Sprachlose' [into the speechless]. These remnants would not only become foreign to the units of meaning that Husserl intends even while seemingly remaining 'recognizable' as words; they would also, in this very ambivalence, become akin to those utterances of which Jakobson speaks when he addresses the difficulty in discerning, during primary language acquisition and aphasic language loss, 'embryo-words' from the 'prelanguage residue' that troubles the distinctions of language by merely resembling them, while resounding from the child's (or patient's) originally unformalized, unsemanticized and therefore – for Jakobson – non-linguistic vocal range.[23] Between meaningful segments of language and fragments of another which may be none at all, the words of poetic language open an 'Intervall' or 'Sprachgitter' [speech-grille][24] with, through and for language, in the all of the senses that Werner Hamacher traces in *Für – die Philologie* [*For – Philology*].[25] This interval permits more and other matters to be articulated than 'all' that would appear through the 'als' [as] which will have determined the 'λόγος als ἀπόφανσις',[26] from Aristotle through Husserl and Heidegger. As Celan writes: 'Es ist alles an-

20 Ibid., p. 99.

21 Ibid., p. 100.

22 Sigmund Freud, *Das Ich und das Es*, in *Gesammelte Werke*, vol. 13, ed. by Anna Freud et al. (London. Imago Publishing, 1940), pp. 235–89, p. 250, my translation.

23 Jakobson, *Child Language*, p. 29; cf. 'Kindersprache', p. 341. They are reminiscent of what Daniel Heller-Roazen, in his brilliant analysis of Jakobson's essay, among others, would call 'the echo of another speech and of something other than speech, [...] which guarded the memory of the immemorial babble that, in being lost, allowed all languages to be': Daniel Heller-Roazen, *Echolalias. On the Forgetting of Language* (New York: Zone Books, 2008), p. 12.

24 Celan, *Der Meridian*, p. 101.

25 Werner Hamacher, *Für – die Philologie* (Weil am Rhein: Engeler, 2009).

26 Martin Heidegger, *Sein und Zeit*, 8th edn (Tübingen: Max Niemeyer Verlag, 2001), p. 33. For a critical reading of this 'Als'-structure, see Werner Hamacher, *Entferntes Verstehen* (Frankfurt a.M.: Suhrkamp Verlag, 1998), pp. 42–43. See also Hamacher, *Für–die Philologie*, p. 43.

ders, als du es dir denkst, als ich es mir denke' [It is all otherwise than as you think it to yourself, than as I think it to myself].[27] Neither an element within the total nexus of Husserl's theoretical world, nor a tool within the existential nexus of Heidegger's being-in-the-world, nor a value within Jakobson's 'phonometic frame', every apparent term would be open-ended and would remain open through its ending. And it is because the poem can thus speak counter to all appearances of its speaking *or* non-speaking that the 'Miterscheinen der Sprache im Gedicht' [co-appearing of language in the poem] can be reformulated – without contradiction – as a 'Begegnung mit der Sprache' [encounter with language] or a 'Begegnung mit Unsichtbarem' [encounter with that which is invisible],[28] within a context where the emphasis will have been placed all along upon the 'gegen' [counter]: 'Das Gedicht ist der Ort, wo das Synonyme unmöglich wird: es hat nur <u>seine</u> Sprache [...] Aus der Sprache hervortretend, tritt ~~die Spr~~ das Gedicht der Sprache <u>gegenüber</u>' [The poem is the place where synonymity becomes impossible: it only has <u>its</u> language [...] Stepping out of language, ~~the lang~~ the poem steps counter to language].[29]

It is in this counterintuitive complexity that the 'with' or 'co' of the 'Miterscheinen der Sprache im Gedicht' [co-appearing of language in the poem] needs to be recognized. Celan may also have seen this in the essay of Émile Benveniste, 'Remarques sur la fonction du langage dans la découverte freudienne' ['Remarks on the Function of Language in Freudian Theory'], which appears cited in Celan's notes beside selections from Husserl, Lukács and Freud, among others, and which culminates in a commentary on 'with' and 'without'. Both 'with'-words fail to 'include [...] contradictory expressions', since 'with', Benveniste claims, consistently indicates *contre*. Even with 'without', he writes, 'the proper sense of with here is "against" (cf. *withstand*) and indicates motion or effort in some direction'.[30] Celan does not directly 'cite' this passage in particular in his notes, but its proximity to his descriptions of poetic language becomes evident when he aligns poetic rhythm with a similarly indeterminate movement and illustrates it with verses from 'Sprachgitter' – or vice versa – : 'Rhythmus – Sinnbewegung auf ein noch unbekanntes Ziel zu. ⌊ → eine Art Tropismus "am

27 Celan, 'Es ist alles anders', in *Die Gedichte*, p. 166, my translation.
28 Celan, *Der Meridian*, p. 105, my translation.
29 Ibid., p. 104.
30 Émile Benveniste, 'Remarks on the Function of Language in Freudian Theory', in *Problems in General Linguistics*, trans. by Mary Elizabeth Meek (Miami: University of Miami Press, 1971), pp. 65–75, p. 70; cf. Émile Benveniste, 'Remarques sur la fonction du langage dans la découverte freudienne', in *Problèmes de linguistique générale* (Paris: Gallimard, 1966), pp. 74–87, p. 81. See Celan, *Der Meridian*, pp. 104, 159.

Lichtsinn errätst du"⌋' [Rhythm – sense-movement toward an as yet unknown goal. ⌊ → a sort of tropism 'by light-sense you guess⌋].[31] As a sheer 'Sinnbewegung auf ein noch unbekanntes Ziel', poetic rhythm moves 'with' and 'without' an aim in precisely the sense of a sheer 'motion or effort in some direction', which may not be guessed in any way other than through an attempt to follow its erratic wandering. Yet beyond these similarities between Celan's and Benveniste's remarks, Celan's formulation exposes another implication of the structure he describes, insofar as sense also *means* direction. The vertiginous consequence therefore follows that the unknown aim of *its* motion is not only indefinite, but also infinite, moving with each movement of sense. This indefinition is already implicit in the way 'erraten', from 'raten' (to advise),[32] comes to resonate in this particular discussion of aimless motion with the utterly erroneous etymon, 'erratum'. And if 'Lichtsinn' [light-sense] may be the trope or tropism for such a 'Sinnbewegung' [sense-movement] – within phrases where 'light' may refer to both the sense-movement and its unknown aim – this movement of sense may be read as a further commentary on the disorientation that is conveyed through the phrases, 'die Sprache als miterscheinender (das Gedicht als durchscheinend~~er~~ ⌊Ge⌋) Hintergrund' [language as co-appearing (the poem as translucent / trans-appearing / ⌊po⌋) background],[33] and it would characterize both instances of appearing as the shining (*Scheinen*) of the φάος, which allows for phenomena or appearances, yet which is itself unseen. But perhaps still more importantly, the appearance of 'Lichtsinn' within Celan's theoretical notes allows these lines from the poem 'Sprachgitter' to be seen as the condensation or *Verdichtung* of the implications of the 'Miterscheinen der Sprache im Gedicht' [co-appearing / co-shining of language in the poem], and it solicits a reading of that poem as a further elucidation of the aphenomenality of language and the language of phenomenality.

SPRACHGITTER

Augenrund zwischen den Stäben.

Flimmertier Lid
rudert nach oben,
gibt einen Blick frei.

31 Celan, *Der Meridian*, p. 101.

32 See Jacob Grimm and Wilhelm Grimm, *Deutsches Wörterbuch*, s.v. 'rathen' and 'errathen', http://woerterbuchnetz.de/cgi-bin/WBNetz/wbgui_py?sigle=DWB&mode=Vernetzung&lemid=GR00934#XGR00934. Accessed 16 May 2019. See also Wolfgang Pfeiffer, *Etymologisches Wörterbuch*, s.v. 'errathen', https://www.dwds.de/wb/erraten. Accessed 16 May 2019.

33 Celan, *Der Meridian*, p. 105.

Iris, Schwimmerin, traumlos und trüb:
der Himmel, herzgrau, muß nah sein.

Schräg, in der eisernen Tülle,
der blakende Span.
Am Lichtsinn
errätst du die Seele.

(Wäre ich wie du. Wärst du wie ich.
Standen wir nicht
unter *einem* Passat?
Wir sind Fremde.)

Die Fliesen. Darauf,
dicht beieinander, die beiden
herzgrauen Lachen:
zwei
Mundvoll Schweigen.[34]

[SPEECH-GRILLE

Eye-round between the bars.

Flitterbug lid
rows upward,
frees a gaze.

Iris, swimmer, dreamless and dim:
the heavens, heartgrey, must be near.

Slanted, in the iron socket / spout / holder
the smoldering splinter.
By its light-sense
you guess the soul.

(Were I like / as you. Were you like / as I.
Did we not stand
under *one* trade wind?
We are strangers.)

The flagstone / tiles. Thereupon,
close by another, the both
heartgrey pools:
two
mouthfuls of silence.][35]

---

34 Celan, 'Sprachgitter', in *Die Gedichte*, pp. 103–4.
35 Paul Celan, 'Speech-Grille', trans. by Pierre Joris (http://www.pierrejoris.com/blog/speech grille-a-celan-poem-for-world-poetry-day/). Translation modified.

Absolved from any contextual scaffolding of the kind which can limit language with other matters, 'Sprachgitter' is a 'Gitter' *of* 'Sprache' which gives voice to a liminal language which opens as it bars and bares itself and which therefore cannot itself be limited or located – say, by a name or a title – but extends from this preliminary to the poem through to its every line. Thus, when the poem opens with an eye – 'Augenrund zwischen den Stäben' [Eye-round between the bars][36] – the 'Augenrund' is not a background somewhere behind the bars. It is another liminal appearance of language 'zwischen' [between] and therefore partially through them,[37] which is why this apparent word also points to the periods that mark the umlaut between the letters – the *Buchstäben* – of the 'Stäbe' [bars], but without being limited to this graphic figure either. As with 'Sprachgitter, 'Augenrund' traces an opening through its contours, whose indefinite scope is emphasized by the absence of any definite or indefinite article before it. However counterintuitive such a claim may seem, then, 'Augenrund' appears more like those other abstract nouns that will pervade Celan's oeuvre – such as water, fire, air or light – which are principally unbounded by any proper form or topos, but are moved and shaped by inconsistent contingencies. Hence, the 'Aug-' [eye-] may be seen to become 'schr*äg*' [slanted] at the opening of the third strophe,[38] and the '-rund' [-round] can go on to lose its morphological definition as well, resounding from the rowing of the lines – 'Flimmertier Lid | *ru*dert nach oben' [Flitterbug lid | rows upward] through to the 'zwei | *Mund*voll Schweigen' [two | mouthfuls of silence]. This last turn of phrase nearly brings the poem full circle while recalling those lines from Georg Büchner's *Dantons Tod* [*Danton's Death*] that Celan will cite in his notes for the *Meridian* – 'Danton, deine Lippen haben Augen ⌊keine Metapher | ein Wissen⌋ | – Der Mund spricht sich dem Aug zu' [Danton, your lips have eyes: ⌊Not a metaphor | a knowing⌋ | – Your mouth speaks itself to the eye].[39]

---

36 It has become a commonplace to note the resonances between this poem and Rilke's 'Der Panther,' on which see Wiedemann's commentary in Celan, *Die Gedichte*, p. 753; and Hendrik Birus, 'Sprachgitter', in *Kommentar zu Paul Celans 'Sprachgitter'*, ed. Jürgen Lehmann et al. (Heidelberg: Universitätsverlag Winter, 2005), pp. 209–24 (p. 212). But the theatre of the eye that Rilke evokes is nonetheless situated and presented as a spectacle within a series of descriptions that indicate the coherence of a figure, whereas the language for vision in Celan's poem yields no such scene.

37 On the role of the 'Auge' in Celan, see also Rochelle Tobias's most insightful commentary in *The Discourse of Nature in the Poetry of Paul Celan* (Baltimore: The Johns Hopkins University Press, 2006), pp. 15, 27.

38 My emphasis here and in the following italicizations of particular word-components in quotations from the poem.

39 Celan, *Der Meridian*, p. 134.

Neither a scene behind bars, nor a section of animal anatomy nor even the minimal geometrical forms of roundness, straightness or obliqueness define the way in which this visual language looks. Yet it is also precisely through those movements by which words parse open and enter into one another that a sort of perception may be seen to occur otherwise than physiology or phenomenology would have it – : namely, through language and, more precisely, through 'Sprachgitter', which captures no perceptual 'Erscheinung' [appearance / phenomenon] but gives way to a broken 'Durchscheinen' [translucence] which elucidates the passing of linguistic phenomena in every sense of the word. Hence, even as the 'Augen*rund*' comes around again in the 'M*und*-', this movement or encounter between the words does not culminate in closure. Rather, the opening word of the poem can circulate and enter the mouth only through the di-visibility by which it alters and vanishes out of sight. This movement is further emphasized by the way in which its redoubled resonance appears between words that indicate a redoubled silence – '*zw*ei | Mundvoll *Sch*weig*en*' [two | mouthfuls of silence] – which, in turn, echo the initial 'zwischen' [between] where the 'Augenrund' [eye-round] was first said to appear. It is, in other words, not merely the nouns, verbs and adjectives which refract through the 'Sprachgitter' [speech-grille] and break away for the ever-speechless language that they are not. From beginning to end, from eye to mouth, the poem also breaks down into the 'Wortreste' [word-remnants] of connectives *and* intervals – *zw-*, *-und-*, *-schen* – whose persistence further exposes the *Schwund* of (poetic) language.

What takes place with 'Augenrund zwischen den Stäben' [eye-round between the bars], however, is only the point of departure for other analyses of the language of vision, a trait which becomes more pronounced as the following words for parts of an eye – 'Flimmertier Lid' [Flitterbug lid], 'Iris, Schwimmerin' [Iris, swimmer] – not only separate from any surrounding organic whole through the rowing and swimming that give them the semblance of assuming a life of their own but also separate from 'themselves' in the same stroke, by means of appositions that draw their connotations away from optics altogether.[40] Despite their nearness to the eye, these animate moving 'parts' appear wholly absolved from any nexus within which every 'content' would be, as Husserl had said, 'inescapably given with many other contents' and 'in a way united to them'.[41] But because the co-appearing names also redouble each subject, said subjects are

40 Jean Bollack also emphasizes that each subject of the first three strophes pertains to the register of the eye in 'Paul Celan sur la langue. Le poème *Sprachgitter* et ses Interpretations', in *Contre-jour. Études sur Paul Celan*, ed. by Martine Broda (Paris: Éditions du Cerf, 1986), pp. 86–115 (p. 90).

41 Husserl, *Logical Investigations*, vol. 2, p. 9.

barred from becoming definite wholes themselves, and it is precisely this multiplication in division that opens these indefinite word pairs to resonate with other words, from the 'Flimmerhaar' [cilia] which Gottfried Benn evoked to describe human sensitivity to words,[42] to the Homeric messenger that shines through the 'Iris', as well as the rainbow that appears after the flood as the sign of the covenant between God and all living flesh in the book of Genesis (Gen. 9:13). Insofar as both anatomical arrangements and nominal identity disintegrate with 'Iris, Schwimmerin' and 'Flimmertier Lid' – which also point to what Celan will later call 'Lieder [...] jenseits des Menschen' [songs beyond the human][43] – the poem can therefore be seen to part with the phenomenological thesis of a 'co-appearing objective background'[44] so as to allow for the 'Miterscheinen der Sprache im Gedicht' [co-appearing of language in the poem].[45] Yet just as this 'Miterscheinen der Sprache' would seem to extend in recognizable ways to other words – and particularly to others' words *for* language, from Benn to the Bible – the language of the poem also speaks counter to even its more conspicuous references. Neither the 'Iris' nor the 'Flimmertier Lid' comes to send or receive a message or vision, but instead performs an intransitive motion such as rowing or swimming. And so as to clarify that this absence of messages and images is not merely circumstantial, but pertains to the subjects of these movements themselves, Iris is said to be 'traumlos und trüb' [dreamless and dim], with no more of an inner, oneiric vision than she has a clear view of the outside. If anything, both the 'Iris' and the 'Lid' may be seen to bear the minimal light of the *I* that shines through them, which has often been aligned with the brightest point on what Jakobson calls the 'grey series' of vowels,[46] but which is broken in turn by their countertendency towards obscure regions 'oben' [above] or the 'herzgrau[en]' [heartgrey] skies. And in the last analysis, even these distinctions dissolve, as the innermost core of the heart and the outermost expanse of the sky blend into one shade, and as this horizon itself comes to swim with waters, 'nah sein' [being near] coming to close to 'naß sein' [being wet].[47] But if all infra- and

42 Gottfried Benn, *Probleme der Lyrik* (Wiesbaden: Limes Verlag, 1951), p. 24, my translation. For a reading of the distinctions between Celan's 'Flimmertier' and Benn's 'Flimmerhaar', see Judith Ryan, 'Monologische Lyrik. Paul Celans Antwort auf Gottfried Benn', *Basis. Jahrbuch für deutsche Gegenwartsliteratur*, 2 (1971), 260–82 (p. 265).

43 Celan, 'Fadensonnen', in Celan, *Die Gedichte*, p. 183, my translation.

44 Husserl, *Logical Investigations*, vol. 2, p. 9.

45 Celan, *Der Meridian*, p. 105.

46 Jakobson, *Child Language*, p. 75; cf. 'Kindersprache'. pp. 379–80.

47 Menninghaus speaks to a similar phenomenon when he addresses the motif of 'Schwimmen' in Celan's poetic oeuvre as 'die semiologische Bewegungsform des angestrebten "Sprechens"' which dissolves definitional semantics (Menninghaus, *Paul Celan*, p. 104).

extratextual articulations of seeing and speaking no sooner begin to emerge than they dissolve into a wash and pass away, it is also this movement that frees 'einen Blick' [a glance], in freeing what is called a gaze from every ego-origo of phenomenological intentionality, from every assumption of given perceptual data and from every visible aim.

It is in this way that the poem runs its course as the 'Sinnbewegung auf ein noch unbekanntes Ziel' [sense-movement toward an as yet unknown goal] which Celan will go on to call 'Lichtsinn' [light-sense] both here and elsewhere.[48] This is not to say, however, that this 'course' would be straightforward. Although 'Lichtsinn' should indicate a vital impulse – nothing less than *the* anima, *the* soul – it arrives in the poem only after the luminous, animate subjects of the first three strophes have been left behind or reduced to a 'blakende[n] Span' [smouldering splinter], suggesting a movement towards extinction in more than one sense.[49] If 'Lichtsinn' should convey a shimmer of life despite this tendency towards its extinction, the latter would have to indicate a difference internal to life itself, one that draws life towards the anorganic,[50] to the point of being barely distinguishable from a blackout. Counterintuitive as it may seem, it is precisely this latter possibility that Sigmund Freud suggests in his reading of Ewald Hering's *Grundzüge der Lehre vom Lichtsinn* [*Foundational Traits of the Theory of Light-Sense*] when he alludes to Hering's arguments that sensitivity to light and dark are contingent upon the assimilating and dissimilating 'vital processes', so as to substantiate his hypothesis on the dualism of the drives. 'According to E. Hering's theory', he writes,

> two kinds of processes are constantly at work in living substance, operating in contrary directions, one constructive or assimilatory and the other destructive or dissimilatory. May we venture to recognize in these two directions taken by the vital processes the activity of our two instinctual impulses, the life instincts and the death instincts?[51]

---

48 Celan, *Der Meridian*, p. 101.
49 Here, I refer to both the inorganic matter of a 'Span', as well as the ambivalence of 'blaken', which may mean 'to glow' or 'to smoke'. Birus points to this ambivalence in his commentary (Birus, 'Sprachgitter', pp. 216–17).
50 Celan, *Der Meridian*, p. 99.
51 Sigmund Freud, *Beyond the Pleasure Principle*, trans. by James Strachey (New York and London: W.W. Norton & Company, 1961), p. 43. Cf. Sigmund Freud, *Jenseits des Lustprinzips*, in *Gesammelte Werke*, vol. 13, ed. by Anna Freud et al. (London: Imago Publishing, 1940), pp. 1–69 (p. 53). The relevant pages in Hering's book can be found in Ewald Hering, *Grundzüge der Lehre vom Lichtsinn* (Berlin: Springer, 1920), pp. 101–2.

To all intents and purposes, life and death should still, of course, be opposites, but this passage implies that death itself can only ever be a dissimulated, ideal limit towards the more obscure end of a spectral continuum, whose structure as a differential, continuous dynamic excludes the attainment of either extreme. All substance would therefore have to be understood as a matter of life *and* death, in which case 'Lichtsinn' may well be operative even in those anorganic matters such as a 'blakende[n] Span' [smouldering splinter] which would hardly appear to have anything like a lifespan.

Celan may or may not have known of Hering's text when he wrote 'Sprachgitter', and he may or may not have noticed the relation of 'Lichtsinn' to the theory of the drives offered by Freud, who does not himself use the word in his citation of Hering. With or without entering into this grey area of sources, however, Celan's notes for the *Meridian* suggest that he had considered 'Lichtsinn' along the lines of Max Scheler's *Die Stellung des Menschen im Kosmos* [*The Human Place in the Cosmos*],[52] where the trope appears within the course of psychophysical, psychoanalytic and phenomenological arguments to designate a movement so radically indeterminate that it would suspend any decision over life or death, and where its explicit relation to rhythm invites the connections that Celan will draw between this 'sense' and the animate-anorganic dimensions of poetic language. Shortly before his note on 'Lichtsinn' as a 'Rhythmus' [rhythm] and 'Sinnbewegung auf ein noch unbekanntes Ziel' [sense-movement toward an as yet unknown goal], Celan had written: 'Rhythmus: Zeitgestalt, deren Teile sich gegenseitig fordern (Scheler)' [Rhythm: time figure, whose parts mutually require each other (Scheler)],[53] most likely with reference to the passage where Scheler writes of instinct:

> We do not find such rhythms, such time figures whose parts mutually require each other among movements that are *acquired* and then take on meaning through association, practice, and habit [....] The meaning of the instinctual need not relate to a present situation, and instincts can aim at those at faraway spatial and temporal distances. For instance, an animal may make meaningful preparations for an oncoming winter [...], although it had demonstrably never experienced a similar situation before. [...] The animal behaves similar to an electron in quantum mechanics, acting 'as if' it foresaw a future situation.[54]

---

52 Scheler's book is one of the more frequently cited texts in Celan's notes for the *Meridian* (Celan, *Der Meridian*, pp. 100, 189–90).

53 Ibid., p. 101.

54 Max Scheler, *The Human Place in the Cosmos*, trans. by Manfred S. Frings (Evanston, IL: Northwestern University Press, 2009), p. 12, translation modified; cf. Max Scheler, *Die Stellung des Menschen im Kosmos* (Munich: Nymphenburger Verlagshandlung, 1947), pp. 17–18.

According to these assertions, the 'Zeitgestalt' [shape of time] of an instinct would install itself in lived time as a movement without precedents, self-presence or projected aims, and thus as a movement that remains alien to temporal experience and to all life as it may be consciously lived. Because such movements take place in dead time,[55] they can be found in the behaviour of electrons as well as the behaviour of animals. And because they occur before or beyond the very life that they may or may not eventually support, they render any living being that should perform them beside itself and utterly in the dark as to its doings.

In all of these respects, what Scheler calls instinct furthers his earlier discussion of unconscious impulses – which he illustrates solely with a blind drive towards light – as the distinguishing features of animate, psychic life:

> The lowest level of the psychic world – the steam, as it were, which pushes forward and up into the highest stages of spiritual activities and which provides energy to the most tender acts of lucid goodness – is impulsion [*Drang*] devoid of consciousness, sensation, and representation. In impulsion 'feeling' and 'drives' are not yet separated (drives always have a direction and tendencies 'toward' ends [...]). A sheer 'toward' light, for example, and an 'away from', as well as a pleasure and suffering without objects are the only modes of impulsion.[56]

Despite Scheler's evocation of pleasure and suffering, where his arguments lose some steam, the basis for animate life that he describes as a pressure 'devoid of [...] sensation' proves incapable of distinguishing between animate or inanimate substances, nor could it, for that matter, ground a notion of substance or subject. At the same time, the radical indeterminacy of a 'sheer "toward"' or 'an "away from"' would render any object of aversion or attraction, such as light, unknown and unsighted, distant and absent, as the situations for which instincts prepare. Celan's notes on 'Lichtsinn' as a 'Sinnbewegung auf ein noch unbekanntes Ziel' [sense-movement toward an as yet unknown goal] and towards 'Rhythmus' as a 'Zeitgestalt, deren Teile sich gegenseitig fordern' [shape of time whose parts mutually require each other][57] could thus be seen to condense both of these passages from Scheler's book, while his evocation of 'Lichtsinn' in 'Sprachgitter' – just after all light and life seem to have gone down the tubes – exposes the ambiv-

55 I borrow this phrase from Elissa Marder's *Dead Time. Temporal Disorders in the Wake of Modernity (Baudelaire and Flaubert)* (Stanford: Stanford University Press, 2001).
56 Scheler, *The Human Place in the Cosmos*, p. 7, translation modified; cf. Scheler, *Die Stellung des Menschen im Kosmos*, p. 12.
57 Celan, *Der Meridian*, p. 101.

alences that shine through Scheler's text, despite his most likely very different argumentative intentions.

More radically indefinite than in Freud's and Hering's rhetoric of substance, the 'Lichtsinn' that Celan addresses in departing from Scheler names a directionality or a-directionality whose supposed psychic substrate can only be guessed (*erraten*) – and can always be erroneous – but whose operations open the horizon of temporal experience to an unlived and unheard of time, and thus to an utterly non-restrictive field where all possible matters could come to life, but only because, as in language, 'every present subject can be absent'.[58] It is in this light that 'Lichtsinn' would appear to be another name for what Celan will call an 'Auf-die-Sprache-Gerichtetsein' [Being-directed-towards-language], whose aim would never directly appear and whose subject may never be there, even should certain behaviours come to light 'as if' there were such phenomena. Hence, when it comes to direct speech in the poem 'Sprachgitter' – when it comes to an 'ich' [I] and a 'du' [you] – these figures which immediately follow upon Celan's evocation of 'Lichtsinn' will appear suspended within parentheses, and their appearance will be virtualized through the subjunctive:

> (Wäre ich wie du. Wärst du wie ich.
> Standen wir nicht
> unter *einem* Passat?
> Wir sind Fremde.)
>
> [(Were I like / as you. Were you like / as I.
> Did we not stand
> under *one* trade wind?
> We are strangers.)]

With this, the poem brings to light perhaps most clearly the radical difference between phenomenological intentionality and the disorienting directionality of the light sense that appears to be another name for the movement of poetic language. For if the parentheses may be seen to reduce what appears within them to a mere appearance of a claim to be, this very claim is also rendered in the *irrealis*, such that the phrases, 'Wäre ich wie du. Wärst du wie ich' [Were I like / as you. Were you like / as I], not only indicate that the 'ich' and the 'du' do not share the same manner of being; nor do they merely allow the question 'Wer?' [who?] to shine through each inflection of being ('wär-', [were]); rather, they also suggest that the 'ich' or the 'du' may not be at all. As if to say what would be impossible according to any logic that rests upon the principle of (subjective) identity

---

58 Derrida, *Edmund Husserl's* Origin of Geometry, p. 88.

and non-contradiction, but what is more than possible according to the errant movements of sense through the poem, the verses may also translate to the wishes: 'If only you were to exist (as I do). If only I were to exist (as you do).' This *lectio difficilior* is supported rather than contradicted by the subsequent question, 'Standen wir nicht | unter *einem* Passat?' [Did we not stand | under *one* trade wind?], insofar as the 'we' that stands under the passage with 'ich' and 'du' may be read in light of that very passage, namely, as the poetic condensation of the 'wie' [as] and the 'wär-' that it could also be (beside 'itself') and therefore as the designation of a sheer modal being that would withstand the absence of all subjects, without barring their arrival either. All of these words occur, moreover, within the 'Zeitgestalt' [shape of time] of the choriamb (–⏑⏑–) that structures both the choral utterance of the 'we' ('Standen wir nicht' [Did we not stand]), that modulates the voice and breath in the passage that precedes it ('Wär ich wie du. Wärst du wie ich') and which may therefore itself be the trade wind or 'Passat' which allows 'ich' , 'du' and 'wir' to exchange places and pass away, while leaving room for innumerable other subjects and objects to catch the drift and assume this metrical shape.[59]

Any 'wir' that should emerge through such a blind rhythm could only be strange – 'Wir sind Fremde' [We are strangers] – and in such a way where not only each member of this apparent first-person plurality (or conjunction of 'wäre' and 'wie') but also each further word of its being and character ('sind' [are] and 'fremd' [strange]), would have to be foreign to 'itself'. It was precisely this estrangement of the one *as* the other – in distinction to the phenomenological elucidation of 'etwas *als* etwas' [something *as* something][60] – that Derrida would emphasize as well in his reading of this poem.[61] But if all that is involved in these verses becomes foreign, then 'foreign' would also have to mean something other than a term demarcating the different from that which is proper or shared. The utterance, 'Wir sind Fremde' [We are strangers], would thus speak not merely 'in fremder [Sache]' [on behalf of a stranger('s) (cause)], but perhaps, as Celan will say in the *Meridian*, 'in eines *ganz Anderen* Sache' [on behalf of *a totally other*],[62] and it would certainly cross through all meanings, phenomena

59 Wiedemann draws a connection between this word for wind and the preterite tense, in Wiedemann, *'Sprachgitter'. Paul Celan und das Sprechgitter des Pfullinger Klosters* (Marbach am Neckar: Deutsche Schillergesellschaft, 2014), pp. 11–12. Birus also draws attention to the choriambs of the verse, 'Wär ich wie du. Wärst du wie ich', but does not remark upon the further instances of this rhythm in the same strophe (Birus, 'Sprachgitter', p. 218).

60 Heidegger, *Sein und Zeit*, p. 159.

61 Derrida, *Schibboleth, pour Paul Celan* (Paris: Galilée, 1986), pp. 92–93.

62 Celan, *Der Meridian*, p. 8.

and communicative expressions which could be put in the service of the phenomenological imperative: 'zu den Sachen selbst!' [to the things themselves!].[63]

The suspension of luminosity, appearances and vision which occurs through 'Sprachgitter' culminates in a reduction of its speakers and therefore a reduction of the speech of the poem 'itself'. Hence, as the poem extends down the page and seems to land upon a word that would indicate the supporting surface for something – 'Die Fliesen. Darauf, | dicht beieinander, die beiden | herzgrauen Lachen' [The flagstone | tiles. Thereupon, | close by another, the both | heartgrey pools] – even the most solid grounding that has appeared thus far verges upon liquidation through the near-homophony of 'Fliesen' and 'Fließen'. Moreover, Celan's lapidary syntax does not allow for any decision as to whether 'Darauf' [thereupon] refers to that which rests upon the nominal tiles or whether it refers to what merely follows as the poem moves from one word to the next. But apart from the question of whether and how the tiles and pools may be situated in relation to one another, there is no getting to the bottom of the pools either: for in addition to pools of water that would mirror the 'herzgrauen' [heartgrey] sky from above, 'Lachen' [pools] signifies the drop out of a surface, whether one were to derive it from 'lacuna,' with Jakob and Wilhelm Grimm;[64] or 'lacca', with Friedrich Kluge;[65] or simply 'leck', with Wolfgang Pfeiffer, which is to say: 'undicht, wasserdurchlässig' [leaky, not watertight]'.[66] None of these etymologies need necessarily be true, but if the word for these waters so much as allows for the reading 'wasserdurchlässig', then it would open another interval in 'Sprachgitter' – another 'Loch' [hole] or 'Lücke' [gap] – and perhaps even an outburst of dark humour and silent laughter ('Lachen' [laughing]) that draws the appearance of language towards its withdrawal.

This would seem to be the thrust that leads to the final verse: 'zwei | Mundvoll Schweigen' [two | mouthfuls of silence]. Yet because this withdrawal happens with and through the very words that appear, it does not and cannot coincide with an absolute silence or muteness. Even the 'zwei | Mundvoll Schweigen' speak as the remainder and reminder of another silence that will have escaped it, both through the way in which 'Schweigen' [silence] – counter to the sense of the word – prolongs the speech of the poem and through the way in which si-

63 This exclamation is underscored in Celan's copy of *Sein und Zeit*, according to *La bibliothèque philosophique*, p. 374.

64 Grimm and Grimm, *Deutsches Wörterbuch*, s.v. 'lache'. (http://woerterbuchnetz.de/cgi-bin/WBNetz/wbgui_py?sigle=DWB&mode=Vernetzung&lemid=GL00069#XGL00069)

65 Friedrich Kluge, *Etymologisches Wörterbuch der deutschen Sprache*, 6th edn (Straßburg: Karl J. Trübner, 1899), p. 234.

66 Pfeifer, *Etymologisches Wörterbuch*, s.v. 'leck'. (https://www.dwds.de/wb/leck)

lence also arrives before the end of that very word, as 'Schweig-' swallows the 'zwei' [two] that precedes it and strangles this internal rhyme with the guttural: 'g'.[67] For all the talk of silence in Celan, and in 'Sprachgitter' in particular,[68] it is neither in the word 'Schweigen' nor in the silence which may or may not follow it that the movement of the poem 'ins Sprachlose' [into the speechless] – which is nothing less than its movement towards 'Sprache' [language] – could have definitively occurred. But traces of such an occurrence may intermittently shine through this passage and around its impasses – such as the 'g' – which bare *and* bar the appearance of the (speechlessness of) language and thereby allow the poem to go on past both the fullness of rhyme ('zwei', 'Schwei-') and the strictest occlusive with the '-en' which reopens a narrow margin for voicing. The ultimate trace in the poem of a 'Begegnung mit Unsichtbarem' [encounter with that which is invisible][69] may be not expression or muteness, but this 'eine, wortfremde Silbe' [single, word-estranged syllable] which will have been inconspicuously implied from the opening 'Aug*en*-' [eye-][70] and which persists as an instance of what Michael Levine has identified as Celan's exposure of the divisibility of language through even its seemingly minimal elements or atoms.[71]

In light of its multifarious functions in German morphology, from verb conjugations to markers of number and case, this last phenomenon would appear to be the least significant of all; a mere background for the more meaningful elements of 'Sprachgitter'; and an add-on suffix whose co-appearance could simply be disregarded. But despite all evidence to the contrary, it may nonetheless be with the '-en' that 'etwas vom Vorwissen der Sprache' [something from/of the pre-knowledge of language] could fall to the attentive through the liminal language of 'Sprachgitter'.[72] *A limine*, there could, of course, be no evidence or grounds to decide for or against such a suggestion. But if we look beyond 'Sprachgitter', we will find a most emphatic 'en' in 'Das Flüsterhaus' ['The Whisperhouse'], a later poem from the cycle, *Zeitgehöft* [*Timestead*], which is inter-

---

67 Hamacher similarly reads the 'uvularen Frikativen und Okklusiven' in Celan's 'Todtnauberg' as the inscription of strangling into the language of the poem (Werner Hamacher, 'WASEN. Um Celans Todtnauberg', in Werner Hamacher, *Keinmaleins. Texte zu Celan* [Frankfurt a. M.: Klostermann, 2019], pp. 93–141 [pp. 114–15, 111]).

68 See, for example, Corbert Stewart, 'Paul Celan's Modes of Silence. Some Observations on "Sprachgitter,"' *Modern Language Review*, 67.1 (1972), 127–42 (p. 139).

69 Celan, *Der Meridian.*, p. 105.

70 Ibid., pp. 123–24.

71 Michael Levine, *Atomzertrümmerung. Zu einem Gedicht von Paul Celan* (Vienna and Berlin: Turia + Kant, 2018).

72 Celan, *Der Meridian*, p. 105.

spersed with 'citations' from Jakobson's study of phonology in language acquisition, as well as language loss: 'es bürgert | den Enge-Laut ein' [it naturalizes | the fricatives].[73] There, 'Enge-Laut' refers first of all to the fricatives which, as Jakobson would write, are not to be found in all 'linguistic systems of the world',[74] and which take longer to become 'eingebürgert' [naturalized] into the child's tongue within those languages that contain it.[75] Yet when he rearticulates this element of the 'phonometic frame' for all meaningful linguistic differences which Jakobson seeks to establish, so as to bar any confusion between linguistic and acoustic phenomena,[76] Celan both raises the bar into relief and lifts it with a hyphen, which not only highlights the heterogeneity that persists in the conjunction between the distinctive 'Enge' (narrow) and the sheer 'Laut' (sound) but also underscores the possibility of other word breaks, whose range could extend from the evocation of angels – 'Engel-Laut' (angel-sound) – down to the 'En-Laut' (en-sound), which is, according to Jakobson, one of the 'nasal consonants' that 'exist in all languages',[77] and which therefore 'belongs' as the citizen of none. For this same reason, moreover, the 'En-' may also be indistinguishable from the very 'prelanguage residue' that Jakobson would relegate to the background of phonetics and, in this way, 'En-' exposes yet another passage where the 'durchscheinender Hintergrund' [translucent background] of poetic language opens to the 'miterscheinender Hintergrund' [co-appearing background] of the language it is not. As a consequence, this marginal-because-universal linguistic phenomenon could also be none; it could appear and not appear in the same stroke; and it could appear as another, such as the אין that signifies 'not', 'nought' and 'without' in Biblical Hebrew and which differs only by a single consonant from the word for the 'eye' עַיִן.

In the end, every poem, word or part thereof could only ever be another beginning and the beginning of another, because every linguistic phenomenon, from the lexicon of phenomenology to the differential elements of phonology, opens from a within to a without – to the without-language which is implicit in the 'Miterscheinen der Sprache im Gedicht' [co-appearing of language in the poem].[78] And because this language may never appear, it cannot be intend-

---

73 Celan, 'Das Flüsterhaus', in *Die Gedichte*, p. 563. Paul Celan, 'The Whisperhouse', in Paul Celan, *From Breathturn into Timestead. The Collected Later Poetry*, trans. by Pierre Joris (New York: Farrar Straus Giroux, 2014), p. 419.

74 Jakobson, *Child Language*, p. 51; cf. Jakobson, 'Kindersprache', p. 360.

75 Jakobson, 'Kindersprache', p. 366, my translation.

76 Ibid., p. 377, my translation.

77 Jakobson, *Child Language*, p. 57; cf. Jakobson, 'Kindersprache', p. 366.

78 Celan, *Der Meridian*, p. 105.

ed, but only attended by following those movements of sense which disrupt what would otherwise appear to be language and which leave off unfinished or phase out indiscernibly, in an *en*–

Christine Ivanovic

Breath Turn, Linguistic Turn, Political Activism. Reading Celan's Poems of 1967

The year 1967 is widely recognized as a year of 'turns' with respect to both political and theoretical movements.[1] It likewise marked a major juncture in Paul Celan's late poetry. Today, we recognize a significant divide between the body of Celan's poetry that had gained public recognition by that point and the enormous number of poems he composed at the same time but did not release to the public. To be precise, the prolific period of 1967 resulted in a total of 157 of Celan's poems, most of which long remained obscure owing to their delayed publication across several volumes in subsequent years. Many of the poems only found recognition in the wake of Celan's untimely death. In most cases, it was almost impossible for the reader to re-contextualize the acute moments referred to by the poems, much less to reconfigure what had happened both in his life and in the world throughout the year in question.

Now that Barbara Wiedemann's meticulously annotated edition of Celan's complete poetic oeuvre offers easy access to an abundance of information relating to the creation of each poem, it has become possible to carry out close readings of all of Celan's poems within their historical and biographical contexts.[2] This comprehensive material draws our attention to this period as an extremely fraught time in Celan's life and suggests the possibility of considering this time as a turning point, something which this chapter will investigate.

First, I would like to highlight the year 1967 as the apex of Celan's poetry. Secondly, I will consider the concept of a 'breathturn', a term widely used to characterize the late period of Celan's writing in relation to the theoretical and political 'turns' which marked the same historical period. Thirdly, I will revisit three poems composed by Celan, all written in 1967 but published in three different volumes in three different years: 'Denk dir' ['Imagine'] (*Fadensonnen* [*Threadsuns*], 1968), 'Todtnauberg' (*Lichtzwang* [*Lightduress*], 1970) and 'Du liegst' ['You lie'] (*Schneepart* [*Snow Part*], 1971). These three poems are of exceptional value within Celan's oeuvre, and each of them has already been intensively addressed by scholarship. Thanks to the availability of external information

1 Robert Stockhammer, *1967. Pop, Grammatologie und Politik* (Munich: Fink, 2017).

2 Paul Celan, *Die Gedichte. Neue kommentierte Gesamtausgabe in einem Band*, ed. by Barbara Wiedemann (Frankfurt a. M.: Suhrkamp, 2017) = NKG. See also *Paul Celan. Breathturn into Timestead. The Collected Later Poetry*, ed. by Pierre Joris (New York: Farrar Strauss & Giroux, 2014).

https://doi.org/10.1515/9783110658330-011

(which is not the case for the majority of Celan's work), these poems were subject to in-depth analysis from early on, with special attention paid to the precise historical and biographical events to which they relate: the Six-Day War in Israel, Celan's first personal encounter with Martin Heidegger and his only visit to Berlin. Taking the poems as immediate statements on those events has revealed them as ideal opportunities for discussing the gap between what we are supposed to know when we read Celan's poems and what the texts literally tell us (the related information is not necessarily made explicit within the poems). At the same time, this practice has generated a model for how to read Celan's work, namely as that of the eminent poet of the Holocaust in German literature: sympathetic towards the state of Israel's struggle for survival, sceptical of (not only) Heidegger's unresolved Nazi past and puzzled by contemporary Berlin. Reading the poems within the broader context of the enduring political and theoretical changes of 1967, we become even more aware of how much Celan paradigmatically represents the post-Holocaust condition. His struggle with the trauma of the Holocaust extends to what had happened to him, his family, his friends and his homeland during the early 1940s; and to what he experienced in the course of the 'Goll Affair', namely the accusations of plagiarism first raised and spread by Yvan Goll's widow Claire Goll; and, finally, to the impact of these events on both his own mental health and the public reception of his work during the 1950s and 1960s.[3] Reading his poems of 1967 not only helps us to better understand the ways in which Celan was confronted by and struggled with the trauma of the Holocaust; it also affords us a stronger grasp of his engagement with the global political unrest of that year as well as the changes it saw in theoretical discourse. It was in 1967 that Celan eventually made his own attempts to position himself within post-war society, mirrored in a split world where the generational gap, the unresolved legacy of the Holocaust and the Second World War, and the global escalation of the Cold War gave rise to fresh acts of open violence. Reading Celan's poems within this framework opens up a new way of understanding what his poems were aiming at: 'actualized language'.[4] One paradigmatic example of this is Peter Szondi's reading of one of Celan's last poems of the year, 'Du liegst', in which he eventually demonstrates the extent to which Celan's writing and the emergence of critical reading were already thoroughly intertwined.

---

3 *Die Goll-Affäre. Dokumente zu einer 'Infamie'*, ed. by Barbara Wiedemann (Frankfurt a.M.: Suhrkamp, 2000).

4 Paul Celan, *Gesammelte Werke in fünf Bänden*, Dritter Band: Gedichte III. Prosa. Reden (Frankfurt a.M.: Suhrkamp, 1983) = GW III, p. 197.

The year 1967 as the apex of Celan's poetry

'*Dichtung:* das kann eine *Atemwende* bedeuten' [Poetry: that can signify a breath turn], Celan famously asserted in his Büchner Prize speech of 1960.[5] This turning of the breath from inhaling to exhaling has since been taken as a topical metaphor of a turn within Celan's oeuvre as a whole, while his fifth volume of poetry, correspondingly titled *Atemwende* [*Breathturn*], is usually perceived as the manifestation of such a 'breathturn'. In retrospect, *Atemwende* marks the halfway point of Celan's work, with four more volumes of poems appearing in the years to follow. However, when *Atemwende* was published in 1967, almost no one recognized that the poems within it had in fact been composed years earlier. Some of them dated back to the time of Celan's first breakdown in 1963, while later poems had been composed in 1965.[6] It is the follow-up volume *Fadensonnen* (1968) that covers the period from 1965 to 1967. We have to be aware of how much the poetry we learn of in or after the year 1967 is part of Celan's struggle with his mental illness and its clinical treatment, which began in 1963, the year *Die Niemandsrose* [*No One's Rose*] was published. Most notable, but still widely unrecognized in the public eye, was Celan's hospitalization for the larger part of 1967.[7] After an unexpected encounter with Claire Goll at the Paris Goethe Institute on 25 January, Celan suffered a mental breakdown. A suicide attempt at the end of January resulted in admission to a surgical clinic. He then remained in a psychiatric care facility until the middle of October, although he was allowed to leave periodically from the end of April.[8] The rather optimistic tone sounded by the poem 'Denk dir', which would become the closing poem of the volume *Fadensonnen,* marks a clear change dating to the middle of 1967.[9] It might have been this poem that made Celan confident that *Fadensonnen* would be completed by the beginning of June, still far ahead of the release of *Atemwende*. The second half of 1967 saw significant progress in Celan's recovery. Although still in clinical treatment and supervision, he was allowed to resume travel abroad: in July, he accepted an invitation to deliver a lecture in Freiburg and prolonged his trip to see his publisher in Frankfurt, where he sketched the impressions of his first per-

5 Ibid., p. 195.

6 NKG, p. 846.

7 For the timeline for this year cf. Paul Celan – Gisèle Celan-Lestrange, *Briefwechsel*, ed. by Bertrand Badiou and Eric Celan, trans. by Eugen Helmlé and Barbara Wiedemann (Frankfurt a. M.: Suhrkamp, 2001) = PC/GCL II, pp. 469–77.

8 Ibid., p. 470; NKG, p. 926.

9 Ibid., p. 266.

sonal encounter with Martin Heidegger in the poem 'Todtnauberg'.[10] Another trip in August took him to London for his annual reunion with his aunt Berta Antschel, where he composed poems such as 'Highgate' and 'Blitzgeschreckt' ['By lightning scared'].[11] Later that year, he visited friends in Switzerland and attended the Frankfurt Book Fair to promote his newly released volume *Atemwende* as well as an anthology of his translations of Shakespeare's sonnets, *Einundzwanzig Sonette.*[12] One further trip in the fall of 1967 took Celan to Cologne for a TV shoot.[13] This intense period of travel as well as the eventual resumption of his teaching duties at the École Normale Supérieure (ENS) was also when Celan composed all of the poems of *Lichtzwang* (1970) within just six months. The last poem of that volume, 'Wirk nicht voraus' ['Do not work ahead'], was conceived on the very day on which Celan signed off on the final manuscript of *Fadensonnen*, 6 December 1967.[14]

Close to the end of 1967, Celan took a flight to Berlin for the first and only time in his life.[15] Traveling to Berlin from Paris somehow mirrored, if not reversed, his first trip abroad. That had taken place in the autumn of 1938, at the exact same time of the infamous November pogroms, when Celan was a prospective student of medicine at the University of Tours. On that occasion, he had crossed Europe, coming from Czernowitz and passing through Berlin. Celan's visit to Berlin at the end of 1967 marked another caesura: his forced separation from his family due to his illness and the beginning of the final period in his writing. Discharged from the hospital on 17 October, Celan eventually had to move into an apartment of his own. He chose Rue Tournefort.[16] In the following weeks, he was busy finishing the manuscripts of both *Fadensonnen* and *Lichtzwang*. During his trip to Berlin at the very end of the year, Celan composed several more poems, such as 'Du liegst'. They form the opening of what would become his first posthumous volume, *Schneepart* (1971). The final separation from his family also separates Celan's authorized work from all the poems which he would ultimately not be able to prepare for publication himself, such as those in the volumes *Schneepart* and *Zeitgehöft* [*Timestead*]. Wiedemann considers those last poems as part of Celan's legacy.[17] I propose a different classification, analogous to the one applied usefully

10 Ibid., p. 991.
11 Ibid., p. 996.
12 PC/GCL II, p. 475; ibid., p. 475 f.; NKG, p. 1010.
13 PC/GCL II, p. 476.
14 NKG, pp. 979, 1024.
15 Ibid., p. 1132.
16 PC/GCL II, pp. 471, 476.
17 NKG, p. 615.

to the poetry of R. M. Rilke, and call them 'latest poems' ('späteste Gedichte') to distinguish it from his later poetry ('Spätwerk'), which culminates in 1967. For Celan, the year 1967 was a year of great pain owing to his illness and the damage it caused his private relationships. However, it also proved to be the year of Celan's greatest productivity, the year in which most of his completed later poetry was either released or composed. It is in this respect that it also marks the turning point for what would become his 'latest poems'.

'Linguistic turn' and political activism in 1967

1967 was a year of change in many respects. At the same time that we can identify a definite turning point in Celan's life and work, the world around him was facing, on the one hand, a new escalation of violent conflicts and, on the other, a significant turn in cultural theory and practice. The Vietnam War, race riots in the United States and the beginning of student protests, pop culture and post-structuralism were all defining moments of the time.

In June 1967, the growing tensions in the Middle East were unleashed in the Six-Day War (5–11 June). At the same time, violence escalated in Germany, and protests against the visit of the Shah of Persia were brutally suppressed by police, who shot the student Benno Ohnesorg in Berlin (2 June). Celan explicitly references these developments in his poetry. In 'Denk dir' he reacts to the events in Israel. In 'Einem Bruder in Asien' ['To a brother in Asia'] , composed ten days after he sketched 'Todtnauberg', Celan comments on the war in Vietnam.[18] Other events, however, go conspicuously unmentioned, in particular the shooting of Benno Ohnesorg, which had become a major public talking point in Germany during the latter half of 1967 and would remain so in the years to come. Celan was undoubtedly aware of this and had been informed not only by media reports but also by personal testimonies, such as that of Gisela Dischner, who had been a student of Max Horkheimer in Frankfurt at the time.[19] On the side of academia, both Theodor W. Adorno and Peter Szondi were not only engaging theoretically with the debate on violence and a 'free university' but were also directly involved in it.

On the other hand, 1967 was also a milestone in the realm of cultural theory and practice. It was the year in which Richard Rorty's anthology *The Linguistic*

18 Ibid., p. 287.

19 Paul Celan – Gisela Dischner, 'Wie aus weiter Ferne zu Dir'. Briefwechsel, ed. by Barbara Wiedemann and Gisela Dischner (Berlin: Suhrkamp, 2012) = PC/GD, pp. 46, 144.

Turn documented a decisive development in the philosophical history of the twentieth century, providing a landmark term for contemporary debates.[20] At the same time, the publication of Derrida's *De la grammatologie*, *La Voix et le Phénomène* and *L'Écriture et la difference* [*Of Grammatology*, *Speech and Phenomena*, *Writing and Difference*] marked the transformation in French cultural theory from structuralism to post-structuralism.[21] Celan's employer at the time, the ENS, was at the centre of this paradigm shift. Both Louis Althusser and Jacques Derrida were working there, and it was also where Jacques Lacan held his famous Séminaire hebdomadaire. In 1967, Lacan invited Michel Foucault to the ENS to present his newly published book *Les mots et les choses* [*The Order of Things*] (1966).[22] To what extent Celan was aware of these events given his ongoing illness remains unclear. However, he reportedly did have an exchange with Heidegger about contemporary French philosophy during his trip to Freiburg.[23] A serious personal discourse between Celan and the representatives of the historical turn employed at the ENS at the time does not, however, appear to have occurred. Nevertheless, Celan's longstanding connection to contemporary French authors becomes evident in 1967 with the publication of the new journal *L'Éphémère*, initiated by the Fondation Maeght.[24] The first issue contains Celan's Büchner Prize speech, 'Le Méridien' [*Der Meridian* (*The Meridian*)], in French translation by André du Bouchet. In the same year, the fourth issue of *L'Éphémère* contained a French translation of Celan's seminal poem 'Engführung' ['Stretto'], translated by Jean Daive ['Strette']. It forms the basis of Szondi's first major Celan essay, 'Lecture de Strette', written in French and published in France in 1971, though

---

20 Richard M. Rorty, *The Linguistic Turn. Essays in Philosophical Method* (Chicago: The University of Chicago Press, 1967).

21 Jacques Derrida, *De la grammatologie* (Paris: Les Éditions de Minuit, 1967); *La Voix et le Phénomène* (Paris: Presses universitaires de France, 1967); *L'Écriture et la différence* (Paris: Seuil, 1967).

22 Jacques Lacan, *Séminaire hebdomadaire 1966–1968 'La logique du fantasme (S XIV)'* http://staferla.free.fr/S14/S14%20LOGIQUE.pdf; *'L'acte psychanalytique (S XV)'* http://staferla.free.fr/S15/S15%20L'ACTE.pdf

23 John Felstiner, *Paul Celan. Poet, Survivor, Jew* (New Haven and London: Yale University Press, 1995), p. 245.

24 Cf. PC/GCL II, p. 469. *L'Éphémère* was published by poets close to Celan: Yves Bonnefoy, Jacques Dupin and André du Bouchet; as well as by Gaëtan Picon and Louis-René Des Forêts. Celan became part of the editorial board in 1968. The journal ceased publication in 1972. Cf. Alain Mascaraou, *Les cahiers de 'L'Éphémère' 1967–1972. Tracés interrompus* (Paris: L'Harmattan, 1998); Dirk Weissmann, *Poésie, judaïsme, philosophie. Une histoire de la réception française de Paul Celan, des débuts jusqu'à 1991.* Dissertation, Université de la Sorbonne Nouvelle, Paris-III, 2003. Vol 2. (http://edocs.ub.uni-frankfurt.de/volltexte/2009/13938/).

conceived of and begun in 1967.[25] In this landmark essay, Szondi for the first time makes Celan's poetic works accessible to French post-structuralism as a subject of philological analysis. Szondi had been an important point of connection for Celan ever since their first meeting in 1959. He remained a constant companion throughout Celan's development in the 1960s as well as an important conversation partner, who had shared Celan's experience of persecution by the Nazis. Szondi was also close to Adorno, whom he had invited in summer 1967 to participate in a seminar at the Free University of Berlin about Celan's 'Engführung'. This seminar not only formed the nucleus for Szondi's 'Lecture de Strette' but also provided fertile ground for Adorno, who planned to write an essay on Celan's poetry after the seminar, something eagerly anticipated by Celan.[26] Celan met with Szondi once more during a trip to London. The discussions they had there encompassed his poems and the political developments in Germany. On the eve of his departure to Berlin, however, Celan sketched a note in which he made Beda Allemann, who had just become a professor in Bonn, the executor of his works.[27] Allemann had received his PhD with Staiger in Zurich the year before Szondi with a thesis on Heidegger and Hölderlin. From 1957 to 1958, he had been a lector teaching German at the ENS, and Celan remained in friendly contact with him. He also wrote the afterword to the 1968 edition of Celan's select poetry published by Suhrkamp Verlag, a seminal collection that would define the poet's reception for decades to come.[28]

By formally installing Allemann as his literary executor at that time, Celan seems to have made a strong decision in favour of the non-Jewish Hölderlin-Heidegger reading of German poetry and against Adorno and Szondi, who saw the es-

---

25 Paul Celan, *Strette*, trans. by d'André du Bouchet, Jean-Pierre Burgart and Jean Daive (Paris: Mercure de France, 1971). Peter Szondi, 'Lecture de Strette. Essai sur la poésie de Paul Celan', *Critique*, 288 (May 1971), 387–420. Cf. Dirk Weissman, 'La publication de 'Strette' de Paul Celan, moment inaugural de sa réception en France', in *Eclats d'Autriche. Vingt études sur l'image de la culture autrichienne aux XXe et XXIe siècles*, ed. by Valérie de Daran and Marion George (Bern and Vienna: Peter Lang, 2014), pp. 345–62.

26 See his letter to Celan from 9 February 1968. Theodor W. Adorno und Paul Celan, *Briefwechsel 1960–1968*, ed. by Joachim Seng, *Frankfurter Adorno Blätter*, 8 (2003), 177–202 (p. 197–98.). Adorno's sudden death in 1969 prevented this plan.

27 Handwritten testation in a letter from 15 December 1967 to Beda Allemann (legacy Allemann at DLA Marbach). Cf. Gunter Martens, 'Celan-Editionen', in *Editionen zu deutschsprachigen Autoren als Spiegel der Editionsgeschichte*, ed. by Bodo Plachta (Tübingen: Niemeyer, 2005), p. 32. On the same day, Celan, in a different handwritten manuscript, also appointed his son Eric Celan as the sole holder of the rights to his work; PC/GCL II, p. 477.

28 Paul Celan, *Ausgewählte Gedichte. Zwei Reden. Nachwort von Beda Allemann* (Frankfurt a.M.: Suhrkamp, 1968).

calation of public violence as a clear sign of the connections between the student movement and the unresolved anti-Semitic ideas of the preceding era. Celan's will and testament (written prior to taking the risk of air travel) might well have been prompted by the awareness of having reached a turning point in his personal life. However, it can also be seen as a consequence of the political unrest of the year 1967, which severely affected academic discourse. While Allemann would lay the groundwork for a historical-critical edition of Celan's oeuvre yet to be accomplished by his successors, it was Szondi who, in Germany as well as in France, paved the way for a reading of Celan's poems within the framework of emerging critical theory, a reading which itself also dates back to that fateful year of 1967.

'Denk dir': Violence, resistance and rescue

Denk dir

Denk dir:
der Moorsoldat von Massada
bringt sich Heimat bei, aufs
unauslöschlichste,
wider
allen Dorn im Draht.

Denk dir:
die Augenlosen ohne Gestalt
führen dich frei durchs Gewühl, du
erstarkst und
erstarkst.

Denk dir: deine
eigene Hand
hat dies wieder
ins Leben empor-
gelittene
Stück
bewohnbarer Erde
gehalten.

Denk dir:
das kam auf mich zu,
namenwach, handwach
für immer,
vom Unbestattbaren her.[29]

29 NKG, p. 266.

One of the few poems by Celan that reacts directly to politically impactful events is the poem 'Denk dir'. The history of its conception and publication points to it being a direct positioning with respect to the Six-Day War.[30] Celan sent copies of the poem to several of his correspondents in Germany, England and Israel. Those letters attest to the immense personal importance Celan ascribed to the poem,[31] which was first published on 24 June 1967 with a commentary by Werner Weber in the Swiss newspaper *Neue Zürcher Zeitung*. Weber explicitly references a personal remark by Celan that seems to suggest that 'Denk dir' is an avowal of Israel as a 'rediscovered home'.[32] Refuting this interpretation, however, Marlies Janz was the first to point out that the poem itself does not provide any actual hints at such a context.[33] A close reading shows that the poem does not refer directly to the events of the war, but rather presents a performative process of contemplation sparked by news of the events in a way that allows readers to retrace the experience through their own reading of the poem. This of course makes the poetic gesture itself inseparable from the historical context of the poem's conception while at the same time refusing to yield to ideological appropriation, a marked difference from any form of pamphlet or political speech in general.

Of crucial importance is the location of the poem's narrative within the overall scope of Celan's poetry, always characterized by the way that it unites poetic thought as extrapolated by Heidegger, the *Andenken/Eingedenksein* of Hölderlin and 'Zahor!', the Jewish commandment to remember. The title and the beginning of each stanza contain the imperative 'Denk dir' in fivefold repetition, akin to a magical rite. It is a call for contemplative thought, for collecting oneself, for observation and introspection; it is not a call for action. The beginning of the poem retraces the movement of thinking and remembering that had been a recurring theme in Celan's work since his *Bremer Rede* [*Bremen Speech*]. Here as much as there, he may be referencing Heideggerian concepts, such as the phrase 'Memory is the gathering of thought', as he wrote in the first of his lectures on 'What Is called Thinking?'[34] Such 'gatherings' of thought had already been de-

30 NKG, p. 967.

31 PC/GCL p. 531; PC/GD pp. 48, 208; Paul Celan – Franz Wurm, *Briefwechsel*, ed. by Barbara Wiedemann in collaboration with Franz Wurm (Frankfurt a.M.: Suhrkamp, 1995), pp. 73 ff.

32 Werner Weber, *Forderungen. Bemerkungen und Aufsätze zur Literatur* (Zürich, Stuttgart: Artemis, 1970), pp. 199–202.

33 Marlies Janz, *Vom Engagement absoluter Poesie. Zur Lyrik und Ästhetik Paul Celans* (Frankfurt a.M.: Syndikat, 1976), p. 233, footnote 194.

34 It was the first lecture that Heidegger gave after his retirement and his return to Freiburg University. It was held in the winter semester of 1951/52. Cf. Martin Heidegger, *Gesamtausgabe Abt. 1 Veröffentlichte Schriften Bd. 8. Was heißt Denken?* (1951–1952), ed. by Paola-Ludivika Coriando (Frankfurt a.M.: Vittorio Klostermann, 2002), p. 5.

manded by the first poem in *Fadensonnen*, 'Augenblicke', written two years prior to 'Denk dir' but in direct conversation with it, appearing at the end of the same volume. In 'Augenblicke', we similarly find the directive to 'collect yourself' in the last two verses: 'sammle dich, | steh'.[35] Wiedemann points out that 'Augenblicke' should be read in connection with a note written by Celan's at the time pertaining to his reading of the Tao Te Ching, which reads: 'Truly: when two take up arms against one another, he who mourns will triumph.'[36] Wiedemann comments on this passage in 'Augenblicke', stating that 'the theme of Jewish resistance and struggle is expressly manifested in the poems of the first cycle of *Fadensonnen*, written in a period of serious psychological difficulties (at least since the middle of September [1965])'.[37] A look at the references within the volume as well as earlier poems by Celan makes apparent how deeply connected his mental illness was with the trauma of fascism and how Celan saw the 'fight for freedom' in Israel as a reflection of his own struggle to prevail against an affliction inextricably linked to the annihilation phantasms of Nazi terror. The poem brings together what happened and what is happening, cancelling great temporal as well as spatial distances in the gathering of thought. This contemplative process 'strengthens'. It relates to the contemporary event of reconquering Jerusalem as much as it does to the memory of the mass suicide committed by the Jewish inhabitants of the fortress of Masada in 73 CE in the face of defeat by the Romans. However, the poem's evocation of the song 'Die Moorsoldaten' ['Peat Bog Soldiers'] composed by the prisoners interned in the concentration camp Papenburg-Bögermoor from 1933 also references another important thought for Celan. At that time, the prisoners of Bögermoor were political opponents of the Nazi regime, mostly socialists and communists.[38] The song that they composed there soon spread beyond the camp and was later put to music and translated into many different languages, eventually becoming popular as a revolutionary song in the Spanish Civil War. This reference to 'Moorsoldaten' repre-

35 NKG, p. 225.

36 Ibid., p. 899. 'Wahrlich: | Wenn zwei die Waffe gegeneinander erheben, | Wird der, der trauert, siegen.'

37 Ibid.

38 The first report of their suffering came from director and actor Wolfgang Langhoff – who had been arrested in 1933 but received amnesty in 1934 and fled to Switzerland – in his book *Die Moorsoldaten. 13 Monate Konzentrationslager* (Zürich: Schweizer Spiegel Verlag, 1935). An English translation by Lilo Linke with a foreword by Lion Feuchtwanger was published the same year in London under the title *Rubber Truncheo. Being an Account of Thirteen Months Spent in a Concentration Camp* (London: Constable, 1935). Langhoff's report was one of the first testimonies on Nazi concentration camps. Though the song was circulated through many sources, Weber explicitly refers to the report by Langhoff.

sents resistance movements against fascism throughout Europe. Celan thus extends his references to Jewish history by adding another dimension, as he had already done previously in other poems, most prominently 'Shibboleth' and 'In eins' ['In one'].[39] The war in Israel allows Celan to draw a connection between 'Peat Bog Soldiers' and 'Masada', illustrating a painful learning process ('bringt [...] sich bei' – an ambivalent process of learning and inflicting wounds) centred around the term 'homeland'. Here, homeland is not a concrete, palpable place, but a mental process of solidarity with the peat bog soldiers as well as the desperate denizens of Masada, a contemplative gathering of thought that can now resist all attempts at internment and annihilation ('aufs | unauslöschlichste'). The movement in the second stanza then ultimately enables convalescence: 'du erstarkst und | erstarkst'.

'Denk dir' formulates Celan's anticipation of the events unfolding in Israel at that very moment in an almost mystical experience that recognizes in the history of Jewish suffering his own suffering. Through solidarity with the fighters of the past and the present, Celan experiences this moment as a liberation, a transgression. Unlike the events of the war, however, this is not an act of violence or a call for violence, but a moment expressed purely through personal collection and recollection: 'denk dir'. The experience is filled with awe and wonder and reported like a miracle: 'denk dir'. And it can be retraced only through a similar act of thinking and remembrance, demanded by the poem that has become a monumental: 'Denk dir'. As such, the poem ultimately transcends the person Celan and reaches further out.

'Todtnauberg': History and hagiography

Todtnauberg

Arnika, Augentrost, der
Trunk aus dem Brunnen mit dem
Sternwürfel drauf,

in der
Hütte,

die in das Buch
— wessen Namen nahms auf
vor dem meinen? —,
die in dies Buch

39 NKG, pp. 87, 157.

geschriebene Zeile von
einer Hoffnung, heute,
auf eines Denkenden

kommendes
Wort
im Herzen,

Waldwasen, uneingeebnet,
Orchis und Orchis, einzeln,

Krudes, später, im Fahren,
deutlich,

der uns fährt, der Mensch,
der's mit anhört,

die halb-
beschrittenen Knüppel-
pfade im Hochmoor,

Feuchtes,
viel.[40]

The 'strengthening' Celan experienced at the beginning of June prompted him to accept an invitation that had been extended in the autumn of the previous year by the Freiburg Professor of German, Gerhard Baumann.[41] Celan himself insisted on holding a lecture at very short notice. Over a thousand people attended his lecture in the great hall of the Collegiate Building II at Freiburg University, a building erected only a few years earlier, between 1957 and 1962, on the grounds of the synagogue destroyed during Kristallnacht [the Night of Broken Glass] in 1938. A plaque in the courtyard in front of the building still commemorates that event. Celan's poem references his first visit to Freiburg but not the events of those dates. Instead, it focuses exclusively on the small village of Todtnauberg, located outside of the city of Freiburg in the Black Forest and home to Heidegger's private cabin. Celan insisted on a trip to that cabin during his visit and was brought there by car the day after the lecture; Baumann's assistant at the time, Gerhard Neumann, was the driver. Heidegger himself had retreated to his cabin for several years after having been suspended from his university post

40 Ibid., p. 286.
41 Whether Celan was aware that Baumann, who was Celan's age, had been a member of the NSDAP from 1937 is unknown. Baumann remained rather quiet about his own involvement in the Nazi regime. Cf. Arno Barnert, Chiara Caradonna and Annika Stello: 'Im Reich der mittleren Dämonen – Paul Celan in Freiburg und sein Briefwechsel mit Gerhart Baumann', *Text. Kritische Beiträge*, 15 (2016), 15–115.

by the Allied forces (1946 – 1951). French intellectuals such as Jean Beauffret (and with him his former student Jean-François Lyotard and others) had visited Heidegger there during that time and contributed notably to his international rehabilitation. Among the later visitors was a poet to whom Celan was close for a time, the former French Résistance fighter René Char, who came to Todtnauberg in 1955 and met with Heidegger several times over the years, until a falling-out in 1973. What Celan was also aware of before his visit on 25 July 1967, according to Otto Pöggeler, was that Heidegger had allowed his cabin to be used by the Nazi regime for training camps conducted by the SS Organisation Todt.[42]

Celan went to Heidegger with 'Denk dir' in his mind. However, despite the evident topicality of recent events in Israel, it appears that they were not part of their conversations. Nevertheless, connection points remained. A number of central phrases and words from 'Denk dir' reappear only weeks later in the poem 'Todtnauberg': homeland, thinking, eyes, names, peat bog. The 'gathering of thought' in a Heideggerian sense, of which the earlier poem says: 'Denk dir: | das kam auf mich zu', corresponds with the expressed 'Hoffnung, heute | auf eines Denkenden | kommendes | Wort | im Herzen' from 'Todtnauberg', provided that we take seriously the dialogic character of Celan's poem, where speech is directed at the Other and longs to reach the Other through speaking.

Celan had developed the idea of the poem as a place that transcends the schema of signified/signifier as early as in 1960 in his Büchner Prize speech: the poem is the very place it references through its speech, a place where language becomes an event unto itself. The movement of the speaker marks this place as a passage, as formulated in the 1958 *Bremer Rede* or as a circular movement, as formulated in *Der Meridian* (1960). In the poem 'Todtnauberg', Celan's reference to a real place marked by the traces of history provokes the 'experience of thought', as Heidegger sought to express it, in the way in which he unites speaking and remembering, and relates both (in updated form) to the present.

The poem 'Todtnauberg' reflects Celan's visit to Heidegger and can be read as a recapitulation of his excursion. The various stages can be clearly gleaned from the text: the situation in front of the cabin, making an entry in the visitor's log, the walk through the bog, the discussion on the drive back.[43] The final conversation during the car ride back does not, however, mark the end point; rather,

42 'Als Parteimitglied und Freiburger Rektor organisierte [Heidegger] auch im Herbst 1933 in Todtnauberg sein nationalsozialistisches Schulungslager' [As party member and rector of Freiburg university he (Heidegger) again organized a national socialist training camp in autumn 1933 in Todtnauberg]. Otto Pöggeler, *Spur des Worts* (Freiburg: Alber, 1986), p. 261.

43 Celan quoted Gerhard Neumann in a letter to his wife as referring to the conversation to be of 'epochal importance' during their car ride; PC/GCL I, p. 536.

it is embedded within an evocation of the previous trip to the bog as a central space of remembrance, the same one referenced before in 'Denk dir'.

Celan dated the publication of the poem 'Todtnauberg' as 'Frankfurt a. M., 1. August 1967' and invested in an expensive private print.[44] The first of the 50 numbered prints (printed on 12 January 1968 in Vaduz) he sent to Heidegger. Number 46 he personally handed to Gerhard Baumann in the spring of 1968.[45] The poem was at first circulated exclusively within a very small circle. It was not available to the public until the appearance of *Lichtzwang* in June 1971, a few months after Celan's suicide. Its striking position in the middle of the second section stands in contrast to the exclusivity of the first publication.[46]

The witnesses to the Todtnauberg encounter, Baumann himself, but in particular Neumann, maintained their silence about the events for decades. Baumann's *Erinnerungen an Paul Celan* were published in 1986, while Neumann's account appeared posthumously only in 2018.[47] Among the first commentators not involved in the events were Hans-Georg Gadamer, Otto Pöggeler and George Steiner.[48] Since the 1990s, there has been an ongoing debate surrounding Heidegger's involvement in National Socialism. Celan's visit to Todtnauberg has become an event of symbolic importance in that debate, an event that the poem itself represents.[49] In light of this fact, readings that ignore reports about Celan's visit to Freiburg and Todtnauberg seem impossible. Philippe Lacoue-Labarthe critically coined the term 'birth of a hagiography' in reference not only to the lengthy debate surrounding the poem and the details of Celan's relationship

---

44 NKG, p. 991.

45 Barnert, Caradonna, Stello, 2016, pp. 37 f.

46 NKG, p. 286.

47 Gerhard Baumann, *Erinnerungen an Paul Celan* (Frankfurt a. M.: Suhrkamp, 1986); Gerhard Neumann, *Selbstversuch* (Freiburg: Rombach, 2018), pp. 307–26.

48 Hans-Georg Gadamer, *Philosophische Lehrjahre* (Frankfurt a. M.: Klostermann, 1977), p. 220–21; Otto Pöggeler, *Spur des Worts* (Freiburg: Alber, 1986), pp. 245–51, 259–71; cf. also Otto Pöggeler, *Der Stein hinterm Aug* (Munich: Wilhelm Fink, 2000), pp. 159–88; Otto Pöggeler 'Die Mittagslinie. Paul Celan und Martin Heidegger', in *Geist und Literatur*, ed. by Edith Düsing and Hans-Dieter Klein (Würzburg: Königshausen & Neumann, 2008), pp. 327–38; George Steiner, 'Heidegger, abermals', *Merkur*, 480 (1 February 1989), 93–102.

49 Cf. Jean Bollack: 'Vor dem Gericht der Toten. Paul Celans Begegnung mit Martin Heidegger und ihre Bedeutung', *Die Neue Rundschau*, 108 (1998), 127–56; Pierre Joris, 'Celan/Heidegger: Translation at the Mountain of Death', in *Poetik der Transformation. Paul Celan – Übersetzer und übersetzt*, ed. by Alfred Bodenheimer and Shimon Sandbank (Tübingen: Max Niemeyer, 1999), pp. 155–166; Werner Hamacher: 'WASEN. Um Celans Todtnauberg', in *Keinmaleins. Texte zu Celan* (Frankfurt a. M.: Vittorio Klostermann, 2019), pp. 93–141.

to Heidegger but also to a hagiography that had lasting effects on the reading of Celan's work in general.[50]

The singularity of the poem, which Celan emphasized by having it printed on its own, stands in contrast to the contextualization of its later publication in the volume *Lichtzwang* – or so it would appear. Wiedemann, however, points out that the otherwise strict chronological sequence in the second section of this volume, the midpoint of which is marked by 'Todtnauberg', is strikingly disturbed. *Lichtzwang* is the last volume that Celan himself put together. It begins with two poems composed, like 'Denk dir', during the Six-Day War. An additional poem created during that historic moment, 'Seit langem' ['Long ago'], flouts the otherwise regular chronological order, appearing just before 'Todtnauberg', juxtaposed on opposite pages of the original edition of *Lichtzwang*. This arrangement visually confronts the journey to the memory space of the peat bog with a text that evokes a landscape of 'Schlamm' [mud] in which past events ('Seit langem bestiegener Schlammkahn') are called into question in the face of current experiences in the context of war in Israel ('die Stunde [...] | hebt ihre Welt aus den Angeln'). What Celan's poem 'Todtnauberg' makes audible in the form of visible silence is more than merely the missing explanations from Heidegger. In contrast to the emphatic act of talking to the Other in 'Denk dir' that unites the contemporary and the remembered, the meeting that this poem longs for cannot be found, neither in the entry in the visitor's log in Heidegger's cabin nor in the conversation during the drive. Unlike the acutely apprehended term 'homeland' from the earlier poem, 'Todtnauberg' can only summarize what was seen, thought, said with the indeterminate collective adjective 'viel' [many], with which the poem ends. It is a reference to Hölderlin's 'Mnemosyne' ('viel | hat erfahren der Mensch') but it is also affected by the 'Feuchten' [moistening] which Celan's own poem 'Engführung' talked about at an earlier juncture: 'Zum | Aug geh, zum feuchten'.[51]

'Du liegst': Berlin revisited, reenacted

Du liegst im großen Gelausche,
umbuscht, umflockt.

Geh du zur Spree, geh zur Havel,
geh zu den Fleischerhaken,

50 Philippe Lacoue-Labarthe, *Poetry as Experience*, trans. by Andrea Tarnowski, (Stanford: Stanford University Press, 1999), pp. 92–97.
51 NKG, pp. 118 f.

zu den roten Äppelstaken
aus Schweden –

Es kommt der Tisch mit den Gaben,
er biegt um ein Eden –

Der Mann ward zum Sieb, die Frau
mußte schwimmen, die Sau,
für sich, für keinen, für jeden –

Der Landwehrkanal wird nicht rauschen.
Nichts
stockt.[52]

During his last trip in 1967, his first visit to Berlin, Celan wrote several poems.[53] They would later form the opening of the first posthumous volume, *Schneepart* (1971), but had already been published while he was alive in an anthology dedicated to fellow poet Peter Huchel.[54] Peter Szondi, one of the acquaintances who accompanied Celan while he was in Berlin, wrote an eight-page manuscript fragment about the creation of 'Du liegst' in 1971, in which he reflects on the fundamental hermeneutic problem that his reading reveals. Szondi's text was first edited posthumously by Jean Bollack.[55] In an academic context, it has since become almost impossible to read 'Du liegst' without taking into account Szondi's reflections on it.

Szondi shares at least in part the experience of the author Celan, allowing him to identify some of the circumstances that it references.[56] Aside from that, however, he can also reconstruct the creation of the text as that movement through which Celan manages to wrest the poem's autonomous aesthetic content from his own perceptions. In Szondi's reading, we experience the poem's blend-

52 Ibid., pp. 485 f.

53 Ibid., pp. 1132–36.

54 *Hommage für Peter Huchel*, ed. by Otto F. Best (Munich: Piper, 1968), p. 16.

55 First in French translation by Jean and Mayotte Bollack in *L'Éphémère* no. 19/20 (hiver/printemps 1972/73), 416–23; the original in the literature section of the NZZ from 15 October 1972, then in Peter Szondi, *Celan-Studien* (Frankfurt a. M.: Suhrkamp), 1972. Quotations follow the English translation: *Celan Studies*, trans. by Susan Bernofsky with Harvey Mendelsohn (Stanford University Press 2003), pp. 83–92.

56 It was decades later that Marlies Janz, another witness of several of the events and impressions which would inspire Celan's Berlin poems, delivered a slightly revised report. Szondi's sketch widely borrows not from his own but from Janz' testimony who at that time was his PhD student. Cf. Janz, *Vom Engagement absoluter Poesie*, pp. 190–200; Janz, '"... Noch nichts Interkurrierendes". Paul Celan in Berlin im Dezember 1967', *Celan*-Jahrbuch 8 (2001–2002), 335–45.

ing and compression of historical reminiscence, which, together with the personal dimensions, functions as a double re-enactment: a reconstruction of Celan's path through Berlin just before Christmas 1967 and a reconstruction of the arrest, torture and murder of Karl Liebknecht and Rosa Luxemburg in Berlin in January 1919. This historical frame of reference was initiated by Szondi himself, who had given Celan a recently published collection of documentary material to read while in Berlin.[57] In the poem, the various locations Celan visited in pre-Christmas Berlin are melded with the places related to Liebknecht and Luxemburg, and with quotations from Heinrich Hannover's volume (V 8–11). The place of the poem's creation is identified by Szondi as Celan's accommodation at the Academy of the Arts at the Tiergarten (V 1f.). Szondi also recounts a visit to the memorial at Plötzensee as well as to a Christmas market, where 'Celan saw an advent wreath made of wood painted red and with apples and candles on it'.[58] During a car ride through the city, Szondi reports that he showed Celan the Eden apartment building, which had been constructed on the site of the old Eden Hotel, where in January 1919, when it was serving as headquarters of the Garde-Kavallerie-Schützen-Division [Division of Cavalry and Riflemen], Rosa Luxemburg and Karl Liebknecht spent the last hours of their lives: 'While we were driving, we spoke of the contempt it showed for the memory of the two people who had been murdered here that the name "Eden" had been retained for these luxury apartments'.[59]

The process of compression takes place through a visual blending of disparate events and historical strata reaching all the way to the immediate, personal present. However, it also shows the form of a mimetic transformation that dissolves the traumatic image: the 'du' stands for Berlin, on the Spree and the Havel. Celan shifts the 'Gerausche' [roaring] of both rivers into a 'Gelausche' [hearing], a process of perception that takes in everything around it, retracing the movement through the city like a historical re-enactment, a dynamic ('geh', 'geh', 'geh'; 'es kommt', 'er biegt um') that ultimately unloads into the terror of the historic image. The recorded images foreshadow the act of language that accompanied the murder and its correlative: the silence that the poem ultimately manages to transform from hearing into speaking: 'Der Landwehrkanal wird nicht rauschen.' That which is already anticipated as missing echoes through the poem's language in the form of the illogical phonetic chain 'Schweden' – 'Eden' – 'jeden', a collection of fragments of a day that showcases char-

57 Heinrich Hannover and Elisabeth Hannover-Drück, *Der Mord an Rosa Luxemburg und Karl Liebknecht. Dokumentation eines politischen Verbrechens* (Frankfurt a.M.: Suhrkamp, 1967).
58 Szondi, *Celan-Studien*, pp. 86f.
59 Ibid., p. 87.

acteristic compressive dreamwork, as Sigmund Freud described it. The poem has no lines that are not connected to another line through rhyme or at least through assonance. It is this degree of connection that allows the poem to counteract the moment of hesitation inherent in the crass break of 'Nichts | stockt', overcoming the gap and continuing to speak.

Szondi's report was published one year after *Schneepart* and had a somewhat shocking impact, first of all because it caused a jolt of realization when it revealed the abundance inherent in Celan's poetry. One late reaction to that jolt was the ongoing practice of accessing his poems through commentary, as found in the commentaries on Celan's volumes *Sprachgitter* [*Speech-Grille*] and *Die Niemandsrose*, as well as on the complete collection of his poetry by Wiedemann. A second reaction was scepticism towards the underpinnings of the poem, which turned out to be the abyss of history and, consequently, a denial of possible knowledge and a plea for an *absolute* poem. A third alternative, however, was to persist with Szondi's method of reading, as Derrida did. What Szondi makes explicit at the beginning of his commentary, namely that the evident and the retracted dating of a poem may co-exist, recurs in Derrida's reading, in which the latter sniffs out the various circumstances and their absorption into the poem. Derrida later develops a 'poetry without navigators', a process very much analogous to Szondi's, as it seeks out the traces of life circumstances in the poem.[60] Derrida is one of the few who managed consistently to continue Szondi's thinking. Like Szondi, he knew Celan personally but was not especially close to him. Unlike many other critics, however, Derrida as well as Szondi shared with Celan the poem's background of historical experience. Celan visited Berlin at the end of a year during which the city had once again experienced extensive violence, culminating in the shooting and death of Benno Ohnesorg, a protester against state power, while the Springer press fanned the flames of controversy with derogatory phrases. Celan's 'Du liegst im großen Gelausche' could also be a reference to the precarious situation of surveillance in a city surrounded by both American and Soviet secret services, a city in which capitalism and Marxism, revolutionary movement and bourgeoisie appeasement, had once again come to a violent head.

60 Jacques Derrida, *Schibboleth. Für Paul Celan* (Vienna: Passagen, 1986), pp. 39f.

Conclusion

The collection of information on Celan's poems such as the one that Barbara Wiedemann presents us with in *Die Gedichte. Neue kommentierte Gesamtausgabe in einem Band* is no doubt helpful when reading Celan, especially his late work. However, as Szondi's reading of 'Du liegst' makes apparent, these 'data' are not simply the materials of an independent construct in its own right. The unique gesture through which Celan's poems make them into 'actualized language' connects existential and historical experience, and endows them with an ultimately political impulse. The aesthetic of linguistic expression thus always remains in the act of speaking the coming word.

Written in early June 1967, the poem 'Denk dir' is about the ambivalence of the suddenly *apprehended* word 'homeland'. Its publication is grounded in a sympathetic moment of remembrance that transcends spatial and temporal distance. It also ultimately generates an experience of (inner) 'strengthening' as it unites the individual struggle for survival (of the mental illness resulting from the attempts at annihilating the poet and his kind) with the struggle for freedom fought in Israel. Though the German 'Heimat' may echo the Hebrew cheer 'Le-Chaim!' to the right ear, when spoken in German the term retains a certain amount of ambivalence expressed in the double meaning of 'bringt sich bei'.

In a very different way, the poem 'Todtnauberg' localizes past events as still pertinent in the space of the present. While the writer expects his mute counterpart to utter that 'Gegenwort' which 'den Draht zerreißt' [tears the wire], as Celan formulates it in *Der Meridian*, the poem serves as proof of the stubborn silence that resists the desired liberation.[61] It is in this poem that Heidegger's non-speaking becomes a document that questions the tradition of Hölderlin echoed in the poem ('Viel hat erfahren der Mensch') which Heidegger's own thinking professes to invoke. Celan's insistence on 'einer Hoffnung, heute, | auf eines Denkenden | kommendes | Wort' allows him and his poem to stand against the silencing.[62] At the same time, assigning Beda Allemann to be his literary executor demonstrates that he is not willing to give up the continuity of thought that stands in this tradition.

While Heidegger never commented on the 'epochal' conversation at the centre of 'Todtnauberg', Peter Szondi became the posthumous commentator on a poem to which he himself contributed as it was being created. He makes Celan's works accessible to all those who were part of the turning point in the wake of

---

61 GW III, p. 189.
62 NKG, p. 286.

the 1967 'linguistic turn'. Szondi's reading of Celan's 'Engführung' and his meticulous analysis of the linguistic movements in the poem 'Du liegst' reveal a process that does not simply reconstruct Celan's poem from historical data, but which seeks to comprehend its form as the realization of events *in statu dicendi*. Szondi succeeds for many reasons, one of which is his astute use of Benjamin's concept of 'intention on language' which he applied first to Celan's 1967 translation of Shakespeare and then to his poem. It is the approach Szondi developed in the summer of 1967 that attempts to read Celan's poems in the spirit of the theoretical turn that crystallized in that same year, especially through the writings of Derrida. 'Du liegst', composed in December 1967 in Berlin, is a poem whose creative context Szondi influenced, accompanied and meticulously documented. It becomes an exceptional example not just of a different way of writing, but a corresponding way of reading Celan's poems. Szondi's reading has become inseparable from the poem itself and, through it, the turmoils of 1967 come together in a paradigmatic way. They changed Celan's life and work, changed the way we read his poems and also changed the political landscape of postwar society as much as the language of the poetry in which they appear.

Chiara Caradonna

Beyond Poetry. Celan's Red Folder, May 1968

The Red Folder

Among Celan's papers preserved at the German Literary Archive there is a red folder on which Celan wrote 'Mai 1968' (signature D 90.1.295). It contains twenty-three sheets of the same kind of French A4 paper (OCF Savoyeux). On them, Celan noted down a wide array of seemingly inconsistent textual passages in various languages. Most of them are quotations from different sources and genres (poetry, a novel, diaries, essays, theatre, newspapers); a few are observations on the events taking place around him; and some are notes of a more personal or, by contrast, abstract, philosophical character. Most of them were written on the recto page of the sheet, while the verso page was left blank, in a manner that seems to betray a deliberate composition. The first page bears the date 13 May 1968, with an exact indication of the hour, 11:10 pm.[1] It had been the day of a massive general strike that had ended with the occupation of the Sorbonne. There had been a counter-demonstration by the extreme-right Mouvement Occident, which included nationalist chants and exhortations to execute the Jewish leader of the student movement, Daniel Cohn-Bendit.[2] It is also the final date to

1 Only two other notations are accompanied by the indication of the time of day, on p. 8v (in pencil, a note regarding Celan's son cutting a conversation on the phone short at 6:45 pm) and on the following p. 9r (blue ink, 10:45 am, an observation on the sound of sirens in the streets 'of ambulances – or police patrols?'). Neither sheet bears a date. The passages that are not quotations have been published in the volume: Paul Celan, *Mikrolithen sinds, Steinchen*, ed. by Bertrand Badiou and Barbara Wiedemann (Frankfurt a. M.: Suhrkamp, 2005), pp. 123–24 and 607–12. There, the commentary provides some information about the context from which they were extrapolated. Further information about the folder can be found in the commentary on the correspondence between Celan and the German student Gisela Dischner. There is a partial overlap between the quotations in the folder and those that Celan integrated into his letters to Dischner and to his friend Franz Wurm from the same period. Finally, some of the material from the folder found its way into poems, as commentaries in the Tübinger edition of *Schneepart* as well as in the complete poetry collection edited by Barbara Wiedemann explain. I am grateful to Bertrand Badiou and Eric Celan for allowing me to read and study this material. This article was written during my time as a Fellow of the Martin Buber Society of Fellows at the Hebrew University of Jerusalem.

2 Cf. Monique Suzzoni, 'Chronologie générale', *Matériaux pour l'histoire de notre temps. Mai-68. Les mouvements étudiants en France et dans le monde*, 11–13 (1988), 284–303 (p. 294).

https://doi.org/10.1515/9783110658330-012

be documented in the folder. The last page bears the date 4 May 1968: after violent clashes between protesters and police in the Quartier Latin the previous day, the police had occupied the area. This, in turn, is the earliest date to be written down: the sheets are thus ordered – upon opening the folder – backwards, from the most recent to the oldest. This is, in fact, the way in which material usually accumulates over time in a folder, as one sheet is laid on top of the other. This trivially pragmatic circumstance illustrates a conventional, linear movement in time towards a future that becomes a past as soon as a point of rest – an intentional interruption – is reached (13 May). From there, the reader turns backwards, opening the folder as if it were a book and going through the collected textual debris of this section of time.

This movement in time corresponds to a development in the material. While the early notes mainly contain political commentary (pp. 20 recto, 22)[3] or excerpts from newspaper articles published on those days (pp. 19, 20 recto), halfway through they are gradually, though never entirely, replaced by quotations from books on subjects that have no direct connection to the protests. The material not only gradually assumes a more compact, less cursory character, but it also detaches itself from immediate events on the streets and from their description in the media (the present) and turns instead to a more distanced and indirect commentary that tackles fundamental problems of political participation, testimony and historical narration through texts from the past. Put differently: the closer the present events become, the further back in time the quoted passages lie. These in turn acquire a political dimension as they assume the function of commenting on present circumstances.

The shift in orientation in time is signalled by the first passage – going by the folder's internal chronology – that is taken from a book: a set of words and expressions from Achim von Arnim's *Die Kronenwächter* [*The Crown Guardians*] published in 1817 (p. 20 verso and p. 21 recto). Significantly, it is a (highly fictionalized) historical novel. Celan collected excerpts from both the theoretical preface – notably, a lengthy reflection on 'Dichtung und Geschichte' [poetry and history] – and from the second part of the novel (the 'Anton book').[4] However, as

3 Henceforth I will refer to the number of the sheet in the folder in brackets, specifying whether the notation is on the recto or verso page only when Celan wrote on both sides. Cf.Celan, *Mikrolithen sinds, Steinchen*, p. 123.

4 The poems 'Auch der Runige' ['The runic one too'] (May 4–5) and 'Deinem, auch deinem' ['Your, even your'] (May 7, 14) contain many words that Celan excerpted from Arnim's novel, as well as references to other passages from the Red Folder. For a brief interpretation of 'Auch der Runige', cf. Barbara Wiedemann, '"Vom Unbestattbaren her". Die Auseinanderset-

the direction of reading when opening the folder is counter-chronological, the collection appears to move from the literary quotations (the actualized past) to impromptu observations on the present, from more cohesive to less cohesive text. While at the time of the folder's formation the impressions created by the events seemed to call for a detached, mediated reflection, after the folder's closure the reading and understanding of the last notes is informed by the previous ones. In a way, the latter prepare the ground for their own dissolution into the former, and commentary returns into the shell of occurrences in time.

The textual disposition inside the folder thus obeys a dialectical principle, in which texts from the past and texts from the present, and the present and past, alternate. Chronological linearity is subverted in the frame of a textual unity that, from the perspective of the present in which it is read, belongs as a whole to the past. Additionally, the transformation that much of the material undergoes in the poems that make use of it adds a future dimension to them which consists in their recurrence as remembrance.[5]

Why didn't Celan continue collecting material? The unrest in the area in which he lived and worked was far from over. In fact, he kept collecting flyers even after that date, and the most explicit poems on the matter were written during the second half of May.[6] While this abrupt halt might be explained on the grounds of Celan's growing disillusionment with the student movements both in France and Germany, their political tenets and the slipping of their linguistic creativity into political jargon,[7] it can also be traced back to the collection's experimental nature. Time restrictions are a necessary condition for any experiment in order for its results to be assessed. The Red Folder's contents span ten calendar days recorded in a variety of ways. This is where the notes are located on the line of measured and commonly accepted time. The issue at stake, how-

---

zung mit linkem Antisemitismus in Paul Celans Spätwerk', *Internationales Archiv für Sozialgeschichte der Deutschen Literatur*, 40 (2015), 84–109 (pp. 88–90).

5 See Walter Benjamin's theoretical notes on the dialectical image from his *Arcades Project*, which Celan could not have known, because they were first published in 1982.

6 Another folder deposited at the archive in Marbach am Neckar (D 90.1.3635) contains further material from May 1968, such as newspaper articles and leaflets produced by the student movement.

7 On 13 May, the last date recorded in the Red Folder, Celan wrote to Franz Wurm: 'es ist vorbei, die KP, genauer: le PCF, auch sie, auch er, hats gefressen' [it is over, the CP, more precisely: le PCF, she too, he too, devoured it] (Paul Celan and Franz Wurm, *Briefwechsel*, ed. by Barbara Wiedemann [Frankfurt a.M.: Suhrkamp, 1995], p. 150). Compare Wiedemann, 'Vom Unbestattbaren her', 90, and Barbara Wiedemann, '"ausgerechnet jetzt". Der Mai 68 und die Jüdische Katastrophe', in *Celan und der Holocaust. Neue Beiträge zur Forschung*, ed. by Ruven Karr (Hannover: Wehrhahn Verlag, 2015), pp. 9–30.

ever, is the poetic 'Unmaß' [non-measure] that Celan allows to interact with conventional measure.[8] The urgency and closeness of the events called for a kind of writing beyond poetry, a form of an even more experimental, indirect kind – a form that could respond, at least partially, to a question that Celan had raised among his preparatory notes for the *Meridian* speech eight years earlier: 'Womit, so frage ich, will man Gegenwart ~~des~~ messen?' [With what, I ask, does one want to measure the present ~~of~~?][9] The question presupposes an understanding of how to measure the past, considering that, as Celan's summary of a passage from Husserl's *Zur Phänomenologie des inneren Zeitbewußtseins* [*Phenomenology of Internal Time Consciousness*] states: 'Das Gegenwärtige: ein zukünftig Gewesenes' [what is present is a future past].[10]

Clearly, this collection was intended for private use only and not for publication. But this private dimension allowed for a kind of experimentation that is worth looking at in greater detail. As a whole, the folder addresses issues that were of great topicality while the student protests were taking place. The task of measuring writing by the yardstick of occurring events (and vice versa) required a clarification of the underlying conception of time, history and historiography. It then implied a reflection on the relationship between the individual and the collective, between individual experience and collective event. This in turn raised questions about the nature of historical knowledge that emerges from experience, of whether and how it is shareable. And if what remains to be shared is more than just the individual experience of particular, transient events, then the core of the endeavour lies in exposing the truth of that present which, in the act of writing, has already slipped into the past. All of the passages collected in the Red Folder, whether of foreign origin or not, revolve around this philosophical core.

The individual and revolution

Upon opening the Red Folder, the series begins with the following sentence written at the top of the first page: 'Nimm mich, nimm mich, Geflecht aus Narrheit und Schmerz' [Take me, take me, net of folly and pain]. Underneath the quota-

8 'Das Gedicht ist das Ungemäße'. Paul Celan, *Der Meridian. Endfassung – Entwürfe – Materialien, Tübinger Ausgabe*, ed. by Bernhard Böschenstein and Heino Schmull (Frankfurt a.M.: Suhrkamp, 1999), p. 165.

9 Ibid.

10 Cf. Edmund Husserl, *Vorlesungen zur Phänomenologie des inneren Zeitbewusstseins*, ed. by Martin Heidegger (Tübingen: Max Niemeyer, 1928), p. 378.

tion, Celan noted its provenance: 'Kafka, Tgbr, S. 505' – cited as a quotation from Kafka's diaries, which Celan read in the 1951 edition edited by Max Brod.[11] Significantly, Celan added the place, date and time that he wrote down the phrase, not the date on which Kafka himself wrote it (July 1916). The originally diaristic notation bears a trace of its provenance and yet gets severed from it in order to become part of a new entity.

Both 'Schmerz' and 'Narrheit' are indeed recurring motifs in the folder's textual material. Pain is explicitly present as individual suffering ('Leiden') in a quotation from the first version of Hölderlin's *Empedokles* (p. 6), in which Empedocles and his disciple Pausanias discuss whether and how individual suffering can be understood by others. While Pausanias aspires to understand Empedocles' pain rationally and thus demands a clear explanation, Empedocles appeals for an empathic approach not mediated through language when he exclaims: 'Siehest du denn nicht?' [Don't you see?] Celan omits the sentence that follows, in which Empedocles wishes that Pausanias could ignore him and his pain.[12] On the folder's following page a Goethe quotation taken from Margarete Susman's essay on Gustav Landauer (p. 7 recto) warns that the collective has always gladly punished and hurt those who share their hearts fully and openly.[13] It serves as a paraphrase of Empedocles' wish by moving it onto a more general plane.

On the verso page of the same sheet, a quotation from Arnim's introduction to *Die Kronenwächter* adds an even broader theoretical dimension to the question of understanding the Other and his or her suffering: 'Only the spiritual we can understand fully, and wherever it is embodied, it simultaneously conceals itself'.[14] The passage underlines the necessary opaqueness of all earthly

11 Franz Kafka, *Tagebücher*, ed. by Hans-Gerd Koch, Michael Müller and Malcolm Pasley (Frankfurt a.M.: S. Fischer, 1990), p. 794. On Celan's readings of Kafka during this period see Florian Welling, *'Vom Anblick der Amseln'. Paul Celans Kafka-Rezeption* (Göttingen: Wallstein, 2018), pp. 476–86.

12 Friedrich Hölderlin, *Empedokles I*, ed. by D.E. Sattler (Frankfurt a.M.: Roter Stern, 1985), p. 106. Celan read it in the following edition, initially curated by Norbert von Hellingrath: Friedrich Hölderlin, *Sämtliche Werke. Dritter Band*, ed. by Ludwig von Pigenot (Berlin: Propyläen-Verlag, 1943), p. 95.

13 Margarete Susman, 'Gustav Landauer', in *Vom Geheimnis der Freiheit. Gesammelte Aufsätze 1914–1964*, ed. by Manfred Schlösser (Darmstadt, Zurich: Agora, 1965), pp. 255–70 (p. 256). Susman does not – probably on account of its celebrity – add that the passage she quotes in prose is derived from the nightly scene at the beginning of Goethe's *Faust*, Part one (vv. 591–93).

14 Before these lines Celan wrote the words 'Die Feder als Pflugschar', which he then crossed out with pencil, adding the surname of the French writer André du Bouchet. Celan's translation of du Bouchet's *Dans la chaleur vacante* appeared in 1968. There, he translated the more general 'lame' [blade, knife] from du Bouchet's poem 'Le nouvel amour' with 'Pflugschar'. Cf. in detail

things, events and human beings alike. Underneath, Celan added a sentence that he found in Susman's essay on Rosa Luxemburg: 'Über die Parteidisziplin geht die Internationale' [The Internationale surpasses party discipline].[15] This addition leads the ethical and epistemological discussion back to the political, tying the three levels together. They jointly maintain the individual's inalienable right to autonomous decision-making and even to a withdrawal into opacity. At the same time, they appeal for alternative ways of understanding one another and underline the individual's solidarity with and participation in the collective, which is oppressed humanity beyond party allegiance, according to the socialist anthem which Celan chanted on the streets in those days: 'Le monde va changer de base: Nous ne sommes rien, soyons tout!'[16]

A passage from another essay by Susman from the same volume, *Vom Geheimnis der Freiheit*, entitled 'Der Einzelne und der Staat' ['The Individual and the State'] (p. 13), returns once more to the fracture in the relationship between individuals, although here the suffering is – paradoxically – caused by everything that the person 'we truly love' is not.[17] Unlike most of the others, this quotation comes without any information about its provenance. The sentence is left incomplete and ends with an ellipsis, which conceals the second part of the comparison with which the quotation begins: the state.[18] According to Susman, both a beloved person and the state often fail to embody the ideal that we expect them to fulfil. Still, in spite of disappointments, we are responsible for 'what the state [...] should be'.[19] In the Red Folder, the quotation is immediately followed – on the same sheet – by an observation that refers to the irruption of

---

Wiebke Amthor, *Schneegespräche an gastlichen Tischen. Wechselseitiges Übersetzen bei Paul Celan und André du Bouchet* (Heidelberg: Winter, 2006), pp. 70 – 91.

15 Margarete Susman, 'Rosa Luxemburg', in *Vom Geheimnis der Freiheit*, pp. 270 – 83 (p. 275). Celan ascribes the sentence to Karl Liebknecht, although in Susman's essay this attribution is not univocal. Rosa Luxemburg, who in 1915 co-founded the journal *Die Internationale* as a splinter group of the SPD (which in 1916 became the Spartakusbund), wrote a vehement declaration titled 'Parteidisziplin' ['Party Discipline'], in which she discussed the conditions under which it is just and necessary to go against the party line; cf. *Spartakus im Kriege. Die illegalen Flugblätter des Spartakusbundes im Kriege*, ed. by Ernst Meyer (Berlin: Vereinigung Internationaler Verlagsanstalten, 1927), pp. 28 – 30.

16 Celan is known to have marched along with the students in Paris, singing the 'Internationale', cf. Stéphane Mosès, *Momentaufnahmen – Instantanés* (Berlin: Suhrkamp, 2010), p. 83, and Celan in a letter to Dischner, 4 May 1968, in Celan, Dischner, *Wie aus weiter Ferne zu Dir. Briefwechsel*, ed. by Barbara Wiedemann (Frankfurt a.M.: Suhrkamp, 2012), p. 89.

17 Margarete Susman, 'Der Einzelne und der Staat', in *Vom Geheimnis der Freiheit*, pp. 49 – 55 (p. 49).

18 Ibid., p. 53.

19 Ibid., p. 54.

events into the process of writing: 'Während ich die Helikopter | schwirren höre – nicht über | meinen Kopf' [While I hear the helicopters | whirring – not over | my head]. The date, 10 May 1968, is emphatically underlined many times. According to Norbert Frei, in this 'night of the barricades'[20] 'France experiences [...] one of its most violent confrontations since the end of WWII'.[21] Thousands of university and high school students gather, the Quartier Latin is occupied, barricades are built with pavement stones, cars and other objects.[22] Overnight, the violent police intervention leaves many wounded; the École normale supérieure temporarily becomes a sick bay.[23] Celan's underlining of the possessive adjective reveals – at the very least – a fundamental gap between an individual sensory perception that is collective, and a collective experience from which the writing individual is excluded. Just like the students in the streets, Celan, too, heard the noise of the security forces' helicopters hovering over the Quartier Latin, but since he was reading and writing while it happened, he was not actively partaking in the protest and thus objectively was not amongst the police targets. On the other hand, had he been a target, he would not have been at his desk reading or writing, and there would be no note testifying to this situation of high social tension with such immediacy. Collective (revolutionary) action suspends individual, isolated intellectual activity as much as writing suspends collective action – they are mutually exclusive. During a revolution, there can be no full concomitance of action and testimony, the latter always being delayed in respect to the former. Remarkably, it is the third, supposedly all-inclusive and yet antagonistic instance (the state), that makes perceivable this divide between the one ('der Einzelne') and the many. In turn, on a textual level, the juxtaposition of Susman's lines with the reference to the state's intervention justifies the omission of Susman's explicit reference to the state. Indeed, the authorities' repressive behaviour during the 'night of the barricades', symbolized by the whirring helicopters, falls significantly behind the moral ideal that they should represent. The two heterogeneous passages, past and present, complement each other and form a new unity of

---

20 Suzzoni, 'Chronologie générale', p. 293.

21 Norbert Frei, *Jugendrevolte und globaler Protest* (Bonn: Bundeszentrale für politische Bildung, 2008), p. 15.

22 Cf. Celan, Wurm, *Briefwechsel*, p. 149.

23 Cf. Malte J. Rauch and Samuel H. Schirmbeck, *Die Barrikaden von Paris. Der Aufstand der französischen Arbeiter und Studenten* (Frankfurt a.M.: Europäische Verlagsanstalt, 1968), pp. 72–84.

meaning, carrying both present and past into a present and future 'now' of critical reading.[24]

Celan quotes a further famous passage from Kafka's diaries in which Kafka focuses precisely on the incompatibility of 'Tat' [action] and 'Beobachtung' [observation] and identifies writing as a 'dangerous, maybe redeeming consolation', for it allows a jump out of the 'Totschlägerreihe' [murderers' row] (p. 8 recto).[25] In itself a form of (non-violent) action, this jump should lead to a 'higher [...] more independent' kind of observation which is action and movement in and of itself (in one word: 'Tatbeobachtung'). The Red Folder may be considered an attempt to gain such a higher vantage point. On the verso page of the same sheet, an earlier entry from Kafka's diaries describes the space that has to be crossed to reach this point, namely the 'Grenzland zwischen Einsamkeit und Gemeinschaft' [border region between solitude and community] which 'I have left extremely seldom' and in which 'I arranged myself more than in solitude itself'.[26] Celan brings this passage together with a third observation by Kafka regarding metaphors that 'draw me to desperation when writing'. Here, too, the juxtaposition is eloquent, as the second sentence becomes – disrupted from the original context – a commentary on the previous two and, in particular, on the metaphorical use of the term 'Grenzland' [border region], questioning its use for the description of the relationship between individual and collective, in a gesture of affirmation, doubt and self-critique that ultimately explains the abandonment of the Red Folder project.

Further implicit references to the motif of suffering are included in the first verse of the last strophe of Rilke's poem 'Aus einer Sturmnacht' ['From a Stormy Night'] (p. 12), from the early collection *Das Buch der Bilder* [*The Book of Images*]: 'In solchen Nächten wächst mein Schwesterlein' [In nights like these my little sister grows], which Celan also annotated on 10 May. The poem is divided into eight 'sheets' which, apart from the first 'title page', all begin with the same words 'In solchen Nächten'. The common thread is the exceptionality of these particular nights. Each stanza describes a subversion of the linear order of time, of the succession of past, present and future, and of life and death. Prisons open and 'through the guard's evil dreams | laughing silently walk | those who despise their violence'. The impossible becomes possible; the dead rise and Rilke's 'little sister', who had died shortly after birth, grows older: 'soon someone will court

---

24 Cf. Walter Benjamin, *Das Passagen-Werk, Gesammelte Schriften V, 1*, ed. by Rolf Tiedemann (Frankfurt a. M.: Suhrkamp, 1982), p. 578.

25 Kafka, *Tagebücher*, p. 892.

26 Ibid., p. 871.

her'.[27] For some hours, the 'night of the barricades' also seemed to be such a night. In a small volume of 1907 titled *Die Revolution*, which Celan kept 'within reach' between dictionaries during those days, Gustav Landauer had written that 'in the world of man [...] it has always been the impossible that creates new realities'.[28]

Under Rilke's verse Celan added a further quotation, taken from Margarete Susman's essay 'Früheste Deutung Franz Kafkas' ['Earliest Interpretation of Franz Kafka'], in which she discusses the important role that the 'Boten eines Unveränderlichen' [messengers of an unchangeable] play in Kafka's stories. They are – according to Susman – the 'basest representatives' of the mysterious, ominous and incomprehensible power that rules over Kafka's protagonists.[29] The combination of these two radically opposite quotations that bluntly contradict each other turns into a valid description of the events unfolding in the Quartier Latin during that night, which saw the emergence of a revolutionary movement promising radical change and the subsequent effective repression at the hands of 'Boten eines Unveränderlichen'. Far from denoting a retreat into a realm of fiction disconnected from reality, these quotations not only show participation – albeit indirect – in the events but also expose the relevance of the quotations in the present, in their actuality. They provide a language in a moment of acute need, serve as commentary, and poignantly and succinctly show the conflict at hand.

From Susman's essay on Kafka, Celan extracts four more passages that are located – in counter-chronological order – on the previous sheets (pp. 10, 11), but which were, in all likelihood, written down later. The first passage (p. 11) returns to the question of the recognition of the Other, as there 'is no gradual getting closer [Annäherung] among men, everything is decided immediately, in the first instant.'[30] This echoes Empedocles' appeal not to expect explanatory, mediating speech to lead to a true understanding of the other person (p. 6), as well as Arnim's lines on the gradual darkening of the spiritual in its embodiment (p. 7). The following, bitter and disillusioned passage once again discusses the question of shared experience and shared collective justice, defining them both as

27 Rainer Maria Rilke, *Gedichte. 1895 bis 1910*, ed. by Manfred Engel and Ulrich Fülleborn (Frankfurt a.M., Leipzig: Insel Verlag, 1996), pp. 333–337.

28 Gustav Landauer, *Die Revolution* (Frankfurt a.M.: Rütten & Loening, 1907), p. 109. Cf. Celan, Dischner, *Wie aus weiter Ferne zu Dir*, p. 89.

29 Celan read the essay in the volume *Gestalten und Kreisen* (Stuttgart, Konstanz: Diana Verlag, 1954), pp. 348–66. It was first published under the title 'Das Hiob-Problem bei Franz Kafka', *Der Morgen* 5 (1929), 31–49.

30 Susman, 'Das Hiob-Problem bei Franz Kafka', p. 45.

unattainable – in Kafka's literary world and in the world in general. Access to common human justice, according to Susman, cannot be reached in today's world, because each 'life has its own particular time' that 'cannot be measured through any common time', thus leaving each individual radically isolated in his or her experience of time and space: 'From men nothing at all can be expected for men anymore'. As part of a folder titled 'May 68', the passages question the possibility of carrying out any successful common action aimed at a more just society, if in fact a common ground is not given. However, if we proceed and return to Rilke's verse (p. 12), scepticism turns once more into cautious reliance. The simultaneously chronological and counter-chronological movement that characterizes the collection corresponds to the constant oscillation between vehement support of and disillusionment with the student protests of May 1968 in particular and of societal change in general.

The very first quotation on the first page of the folder – which, again, was probably written last – sets the tone and names those concerns that hold the passages together thematically. The emphatic imperative 'nimm mich, nimm mich' [take me, take me] may actually be considered, in hindsight, a sign of acceptance of the 'Geflecht' [net, network] of textual debris that accumulated during those ten days. Standing at the end and yet at the beginning of the collection, Kafka's words define this sequence of heterogeneous passages as a 'Geflecht aus Narrheit und Schmerz' [net of folly and pain], by which one is taken, both as a writer and as a reader, without further specification regarding the nature of the suffering or the folly that is at stake. These can – as the epistemological passages explain – only be recognized without mediation, through a kind of direct and unfiltered viewing [Schau] that acknowledges those aspects that remain in the shadow.

Kamalatta language

If we proceed with the counter-chronological reading, the three quotations that follow Kafka's exhortation (pp. 2–4) can be understood as an immediate commentary on the question of madness that it raises, its linguistic texture, as well as the Red Folder's language as a whole. On the second page there are two fragments from a book entitled *Der kranke Hölderlin* [*The Sick Hölderlin*], in which Erich Trummler gathered documents and testimonies from the time of Hölderlin's 'Umnachtung' – literally, the time of darkness (Arnim's 'Verdunkelung' or 'gradual obscuration') – when night obscured his mind (to himself, but most of all to the comprehension of others). They refer either to Hölderlin's own words as reported by a third party ('Das ist Kamalattasprache' [That is kamalatta language]) or to his way of speaking half in German, half in French when asked about his time in Frankfurt.[31] Hölderlin allegedly used the Greek-sounding neologism 'kamalatta language' when verses from Aeschylus in the original Greek were read aloud to him – verses that he knew well. Instead of signalizing recognition and reacting as his companion might have expected, for example by way of an impromptu translation or of a learned, educated conversation on the topic, he burst into laughter, exclaimed 'I don't understand that!' and described the Greek as 'kamalatta language'.[32]

At a first glance both quotations show a situation of mutual misunderstanding. What Hölderlin appears to be doing on these occasions, however, is more refined than a simple refusal to play the part that is expected of him and to act according to the accepted norms of behaviour. The use of a word that sounded Greek (possibly a metathesis of 'Kalamata'?) must have confused the guest, who for a moment may even have gone through his mental vocabulary, asking himself if he knew the word and could discern its meaning. Cornered as a circus animal into performing a translation on request, Hölderlin, in a perfect surrealist gesture *ante litteram*, throws the ball right back at his interlocutor, forcing him into a translating task that is impossible to solve because, instead, its function lies in opening a field of reflection on the situation at hand. Hölderlin's exclamation 'I don't understand that!' then becomes the exclamation of the interlocutor himself, who is confronted with a word that he really cannot understand. Apparently, the subversive potential of Hölderlin's provocative retreat into opacity for the sake of a change in the conditions of interpersonal encounter was not recognized.

However, in its newly found position after Kafka's invocation, Hölderlin's answer also comes to define – through the deictic demonstrative pronoun – Kafka's words quoted by Celan: they too are, after all, 'Kamalattasprache', a language so full of pathos that it needs relativization and a dose of irony to be savoured properly. What Hölderlin did – whether consciously or not is ultimately irrelevant – was to refuse to comply, though in such a subtle way that it remained almost imperceptible.

On the following (previous) page Celan adds a further twist to this reflection on language and understanding by quoting Hölderlin directly, specifically from a

---

31 *Der kranke Hölderlin. Urkunden und Dichtungen aus der Zeit seiner Umnachtung*, ed. by Erich Trummler (Munich: O. C. Recht, 1921), p. 81 and p. 93. The pun that lies in speaking in French when asked about *Frank*furt was probably lost on Hölderlin's guests. Celan sends both quotations to Dischner on 13 May, adding both the time and place of notation (Celan, Dischner, *Wie aus weiter Ferne zu Dir*, p. 93).

32 *Der kranke Hölderlin*, p. 81.

text written at a time in which his eloquence was at its height and not yet impaired by signs of 'Umnachtung'. The few lines stem from the theoretical essay 'Grund zum Empedokles' ['Ground for Empedocles'], which Hölderlin left as incomplete as the tragedy itself. They refer to Empedocles and his predisposition to 'always penetrate his object so beyond measure [übermässig] that he lost himself in it as if in an abyss'.[33] On one level, the juxtaposition of these passages shows different forms of linguistic articulation by an individual, firstly, as reported by others, along with a judgment on the speaker's mental sanity, and secondly, as it has been transmitted to us in the form of edited and printed handwritten text that in turn passes on a judgment on a historical, fictionalized figure (Empedocles), who has often been interpreted as an alter-ego of Hölderlin himself. In fact, through Celan's juxtaposition, Hölderlin's statement on Empedocles becomes a statement on Hölderlin himself and an explanation of his mind's 'obscuration'. The loss of the self is the consequence of a complete abandonment to the object of enquiry. According to the dialectical movement of Hölderlin's own argumentation, though, the reversal of this sinking into objectivity would be a language that is radically individual for having passed through the general – indeed, a kamalatta language that is used neither for the expression of an alleged subjectivity nor for communicating information, but lies beyond all instrumentality, testifying purely to the presence of an individual as part of a collective.

The material collected in the Red Folder can be seen as striving for this kind of language. The object (May 1968) is dominant in that it absorbs every passage contained in the folder into its epistemic horizon. However, only few utterances refer directly to the object itself. Given the risk of losing oneself in it, distancing is required through text that is foreign both to the object and the subject. The collage itself thus destabilizes the very opposition of subject and object, as well as the claim that events can be recorded in a detached and objective manner. The individual is present indirectly, in the choice and distribution of the material, which also responds to a logic of chance that is neither foreseeable nor entirely controllable.

The first note of the collection, dated 4 May 1968, is written on the sheet that lies at the very bottom of the folder. It summarizes these reflections in an apodictic demand which articulates the concern that lies – literally – at the folder's base: 'Das Recht auf Fremdheit' [The right to foreignness].

33 Hölderlin, *Empedokles I*, p. 437.

The memory of contingence

Two passages epitomize this right to foreignness, for they are written in foreign languages other than German: English and French, respectively. They both thematize the impact of time's passing on an individual and the conditions under which memory can thrive. Two lines from Emily Dickinson's poem 'You cannot make remembrance grow' (p. 5) break the sequence of Hölderlin quotations with a female voice, declaring: 'real memory, like cedar feet | is shod with adamant'. Through the metaphor of the tree plunging its roots into the earth, Dickinson distinguishes false from real memory. False memory is characterized by its superficiality and lack of depth. From it, nothing can develop further; its stability is illusory, and it is therefore fleeting and unreliable. As banal as the tree metaphor may seem at first, it takes an unexpected turn precisely in those central lines that Celan chose to quote. The metaphoric, personifying use of feet to describe the cedar's roots, the paradoxical description of the shoes on these feet as being made of the hardest stone possible, and the simile between these 'cedar feet' resting on solid ground and 'real memory' lead to a chain of associations that leaves the sphere of the purely organic (the tree's growth) and combines it with its opposite, inorganic matter, stone (adamant) and, later, iron. The placement of Dickinson's verses in between quotations from Hölderlin's *Empedokles* may be seen as a subtle hint to the fact that they both rely on the dialectical contrast between these two categories (albeit with different meanings), for it is famously in the 'Grund zum Empedokles' that Hölderlin discusses the opposition between art and nature as the opposition between 'aorgisch' [aorgic] and 'organisch' [organic]. As these two opposites dissolve in death and unite in the character of Empedocles, so the organic and inorganic, caducity and persistence, come together in a conception of 'real memory' which consists both in preservation and growth, development into the past as well as towards the future (the tree of remembrance develops 'Iron buds' that 'will sprout anew | however overthrown –').[34] This conception of remembrance (also) informs the collection of material contained in the Red Folder, inasmuch as the historical quotations are retrieved and exposed as the layer on which the memory of the present stands.

By way of demonstration, on page 16 a rather unusual notation dated 10 May 1968 is inserted between an observation regarding Louis Aragon's conversation

34 Emily Dickinson, *The Complete Poems*, ed. by Thomas H. Johnson (Boston, Toronto: Little, Brown & Co., 1951), p. 1508.

with protesting students on Boulevard St Michel on the previous day (p. 15)[35] and quotations from Margarete Susman's *Das Buch Hiob und das Schicksal des jüdischen Volkes* [*The Book of Job and the Destiny of the Jewish People*] (p. 17). The brief text is an ekphrasis – in French – of a late, remarkable and enigmatic self-portrait by Rembrandt that hangs in the Wallraf Richartz Museum in Cologne (*Self-Portrait as Zeuxis*, ca. 1662). The description is introduced by its logical and phenomenological premise, namely the act of seeing, in a linguistic gesture that is as redundant as it is significant: 'Je regarde l'autoportrait | de Rembrandt (celui de Cologne)' [I observe the self-portrait | of Rembrandt (the one of Cologne)].

This is significant, for one, because the chronologically previous quotations by Susman revolve around the question of the limits of visual representation, with references to Vincent van Gogh's refusal to paint Christ (the divine made human or, again in Arnim's phrasing, the embodied and therefore obscured spiritual) at a time when the divine has withdrawn from the world,[36] and a sentence according to which 'Israel's part is not seeing but hearing'.[37] Life and its representation in 'image and simile'[38] ['Bild und Gleichnis'] constitute two opposite poles that cannot be reconciled, thus a further quotation from the same page. Vision calls for the reproduction of what is seen while at the same time confronting us with the boundaries of representation as it reveals the divide between the visible and the invisible. Hearing, Susman argues, does not lead to the urge to represent the divine, but rather to its immediate experience.[39]

And yet, since these excerpts are isolated from their original context and inserted into a new one, the question of representability loses its focus on the divine and transforms into the question of representability as such. Events occurring in time are, from the point of view of their representation, just as invisible and elusive as the divine. And just as representing the divine prevents its experience, similarly the representation of events in writing excludes, as I mentioned already, participation in them. Accordingly, in the Red Folder, where one of the main topics of enquiry is the possibility of preserving the memory of current events from a perspective that is individual and therefore partial, but still relevant because of its uniqueness, what is heard is also subjected to the principle

35 Cf. Suzzoni, 'Chronologie générale', p. 291.

36 Celan writes down only van Gogh's name (underlined), the book and the page in which the name occurs. Cf. Margarete Susman, *Das Buch Hiob und das Schicksal des jüdischen Volkes* (Freiburg im Breisgau: Herder, 1968), p. 177.

37 Ibid., p. 178.

38 Ibid.

39 Ibid., p. 179.

of representation in and as script. The passage that chronologically follows the ekphrasis records something that has been heard, namely Aragon's sentence: 'Je suis un homme qui n'a pas plié.' Susman's reflection provocatively touches on the heart of the matter, as it demands a response to the systematic violation of the *Bildverbot* [aniconism] both in the folder and in poetry.

The explicit reference to the gaze directed towards the painting seems openly to contradict Susman's observations, all the more so considering the passage's continuation, in which the gaze of the viewer is reciprocated by the gaze of the painter on the canvas ('son regard et sa bouche' [his gaze and his mouth]), who in turn is gazing at himself while painting this self-portrait. Both painter and spectator are following Empedocles' emphatic exhortation to look at the Other. Together, the passage on Rembrandt's painting and Aragon's statement illustrate the respective possibilities of representation through hearing and seeing that the previous quotations had questioned. Both experiences undergo a translation into writing; both take the detour of a foreign language to reflect on them, a language that is in fact foreign in the context of the folder and of Celan's poetic oeuvre, but not in relation to the city in which the writing took place. The non-German inserts in the folder underline the polemical gesture – the 'spirit of contradiction' – that characterizes the folder's material and which is most evident in the double direction in which the textual sequence can be read. Indeed, if we reverse the succession of pages 15–17, thus reading Susman's quotations last, the latter become an admonition on the precariousness of any representation, after an attempt has nonetheless been made.

The ekphrasis develops in an articulated way, animated by the exchange of gazes with which it began. The repetition of the homophonic verb 'regarde' and the noun 'regard' in the first three lines sets the tone for a train of observations that is sustained mainly by repetition and alliteration:

> Je regarde l'autoportrait
> de Rembrandt (celui de Cologne),
> son regard et sa bouche
> distendus par les contingences,
> sa tête et un peu de son
> son manteau dorés par les
> contingens[c]e[s], s[b]ougés[40] par elles, songés par elles,
> son bâton éclaboussé de deux
> gouttes, trois gouttes de cette
> même substance.

---

40 The letters in brackets indicate a substitution in the manuscript.

[I observe the self-portrait
of Rembrandt (the one of Cologne),
his gaze and his mouth
smoothed out by contingencies
his head and a bit of his
his coat made golden by
contingencies, moved by them, dreamt by them,
his stave besprinkled with two
drops, three drops of this
same substance.]

The repetitions reproduce on a textual level the effect that the many layers of oil paint have on Rembrandt's canvas, creating a texture that is of poetic rather than prosaic nature. The recurring phrasing 'par le contingences'/'par elles' structures the passage and lends it its rhythm; the word 'contingences' acquires a centrality that is echoed by the alliterating verbs 'bougés', 'songés'; finally, through the double recurrence of the word 'gouttes' the two drops are literally present in the text, while the repetition of the plosive sound in the same line ('gouttes', 'gouttes', 'cette') reproduces onomatopoetically the steady sound of drops falling.

The ekphrasis takes an unusual turn, as surprising as the development of the comparison in Dickinson's poem. Instead of plainly describing what is seen, the description shifts to an identification of the causes that led to the portrait appearing as it is. But the causes themselves are not specified in detail. Instead, the passage provides information about their nature, which is said to be contingent. The events that shaped Rembrandt's face in the portrait, that gave his coat its shape and golden hue, and that sprinkled 'that same substance' on his stave, are events that could have, but also could not have happened. Instead of referring to any kind of artistic intentionality in the arrangement of the colours on the canvas, Celan emphasizes their fortuity in a way that does not say unequivocally whether he is referring to the pictorial process or to Rembrandt's life captured in the image. The distribution of material on the canvas is as contingent as the events that shape a life over time and leave their mark on faces and objects alike, and as contingent as the textual passages that accumulate over the course of ten days in the Red Folder, while contingent events are taking place, outside, on the street.

But contingencies do not only colour Rembrandt's 'head and a bit of his coat'. Most importantly, and unexpectedly, they are the product of the contingencies' imagination, of a reverie in which the frontier between life and art, experience and reflection is blurred ('songés | par elles'). Walter Benjamin formulated a concept of historiography as the 'art of experiencing the present as the waking state to which the dream that we call the past truly refers'.[41] Celan takes into consideration a similar relation of dream and waking, according to which the tiniest and yet visible signs that events leave behind are a dream through which, upon awakening (i.e. looking, 'regarder'), we recognize not only their occurrence but also their contingency, the fact that they could have occurred otherwise or could not have occurred at all. Celan does not, as is often the case in discussions of this self-portrait, wonder about Rembrandt's enigmatic smile, but rather gradually zooms in on the smallest, most imperceptible detail that barely stands out on the painting's dark background. The golden drops on Rembrandt's stave are almost indiscernible, all the more so in a reproduction. To be detected, they require an attentive yet wandering gaze that does not simply focus on the main, centrally positioned object of representation (the artist's ageing face). Were it not for the golden drops, the painter's stave, the only recognizable sign of the portrayed man's craft, would be invisible and his identity even more mysterious than it already is. The few delicate brushes raise this significant object – without which the painting itself would not be – from invisibility to visibility, from absence to presence, from non-existence to existence. In the left lower corner of the canvas the issue of representation is addressed at the same time from the point of view of its precariousness and power. A hint is sufficient to record the existence of an object, but also to remind us of the fugacity of its appearance in the world, of the ease with which, quite literally, it can dissolve into darkness and oblivion. Art, Celan's note seems to suggest, can and might be the space where the smallest, yet most significant objects and events (objects as events) are recorded in their momentary passing before their disappearance. They are gathered and represented as fleeting, and there is no necessity to their appearance. The fact that they are defined as contingent, that they might as well not have been, or might have been and been represented differently, points both to their inherent frailty and to the alternative possibilities that may arise at any given moment. This openness serves as the premise of change and memory; the contingent collection of contingent material from the past as well as in the present does not have a museal, but rather – akin to Benjamin's understanding – a revolutionary function.

The Red Folder was an experiment restricted in time, as provisory and contingent as the drops on Rembrandt's canvas and as the events taking place in the streets of Paris. They were neither necessary (as may at times be said of a poem, or as events might appear in hindsight or in conventional historical accounts), nor did they possess a clear and univocal purpose. Gathered from the newspa-

41 Benjamin, *Passagen-Werk*, p. 491.

pers, books, images and reflections at hand, 'within reach', they could definitely have been different – and indeed they produce different meanings depending on the order of reading. Only the folder's closure introduced a degree of stability that allows for interpretation; only then the scattered material formed a unity in which the single passages interact and illuminate one another. As the painter's stave in Rembrandt's self-portrait, they might even have disappeared, were it not for the conservational intervention of the archivist, who preserves every written document formerly belonging to the poet, even if it is not strictly a poem. It was only possible for the Red Folder, as we can read it today upon visiting the archive, to come into being at that specific time, in the first half of May 1968, in that specific place, the Quartier Latin. Only in this particular framework could such diverse textual material be read as providing a theoretical background in order to understand and articulate a position towards the momentous events of May 1968. Only then and there could they become their own commentary, and only then could they indirectly express the problems and concerns that arose with and during those very events. However, their significance for a possible future of reading is not limited to that specific time and space.

As much as the Red Folder can be considered no more than the vestibule for the poems that were written in the same period, it nonetheless illustrates in a more extensive way the principle on which the poems themselves are often based. As they draw on different material, they each collect and compose it into a new unity that is independent from the original context and yet bears its trace. At the beginning of his essay on revolution, Landauer had claimed that the 'past [...] that we construct from remains [Überreste] [...] should from time to time be revised, overthrown and built anew in a revolution of historical contemplation [Revolution der Geschichtsbetrachtung]'. He then added that this past 'builds itself up for each individual in a particular way: each individual perceives the images differently, depending on how the real affecting past in their chest propels them forwards and sends them on their way.'[42] The Red Folder can be understood as an experimental translation of Landauer's statement, as an attempt at an alternative historiography that reflects on its premises and is aware of its limits. In the midst of a revolution taking place on the streets, it seeks to realize a revolution in the way we testify to a revolution, as well as to its imminent failure. This revolution in writing is not an alternative to the revolution on the streets – they are complementary – and no change in the conditions of human life, Celan seems to suggest alongside Landauer and Benjamin, can be brought about without the recognition that 'everything that happens at

42 Landauer, *Die Revolution*, p. 28.

any moment anywhere is the past' and that 'the past that is alive inside us rushes in every instant into the future'.[43]

The Red Folder, hidden in an archive for decades and never published in its entirety, poses but does not solve the question of how this individual recognition can be shared and become a common good. Interpretation, a work of recovery and rewriting in and of itself, which is the fruit of contingent discovery and understanding, becomes a part of its object's history, while also being affected by it. It aspires to contribute to the material's revolutionary impetus through condivision, exposing the alternative ways of narration that are possible in between the constraints of convention.

43 Ibid.

Sue Vice

Paul Celan's Successors. From Reverence to Transduction

It might seem that the influence of certain poets on the work of Paul Celan, including the French surrealists, Osip Mandelstam and Rainer Maria Rilke, has been more widely acknowledged than Celan's own influence on later writers.[1] However, despite Celan's own conviction that he had been poetically 'snubbed' in the USA, his influence is, rather, distinctive for its wide-ranging effect on an eclectic group of writers from various generic and national contexts.[2] In the present article, I will ask which elements of Celan's poetic practice have shaped the work of later writers, and what kind of image of his legacy is constructed by this means. The modes of such an influence as shown by the successive generations of writers range from close readings and direct quotation, as part of which Celan is both cited and named, to implicit allusion and free translation, in each case coming to form part of another artwork.

This chapter starts with the US poet Stanley Kunitz, whose appreciation of Celan's work sets the scene for the other, more direct homages that follow. Kunitz's reverence towards Celan as what he calls a Holocaust poet means that he has avoided explicit reference either to that topic or to the other poet's work, except in the form of a new version of an English translation of 'Todesfuge' ['Death Fugue']. These apparently conflicting strategies, of viewing Celan's writing as untouchably historicized, yet so tentatively rendered into English that his poetry demands reworking, are extreme versions of Celan's legacy, as is apparent in all the instances that follow. These include the constructed Hiroshima poet Araki Yasusada, the Norwegian author Karl Ove Knausgaard, and the poets Ciaran Carson, Geoffrey Hill and Courtney Druz. In each instance, Celan's influence can be perceived at the broadest level as well as within individual examples of word-choice.

1 Hugo Bekker, *Paul Celan. Studies in His Early Poetry* (Leiden: Brill, 2008), pp. 14, 22.
2 Matthew Hofer, '"Between Worlds". W.S. Merwin and Paul Celan', *New German Critique*, 91 (2004), 101–15 (p. 101).

https://doi.org/10.1515/9783110658330-013

Diffident homage: Stanley Kunitz

In a tribute to Celan written for the Poetry Society of America, the Massachusetts-born Stanley Kunitz describes the importance of the other poet's work in defining his own practice. Although this finally takes the form of the creative translation of Celan's poetry, Kunitz shrinks before what he sees as the other writer's historical position. Kunitz describes an affinity felt for Celan on account of his 'heritage', as the son of Jewish immigrants who left Lithuania and Russia for the USA at the end of the nineteenth century, and his own story during the Second World War as a conscientious objector.[3] These experiences are united in Kunitz's 1943 poem 'Reflection by a Mailbox', with the effect that a young man waiting for his call-up papers keenly imagines the temporal and geographical proximity of his forebears:

> One generation past, two days by plane away,
> My house is dispossessed, my friends dispersed,
> My teeth and pride knocked in, my people game
> For the hunters of man-skins in the warrens of Europe.[4]

The setting for the poem is what Kunitz describes as the 'conflict in feelings' about his impending conscription following the US entry into the war in 1941: 'On the one hand, I am against war in principle; on the other, I have spent a good part of my life opposing fascism and anything that resembles it'.[5] In the poem, the everyday image of 'the red-haired postman with the smiling hand' represents such a tension for the speaker, whose 'familiar' life is about to be disrupted.

Kunitz's debt to Celan is therefore not one that is directly reflected in his writing, even though it prompts him to reconsider his own wartime verse. Rather, as his tribute makes clear, Celan's writing delineates work of a kind to which Kunitz felt he could never aspire. Although he values the rooting of Celan's work in twentieth-century history, Kunitz clarifies that, 'I have never written a poem about the Holocaust, because it has been my feeling, *especially after Celan*, that the Holocaust belongs to those who have suffered it directly' (my italics).[6]

---

3 Stanley Kunitz, 'On Paul Celan and the Poetry of the Holocaust', in *Poets on Poets*, https://www.poetrysociety.org/psa/poetry/crossroads/tributes/stanley_kunitz_on_paul_celan_and/attachment.pdf
4 Kunitz, 'On Paul Celan', p. 6.
5 Kunitz, 'On Paul Celan', p. 6.
6 Ibid., p. 6.

Nonetheless, the poet concludes with his realization that, 'the Holocaust has been the basic subtext of a good part of what I have produced in poetry.'[7] If Celan is the touchstone for this perception, it suggests that his influence is felt by Kunitz in the form of a boundary, beyond which he will not venture. Celan is from that world which is for the speaker in Kunitz's poem, 'One generation past, two days by plane away'.

In his tribute, Kunitz invokes Celan's poem, 'There was earth inside them, and they dug', after his mention of the death of the latter's parents in a Transnistrian labour-camp. In addition, a reference to the poet's suicide in 1970 is followed by his citation of Celan's 'Fadensonnen' ['Threadsuns'], in John Felstiner's translation, for its contrast of the hopeful final sentiment – 'there are | still songs to sing | beyond mankind' – which, as Felstiner reminds us, is often quoted without its bleak opening reference to 'the gray-black wasteland'.[8] In both instances, an absolute link is assumed to exist between Celan's biography and his poetic writings. It is this which, Kunitz implies, cannot be emulated in the era 'after Celan', as he phrases this more specific version of the Adornean proscription of lyric poetry 'after Auschwitz'.

Although Kunitz claims that he could not allow his writing to be affected by Celan's poetry in the post-war era because of the existential gulf between them, we witness a different kind of reaction in relation to Celan's 'Todesfuge'. In an interview conducted in 1995, Kunitz describes this as the only poem 'great and terrible enough to evoke the smell of evil, the delirium, of the death camps', and his tribute takes the form of a later poet's reconsideration of its English-language version.[9] Kunitz quotes Celan's best-known poem in its entirety, but in a new form. 'Death Fugue' appears as what he calls 'a combination' of the translations by John Felstiner and Michael Hamburger, to which Kunitz has 'contributed some occasional modifications'.[10] However, although it is only as an annotator or modifier of its rendering into English that Kunitz claims he can approach Celan's writing, his changes to the translation of 'Death Fugue' are more radical than this makes them sound. In the opening lines alone, Kunitz alters the diction and tenses used by Hamburger and Felstiner to an effect that is striking in its newness for any reader familiar with the canonical translations:

---

7 Ibid., p. 6.

8 Ibid., p. 13; John Felstiner, *Paul Celan. Poet, Survivor, Jew* (New Haven: Yale University Press, 1995), p. 218.

9 Gary Pacernick, 'Interview with Stanley Kunitz', *Michigan Quarterly Review*, https://sites.lsa.umich.edu/mqr/2016/11/from-the-archive-an-interview-with-stanley-kunitz/

10 Kunitz, 'On Paul Celan', p.11; Paul Celan, *Selected Poems*, trans. by Michael Hamburger (London: Penguin), 1996, pp. 63, 64; Felstiner, *Paul Celan*, pp. 31–32.

Black milk of daybreak we drink it at nightfall
we drink it at midday and morning we drink it at night
drink it and drink it
we are digging a grave in the sky there's plenty
of room there[11]

Kunitz's version makes the poem's discourse simpler and more colloquial than the well-known versions. While Hamburger translates 'abends', the final word of the original's first line, as 'sundown', and Felstiner has it as 'evening', Kunitz prefers 'nightfall'. In this way, he matches it to the term used in the following line's description of the perpetual act of drinking, which takes place at all times of the day and also 'at night'. The fourth line of the original, 'wir schaufeln ein Grab in den Lüften', uses the German present tense to convey immediacy. Its English equivalent is Hamburger's simple present utterance, 'we dig a grave', and Felstiner's 'we shovel a grave'. Yet Kunitz instead uses a continuous present in his new version, where his phrase 'we are digging' transforms the action into one which takes place even as we read. In the last of these opening lines, the challenge of Celan's terse, monosyllabic phrase, 'da liegt man nicht eng', becomes in Kunitz's hands the discordantly direct, 'there's plenty | of room there'. There is extra irony in the enjambment, which makes 'plenty' sound at first like a noun, suggesting the presence of an abundance, before revealing it to be an adjective, one qualifying the limitlessness of death. This contrasts with Hamburger's 'there one lies unconfined', in which the phrasing of both person and location sounds archaic, and Felstiner's 'you won't lie too cramped'. Felstiner claims that he tried 'for years' to bring this phrase of Celan's into 'direct, idiomatic English', and eventually he chose 'cramped' for its final hard consonant, a 'harsh cutoff' matching that of Celan's 'eng'.[12] Yet Kunitz's wording is even more idiomatic, since it gets around Felstiner's having awkwardly to use the adjective 'cramped' as an adverb. In Kunitz's version, the prospect of being turned loose in the form of smoke in the sky is put in terms of the deceptively inviting and everyday offer of 'plenty of room'.

Self-conscious influence: Araki Yasusada

An assertion of poetic diffidence of the kind made by Kunitz in the face of the extremes of Celan's life, and his assumptions about the role of that experience

11 Kunitz, 'On Paul Celan', p. 11.
12 Felstiner, *Paul Celan*, pp. 35–36.

in Celan's art, is certainly not unique. Such self-effacing homage often takes the form of the free translation or rewriting of Celan's poems by others, as much as original work inspired by them. In the following instance of Celan's effect on the writer Araki Yasusada, the notion of the 'witness-poet' is itself the subject of literary scrutiny. The case of the so-called Hiroshima poet Araki Yasusada exhibits a high degree of self-consciousness about the notion of poetic influence, a pattern into which Celan is overtly incorporated. The poetry allegedly by the late Yasusada appeared in 1996 in two high-profile Anglophone contexts, in each case accompanied by a biographical introduction. These were *Stand* magazine in the UK, where seven poems by Yasusada were published under the title 'Poems from Hiroshima', and *American Poetry Review*, in which the selection of fourteen poems was called 'Doubled Flowering. From the Notebooks of Araki Yasusada'. These publications marked the fullest and most prominent appearance of Yasusada's work in the public realm and also precipitated its exposure as an aesthetic stunt.

Although Yasusada's poetry and the biographical material in the form of annotation and extracts from his notebooks that appeared alongside it suggested that he was an eyewitness to the atomic attack on Hiroshima, his oeuvre has been shown to be an elaborate literary deception. No such person as Yasusada exists, and his works are not translations from the original Japanese, but English-language texts by an American writer. The deception takes the form of what Brian McHale calls an 'entrapment hoax', the effect of which relies upon its eventually being revealed.[13] Yet even the exposure of Yasusada's non-existence is characterized by an 'attributional indeterminacy',[14] since its actual author has not been formally identified. Yasusada's oeuvre is judged likely to have been written by Kent Johnson, a Spanish instructor at a college in Illinois, who is named as the translator or co-translator of Yasusada's work. *Doubled Flowering*, the 1997 book-length collection of his writings, was published under Yasusada's authorship but in full knowledge of the imposture, and Johnson is listed as the copyright-holder. The satirical effects of the hoax's exposure in this case are several, including the confrontation of readers and editors with their own orientalist gullibility where eyewitness writing is concerned, as well as the constitution of a means for Johnson to have his work more widely celebrat-

---

13 Brian McHale, '"A Poet May Not Exist". Mock Hoaxes and the Construction of National Identity', in *Faces of Anonymity. Anonymous and Pseudonymous Publication from the Sixteenth to the Twentieth Century*, ed. by Robert J. Griffin (New York and Basingstoke: Palgrave 2003), pp. 233–52 (pp. 236–37).

14 Kent Johnson, 'Some Thoughts on Araki Yasusada and the Author', *Wag's Revue* (2008), 125–36, http://wagsrevue.com/Download/Issue_6/125-%20Yasusada.pdf

ed than seemed possible under his own name. Even in the present brief account of the 'Yasusada project', as Eliot Weinberger has called it,[15] the kinds of questions about the relevance of biography and history to poetic writing in the aftermath of atrocity, as these are also customarily posed concerning Celan, clearly take centre-stage.

Yasusada's oeuvre as a whole could be viewed as a mixed-genre life-writing, consisting as it does of poetry, letters and notebook entries, yet its invented nature prompts us to examine the biographical quotient of any such poetry. For instance, in the poem 'Loon and Dome', dated 1 January 1947, the image of the 'plaster chambers | of the giant Model of the Heart', into which the speaker strolls with his wife Nomura, has been identified as one inspired by that in Chicago's Museum of Science and Industry, rather than Hiroshima's 'Industrial Promotion Hall' of the poem's ostensible setting.[16] This giant heart is one of many poetic references which have a double significance in Yasusada's work: as poetic imagery which is necessarily free of the demands of factual accuracy and as clues to the imposture.

In an elaboration of this pattern, in which the presence of such detail signifies the inventive deployment of fact, the deliberately misleading details of Yasusada's intellectual biography include references to the writers who are said to have influenced him. These are listed as the critic Roland Barthes along with the poets Jack Spicer and Paul Celan. The claim that he was influenced by any of these writers, including Celan, given the dates of Yasusada's poetic activity in the pre-war era, is an impossibility.[17] It is one of the self-advertising anachronisms, or more specifically the prochronisms, in the sense of events that are placed too early, that characterize his work. In support of the story of Yasusada's poetic forebears, those described as the translators of the original Japanese in *American Poetry Review* claim that he wrote 'undated haiku' which 'unmistakably bear the stamp of the famous poet, and Holocaust survivor, Paul Celan', whose writing was read in the pre-atomic attack era 'by the Layered Clouds [po-

15 Eliot Weinberger, 'Can I Get a Witness?', in *Scubadivers and Chrysanthemums. Essays on the Poetry of Araki Yasusada*, ed. by Bill Freind (Exeter: Shearsman 2012 [1998]), pp. 16–22 (p. 19).
16 Araki Yasusada, *Doubled Flowering. From the Notebooks of Araki Yasusada*, ed. and trans. Toso Motokiyu and others (New York: Roof Books, 1997), p. 15; David Wojahn, 'Illegible Due to Blotching. Poetic Authenticity and its Discontents', in *Scubadivers and Chrysanthemums*, pp. 286–311 (p. 303).
17 Marjorie Perloff, 'In Search of the Authentic Other. The Poetry of Araki Yasusada', in *Scubadivers and Chrysanthemums*, pp. 23–50 (p. 39).

etry] group and critically discussed by them'.[18] Yet Celan's work was not published even in German until the early 1950s, 'Death Fugue' appearing in English translation only in 1955, disrupting any possibility that a Japanese literary coterie of the 1930s could have discussed it. Although this does not mean that Celan's 'stamp' on the writing itself is not perceptible, even if it is fictive or performative, the very mention of his name is a signifier for Yasusada's invented status as a witness-poet. However, the poetry as it stands could indeed be indebted to Celan, since it is the product of a writer who was not born in Japan in 1907, as Yasusada is said to have been, but one born in the USA of the mid-1950s. Yasusada, as constructed by Johnson, has taken from Celan's example several threads of signification that allow for his being named as an influence. These include the notion of the poet as retrospective eyewitness to barbarism, an allegiance to and self-consciousness about national language, its counterpart of silence leading to paradoxes about the impossibility of utterance. Yasusada's habit of incorporating cultural detail and location into writing that is otherwise abstract and oblique suggests a particular debt to Celan's early writing.

For these reasons, we might wonder which are the 'undated haiku' to which the translators' note refers, and whether the aesthetic or mock hoax of the Yasusada project extends so far that they also exist. The published collection *Doubled Flowering* includes several examples of undated haiku, some of which show evidence of an uneasy juxtapositions of everyday and elevated discourse, while others explicitly invoke the bombing of Hiroshima. Some, however, as the following examples show, draw on the imagery of geology, astronomy and silence, as a way of reflecting on poetic practice which seems to be an invocation of Celan's:

Tirelessly, tirelessly,
moon is breathing
mountain-side lake's birth

In the temple's silence
shaped like a hammer
the hammer's silence[19]

The references in this pair of poems to the moon and to silence draw on both Japanese and 'Celanesque' imagery, in Matthew Hofer's phrasing,[20] calling on the reader's recognition of the seemingly productive conflict between them.

18 'Doubled Flowering. From the Notebooks of Araki Yasusada', *American Poetry Review*, 25.4 (1996), p. 24.
19 Yasusada, *Doubled Flowering*, p. 76.
20 Hofer, '"Between Worlds"', p. 102.

Such awareness would have taken a different form before the exposure of Yasusada's non-existence, where it might have suggested the presence of cultural hybridity, while afterwards it reveals instead how such a hybridity might be constructed. The 'breathing' moon in the first haiku invokes a mixture of Buddhist and Shinto attitudes to the natural world, set against a recall of Celan's 'deromanticized' use of the same image in such poems as 'Evening of Words'.[21] The second haiku implies the possible disruption of a temple's traditional silence by a hammer, the word's repetition itself having a Celanian sound, as an agent of either violence or creativity, before it falls silent itself. This scenario implies a tension between traditional culture and wartime inhumanity, figured by the intrusion of a hammer into a temple. Celan likewise uses the axe as an image of an object which, like the hammer, can be either a tool or a weapon. Thus, we read in Celan's 'Playing with Axes' the utterance, 'I hear that the axe has flowered', even if such redemption is possible only through the indirection of hearsay. In 'Playing with Axes', the implement suggests the dangerous nature of certain kinds of memory or writing, as the speaker claims:

> at your head the pageantry of the unspoken,
> at your feet the beggary of words,
> you lie there, playing with the axes–
> and at last you are shiny like them.[22]

The final line suggests that progress has been made, since the figure addressed in the second person has started to reflect light in the same way that the 'shiny' axes do.[23] This light might constitute the poetic language which is 'at last' visible as a mediation between 'the pageantry of the unspoken' and the 'beggary of words'. It is the experience of reading Celan's image through Yasusada's reception of it that makes the former's verse seem inexorably to reference only wartime barbarity.

The fleeting instantiations of a Celanian practice in Yasusada's haikus act at first to offer 'authenticity and authority' to the latter's verse,[24] but, given our knowledge of that poet's non-existence, these echoes act instead as a model or enactment of what such influence might look like. They also present a warning against simple biographical reading. Indeed, we might wonder wheth-

---

21 Ibid., p. 113.

22 Paul Celan, 'Playing with Axes', quoted in Yoko Tawada, 'Paul Celan Reads Japanese', *The White Review*, http://www.thewhitereview.org/feature/celan-reads-japanese/

23 Ibid.

24 Hofer, '"Between Worlds"', p. 104.

er there is a retroactive construction present here. It is as if the concept of a Japanese poet, who used the traditional verse-forms of haiku and the collaborations of *renga*, in which writers take turns composing stanzas, as a way to represent contemporary atrocity, was one which itself emerged from its creator's sense of Celan's apparently haiku-like style. Yoko Tawada sees Celan's 'threshold' poems such as 'Playing with Axes' as those already 'peering into Japanese' in their concern with the 'gates' or borders between states of mind and being. In this case, Celan's writing is itself prochronistic in seeming to anticipate an affinity with the ideogrammatic language into which it would be translated, as Tawada puts it: 'The poet must have sensed the gaze of the translation being cast from the future upon the original text'.[25] In this way, the connection Yasusada's poetry was designed to establish with Celan's seems fitting.

Just as Celan's biography has been detected in refracted form in his poetry, so the details of Yasusada's constructed life appear obliquely in his often dreamlike elegies. For instance, the uncanny imagery of women's hair in 'Todesfuge', invoked in relation to Jewish and German history through the figures of Sulamith and Margarete, reappears in Yasusada's poem 'Mad Daughter and Big-Bang', the representation of a father driven to hallucination by grief for his dead daughter. An editorial footnote strategically ensures the reader's impression of biographical significance by glossing the poem's location in the 'foothills of the Chugoku mountains', one often chosen by survivors in the 'aftermath of the bombing'.[26] The poem's opening stanzas set the scene for such an aftermath:

> Walking in the vegetable patch
> late at night, I was startled to find
> the severed head of my
> mad daughter lying on the ground.
>
> (From a distance it had appeared
> to be a stone, haloed with light,
> as if cast there by the Big-Bang.)[27]

Yasusada's mixture of everyday with otherworldly discourse echoes Celan's practice, in this case in the form of a bad-tempered family exchange. The 'startled' father declares that his daughter 'look[s] ridiculous' and demands, with almost literal force, 'what on earth' she is doing in the garden. His daughter replies, with, as Marjorie Perloff notes, a possible reference to the US Air Force crew

25 Tawada, 'Paul Celan Reads Japanese'.
26 Yasusada, *Doubled Flowering*, p. 11.
27 Ibid., p. 11.

who dropped the atomic bomb,[28] that 'some boys buried me here', after which we encounter the father's perception:

> Her dark hair, comet-like, trailed behind ...[29]

By contrast to Celan's invocation of the Bible and German literary history in 'Todesfuge', as the image of the 'comet' here suggests, Yasusada calls on the history of the cosmos for the image of the daughter in this poem. The phrase 'big-bang' in the title refers both to the atomic blast and, by means of another prochronism on the part of his fabricator, to the creation of the universe.[30] The conversational address alongside a surreal register in Yasusada's writing might remind us equally compellingly of Sylvia Plath's poetry, or of Celan's as mediated through hers, as we see in the concluding lines of 'Mad Daughter and Big-Bang'. They mark the reappearance of the confusion of subjects with objects with which the poem began, using an instance of the same vocabulary as Plath:

> Squatting, I pulled the
> turnip up by the root.[31]

The father's mistaking a turnip for his daughter in an act of traumatized substitution depends on its 'root' resembling her 'dark hair'. In Plath's poem 'You're', the speaker's beloved child, is said to be 'Mute as a turnip'.[32] This use of simile contrasts with the category error that we encounter in Yasusada's poem, where the vegetable is all too vocal in fantasy. The image of the 'root' itself is one that signifies an alien implantation or hidden cause in Plath's work, as it does here in Yasusada's, characterizing in her case not only hair ('Hanging Man', 'Lady Lazarus') but also trees ('Elm', 'I am Vertical'), insemination and ominous telephonic communication ('Daddy'). While there is debate, given the dates of his work appearing in English, about whether Celan could have influenced Plath,[33] it is possible to claim that the Yasusada project and its self-conscious construction of poetic debt draws on their affinities without having to make a judgement about origin.

---

28 Perloff, 'In Search of the Authentic Other', p. 42.
29 Yasusada, *Doubled Flowering*, p. 11.
30 Perloff, 'In Search of the Authentic Other', p. 40.
31 Ibid., p. 11.
32 Sylvia Plath, 'You're', *Collected Poems*, ed. by Ted Hughes (London: Faber, 1981), p. 14.
33 Antony Rowland, *Holocaust Poetry. Awkward Poetics in the Work of Sylvia Plath, Geoffrey Hill, Tony Harrison and Ted Hughes* (Edinburgh: Edinburgh University Press, 2005), pp. 48–49.

Prose readings: Karl Ove Knausgaard

In the case of the novelist Karl Ove Knausgaard, whose *The End* (2011), the sixth and final volume of the series *My Struggle*, includes an almost 60-page anatomy of Celan's poem 'The Straitening' (1958), the poet's presence is felt in a work of prose. The narrator of *The End* claims to have chosen the poem to illuminate his concern with the use of proper names and personal pronouns in literary and political life. This example shows the uncertain boundary between influence and incorporation, since the very act of presenting and analysing the poem is an action within the novel's plot. Yet it equally affects the very discourse of the fiction. Indeed, Knausgaard's narrator opens his act of reading with a claim to unworthiness in the face of the entire genre – as he says, 'I couldn't read poetry, and had never been able to' – resulting in his feeling 'excluded' from this poem, one judged by Felstiner to be 'by far the most demanding' as well as the longest of Celan's works.[34] The narrator resolves this impasse by declaring that the poem's composition, 'not ... of mysteries, but of words', means that 'all that was required was to read them'.[35] Such an apparent truism has significant repercussions for the narrator's keeping to a close linguistic study of 'The Straitening', which depends on his noting 'the possible meanings' of each word and 'the connections between them'.[36] Doing so without recourse to a historicized significance as the final signified of Celan's writing is to present a model of poetic reading, as well as an elucidation of the poem itself.

However, Knausgaard's analysis of this kind is itself fictionalized. Despite the 'chasm'[37] he claims to exist between 'The Straitening' and his ability to comprehend it, he is instantly drawn to Celan's poem in his search for a way to conceptualize the social act of naming, as if already aware of its significance.[38] The importance of such a topic arises from the 'prohibition' placed on the fictive use of Knausgaard's father's name as the result of a family feud, as well as his father's loss of a name in death, as the son observes: 'His body had slid out of his name and lay there without, nameless'.[39] The contradiction between the avowal of poetic ignorance and the reality of this sophisticated, even 'thrill-

---

34 Felstiner, *Paul Celan*, p. 121; Karl Ove Knausgaard, *The End*, trans. by Martin Aitken and Don Bartlett (London: Harvill Secker, 2019), pp. 421–22.

35 Ibid., p. 424

36 Ibid., p. 424.

37 Ibid., p. 424.

38 Ibid., p. 424.

39 Ibid., pp. 418–19.

ing',[40] understanding of Celan's poem, lies partly in the narrative structure of Knausgaard's encounter with 'The Straitening'. It is related as if we are accompanying the narrator on his gradual and real-time reading through the stanzas of Celan's poem, giving the impression that he is 'live-blogging his line-by-line effort to make sense' of the poem, as Ruth Franklin puts it.[41] But the effect of immediacy is one painstakingly constructed with the hindsight not only of the narrator's own cogitations, but of his research into the poem's critical history.

This fictive scenario is clear in a passage where the narrator's finding in Celan's poem a way to express his conviction that 'the very foundation of the name was broken' acts to enfold three lines of poetry:

> I was looking for something I could use in my essay about the name. I found it.
>
> > The place where they lay, it has
> > a name – it has
> > none.
>
> I read.[42]

As this act of subsuming the poetry within prose suggests, 'The Straitening' is valued by the narrator in a way that accords with his particular concerns, part of the reason for its boldly not making the Holocaust the poem's referent. Of these three lines, Knausgaard acutely observes that, 'Something had a name ... and then the fact of it having a name was taken back', in a poem where, unlike 'Todesfuge', 'there wasn't a single name' for a location, person or event.[43] Although this is presented in the novel as the narrator's immediate perception, it is rather a moment of belated understanding. It is clear that he has already set aside such critical responses as Peter Szondi's that the poem is spoken by 'time personified' and has entered into pre-existing debates over diction.[44] Thus the narrator considers whether the poem's opening word, 'verbracht', should be rendered as 'deported' rather than simply 'driven', as it appears in the Hamburger translation he quotes:

---

40 Daniel Mendelsohn, review of *The End*, in the *New York Times*, https://www.nytimes.com/2018/09/24/books/review/karl-ove-knausgaard-my-struggle-book-six.html

41 Ruth Franklin, 'How Writing *My Struggle* Undid Knausgaard', in *The Atlantic*, https://www.theatlantic.com/magazine/archive/2018/11/knausgaard-devours-himself/570847/

42 Knausgaard, *The End*, p. 421.

43 Ibid., p. 421.

44 Ibid., p. 444.

Driven into
the terrain with the unmistakable track:

grass, written asunder.[45]

Felstiner, who translates this opening utterance with a past participle of a less concrete kind as, 'Taken off to the | terrain with the unmistakable track', comments in detail on the matter of vocabulary and what seems to be Celan's deliberately eschewing the Nazi-era euphemism 'deportieren' in preference for the more everyday 'verbringen'.[46] There is no mention of Felstiner's biography of Celan in *The End* nor in the novel's bibliography, and Hamburger's title for the poem is used in preference to the other translator's 'Stretto'. Yet, as if by implicit contrast to Felstiner's full acknowledgement of the historical context of composition, Knausgaard withholds any mention of genocide and war, even in the context of rejecting the term 'deported'. Indeed, only towards the end of his long analysis does he make this omission explicit, by quoting the poet and translator Øyvind Berg in relation to the poem's setting. Berg mentions in his Norwegian 'rendering' of Celan's poetry the deaths of the poet's parents 'in a German work camp known as the Stone Pit', alongside a caveat quoted by Knausgaard about '"historicising interpretations [that] deprive the poetry of contemporary interest"'.[47] Knausgaard's reading fully enacts this invitation to give the poem an 'interest' of a 'contemporary' kind. In this way, his reading of 'the unmistakable track' as 'at once something in its own right, and a sign of something else' allows him to consider it as part of 'the terrain of the poem' in which 'the track is language'.[48] Its location is the poem's own 'field of loss', rather than what a reviewer calls the site of Celan's parents' 'mass grave on earth'.[49]

In keeping with his focus on nomination and signification, and in contrast to the review's literalizing impulse, the narrator of *The End* observes that the grass, described in the opening lines as 'written asunder', has been afflicted by language: 'it is the way the grass is considered that is damaged, rather than the grass itself'.[50] He considers the poem an elegy not just to the poet's parents,

45 Ibid., p. 424.
46 Felstiner, *Paul Celan*, p. 119.
47 Knausgaard, *The End*, p. 464.
48 Ibid., p. 434.
49 Ibid., p. 455; Rika Lesser, 'Paradoxically German', in the *New York Times*, https://www.nytimes.com/1981/04/26/books/paradoxically-german.html
50 Knausgaard, *The End*, p. 425.

but to 'what was lost in their death'.[51] In this way, the narrator both enlarges the poem's significance and turns it into one about his own concerns, ranging from personal bereavement to the 'coming apart' of language in extreme political circumstances. He sees hope in 'The Straitening' with its address to the 'you' that is fatally absent from fascistic thinking, including not only that of the Nazis but also of the Norwegian terrorist Anders Behring Breivik, which constructs itself instead against a 'them'.[52]

The attention paid to Celan's 'The Straitening' in Knausgaard's novel is presented as a search for inspiration as much as evidence of an organic effect on his work. It transforms into a plot device the fact that not only is every instance of poetic influence an exegesis, but so is translation itself. The appearance of Celan's poem is in the form of a translation within a translation, in which Knausgaard's original Norwegian analysis of Berg's version is turned into an equivalent one in English, for which the translators chose Hamburger's edition.[53] The Norwegian original includes 'linguistically reflexive' instances of the narrator's altering Berg's language-use, while the equivalent in the English edition is that of the translators' amendments to Knausgaard's diction to ensure that it fits Hamburger's translation.[54] Such a context gives a meta-translational aspect to Knausgaard's conviction that the poem's very difficulty is its meaning.

Double influences: Ciaran Carson, Geoffrey Hill and Courtney Druz

In the English translation of *The End*, Knausgaard's view of Celan is filtered through Hamburger, while in the Norwegian original it appears via Berg's translation. The following examples, starting with the Northern Irish poet Ciaran Carson, extend this awareness of the poetry's mediation in responding to Celan by means of his intertexts and influences. This has the effect of situating Celan within a poetic lineage rather than as unapproachably addressing a singular event, as well as establishing a distinctive practice of response to his work.

Carson's 2008 collection *For All We Know* is entitled with an ambiguous phrase suggesting both lack of knowledge as well as its totality, one borrowed

51 Ibid., p. 471.
52 Ibid., p. 469.
53 Don Bartlett, personal correspondence, 22 May 2019; Martin Aitken, personal correspondence, 23 May 2019.
54 Aitken, personal correspondence.

from Celan's 1963 poem 'So many constellations'. Carson's sonnets follow the doomed love of a couple set against various European locations, including Dresden, Berlin and the 1970s Belfast of Troubles era, at the end of which the loved one, Nina, is killed in a car-crash, forming an implicit parallel with a version of Celan's own personal losses. The form of *For All We Know* establishes what has been called a 'fugal memory' of repeated details and locations.[55] In this way, the biographical likeness in Carson's collection stands for a compositional one. In a sonnet from *For All We Know*, Carson performs a double citation, invoking a poem of Celan's in which the latter himself quotes an anterior writer, in this case Bertolt Brecht. The notion of the two-way temporality of influence, by means of which a later poem activates the earlier one's potential meaning, makes clear the role of remembering for the future. Brecht's 'An die Nachgeborenen' ['To Those Born Later'], published in 1938, almost exactly thirty years before Celan's poem, asks in its second stanza, 'What kind of times are they, when | A talk about trees is almost a crime | Because it implies silence about so many horrors?'[56]

As Karen Leeder has argued, the challenge issued in the title of Brecht's poem has turned it into the site of explicit reconsideration in post-war German poetry, particularly in its appearing to regret the separation of the ethical from the aesthetic.[57] While for some later writers responding to Brecht, the act of uttering the word 'tree' in the context of ecological threat and private land ownership is a political act, for others the notion of 'conversation' remains paramount. Celan's response reflects on the unreliability of language, or what Knausgaard calls its 'fall',[58] in the post-war era:

A leaf, treeless,
for Bertolt Brecht:
What times are these
    when a conversation
is nearly a crime,
    because it includes
so much being spoken.[59]

55 Timothy C. Baker, 'Second Time Around. Fugal Memory in Ciaran Carson's *For All We Know*', *Review of Irish Studies in Europe*, 1.1 (2016), 1–17 (p. 12).
56 Bertolt Brecht, 'To those born later', *Poems 1913–1956*, trans. by Edith Anderson and others (London: Routledge, 2007), p. 318.
57 Karen Leeder, 'Those born later read Brecht. The reception of "An die Nachgeborenen"', in *Brecht's Poetry of Political Exile*, ed. by Ronald Speirs (Cambridge: Cambridge University Press 2000), pp. 211–40 (pp. 225–29).
58 Knausgaard, *The End*, p. 468
59 Celan, 'A leaf, treeless. for Bertolt Brecht', in *Selected Poems*, p. 339.

The poem itself here is the 'leaf', as if it were a single page from a book, but its anchoring 'tree' is absent, by reason of an overproduction of utterance – the 'being spoken' – in a newly unreliable form. The gulf between Brecht's 1938 and Celan's 1968 is conveyed by his description of what language has witnessed in the meantime.

Carson's poem 'Peace' folds together Brecht's poem with Celan's response:

> What kinds of times are these, you'd say, when a conversation
> is deemed a crime because it includes so much that is said?[60]

John Clegg calls this a 'translation' on Carson's part, one which is 'fairly close' to Celan's original.[61] However, the lineation is significantly different and indeed is itself conversational. The crucial addition of 'you'd say' and the transformation of Celan's 'nearly a crime' into Carson's 'is deemed' a crime distances these notions from the speaker.[62] It is as if the speaker in Carson's poem is seeing the Irish peace process, for which it is named, via Eastern European and wartime history, and includes the idea of an interlocutor ('you') and the absolutist process of law ('deemed').

Carson's practice is in this sense one possible answer to the rhetorical question posed by the poet Courtney Druz in her consideration of Celan, 'How does one convert energy into another form?'.[63] The overdetermined nature of poetic debt where Celan's writing is concerned is foregrounded further in Druz's work, since she explicitly frames her poetry in terms of a double influence. Her method of responding to Celan's verse is inspired by what she calls Geoffrey Hill's method of 'transduction'.[64] Druz uses this term in reference to Hill's revisionings of Celan's poetry, particularly his 'Two Chorale-Preludes. On Melodies by Paul Celan', in the collection *Tenebrae* (1978), which is itself titled after Celan's 1957 poem of that name. As the subtitle which names Celan suggests, Hill's poems take as their subject the other poet's verse, offering 'imitations' of the originals, rather than being simply free translations.[65] In this case, the

---

60 Ciaran Carson, 'Peace', *For All We Know* (Loughcrew: Gallery Press, 2008), p. 55.
61 John Clegg, 'The Eastern European Context of Poetry in English after 1950', unpublished PhD thesis, University of Durham, Durham, England, 2014, p. 81.
62 Ibid., pp. 80 – 81.
63 Quoted in J.K. Gayle, 'Courtney Druz. "Transductions of Celan"', in *Bible, Literature, Translation*, https://bltnotjustasandwich.com/2012/02/28/guest-post-by-courtney-druz-transductions-of-celan/
64 Ibid.
65 E. M. Knottenbelt, *Passionate Intelligence. The Poetry of Geoffrey Hill* (Amsterdam: Rodopi, 1990), p. 249.

poems of Celan's on which Hill draws are 'Ice, Eden' and 'Kermorvan' from *Die Niemandsrose* [*No One's* Rose] of 1963. Hill's poems are framed by his addition of Latin titles, themselves the names of devotional hymns, and take as epigraphs a line from each of the original German of Celan's poems. Celan's poetry is used in each case as a prefatory quotation to a new work which addresses his.

The first of Hill's two poems responds in this way to Celan's 'Ice, Eden', as can be seen by a comparison of their respective opening stanzas. As Celan's title suggests, the poem's imagery concerns religiously inflected notions of consolation and rebirth even in an unpromisingly wintry setting. Celan's poem, in this version translated by Michael Hamburger, sets a scene in which a voice recounts its own death:

> There is a country Lost,
> a moon grows in its reeds,
> where all that died of frost
> as we did, glows and sees.[66]

In Hill's version, translation is subsumed by interpretation. He keeps Celan's use of the first-person plural, but makes the lost world an internal realm:

> I AVE MARIA COELORUM
> *Es ist ein Land Verloren ...*
>
> There is a Land called Lost
> at peace inside our heads.
> The moon, full on the frost
> vivifies these stone heads.[67]

Hill retains the rhyme that is unusual in characterizing Celan's original, which has equally been replicated by Hamburger. The rhyme itself has allowed critics to hear in Celan's version the 'foreign importation' of echoes from a Christmas carol, 'Es ist ein Ros' entsprungen' ['A Spotless Rose'].[68] Hill adds to this usage with the term 'chorale-preludes', in the sense of organ compositions prefacing hymns, so that his poems act as improvisations on the 'melodies' furnish-

66 Celan, 'Ice, Eden', *Selected Poems*, p. 177.
67 Geoffrey Hill, '1. Ave Maria Coelorum', *Tenebrae* (London: André Deutsch, 1978), p. 35.
68 Winfried Menninghaus, quoted in Charlotte Ryland, 'Keeping Faith. Michael Hamburger's Translations of Paul Celan's Poetry', https://www.ingentaconnect.com/content/plg/jfig/2011/00002011/00000002/art00004?crawler=true

ed by Celan.[69] Hill stays close to Celan's German in the opening line quoted above by keeping the English 'land' as the equivalent for Celan's, 'Es ist ein Land Verloren'.[70] Hamburger's contrasting choice of 'country' responds to the ambiguity of the German 'Land', making the word refer to a national and personal loss as well as a mythical realm.

Druz's practice follows Hill's mediation of Celan's poetic signification, although her verse often extends beyond the latter's originals to an extent that suggests inspiration as much as influence. The origin of the term 'transduction' lies in genetics, where it refers to a transfer of material: thus, to transduce is to 'convert variations in (a physical quantity) into an electrical signal, or vice versa',[71] fittingly implying a two-way process. In addition, in the neologistic sense used by Druz to describe Hill's and her own poetic practice, 'transduction' merges the notion of 'translation', in its varied senses where Celan's poetry is concerned, with that of 'deduction'. In this mode, Druz has produced a poem that consists of responses to four of Celan's poems from *Atemwende* [*Breathturn*] of 1967, which she titles 'Notes on some sculptures by Paul Celan'.[72] Celan's 'Thread suns', now entitled thus, which we have already encountered as viewed in biographical terms by Stanley Kunitz, is one of these anterior poems. In a commentary on her compositional method, Druz quotes Hamburger's translation, as below:

> above the grey-black wilderness.
> A tree-
> high thought
> tunes in to light's pitch: there are
> still songs to be sung on the other side
> of mankind.[73]

Celan's poem can be seen as an attempt, like that made in 'Ice, Eden', to reconcile a mystical sense of unified life with the knowledge of its bleakness. Critics have pointed out that the phrase 'the other side | of mankind' ambiguously sug-

---

69 Christoph Bode, 'A Mercia of the Mind', in *Regionalität, Nationalität und Internationalität in der zeitgenössischen Lyrik*, ed. by Lothar Fietz and others (Tübingen: Attempto Verlag 1992), pp. 313–42 (p. 341).

70 Celan, 'Eis, Eden', in *Selected Poems*, p. 176.

71 *Oxford English Dictionary*, 'transducer', https://en.oxforddictionaries.com/definition/transducer

72 Druz, in Gayle, 'Transductions of Celan'.

73 Celan, 'Thread suns', quoted in Gayle, 'Transductions of Celan'.

gests either the vanishing of the species or a transcending of human frailty.[74] The tentatively positive nature of the latter meaning is easier to perceive if the original noun 'Menschen' is translated as 'people' or 'men and women' rather than Hamburger's more abstract and totalizing 'humankind'.

Druz's 'transduction' of 'Fadensonnen' retains Celan's idea of songs extending beyond the purview of humankind. Her calling his originals 'sculptures' is a counterpart to Hill's use of the musical term 'melodies'. However, it seems more apt as a description of her own practice, since Druz's version of 'Thread suns' suggests a three-dimensional object, its movement that of a kinetic sculpture:

> 2. *Thread suns*
>
> The tree on fire throws out its filaments,
> weaves them to an orb with all eight branches
> to keep you out. What we see seems
> a chrysalis, lanterning a pulsing light.[75]

The differences in Druz's version include the title, since her poem is, in a tentative manner, called 'Notes'. Like Felstiner and in contrast to Hamburger, Druz uses a direct counterpart to the German original's 'Fadensonnen' in the invented English compound 'threadsuns', while Celan's 'tree-high thought' takes on the guise of 'The tree on fire'.[76] Such changes make her poem less abstract while abandoning the musical hint that the tree's strings or threads are playing alongside the sun. A note of potential is retained by the image of the 'chrysalis', even if it is subjectively constructed ('seems'). Druz's commentary emphasizes the origin of her version of Celan's poem in the Hebrew Bible, in contrast to Hill's use of Christian imagery, as the reference to an 'eight branche[d]' menorah suggests. As Druz says, 'I ordered those poems according to the Jewish schedule of weekly Torah readings, and placed "Notes" in the position of Parshat Vayera (Genesis 18:1–22:24). This is the biblical passage in which Lot's wife looks back at destruction and solidifies, in which Abraham binds Isaac on the altar.'[77] As Druz implies, both Lot's wife's turning into salt because she could not prevent herself from the movement of a backward look and Isaac's being freed from his bindings present a combination of energy and stasis in this paradox drawn from Celan's original.

---

74 Doug Valentine, 'Paul Celan and the Meaning of Language. An Interview with Pierre Joris', http://www.flashpointmag.com/Doug_Valentine_Interview_with_Pierre_Joris.htm

75 Druz, quoted in Gayle, 'Transductions of Celan'.

76 Felstiner, *Paul Celan*, p. 218

77 Druz, in Gayle, 'Transductions of Celan'.

Conclusion

In each of the cases discussed here, Celan's name, or the foregrounding of quotations from his work, alerts the reader to the presence of his poetic effect. As Langdon Hammer puts it of Geoffrey Hill's rather different debt to the American poet Allen Tate, these are examples of 'conspicuous influence', rather than the kind of 'buried sources' discussed by Harold Bloom in his *The Anxiety of Influence.*[78] The present examples are of an eagerly claimed debt on the part of Hill and the other writers.

The kinds of genre and method taken up by later authors from Celan's practice include examples of literary music, fugal memory, eyewitness and political poetry, self-conscious explorations of language, constructs of home and its loss, as well as the invocation of literary forebears and mythical or mystical history. These varied features can be summed up as the tendency either to emulate Celan's status as an eyewitness poet or to respond to the formal construction of his writing. It is thus not only Karl Ove Knausgaard's narrator who positions himself as a reader as much an inheritor of Celan's poetry. Each of the poets' speakers is likewise constructed as a reflective reader, usually in relation to specific poems by the earlier writer. Such a poet-reader has encountered Celan's work in the form of its best-known translations into English, most often those by Michael Hamburger, although also sometimes the variants put forward by John Felstiner. This is even true of Knausgaard's novel, whose response to Celan draws on Hamburger's translation in its English version, as the novel's copyright page confirms. The widespread practice of altering the detail of the translation, either at the level of individual words and phrases, as Stanley Kunitz does, or to more wholesale effect, as in the case of Courtney Druz, implies attention to Celan's original German versions, albeit as a secondary or supplementary source. Such a compositional method goes beyond even the customary attention paid in free translation to the 'target language', in these cases that of English.[79] Indeed, the conspicuous failure to mention in which language Celan's verse was read by the so-called Hiroshima poet Araki Yasusada is another hint at its imposture.

The example of Yasusada shows that Celan's influence is conspicuous where poets have sought a model for representing historical enormities, as Matthew

78 Langdon Hammer, 'The American Poetry of Thom Gunn and Geoffrey Hill', *Contemporary Literature*, 43.4 (2002), 644–66 (p. 644.)

79 Katharina Barbe, 'The Dichotomy *Free* and *Literal* Translation', *Meta*, 40.3 (1996), 328–37 (p. 328).

Hofer has argued is the case for the Vietnam War, Andres Ajens for the fate of the American Indians in the instance of the Argentinian poet J. C. Bustriazo Ortiz.[80] The examples in the present chapter suggest that it is possible to move beyond a view of Celan's work as determined primarily by his historical moment. At an even greater expansion beyond such a historicized significance, the reading given by Knausgaard of 'The Straitening' accords with Marjorie Perloff's view of the poem's reference to 'any death or painful memory, the poet's Holocaust experience notwithstanding'.[81] Such belated casting of light back on Celan's writing gives us an image of the poet not simply as eyewitness to wartime atrocity, as Kunitz implies in his tribute, but as one whose view of that atrocity allowed him to reconsider the function of language in the aftermath of any fraught, cataclysmic or sublime occurrence and resultant internal state.

80 Andrés Ajens, *Poetry After the Invention of América. Don't Light the Flower*, trans. by Michelle Gil-Montero (New York: Palgrave 2011), p. 51.

81 Marjorie Perloff, 'A Poet's Hope', *Boston Review*, http://bostonreview.net/archives/BR30.6/perloff.php.

Cherilyn Elston

'almost | you would | have lived'. Reading Paul Celan in Colombia

Since his death in 1970 Paul Celan's reputation has been consolidated as 'the greatest German-language poet'[1] or even 'the major European poet'[2] of the second half of the twentieth century. This is in large part due to his status as the 'exemplary postwar poet',[3] read in light of his biography as a Holocaust survivor and held up as the paradigmatic example of how, despite Adorno's dictum, poetry can be still be written 'after Auschwitz'. In this way, his famously difficult, 'hermetic' poems – characterized by silence, aporia and syntactical dislocation – have become the predominant aesthetic model for how to bear witness to the non-representable horror of the Holocaust, registering the catastrophe within the German language. While the complexity of Celan's verse, with its lessons for post-Holocaust critical theory and philosophy, has resulted in a diverse body of critical literature on the poet, it has also meant that Celan – the Holocaust poet – has been largely subsumed within a predominant critical discourse on Holocaust representation. Informed by poststructuralist approaches to history and language, this critical framework saw the incomprehensibility of traumatic experience best served by textual strategies of fragmentation and testimonial failure, of which Celan's 'resistant, modernist aesthetics' are the pre-eminent example.[4]

One of the consequences of this interpretative framework has been, as Marjorie Perloff notes, the placement of Celan 'in a kind of solitary confinement'.[5] Charles Bernstein states that a 'crippling exceptionalism' has isolated the poet 'from any other poetry, contemporary or subsequent', making 'his work a symbol of his fate rather than an active matrix for an ongoing poetic practice'.[6] Yet this isolation seems strange for a poet who, despite his 'hermeticism', in his own statements on poetry actually envisaged it as a 'dialogue' or an 'encounter'; fa-

1 *Paul Celan. Selections*, ed. by Pierre Joris (Berkeley: University of California Press, 2005), p. 3.
2 George Steiner, *After Babel. Aspects of Language and Translation*, 3rd edn (London: Oxford University Press, 1998), p. 191.
3 John Felstiner, *Paul Celan. Poet, Survivor, Jew* (New Haven; London: Yale University Press, 1995), p. xvii.
4 Anthony Rowland and Robert Eaglestone, 'Introduction. Holocaust Poetry', *Critical Survey*, 20.2 (2008), 1–6 (p. 4).
5 Marjorie Perloff, 'A Poet's Hope', *Boston Review*, 1 November 2005 (http://bostonreview.net/marjorie-perloff-paul-celan-a-poets-hope).
6 Charles Bernstein, 'Celan's folds and veils', *Textual Practice*, 18.2 (2004), 199–205 (pp. 200–1).

https://doi.org/10.1515/9783110658330-014

mously 'a message in a bottle, sent out in the – not always greatly hopeful – belief that somewhere and sometime it could wash up on land'.[7] It is furthermore perplexing because, beyond the huge number of intertexts and allusions in Celan's own poetry, his work has consistently been cited across diverse contexts, and in different artistic media, over the last half century. As Jonathan Mayhew argues, updating Benjamin's conclusions on Baudelaire's pan-European influences, the case could be made for Celan as a writer of 'European repercussions', whose relevance is 'obviously not confined to the European continent'.[8] This chapter, consequently, takes up Bernstein's task 'to imagine other, still contemporary, company for Celan'.[9] Specifically, it makes the case for Celan's global relevance by analysing his reappearance far from his own historical, geographical and personal topographies, and in the context of another of the twentieth century's histories of political trauma: the Colombian conflict. The chapter focuses on how two of Colombia's most important female artists, the sculptor Doris Salcedo and the poet María Mercedes Carranza, have dialogued with Celan's poetry as a means of thinking through the role of art in representing violence.

Holocaust studies scholars, however, might be surprised at the claim for Celan's significance in relation to other, geographically diverging histories of trauma, especially in non-European contexts such as Colombia. In recent years there has been a significant move within Holocaust studies to question the global applicability of paradigms derived from the Holocaust. As part of a challenge to what has been termed the field's Eurocentric assumptions, scholars have re-examined the positioning of the Holocaust as a unique and singular event, privileged over other (non-Western) histories of genocide and violence, and have also critiqued the predominant tropes of anti-representation, 'unspeakability' and incomprehension associated with trauma theory and Holocaust literature, such as Celan's poetry. As Stef Craps argues, these paradigms:

> marginalize or ignore traumatic experiences of non-Western or minority cultures, they tend to take for granted the universal validity of definitions of trauma and recovery that have developed out of the history of Western modernity; and they often favour or even prescribe a modernist aesthetic of fragmentation and aporia as uniquely suited to the task of bearing witness to trauma.[10]

7 Felstiner, *Poet, Survivor, Jew*, p. 115.

8 Jonathan Mayhew, *The Twilight of the Avant-garde. Spanish Poetry 1980–2000* (Liverpool: Liverpool University Press, 2009), p.101.

9 Bernstein, 'Celan's folds and veils', p. 200.

10 Stef Craps, 'Beyond Eurocentrism. Trauma Theory in the Global Age', in *The Future of Trauma Theory. Contemporary Literary and Cultural Criticism*, ed. by Gert Buelens, Sam Durrant and Robert Eaglestone (Abingdon, Oxon: Routledge, Taylor & Francis, 2014), pp. 45–61 (p. 46).

According to this framework, the appropriateness of speaking about Celan, the modernist, anti-representational poet par excellence, in relation to other political traumas could be questioned. This chapter, however, argues for a more nuanced reading of Celan's life and oeuvre, which would allow us to understand his impact on a global scale and particularly his relevance in non-Western and postcolonial contexts.[11] Against the predominant critical interpretation, which simply situates Celan in a Western trauma canon or majoritarian European modernist tradition, this chapter argues that Celan's 'complex, migrant fate',[12] his experience of racial segregation, exile and homelessness *within* Europe – which echoes throughout his poetic language – speaks powerfully to both the postcolonial condition and artists working in other contexts, like Colombia, marked by loss and displacement. Drawing upon recent work that has traced the multidirectional links between the Holocaust and other, particularly postcolonial, histories of violence, this chapter demonstrates that the appearance of Holocaust discourses in Colombia is not a Eurocentric imposition of external trauma paradigms. Questioning the idea that anti-representational, fragmented aesthetics are solely part of a European tradition, I argue that Colombian artists have drawn on Celan's work precisely because he provides a model to explore how art can respond to the dynamics of political violence in Colombia. Significantly, this model does not only reflect, as the critical literature would seem to imply, the incomprehensibility of trauma and impossibility of testimony. As scholars have pointed out, Celan's poetry also draws upon an ontological philosophical-poetic tradition, which seeks to find a poetic language that could enact an encounter with the lost 'Other' of the Holocaust. It is here, I argue, that Carranza and Salcedo dialogue with Celan, in their creation of an aesthetic mode that recognises and makes visible the absent presence of the forgotten dead and disappeared of the Colombian conflict.

Decolonizing Holocaust studies and Celan's Holocaust legacy

Alongside the postcolonial critique of trauma theory and modernist aesthetics outlined by Craps, the recent transnational turn in memory studies has sought

---

11 While Latin America is part of the Western hemisphere, the category "non-Western" is understood to refer to those parts of the world outside the historically hegemonic powers of Europe and the United States.

12 Felstiner, *Poet, Survivor, Jew*, p. xvii.

to challenge the singularity of the Holocaust by questioning its separation from other histories of trauma. In particular, Michael Rothberg's work challenging competitive memory models has been key to understanding how Holocaust memory did not develop in isolation but emerged in dialogue with post-Second World War decolonization processes and 'their modes of coming to terms with colonialism, slavery, and racism'.[13] Building on a tradition of intellectual reflection on the Holocaust, beginning with Hannah Arendt, Aimé Cesaire and W.E.B. Du Bois, which conceptually linked the genocide of the European Jews and the history of European colonialism, Rothberg identifies a 'minoritarian tradition of "decolonized" Holocaust memory'[14] that uncovers the connections between postcolonial and Holocaust studies, and analyses the interrelatedness of the Nazi genocide and the broader histories of violence, racial oppression and imperialism which have constituted the 'darker side of Western modernity'.[15] Following on from Rothberg, scholars have now begun to trace the ways in which the Holocaust has enabled us to think through other histories of victimization, and how these traumas, such as the Algerian War of Independence, slavery in the US and British colonialism, among many others, have also informed Holocaust memory in a multidirectional sense.[16]

Within Western memory studies' comparative work, however, the dialogue between Holocaust memory and Latin America's traumatic late-twentieth-century history has received little attention. As Edna Aizenberg notes, beyond the assertion that many Nazis went into hiding in the Southern Cone, Latin America's complex engagement with the Holocaust and Nazism has been 'eclipsed' by a focus on the US, Europe and Israel.[17] This has occurred despite the fact that

---

13 Michael Rothberg, *Multidirectional Memory. Remembering the Holocaust in the Age of Decolonization* (Stanford, CA: Stanford University Press, 2009), p. 22.

14 Rothberg, *Multidirectional Memory*, p. 22.

15 Walter Mignolo, *The Darker Side of Western Modernity* (Durham and London: Duke University Press, 2011)

16 See for example: Eaglestone '"You would not add to my suffering if you knew what I had seen". Holocaust Testimony and Contemporary African Trauma Literature', *Studies in the Novel*, 40.1–2 (2008), 72–85; Craps, 'Beyond Eurocentrism'; Stef Craps and Michael Rothberg, eds, *Transcultural Negotiations of Holocaust Memory*, special issue of *Criticism. A Quarterly for Literature and the Arts*, 53.4 (2011). This also builds upon earlier work, such as Paul Gilroy, *The Black Atlantic. Modernity and Double Consciousness* (London: Verso, 1993); Bryan Cheyette, 'Venetian Spaces. Old-new Literatures and the Ambivalent Uses of Jewish History' in *Reading the 'New' Literatures in a Postcolonial Era*, ed. by Susheila Nasta (Cambridge: Brewer, 2000), pp. 53–72.

17 Edna Aizenberg, *On the Edge of the Holocaust. The Shoah in Latin American literature and Culture* (Waltham, MA: Brandeis University Press, 2016), p. x.

the 'Shoah has a unique echo in Argentina, Chile, Uruguay, and other countries of the South' after the establishment of right-wing military dictatorships in the 1970s.[18] Whilst scholars in Latin American memory studies have shown how the region's own turn to memory in the 1980s was conceptually influenced by Holocaust paradigms and trauma theory – which played a key role in emerging memory debates as post-dictatorial societies struggled to come to terms with the past[19] – this scholarship has largely focused on the Southern Cone dictatorships to the exclusion of other memory models in the continent that do not fit the post-dictatorial model.[20] Thus, the 'echo' of the Shoah in Colombia has received even less attention, notwithstanding extensive evidence of Holocaust discourses and memory paradigms in the country. These range from the use of Holocaust rhetoric to speak about specific acts of political violence in Colombia – for example the use of the term 'holocaust' to refer to the 1985 siege of the Palace of Justice,[21] and naming the assassination of more than 3,000 members of the left-wing Patriotic Union party a 'political genocide'[22] – to the emergence of Nazism and the Second World War as a key theme in recent literary works about the country's past.

While an in-depth analysis of how Holocaust memory dialogues with the Colombian conflict is beyond the scope of this essay, it is clear that Holocaust rhetoric has been articulated in Colombia as part of attempts to confront the country's history of violence. Home to the longest war in the Western hemisphere, since the mid-twentieth century Colombia has suffered the brutal effects of a complex armed conflict between the Colombian government, guerrilla forces, right-wing paramilitary groups and drug traffickers, which has left more than 220,000 people dead,[23] almost 8 million displaced,[24] and more than 60,000 dis-

---

18 Aizenberg, *On the Edge of the Holocaust*, p. 161.

19 Michael Lazzara, 'The Memory Turn', in *New Approaches to Latin American Studies. Culture and Power*, ed. by Juan Poblete (New York: Routledge, 2018), pp. 14–31.

20 Colombia, unlike its Latin American neighbours, did not have a right-wing military dictatorship in the late twentieth century and memory debates emerged later, in the 2000s, and *prior* to the end of the conflict.

21 Sigifredo Leal-Guerrero, '"The Holocaust" or "The Salvation of Democracy". Memory and Political Struggle in the Aftermath of Colombia's Palace of Justice Massacre', *Latin American Perspectives*, 42.3 (2015), 140–61 (pp. 148–49).

22 Andrei Gómez-Suárez, 'Perpetrator blocs, genocidal mentalities and geographies. The destruction of the *Union Patriótica* in Colombia and its lessons for genocide studies', *Journal of Genocide Research*, 9.4 (2007), 637–60.

23 National Centre for Historical Memory, http://www.centrodememoriahistorica.gov.co/en/noticias/noticias-cmh/262-197-muertos-dejo-el-conflicto-armado

24 United Nations High Commissioner for Refugees, https://www.unhcr.org/uk/colombia.html

appeared.[25] In this context, Marta Cabrera points out, violence has become a central theme across literature and the visual arts,[26] as artists have sought ways to represent trauma, bear witness to grief and critically explore the role of art during times of war. In seeking aesthetic languages for this task, certain Colombian artists have looked to the post-Holocaust aesthetic tradition; specifically, they have looked to one artist in particular, Celan, who provided a model of how art could respond to violence. As Julie Rodrigues Widholm emphasises, Celan's poetic exploration of displacement, silence and the possibility of representing absence takes on a particular significance in relation to the specific modes of violence in Latin America:

> Notions of presence and absence on a global scale take on highly charged political meanings when considered in the context of Colombia and other regions of South America, where the violent and widespread phenomenon of 'the disappeared' (*desaparecidos*) has created a culture characterized by profound loss.[27]

However, although Celan's presence in Latin America has been noted in relation to individual artists exploring how to represent traumatic loss – specifically Salcedo's celebrated sculptures and Jewish-Argentinean writer Juan Gelman, whose poetry echoes Celan's creation of neologisms, use of wordplay and fragmented syntax to speak to the disappearance of the poet's son and daughter-in-law at the hands of the 1976–1983 Argentinean military dictatorship – a comprehensive analysis of Celan's significance in Latin America and other non-European contexts has yet to be undertaken.

This is the result of the critical framing of Celan, within which his work has largely been read within the context of a 'nearly nationalistic "Germanistik" tradition'.[28] This has limited analysis of the poet's influence even in his adopted country, France,[29] or on English and American poetry. Moreover, the common ci-

---

25 National Centre for Historical Memory, http://www.centrodememoriahistorica.gov.co/micrositios/hasta-encontrarlos/

26 Marta Cabrera, 'Representing Violence in Colombia. Visual Arts, Memory and Counter-Memory', *Brújula*, 6.1 (2007), 37–56 (p. 45).

27 Julie Rodrigues Widholm, 'Presenting Absence. The Work of Doris Salcedo', Museum of Contemporary Art, Chicago, IL (https://www3.mcachicago.org/2015/salcedo/texts/presenting-absence/index.html)

28 *Paul Celan. Selections*, pp. 14–15.

29 An exception to this is Benjamin Hollander, *Translating Tradition. Paul Celan in France* (San Francisco: Acts, a Journal of New Writing, 1988) and Dirk Weissman's doctoral thesis: *Poésie, judaïsme, philosophie. Une histoire de la réception de Paul Celan en France, des débuts jusqu'à 1991* (Université de la Sorbonne-Nouvelle, Paris, France, 2003).

tation of Celan within the 'trauma canon consisting of non-linear, modernist texts by mostly Western writers',[30] and the recent arguments against the appropriateness of these aesthetic paradigms in the context of other, non-Western political traumas, has inevitably restricted a broader, global study of Celan's influence. This positioning of Celan, however, is strange, for, as John Felstiner states, there are many claims for Celan's identity, all of which point to a 'complex, migrant fate'.[31] Indeed, Celan's biography – as a Romanian-born German-speaking Jew victimized and exiled by the Nazi genocide – complicates the simplistic reading of the writer as representing a predominant European cultural tradition. As Rothberg's multidirectional framework allows us to recognize, 'the experience of Jewish difference within modern Europe – and the frequently violent reaction Jews confronted – foreshadows many of the debates and problems faced by postcolonial societies and by postcolonial migrants in contemporary Europe'.[32] Thus, Celan's own direct experience of marginalization and oppression could be viewed comparably with the subaltern experience of racial segregation, exile and displacement typical of the postcolonial. This is clearly how Celan is viewed by Salcedo. For the Colombian artist, Celan's poetry doesn't just represent an artistic response to the horrors of the Holocaust but a broader exploration of dispossession, racist exclusion and oppression. This was represented in Salcedo's installation of a massive fissure in the floor of the Tate Modern in 2007, its title taken from Celan's poem 'Shibboleth', which itself draws upon the Hebrew word that 'has been used as a measure of belonging or exclusion in different societies'.[33] For Salcedo, 'the crack represents a history of racism, running parallel to the history of modernity'[34] which corresponds to the minoritarian, dialogical tradition of decolonized Holocaust memory identified by Rothberg.[35]

In this way, Celan's exilic status can be seen as clearly speaking to the postcolonial condition and contexts, such as Colombia, characterized by loss and

30 Stef Craps, *Postcolonial Witnessing. Trauma Out of Bounds*, 2nd edn (New York: Palgrave Macmillan, 2015), p. 41.

31 Felstiner, *Poet, Survivor, Jew*, p. xvii.

32 Rothberg, *Multidirectional Memory*, pp. 22–23.

33 Manuel Toledo, 'Doris Salcedo. Canto contra el racismo', *BBC Mundo*, 9 October 2007 (http://news.bbc.co.uk/hi/spanish/misc/newsid_7035000/7035694.stm)

34 Doris Salcedo, 'Shibboleth', *Tate Modern*, 1 October 2007 (https://www.tate.org.uk/art/artists/doris-salcedo-2695/doris-salcedo-shibboleth)

35 See, for example, the inclusion of Celan as one of the thinkers in the Global Social Theory project, which seeks to challenge the Eurocentrism of the theoretical canon and decolonize the curriculum by 'amplifying the voices and perspectives of those from across the globe' (https://globalsocialtheory.org/).

displacement. Moreover, it also enables us to reflect on why the poet's particular aesthetic has influenced artists responding to other political traumas. While I am in agreement with Craps that there are other ways of representing trauma beyond 'experimental, modernist, textual strategies'[36] – and indeed, within Colombia diverse artistic responses to the conflict can be found – I would argue that we must also take care not simply to assume that certain artistic practices associated with literary texts written about the Holocaust, such as fragmented modernist aesthetics, are solely part of a European tradition or are inappropriate responses to trauma outside of Europe. If the transnational turn in modernist studies has challenged the idea that literary modernism is a Western phenomenon that can be limited to an Anglo-European canon,[37] recognizing the 'border-crossing flows'[38] of memorial forms should provide a space to analyse how and why specific discourses associated with the Holocaust also appear in the context of other political traumas. Indeed, as I will show in the case of Carranza and Salcedo, the artists draw on Celan's anti-representational aesthetics as part of their attempts to find a way of artistically responding to the dynamics of the Colombian conflict, which, as Michael Taussig has influentially stated, is marked by a 'war of silencing' that has prevented the construction of a collective memory of the victims in Colombia.[39] Consequently, their inability to represent the violence in Colombia is not a Eurocentric imposition of post-Holocaust aesthetics but an aesthetic reflection of the dispossession, terror and silencing of the population within a war which 'victims do not easily manage to weave into a narrative with a clear meaning'.[40]

Furthermore, Carranza and Salcedo do not just demonstrate the incomprehensibility of trauma or impossibility of witnessing; through their art they seek to make present the dead and disappeared who have been erased from Colombian history. In this manner their work also engages a different reading of Celan, one which reflects the history of the translation of Celan's verse into Spanish. As Mario Martín Gijón and Rosa Benéitiz Andrés highlight, Celan's appear-

36 Stef Craps, 'Beyond Eurocentrism', p. 50.

37 A crucial part of this work, as Patricia Novillo-Corvalán highlights in her study of modernist networks between Latin America and Europe, *Modernism and Latin America. Transnational Networks of Literary Exchange* (New York: Routledge, 2018), has been to identify the transnational circulation of modernist ideas and practices, as well as analysing how modernism responds to questions of empire and projects of decolonization.

38 Michael Rothberg, 'Afterword. Locating Transnational Memory', *European Review*, 22.4 (2014), 652–656 (p. 652).

39 Michael Taussig, *The Nervous System* (New York; London: Routledge, 1992), p. 26.

40 Daniel Pécaut, 'Memoria imposible, historia imposible, olvido imposible', in *Violencia y política en Colombia. Elementos de una reflexión* (Medellín: Hombre Nuevo Editores, 2003), p. 117.

ance in the Spanish-speaking world was posthumous, with the first translations of his poetry published in the 1970s.[41] The most influential of these translations were those by post-Civil War poet José Ángel Valente, whose reading of Celan formed part of a shift in his work away from his early, politically engaged poetry, towards a more hermetic, 'High Modernist' verse rooted in the Spanish Heideggerian tradition with its 'ontological conception of poetry'.[42] This tradition, as I will show, also influenced late-twentieth-century Colombian verse and points towards another way of understanding Celan's global influence. Against the predominant reading of Celan's poetry as solely displaying the ineffability of the Holocaust, scholars have also argued that Celan's anti-representational breakdown of language actually forms part of a search for language's ability to find a source of meaning. This interpretation draws heavily on Celan's famous poetological statement, the *Meridian* speech, where the poem is described as a place of encounter, a conversation with another: 'The poem intends another, needs this other, needs an opposite. It goes toward it, bespeaks it'.[43] The encounter with the abstract other – comparable with 'l'Autre' of Levinasian and Sartrean philosophy, or Heidegger's 'das Andere'[44] – situates Celan's poetry within the realm of philosophy, influenced by Heiddegger's ontological conception of poetry not as a mimetic reflection of the world but as a space that will respond to Hölderlin's query surrounding the role of the poet in a destitute time. Yet, if for Heidegger poetic language had a mythologizing function and was the dwelling place of the sacred after the disappearance of the gods,[45] Celan's understanding of language was founded on a dialogical relationship, in line with the philosophy of Martin Buber, where poetry became a 'way to measure the measureless suffering of those who have perished, a way to find a resting place to commemorate the

---

41 *Lecturas de Paul Celan*, ed. by Mario Martín Gijón and Rosa Benéitiz Andrés (Madrid: Abada Editores, 2017), p. 1.

42 Mayhew, *The Twilight of the Avant-garde*, p. 87.

43 Paul Celan, 'The Meridian', in *Paul Celan, Collected Prose*, trans. by Rosemarie Waldrop (New York: Routledge, 2003), p. 49.

44 Joanna Klink, 'You. An Introduction to Paul Celan', *The Iowa Review*, 30.1 (2000), 1–18 (p. 9).

45 In the critical literature the influence of Heidegger's philosophy on Celan's poetry has been well established, even if, as Bambach states, 'Celan had a deeply ambivalent relationship to Heidegger' (p. 187): 'if Celan could find deep affinities with Heidegger's critique of the metaphysics of presence and with his emphasis on the need for a philosophical-poetic dialogue on the thematics of loss and abyssal absence, then he could not follow the lines of Heidegger's exclusionary Graeco-German axis of affinity or his inability/unwillingness to enter into dialogue about the fate of European Jewry' (p. 189).

scattered ashes of the dead'.[46] In reaching out to the absent dead, the wholly other, Celan's poetry can be read as part of a counter project which, in the face of Auschwitz, seeks to countervail 'through poetry the very possibility of catastrophe'.[47] I argue that it is this visionary, ontological aspect of Celan's legacy which we can also find in evidence in the work of Colombian artists such as Carranza and Salcedo.

What are poets for? Celan and María Mercedes Carranza

In 1989, the Colombian poet, public intellectual and peace activist María Mercedes Carranza addressed the crowd at a poetry recital in the city of Medellín. Speaking during one of the most violent periods of the conflict, Carranza denounced the social, political and moral crisis which was ravaging the country. As she stated, 'extreme left- and right-wing assassins who have unleashed a war to defend their interests' exist alongside 'the drug-trafficking mafia who want to impose their own laws' and a state that has failed to address the tremendous social inequalities and injustices that are the root causes of the conflict. Asking what role poetry played in the context of this crisis – 'What is the role of poetry in the time of the assassins?' – Carranza responded by making the case for poetry as a communicative, humanistic practice in a nation saturated by conflict. For Carranza poetry was a weapon 'against destruction, against chaos, against horror', which 'provides clarity', 'is feeling' and allows us 'to communicate and dialogue with ourselves and others'. Most importantly, the poetic word 'is a social product, which, on being said, reveals reality in its most essential characteristics'.[48]

In arguing for poetry's essential role in a country ravaged by conflict, Carranza was drawing upon an important poetic tradition. Although largely considered a feminist poet by critics, who have characterized her poetry as provocative and iconoclastic, using a colloquial language drawing upon popular culture, Carranza's defence of poetry in the series of poetic campaigns and editorial pieces

---

46 Charles Bambach, *Thinking the Poetic Measure of Justice. Hölderlin, Heidegger, Celan* (Albany: State University of New York Press, 2013), p. 229.

47 Michael Eskin, *Poetic Affairs. Celan, Grünbein, Brodsky* (Stanford, CA.: Stanford University Press, 2008), p. 25.

48 María Mercedes Carranza, 'La poesía en la hora de los asesinos', *Revista Casa Silva*, 3 (1989), 6–9 (p. 6).

she published from the late 1980s, actually suggests a position close to the High Modernist tradition of poetry, as articulated in post-vanguard Latin American poetry and its 'search for humanist values in a world where they seem to have disintegrated'.[49] Moreover, in querying poetry's role in the time of the assassins, Carranza was also articulating a way of conceptualizing poetry in philosophical terms, which not only dialogued with modernist poetics but with a tradition of thinking about poetry that derives from the German literary-philosophical tradition. Explicitly paraphrasing Heidegger's exploration of Hölderlin's famed question, 'Wozu Dichter in dürftiger Zeit?', Carranza's Medellín speech is evidently influenced by a Heideggerian understanding of poetic language.[50] As Heidegger argued, poetry could become the dwelling place of the sacred in a destitute time, registering the trace of the fugitive gods; Carranza echoed this in her understanding of poetry in Colombia as revealing the truth of the world in the midst of degradation: 'it goes beyond, it doesn't remain in the superficial part of reality, but goes to its essence'.[51]

The influence of the Heideggerian tradition on Carranza's reflections on the role of poetry during the Colombia conflict provides an important link to her most well-known collection of poems, *El canto de las moscas* [*The Song of the Flies*] (1998). Written in the midst of Carranza's poetic campaigns and during the worsening of the conflict during the 1990s, this short volume was the

---

49 Donald Shaw, *Spanish American Poetry after 1950. Beyond the Vanguard* (Woodbridge: Tamesis, 2008), p. 11.

50 From the 1960s German emigres and Colombian intellectuals had promoted greater dialogue between Colombian culture and German philosophy in Colombia, particularly through the influential magazine *Eco. Revista de la cultura de Occidente* [*Echo. Magazine of Western Culture*], which published key German thinkers in translation, such as Benjamin, Adorno, Marcuse, Horkheimer, Arendt, as well as Celan (Claudia Supelano-Gross, 'El contrapeso de la barbarie. Benjamin en Colombia', *Constelaciones. Revista de Teoría Crítica* 2 (2010), 318–41, p. 320). Those who collaborated with the magazine included a new generation of Colombian philosophers, such as Danilo Cruz Vélez and Rafael Gutiérrez Girardot, both of whom had studied under Heidegger in Germany in the 1950s and played a key role in introducing phenomenology and Heideggerian thought in Colombia. Carranza would have been familiar with these intellectuals. Her father, the poet and diplomat Eduardo Carranza, moved in the same intellectual circles as Danilo Cruz Vélez; in her own literary criticism Carranza cited the work of Gutiérrez, who was also an important reader of Celan in the Colombian context, first encountering his work in Germany in the late 1960s and later publishing a number of articles on the poet in the late 1980s (Claudia Supelano-Gross, 'La significación de la poesía. Paul Celan en la obra de Rafael Gutiérrez Girardot' in *Lecturas de Paul Celan*, ed. by Mario Martín Gijón and Rosa Benéitiz Andrés (Madrid: Abada Editores, 2017), pp. 213–26, pp. 204–5).

51 María Mercedes Carranza, 'Por qué la poesía hoy y aquí?', *Lecturas dominicales*, 29 (November 1987), 10–11.

poet's last collection before her death by suicide in 2003. Celebrated as one of the most powerful artistic representations of Colombia's late-twentieth-century violence, *El canto* represented a shift in the style and content of Carranza's verse, being dedicated entirely to 'the evocation of the violence in Colombia'.[52] Consisting of twenty-four short haiku-like *cantos*, each poem is named after a rural town in Colombia where massacres and gross human rights abuses took place in the 1980s and 1990s. For example, the second poem of the collection, 'Mapiripán', draws its title from the town where a horrific massacre of an unknown number of civilians by paramilitary forces was perpetrated in 1997:

Still the wind,
time.
Mapiripán is now
a date.[53]

The historical specificity of the poems and their concentration on the violence has led the few critics who have analysed the collection to define it as a work of political testimony or social protest.[54] Yet, as 'Mapiripán' demonstrates, the aesthetic and formal features of the poems – marked by a sparse, minimalist, austere language – actually suggest a different mode of poetic witnessing which shares affinities with the post-Holocaust anti-representation tradition. With an intense concentration on time, stillness and silence, the four-line poem is unable to describe or represent the horrific event; instead, the poem itself is constructed around the ineffability of the violence, which becomes an irrevocable date in the catastrophe of history.

The rest of the poems, like 'Mapiripán', are similarly characterized by their brevity and silence in the face of horror. Unable to represent the violence evoked in the toponyms of the poems' titles, instead the collection is dominated by images of the natural world, albeit one marked by absence and destruction. In

52 Antoine Ventura, 'La poesía colombiana escrita por mujeres y lo real. Realidad social, lirismo amoroso y estereotipos de género', in *Palabras de mujeres. Proyectos de vida y memoria colectiva*, ed. by Marie Estripeaut-Bourjac (Bogotá: Siglo del Hombre Editores: Friedrich Ebert Stiftung, 2012), pp. 121–45 (p. 127).

53 María Mercedes Carranza, *Poesía completa y cinco poemas inéditos*, ed. by Melibea Garavito Carranza (Bogotá: Ministerio de Cultura; Alfaguara; Casa de Poesía Silva, 2004), p. 186. All translations from Spanish are my own.

54 See for example: Sofia Kearns, 'Political and Toxic Discourse in María Mercedes Carranza's Latest Poems', *Ciberletras. Revista de crítica literaria y de cultura*, 5 (2001), http://www.lehman.-cuny.edu/ciberletras/v05/kearns.html; Enrique Yepes, 'Regiones en vías de extinción. *El canto de las moscas* de María Mercedes Carranza', *Lingüística y Literatura*, 0.61 (2012), 107–27.

'Confines', for example, the desolate imagery of the poem simply represents nothing: 'Rain and silence | is the world in | Confines';[55] in 'Vista Hermosa', the name of the town, which literally means 'Beautiful View', is ironically refigured in the poem's sole image, of a 'spectral, | burnt, stiff, | solitary' plant stalk.[56] It is clear that in deploying such aesthetic features Carranza is not just drawing upon the fragmented aesthetics of post-Holocaust poetry but more particularly on its key exemplar, Celan.[57] In negating any direct representation of scenes of traumatic loss, in transforming catastrophe into fragmented silences and images of destruction, *El canto* echoes the 'negative poetics of silence and absence at the heart of Celan's poetry'.[58] Paralleling Celan's 'very short poems, where terms, phrases seem, by the rhythm of their brevity, undefined, surrounded by blankness',[59] the collection deploys a very Celanian language, allusive and elliptical, which appears to reinforce Adorno's conclusions that the most extreme horror is only expressed by remaining silent. Thus, in death-infused 'Sotavento': 'Like the clouds | death | in Sotavento today. | Deceased whiteness'.[60]

This is not to say that Carranza's deployment of Celanian aesthetics represents the imposition of Holocaust paradigms in Colombia. Elsewhere I have argued that in fact the aesthetics of the collection reflects the 'amnesia surrounding violence and its causes in Colombia'.[61] Indeed, the collection's subtitle, 'version of the events', engages with political scientist Daniel Pécaut's description of the modes of Colombian violence:

> the terror that a great proportion of the population live through, the law of silence that is imposed on them when they find themselves caught in the crossfire, the forced displacement that affects them, the absence of a front in the war, represent extreme but dispersed experiences that engender a memory based on events, that victims do not easily manage to weave into a narrative with clear meaning.[62]

---

55 Carranza, *Poesía completa*, p. 198.
56 Carranza, *Poesía completa*, p. 195.
57 Although Carranza never cited Celan directly in her work, it is not beyond reasonable assumption that she was familiar with Celan's legacy thanks to her association with the movement to promote German post-war philosophy and critical theory in Colombia. Spanish translations of Celan's poetry, including those by Valente, form part of the library of the Silva House of Poetry, the cultural centre founded by Carranza in 1986.
58 William Franke, 'Poetics of Silence in the Post-Holocaust Poetry of Paul Celan', *Journal of Literature and Trauma Studies*, 2.1–2 (2014), 137–58 (p. 137).
59 Maurice Blanchot cited in Franke, 'Poetics of Silence', p. 138.
60 Carranza, *Poesía completa*, p. 203.
61 Cherilyn Elston, *Women's Writing in Colombia – An Alternative History* (New York: Palgrave Macmillan, 2016), p. 135.
62 Pécaut, 'Memoria imposible', p. 117.

However, alongside this deconstructive reading of Carranza's use of language in *El canto*, we can also find another reading of the collection which also demonstrates traces of Celan's influence. As we have seen, at the same time in which she was writing these poems Carranza was also espousing a Heideggerian vision of poetic language that advocated poetry's ability to access truth in a destitute time, as well as arguing for its significance as a dialogical act: 'poetry is above all the desire for dialogue, for communication'.[63] It is here, I argue, that an interesting dialogue between Celan's and Carranza's poetic philosophies emerges. In his *Meridian* speech, Celan also articulated the importance of poetry as a part of a dialogue or encounter. Yet, as scholars have shown, Celan's difficult, hermetic verse, with its rejection of instrumental language, was not aiming at some facile notion of communication. Although drawing upon Heidegger's ontological conception of poetic language, which rejects mimesis in seeking to enable 'the unmanifest symbolic world to break into view',[64] unlike Heidegger Celan's aim was not to access the 'house of Being' but to forge an encounter with the 'effaced Other of the Holocaust'.[65] Bambach similarly states that Celan engaged the work of Heidegger to help him think through 'the uncanny relation of language to the topoi of terror'.[66] Thus, in pushing language to its uncanny limits, Celan sought to enact a form of poetic language that could lead to an impossible encounter with the 'immaterial, yet earthly, terrestrial' traces of the absent dead who populate his poetry:

> the poet seeks in the shadow of the unspeakable to somehow recover what can never be recovered. Within this impossible landscape, this 'topology of the abyss,' as Jean Bollock calls it, Celan dares to suggest that in spite of everything the poem 'remain mindful of its dates'.[67]

It is this Celanian impossible landscape, I argue, that Carranza also seeks to enact in *El canto*. Indeed, the landscape depicted in the collection is not simply defined by absence. As Michael Sisson states, it is 'a deserted landscape, or better said a populated one, but with the dead'.[68] As Celan creates a poetic land-

63 María Mercedes Carranza, '¿A quién le interesa la poesía?', *Revista Casa Silva*, 4 (1990), 6–8 (p. 8).
64 Klink, 'You', p. 9.
65 Eric Kligerman, *Sites of the Uncanny. Paul Celan, Specularity and the Visual Arts* (Berlin and New York: Walter de Gruyter, 2007), p. 26.
66 Bambach, *Thinking the Poetic Measure of Justice*, p. 188.
67 Ibid., p. 194.
68 Michael Sisson, 'María Mercedes Carranza en inglés. Perspectivas de un traductor', *Forma y Función*, 20 (2007), 253–62 (p. 255).

scape characterized by images from the natural world, but within which the uncanny surfaces and the traces of the effaced dead emerge, Carranza guides the reader through an *unheimlich* landscape, occupied by the presence of what is no longer there. In 'Tierralta' the poem is constructed around the image of those who once populated the town – 'This is the mouth that was' – but who now lie buried beneath the ground, 'Now only earth: earth | in the still mouth'.[69] The image of the still mouths of the dead call to mind the repetition in Celan's verse of mouths that cannot speak – 'mouthsfull of silence'.[70] This image is repeated in 'Paujil' where 'the mouths | of the dead' uncannily appear in the flowers that bloom after the violence – recalling Celan's own 'Flower – a blind man's word'[71] – and are paralleled in 'Encimadas' where the 'flowering eyes' are hauntingly conflated with the bodies 'Under the ground' where 'the terror still shines'.[72]

Moreover, drawing upon a Heideggerian language of dwelling and topology, Celan's emphasis on poetry as topos research in his *Meridian* speech and his suggestion that 'every poem is marked by its own "20th of January"'[73] is recalled in *El canto*'s own emphasis on specific place names and dates. Scholars have read the toponyms in the collection as simply reflecting the poet's engagement with history.[74] However, Carranza's mindfulness of the date of Mapiripán, her naming of places that evoke a topography of terror in Colombia, suggests a Celanian positioning 'toward the historical date of the Other's effacement'[75] and an attempt to draw her own meridians to the lost places and the forgotten dead of the conflict. In Celan's verse this topography, as Bambach states, is particularly evoked in his references to moorland and the 'thematic complex of moors', which come to symbolize not only his own youth in Czernowitz but 'the traces of the Jewish dead whose names echo at the margins of these moors'.[76] This is also echoed in the topography of the moorland in *El canto*, which appears in its particularly Colombian formation, the *páramo*. Thus, the 'Moorland desolation'[77] which Carranza depicts in the collection represents not an empty landscape post-catastro-

69 Carranza, *Poesía completa*, p. 191.
70 Paul Celan, 'Language Mesh', in *Paul Celan. Selected Poems*, trans. by Michael Hamburger and Christopher Middleton (Middlesex: Penguin, 1972), p. 50.
71 Paul Celan, 'Flower', in *Paul Celan. Selected Poems*, p. 49.
72 Carranza, *Poesía completa*, p. 189.
73 Paul Celan, 'The Meridian', p. 47.
74 Sisson, 'María Mercedes Carranza en inglés', p. 53; Yepes, 'Regiones en vías de extinción', p.114.
75 Kligerman, *Sites of the Uncanny*, p. 28.
76 Bambach, *Thinking the Poetic Measure of Justice*, p. 227.
77 Carranza, *Poesía completa*, p. 198.

phe but also a symbolic reminder of the dead hidden beneath the ground, many of whom in Colombia, like the millions of murdered Jews, lie in unmarked mass graves.

What are poets for in a destitute time? Carranza responds, echoing Celan by creating a 'topography of landscape as a way of coming to terms with an ethics of remembering the dead'.[78] In turning towards the effaced Other, Carranza creates a poetic space that also becomes a symbolic crypt for the unburied dead of the conflict and imagines their presence in an attempt to countervail the official oblivion surrounding the violence in Colombia. Thus, as the Holocaust dead manifest their impossible presence in Celan's verse – 'A strange lostness was | palpably present, almost | you would | have lived'[79] – in *El canto*, years later and at a different point in the meridional line, 'someone | dreams that they lived'.[80]

Palpable presences: Celan and Doris Salcedo

In 1998, the same year that Carranza published *El canto*, Colombian artist Doris Salcedo exhibited her sculpture series *Unland*. Consisting of three conjoined tables of differing sizes, their surfaces painstakingly drilled with tiny holes through which hair had been threaded, the sculptures deployed an aesthetic language of minimalism and conceptualism typical of Salcedo's work.[81] Since first becoming internationally recognized in the 1990s, Salcedo – now Colombia's most celebrated contemporary artist – has become known for her creation of abstract sculptures, such as *Unland*, characterized by their materiality – represented in the use of found objects, furniture and clothing, which are embedded with organic materials such as human hair, bone and grass. Yet, like Carranza's final collection, Salcedo's abstract sculptures are also intimately related to Colombia's traumatic history. Behind each installation lies a detailed investigation into an aspect of the conflict, often involving interviews with victims or the direct collaboration of victims' groups in the process of artistic production. For example, the first of the *Unland* sculptures, subtitled 'the orphan's tunic', was inspired by the story of a six-year-old orphan whom Salcedo met in northern Colombia who, after witnessing her mother's death, refused to wear anything but the dress her mother had made for her.

---

78 Bambach, *Thinking the Poetic Measure of Justice*, p. 219.
79 Paul Celan, 'Dumb Autumn Smells', in *Paul Celan. Selected Poems*, p. 69.
80 Carranza, *Poesía completa*, p. 187.
81 Cabrera, 'Representing Violence in Colombia', p. 50.

However, in line with her minimalistic aesthetic practice, Salcedo does not translate the testimonies that inspire her sculptures into direct representations of the violence. 'Unland: the orphan's tunic', for example, consists of two conjoined tables, one of dark wood and the other covered in white silk; where they join a thick strand of human hair is woven into the tables' surface. As Andreas Huyssen says, in the girl's testimony 'the dress is a marker of memory and a sign of trauma',[82] which Salcedo metaphorically evokes through the silk covering the table:

> approximating it, never quite getting it, compelling the viewer to innervate something that remains elusive, absent – the violent death of the mother that left the child orphaned, the orphan present only in the residual tunic, which now seems more of a shroud covering part of the table.[83]

As the table metaphorically approximates testimony but is unable to represent directly the violence evoked, Salcedo's art suggests a mode of witnessing that dialogues very clearly with the ineffability of post-Holocaust aesthetics. Mieke Bal notes, analysing another of Salcedo's sculptures, *Atrabilarios* (1991), where the theme of female disappearance in Colombia is explored through the metonym of worn shoes placed in niches, that Salcedo's artistic response to the Colombian violence openly places itself in the lineage of Adorno's discussions of post-Holocaust art and thereby evokes one artist in particular, Celan.[84] Indeed, the 'orphan's tunic' in the subtitle of the first *Unland* sculpture is a direct citation of an untitled poem by Celan from *Lichtzwang* [*Lightduress*] (1970) in which the state of orphanhood – a key theme in Celan's work, where many his poems evoke his mother's killing – is symbolized by a tunic, which is also the orphan's flag, as well as 'his | first | birth-marked, se- | cret-speckled | skin'.[85] As Edlie L. Wong notes, the skin enveloping the orphan in Celan's poem is hauntingly cited in the dress that covers the orphan's body in Colombia, later becoming the skin-like membranes shrouding Salcedo's tables.[86]

82 Andreas Huyssen, 'Unland: the orphan's tunic', in *Doris Salcedo*, ed. by Nancy Princenthal, Carlos Basualdo and Andreas Huyssen (London: Phaidon, 2000), pp. 92–102 (p. 96).

83 Huyssen, 'Unland: the orphan's tunic', p. 101.

84 Mieke Bal, *Of What One Cannot Speak. Doris Salcedo's Political Art* (Chicago: The University of Chicago Press, 2010), p. 17.

85 Paul Celan, 'Night Rode Him', in *Paul Celan. Selected Poems*, p. 98.

86 Edlie L. Wong, 'Haunting Absences. Witnessing Loss in Doris Salcedo's Atrabilarios and Beyond', in *The Image and the Witness. Trauma, Memory and Visual Culture*, ed. by Frances Guerin and Roger Hallas (London: Wallflower Press, 2007), pp. 173–87 (p. 178).

The 'orphan's tunic' is not the only reference to Celan in Salcedo's corpus. Indeed, critics have spoken about an 'ongoing dialogue' between the Colombian artist and the Holocaust poet[87] who is repeatedly cited by Salcedo and referenced across the critical studies produced about the artist.[88] While the links between Carranza and Celan can be read, as we have seen, within the context of the Heideggerian philosophical-poetic tradition in Colombia, Salcedo's dialogue with Celan reflects a closer engagement with post-war European philosophy and the influence of thinkers such as Emmanuel Levinas, Primo Levi and Celan on her approach to trauma and memory.[89] It also demonstrates, in dialogue with scholars such as Eric Kligerman, who have explored the 'ripple effects' of Celan's poetics on 'visual artists who probe the Holocaust',[90] the impact of Celan beyond poetry and on the field of visual culture. Noting Celan's influence on the Colombian artist, scholars have read Salcedo's sculptures in line with Celan's negative poetics, defined by mourning, absence and the impossibility of witnessing. As Carlos Basualdo comments in an interview with the artist, her practice parallels Celan's translation of 'the experience of absence, the horror of the Holocaust precisely through the disintegration of language and its structures'.[91] The title of *Unland*, for example, is a Celan-inspired neologism coined by Salcedo to refer to the loss inherent in the dispossession of war; it replicates Celan's tendency to coin new words and his negation through wordplay, as he pushed against the limits of language. Salcedo herself also directly links her anti-monumental, material images – such as *Unland*'s conjoined tables – to Celan's fragmented, ruptured language, pregnant with silences: 'Celan's poetry involves piecing together from ruptures and dissociations, rather than association and union. This is the way I approach sculpture. I concern myself with the disassembled and diachronic'.[92]

Salcedo's anti-representational aesthetics is moreover reinforced by the second citation of Celan in *Unland*'s subtitles, 'audible in the mouth', which dialogues more explicitly with the ideas of silence and bearing witness associated

---

87 Ángela María Lopera Molano, 'El diálogo que se encamina. La traducción entre Paul Celan y Doris Salcedo', *Hallazgos*, 12.24 (2015), 31–48.

88 In the 2000 survey of Salcedo's work, for example, various poems by Celan are featured as part of the 'Artist's Choice', alongside an extended extract from the Meridian speech.

89 Cabrera, 'Representing Violence in Colombia', p. 50.

90 Kligerman, *Sites of the Uncanny*, p. 5.

91 Charles Basualdo, 'Interview. Carlos Basualdo in conversation with Doris Salcedo', in *Doris Salcedo*, ed. by Nancy Princenthal, Carlos Basualdo and Andreas Huyssen (London: Phaidon, 2000), pp. 8–35 (p. 25).

92 Basualdo, 'Interview', p. 26.

with Celan's work. This quotation refers to an earlier Celan poem, entitled 'An Eye, Open', from *Sprachgitter* [*Speech-Grille*] (1959). As Tanya Barson explains, this, like much of Celan's poetry, is about the act of bearing witness to suffering and the impossibility of articulating this through language.[93] Faced with the inability to describe or even speak of the 'no more to be named', referring to the dead, the poem describes in minute detail the physical movements of the eye:[94]

> Aching depth of the eyeball:
> the lid
> does not stand in its way, the lash
> does not count what goes in.[95]

As Celan's verse is unable to express in language the horrors witnessed – in the poem the images of suffering remain 'audible in the mouth' – Salcedo's sculptures, which never literally reveal the testimonies behind them, are likewise read as aesthetic statements on the failure of testimony: the silence of the victim and the fact that trauma cannot be transformed into narrative. While Salcedo refers to herself as a secondary witness, 'I try to be a witness of the witness',[96] her work is seen as materially embodying the Celanian axiom that 'No one | bears witness for the | witness',[97] for the true witness will either not have survived or will be unable to utter the unspeakable horror. Salcedo has therefore described her art as 'a hopeless act of mourning',[98] representing art's inability to recuperate the lost lives it evokes: 'Art is unable to redeem. In the face of death, art is impotent'.[99]

Yet, similar to *El canto*, Salcedo's deployment of post-Holocaust aesthetics does not mean she imposes Holocaust paradigms on the memory of a very different conflict. Various critics have drawn a connection between Salcedo's aesthetics of absence and silence, and the nature of the Colombian armed conflict. Both Bal and Wong cite the work of anthropologist Michael Taussig, who, like Pécaut, has written about the 'war of silencing' and the 'creation of terror through uncer-

---

93 Tanya Barson, 'Unland. The Place of Testimony', *Tate Papers*, 1 (Spring 2004) (https://www.tate.org.uk/research/publications/tate-papers/01/unland-the-place-of-testimony)
94 Ibid.
95 Paul Celan, 'An Eye, Open', in *Paul Celan. Selected Poems*, p. 56.
96 Doris Salcedo, 'Interview with Charles Mereweather' in *Doris Salcedo*, ed. by Nancy Princenthal, Carlos Basualdo and Andreas Huyssen (London: Phaidon, 2000), pp. 134–45 (p. 140).
97 Paul Celan, 'Ashglory', in *Breathturn into Timestead. The Collected Later Poetry*, trans. by Pierre Joris (New York: Farrar, Straus and Giroux, 2014), p. 62.
98 Basualdo, 'Interview', p. 21.
99 Manuel Toledo, 'Doris Salcedo. Canto contra el racismo'.

tain violence' in Colombia: 'There is no officially declared war. No prisoners. No torture. No disappearing. Just silence consuming terror's talk for the main part';[100] Salcedo herself has spoken of the 'precariousness of thought: an inability to articulate history and therefore form a community' in the midst of conflict.[101] Relatedly, in her influential study, Bal argues that Salcedo's anti-representational aesthetics, while not obviously political, actually creates a space in which the political can be enabled. Drawing upon political theorist Chantal Mouffe's distinction between politics and 'the political', Bal states that in the Colombian context, where 'antagonism is violently silenced',[102] alternative practices are required to open up the spaces of 'the political' and the social life it makes possible. Like Celan, who constructed an alternative aesthetic language in the aftermath of trauma, for Bal Salcedo creates a new aesthetics in the face of Wittgenstein's conclusion that the 'unspeakable must be kept silent'.[103] It is here, Bal states, drawing on Celan, that the political potential of Salcedo's work and a definition of political art can be found: 'To make audible in the mouth whereof one cannot speak: this is as good a description as any for political art today'.[104] Importantly then, Salcedo's anti-representational sculptures do not just enact the psychic experience of trauma; rather, as Wong argues, they seek to transform 'the alienation of a state-imposed silence' into a silence that 'becomes a site of shared collective engagement that preserves the painful inarticulateness of loss'.[105]

This can be clearly seen in the series of large-scale installations that Salcedo has created in recent years – ranging from *Noviembre 6 y 7* (2002), where she lowered chairs down the walls of the Palace of Justice to commemorate those killed in the siege, to *Sumando Ausencias* (2016), where Bogotá's central square was covered in a white shroud stitched with the names of victims in ash. Despite Salcedo's negative conclusions on the role of art in the face of suffering and trauma, these large-scale acts of mourning point to how her artistic practice does not simply imply testimonial failure and traumatic incomprehensibility. Although it is clear that Salcedo's aesthetics reinforce the post-Holocaust limits to representing trauma, this clearly forms part of an attempt to find an aesthetic language appropriate for registering the absence of the disappeared and forgotten dead of the Colombian conflict. As Salcedo herself states: 'When a beloved per-

100 Taussig, *The Nervous System*, p. 26.
101 Basualdo, 'Interview', p. 25.
102 Bal, *Of What One Cannot Speak*, p. 12.
103 Ibid., p. 14.
104 Ibid., p. 28.
105 Wong, 'Haunting Absences', p. 179.

son disappears, everything becomes impregnated with that person's presence. Every single object but also every space is a reminder of his or her absence, as if absence were stronger than presence'.[106] Paralleling, the 'strange lostness [that] was | palpably present' in Celan's verse,[107] Salcedo's deployment of mundane domestic objects in her sculptures, alongside the shoes, clothes and hair of the missing – which are juxtaposed in a very Celanian, *unheimlich* way – powerfully evoke how the material objects left behind after displacement, war and disappearance are incessant, haunting reminders of the absent person. In this way, Salcedo's artworks seek to 'counter acts of disappearance with acts of reappearance',[108] bringing to presence the invisible victims of Colombia's conflict.

Significantly, this practice also suggests another reading of Salcedo's engagement with Celan which is highlighted by the inclusion of the *Meridian* speech as part of Salcedo's 'Artist's Choice'. In Salcedo's own reflections on her artistic practice she echoes Celan's description of poetic language in the *Meridian* speech as an encounter, a 'desperate dialogue', which hopes to speak '*on behalf of the other* [...] perhaps of an *altogether other*'.[109] As Salcedo states, dialogue is crucial to the process of creating the sculpture – 'it is what allows me to know the experience of the Other, to the point at which an encounter with otherness in the field of sculpture is possible'.[110] This process allows not only for 'a form of communion' between the artist and the Other who makes herself or himself present in Salcedo's work,[111] but seeks affectively to bring to presence the trauma, pain and loss of the absent victim for the spectator viewing the artwork. Thus, the traumatized speech that, as Celan expresses, is 'audible in the mouth' of the victim is transformed into the silence of the artist and the viewer who come together in a moment of silent contemplation 'that permits the life seen in the work to reappear'.[112]

---

106 Basualdo, 'Interview', p. 16.
107 Huyssen also draws an explicit connection between Celan's poem 'Dumb Autumn Smells' and Salcedo's work in his analysis of 'Unland: the orphan's tunic'.
108 Rodrigues Widholm, 'Presenting Absence'.
109 Paul Celan, 'The Meridian', p. 48.
110 Basualdo, 'Interview', p. 13.
111 Ibid., p. 17.
112 Salcedo, 'Interview with Charles Mereweather', p. 137.

Eric Kligerman

Between Poetry and Prayer. A *Kaddish* for Paul Celan

When I was first asked to contribute to this Celan anniversary volume I was hesitant. After spending many years immersed in his poetry, I have neither written about Celan nor taught on his work in over a decade. In fact, my research has shifted to Franz Kafka. My return to Celan's poems is reminiscent of Walter Benjamin's description of encountering Kafka's creature Odradek from 'Die Sorge des Hausvaters' ['Cares of the Family Man']. Benjamin describes how the distorted Odradek

> [p]refers the same places as the court of law which investigates *Schuld* [guilt and debt]. Attics are the places of discarded, forgotten objects. Perhaps the necessity to appear before a court of justice gives rise to a feeling similar to that with which one approaches trunks in the attic which have been locked up for years that we would like to put off until the end of time.[1]

Odradek flashes up at different moments in history, compelling us to interrogate the past in relation to the present. In Benjamin's comparison of Odradek to a locked trunk, the past is no longer conceived of as a fixed point in time. Instead, Benjamin perceives history as incomplete; the dead are not actually dead but are suspended in an in-between state, whose completion is contingent on a vigilant tarrying with the unfinished past.

Similarly, my return to Celan's poetry entails this three-fold meaning of *Sorge:* it is marked by care, anxiety and sorrow. How does one begin to read anew, let alone think about the meaning of Celan's poetry after such a long hiatus? At the close of his Odradek analysis Benjamin concludes, 'Even if Kafka did not pray – and this we do not know – he still possessed in the highest degree what Malebranche called "the natural prayer of the soul: attentiveness [Aufmerksamkeit]."'[2] Benjamin's use of 'Aufmerksamkeit' conveys multiple meanings, including being thoughtful, alert and the act of giving a small gift ('kleine Aufmerksamkeit'). The resonance I hear between Celan and Odradek is not coincidental. In his 1960 Georg Büchner Prize speech, *Der Meridian*, Celan used Benjamin's line on Kafka's attentiveness to describe the task of poetry.

1 Walter Benjamin, 'Franz Kafka. On the Tenth Anniversary of his Death', in *Illuminations*, ed. by Hannah Arendt, trans. by Harry Zohn (New York: Schocken Books, 1968), pp. 111–45, p. 133.
2 Benjamin, 'Franz Kafka', p. 134.

https://doi.org/10.1515/9783110658330-015

Characterizing how every poem is inscribed with its own 20 January, Celan depicts how poetry's attentiveness is 'aller unserer Daten eingedenk bleibende Konzentration' [a concentration that stays mindful of all our dates]. Right after using the ominous word 'Konzentration', Celan quotes Benjamin's line on Kafka, 'Aufmerksamkeit ist das natürliche Gebet der Seele' [Attentiveness is the natural prayer of the soul].[3]

In addition to being the fictional date on which Büchner's Lenz gets lost in the mountains, Celan also has in mind the Wannsee Conference of 20 January 1942, when the Nazis implemented the Final Solution. The poem, originating from a date of historical violence, neither transcends time nor faces the divine; instead, it remains part of our terrestrial realm. In turn, Celan insists that the recipient must be attentive to both the poem and its date. If I have learned anything from Celan, it is that our encounter with a text requires our own *Aufmerksamkeit.*

Although Kafka is mentioned only once in the final draft, Celan included multiple references to Kafka and prayer in his *Meridian* notes. In another fragment Celan writes, '"Schreiben als Form des Gebets", lesen wir – ergriffen – bei Kafka. Auch das bedeutet zunächst nicht *Beten*, sondern *Schreiben:* man kann es nicht mit gefalteten Händen tun' ['Writing is a form of prayer', we read – seized by emotion – in Kafka. Though this does not mean prayer in the first instance, but writing: you cannot do it with folded hands].[4] In his explication of the fragment, Celan juxtaposes two sets of hands: just as writing requires attentive hands, so too is the act of reading marked by *Aufmerksamkeit.* Instead of futilely searching for an absent god, the poem seeks a meridian between itself and an attentive reader. Celan demands 'Die Aufmerksamkeit des Lesers: eine Zuwendung zum Gedicht' [The reader's attentiveness: a turning towards the poem].[5] Extending one's hand towards the poem, the reader pulls the *Flaschenpost* [message in the bottle] from its indefinite journey and tarries with its meaning.

In what follows I will examine the interplay between prayer and poetry. I will focus on one specific prayer that Celan interrogates and its relation to a poetic genre. What is the connection between the Jewish prayer for the dead, the mourner's *Kaddish*, and the poem of loss, the elegy? How does Celan dismantle the traditional modes of liturgical and poetic mourning? In his glossary of poetic terms, Edward Hirsch writes,

---

3 Paul Celan, *Der Meridian. Tübinger Ausgabe. Endfassung, Vorstufen, Materialien*, (Frankfurt a.M. Main: Suhrkamp, 1999), p. 9.

4 Ibid., p. 72.

5 Ibid., p. 132.

> The elegy does what Freud calls 'the work of mourning.' It ritualizes grief into language and thereby makes it more bearable. It turns loss into remembrance and delivers an inheritance. It opens a space for retrospection and drives a wordless anguish toward the consolations of verbal articulation and ceremony.[6]

Contrary to Hirsch, Celan's poetry refutes this definition; devoid of consolation, Celan deforms both language and ritualized mourning. Instead of passing on an inheritance, his poems transmit an unpayable *Schuld* – in German 'guilt' or 'debt' – to the reader, thus subverting elegy's compensatory logic in the aftermath of mechanized death.

In addition to Hirsch's definition of elegy, I wish to break free from such works as Peter Sacks' *The English Elegy* and Jahan Ramazani's *Poetry of Mourning*, which also foreground the psychic economy of mourning. While Sacks examines elegy's normative modes of mourning, Ramazani turns to mourning's failure – melancholia – in the face of modern death.[7] Avoiding such reductive psychoanalytic frames of mourning, melancholia and entombed traumas often used to probe elegy's relation to catastrophic loss, I will explore how the question of mourning shifts to a poetics of justice, one that lies outside the conventional juridical ramifications of the term. After the Shoah, elegy's function as the privileged genre of mourning has to contend with a new genre. Following Elie Wiesel's claim that survivors of the Holocaust 'invented a new literature, testimony', traditional forms of elegiac commemoration collapse.[8] The intersection between poetry and historical violence is not simply about memorializing the dead; rather – to paraphrase Yosef Yerushalmi in his book on Jewish memory – perhaps the opposite of forgetting is not memory but justice.[9]

I am not suggesting that genocide's magnitude makes the Shoah's victims inaccessible, nor does its scope pose an epistemic or aesthetic limit that warps elegy's traditional generic traits. Instead, it is the degradation of death itself in the camps that transforms the fundamental way in which we speak about the dead. In her *Dying Modern. A Meditation on Elegy*, Diane Fuss examines how the technological and bureaucratic erasure of death in the twentieth century results in the

---

6 Edward Hirsch, *How to Read a Poem and Fall in Love with Poetry* (New York: Harcourt, 1999), p. 278.

7 Peter Sacks, *The English Elegy. Studies in the Genre from Spenser to Yeats* (Baltimore: The Johns Hopkins University Press, 1985); Jahan Ramazani, *Poetry of Mourning. The Modern Elegy from Harding to Heaney* (Chicago: The University of Chicago Press, 1994).

8 Elie Wiesel, 'The Holocaust as Literary Inspiration', in *Dimensions of the Holocaust. Lectures at Northwestern University* (Evanston, IL: Northwestern University Press, 1977), pp. 5–19.

9 Yosef H. Yerushalmi, *Zakhor. Jewish History and Jewish Memory* (Seattle: University of Washington Press, 1982), p. 117.

collapse of traditional forms of poetic and liturgical mourning. Celan's poetry exemplifies what Fuss calls 'the corpse poem'. Describing how such poems depict 'the emptying out of mortality that deprives modern deaths of their singularity and distinction', the dead are given voice not beyond the grave but from within it.[10]

Specifically, within the realm of Holocaust studies the figure of the *Muselmann* has come to embody for poets and philosophers the suspension between the living and the dead. The *Muselmann*, whom Jean Améry described as 'a bundle of physical functions in its last convulsions', refers to those inmates who had been reduced into the non-human and had no chance for survival.[11] Building on Primo Levi's image of Auschwitz's drowned, Giorgio Agamben investigates the mutation of human beings into 'bare life' in the death camps: 'Where death cannot be called death, corpses cannot be called corpses.'[12] Although Celan's poetry does not explicitly represent the *Muselmann*, he positions these broken figures at the centre of drafts to his *Meridian*. Celan removes overt references to the *Muselmann* in his final draft, but by delving into his notes we behold how they suffuse his *ars poetica*.

Just as there is no adequate consolation for the dead through traditional forms of elegy after Auschwitz, so too has the Jewish prayer for the dead been compromised in relation to genocide's irrecuperable bodies.[13] In the *Kaddish* the mourner speaks the following words, 'Blessed be He, beyond all song and psalm, praises and consolations that mortals can utter; let us say, Amen.' Despite being used in mourning rituals, the prayer never mentions the dead. Sanctifying God's name, the prayer centres on the messianic restoration of God's kingdom.

Elie Wiesel captures the fate of *Kaddish* in relation to those exterminated in 'The Death of my Father'. Wiesel recalls his father's death and describes his

---

10 Diane Fuss, *Dying Modern. A Meditation on Elegy* (Durham, NC: Duke University Press, 2013), p. 73.

11 Cited in Giorgio Agamben, *Remnants of Auschwitz. The Witness and the Archive,* trans. by Daniel Heller-Roazen (New York: Zone Books, 2002), p. 41.

12 *Remnants,* p.70.

13 Writers such as Jorge Semprun (*Literature or Life*), Elie Wiesel (*Night*), Rose Ausländer ('Kaddisch und Schiwe') and Imre Kertesz (*Kaddish for a Child Not Born)* all turn to the prayer's significance in relation to the poets' obligation to recollect the dead. In his *Kaddish,* a book comprised of over a thousand black and white images taken from newspapers, postcards and found photographs, the visual artist Christian Boltanski utilizes a Holocaust aesthetics steeped in melancholia. Most recently, *László* Nemes' film *Son of Saul* (2015) centers on a member of the *Sonderkommando*, who searches for a rabbi to recite *Kaddish* over the body of a dead child in Auschwitz.

struggles to recite *Kaddish* in Buchenwald and each *Yahrzeit* commemorating his death: 'There was no link between his death and the life he had led. His death, lost among all the rest, had nothing to do with the person he had been [...]. *He was robbed of his death.*'[14] Acknowledging the dissolution of death's meaning, Wiesel repeats that he cannot interpret his death and differentiates his father's death from that of his father's father. Deprived of individuality, his father's anonymous death 'did not belong to him'.[15] Focusing not on God's absence, but on the transformation to the meaning of death through the degradation of the human, Wiesel searches for new words to help him memorialize his father.

As he struggles to interpret his father's last breath, Wiesel confesses, 'I did not say *Kaddish* [...]. I felt a useless object, a thing without imagination.'[16] On the eve of his father's *Yahrzeit* Wiesel's thoughts shift from mourning to justice in his search for new modes of commemoration.[17] According to Wiesel, 'It would be inadequate, *indeed unjust*, to imitate my father. I shall have to invent other prayers, other acts.'[18] If there is to be justice for his father, Wiesel must go beyond *Kaddish* and invent 'other prayers'. Contrary to being 'a thing without imagination', Wiesel's essay becomes his new prayer. Repeating how 'tomorrow is the anniversary of my father's death', Wiesel stresses that his pursuit of justice is future oriented: next year he will face the same task of having to invent another prayer to do justice for his father.

There is a prevalence of texts that reflect on the relevance of *Kaddish* in Holocaust representations. Writers such as Wiesel, Jorge Semprun and Imre Kertész turn to the prayer in relation to the obligation to recollect the dead. According to Midrash, the recitation of *Kaddish* raises the souls of the dead to a higher level, saving them from the afterlife's lowest strata. Following Adorno's contention that 'After Auschwitz there is no word tinged from on high, not even a theological one, that has any right unless it underwent a transformation', *Kaddish* has undergone a transformation within the domain of Holocaust representations.[19] The prayer's disfiguration attests not only to a missing God but also to the failure

---

14 Elie Wiesel, 'The Death of my Father', in *Legends of our Time* (New York: Random House, 1968), pp. 1–7. P. 2.

15 Ibid., p.3.

16 Ibid., p.5.

17 *Yahrzeit*, a Yiddish term meaning 'time of year', marks in Jewish law the yearly anniversary of a person's death. One recites *Kaddish* and lights a memorial candle for the dead.

18 Ibid., p.7.

19 Theodor W. Adorno, *Negative Dialectics*, trans. By E. B. Ashton (New York: Continuum, 1973), p. 359.

of transporting the soul beyond its purgations in Gehenna. *Kaddish* is replaced with a poetry that laments the limits of its vocation.

If elegies mourn for the dead and *Kaddish* is spoken on their behalf, how does one commemorate the Shoah's victims, who are repeatedly compared to objects, abject creatures or bare life by poets and philosophers? My analysis of the intersection between elegy and *Kaddish* comprises the following sections: first, I begin with a reading of Celan's poem 'Die Schleuse', where the poet descends into the landscape of mourning in search of lost words, including *Kaddish*. Afterwards, I examine the *Atemwende* [*Breathturn*] section in Celan's draft of the *Meridian*; this turn of breath refers to the linguistic disruptions punctuating his poems. While Celan inserts depictions of the *Muselmann* alongside these ruptures, I am struck by his inclusion of Benjamin's Kafka essay in this section of his notes. It is through his allusions to Benjamin's analysis of Odradek that we can uncover Celan's reflections on justice for the undead. In the last section, I examine Celan's posthumous life in poems commemorating his death. How do other writers inherit Celan's *Flaschenpost*, try to elegize his drowning and invent a new *Kaddish* for him?

Finally, within the context of Celan scholarship, 2020 marks a meridian of dates; it celebrates the poet's centennial and memorializes the fiftieth *Yahrzeit* of his death. In the Jewish tradition, the Jubilee year entails the erasure of outstanding debts. Despite this volume's anniversary context, no such *Ausgleichen* – balancing of debts – is possible for the *Schuld* we incur in our encounter with Celan. Like the threads from Odradek's spool entangled across three generations, Celan and his poetry embody the *Schuld* in post-Holocaust discussions of poetry. He inscribes into his poems an irredeemable past that always transfers its debt into the future.

From mourning to justice

Die Schleuse

Über aller dieser deiner
Trauer: kein
zweiter Himmel.

. . . .

An einen Mund,
dem es in Tausendwort war,
verlor –
verlor ich ein Wort,

das mir verblieben war:
Schwester.

An
die Vielgötterei
verlor ich ein Wort, das mich suchte:
Kaddisch.

Durch
die Schleuse mußt ich,
das Wort in die Salzflut zurück-
und hinaus- und hinüberzuretten:

Jiskor.

[The Sluice

Over all this
grief of yours: no
Second heaven.
. . . .

To a Mouth
for which it was a thousandword,
lost –
I lost a word
that was left to me:
Sister.

To
polygoddedness
I lost a word that sought me:
Kaddish.

Through
the sluice I had to go,
to salvage the word back into
and out of and across the salt flood:

Yizkor.][20]

Celan's 'Die Schleuse', completed shortly before he delivered his *Meridian* speech, depicts the breakdown of elegy and *Kaddish.* Structured around a catabasis, or descent into an underworld, the poet goes beneath the poem's perforated line and crosses a body of water in search of lost words. As the poet journeys

20 Paul Celan, *Die Gedichte. Kommentierte Gesamtausgabe in einem Band,* ed. by Barbara Wiedemann (Frankfurt a.M. Main: Suhrkamp, 2003), p. 131; *Poems of Paul Celan*, trans. By Michael Hamburger (New York: Persea Book, 1980), p. 151.

beyond 'die Salzflut' [the salt flood] – an image that invokes the space of tears – the poem depicts a sinking into mourning without salvation: there is no second heaven. The poem's *deus abscondis* is marked by the poet's loss of *Kaddish:* the Aramaic word for 'holy'.

However, at the poem's conclusion the poet rescues the word '*Jiskor*': another prayer associated with mourning. *Yizkor*, Hebrew for 'may God remember', is the opening word to the memorial prayer during the commemorative service for the dead that occurs four times a year.[21] How each prayer memorializes the dead sheds light on their fate in the poem. While *Kaddish* is spoken in a community and exalts God, *Yizkor* is read silently and comprises two parts: a call to God to remember the dead is attached to the mourner's pledge to give charity or perform righteous acts (*tzedakah*) on behalf of the dead. Although one could argue that by rescuing *Yizkor*, Celan finds a name for Jewish memory, I would suggest that *Yizkor's* recuperation shows how the work of memory is bound to justice. I will return to the significance of this juncture from *Kaddish* to *Yizkor*, from mourning to justice, later in this chapter.

While Orpheus is poetry's quintessential elegist, venturing into the underworld to retrieve Eurydice, Celan's descent in 'Die Schleuse' diverges from this path. Instead of providing restitution for the dead, the poem concludes with a debt. Celan ultimately performs the role of Charon, abandoning us in the realm of the dead with two untranslated words: *Kaddish* and *Yizkor*. What might seem to be a form of *Ausgleichen* – rescuing *Yizkor* – is subverted by the lack of translation. In turn, our encounter with this rupture gives rise to an *Aufmerksamkeit* that makes us reflect on what remains untranslated. Even though it is anti-elegiac, the poem does not end in silence; rather, a fragile link of communication arises between poet and reader. A word is transmitted, but the uncertainty of its meaning leaves us with a debt.

For many critics Celan's poetry occupies a space between poetry and prayer. In particular, with its repeated invocations during commemorative events in Germany, scholars such as John Felstiner and Amy Colin refer to 'Todesfuge' ['Death Fugue'] as a secular *Kaddish*.[22] But it is this misappropriation of 'Todesfuge' that Celan ultimately rejected. In his *Meridian* notes Celan lamented how Germany's obsession with the poem's metaphors and fugue-like composition obscured the Shoah's horrors. Celan was wary that the poem's iconization might function as a

---

21 The prayer is recited on Yom Kippur, Shemini Atzeret, the eighth day of Passover and the second day of Shavuot.

22 John Felstiner, 'Mother Tongue, Holy Tongue. On Translating and not Translating Paul Celan', in *Comparative Literature*, 38.4 (Spring 1986), 113–36, p. 122. Amy D. Colin, *Paul Celan. Holograms of Darkness* (Bloomington: Indiana University Press, 1991), p. 45.

Wiedergutmachung that compensated for genocidal loss. His critique of the poem's reception transpires in the *Meridian* notes' *Atemwende* section.

In Celan's trope for the poem's momentary pauses where language breaks down, the reader is compelled to be mindful of its catastrophic date: 20 January. As he develops the *Atemwende*, Celan juxtaposes two figures. Although readers may 'weep' ('nachweinen') for 'Todesfuge's' 'almond-eyed beauty' Sulamith, burying her deeper into forgetting, Celan implores us to turn away from her and towards the 'krummnasigen, bucklichten, mauschelnden und kielkröpfigen Toten' [the crooked-nosed, hunchbacked, yiddy and goitery dead] from Auschwitz, who are located in the poem's intervals.[23] Thus, the forgotten *Muselmann*-like figures reside in the *Atemwende*.

While Agamben asserts that an ethics after Auschwitz must begin with the *Muselmann*, where it 'is forever impossible to distinguish between man and non-man', Celan had already inscribed this juncture into his poetics.[24] The *Muselmann* not only marks the threshold of a new ethics but also constitutes the point where Celan shifts from the conventions of elegy to a search for justice. Although he never explicitly uses the term in the *Meridian*, in his notes Celan gestures to a poetics of justice. We should keep in mind the speech's historical backdrop. There is little doubt that Adolph Eichmann's capture (May 1960) and impending trial (April 1961) were influencing Celan's thoughts. It was during this period when the significance of 20 January 1942 became part of the cultural memory of the Shoah as Eichmann's role at Wannsee came to light.

But in addition to positioning the memory of this date at the *Meridian's* centre, Celan also references multiple concepts that contribute to its juridical tone. From his opening fragment in the *Atemwende* section, Celan links the poem's swerve into silence to a reflection on personal guilt: 'Ich hatte einiges überlebt [...]. Ich hatte ein schlechtes Gewissen; ich suchte [...] meine Atemwende' [I had survived some things [...]. I had a bad conscience: I was searching for [...] my breathturn].[25] Thus, Celan's confession of survivor's guilt prompts the search for his *Atemwende*.

In another fragment Celan writes, 'We have been, each in his own way, witnesses of a process [Zeugen eines Prozesses], which has led us to this circumstance from that which only fifteen years ago still lay true and heavy on our heart: talk of turning instead of change itself, supposed engagement and commitment instead of real responsibility, cultural busy-ness [Kulturbeflissenheit]

23 *Meridian*, p. 128.
24 *Remnants*, p. 47.
25 *Meridian*, p. 123.

instead of simple attentiveness [Aufmerksamkeit]'.[26] With the temporal mark of 'fifteen years ago', Celan does not claim that he witnessed the extermination, but that his poetry bears witness to the process of injustice whereby Auschwitz's dead are buried deeper into forgetting. Although he contends that in 1945 there was profound grief when the Shoah came to light, Celan laments our inability to retain this catastrophe in contemporary memory.

In this complex passage the word 'Prozess' is layered with meaning. First, the fragment testifies to the process in which the Shoah's legacy was obfuscated by discussions on culture. Through his use of such terms as 'Engagement', 'Commitment' and 'Kulturbeflissenheit', Celan alludes to Adorno.[27] Describing how debates on aesthetics had perpetuated the failed engagement with Nazism's legacy, Celan was wary that discussions of *Kultur* obscured all that had transpired. But with his use of such terms as 'Zeugen' and 'Prozess', Celan encodes a literary reference within this historical moment. 'Prozess' conjures up both the deterioration of justice in Kafka's *Der Prozess* and the continued postponement of justice in the shadow of Eichmann's capture.

By employing the term *Aufmerksamkeit* from Benjamin's Kafka study, Celan goes beyond a conventional understanding of justice. Instead of offering up a prayer for the dead, poetry's breathturn struggles with an act of justice as it attempts to bear witness to the *Kreatur*'s disfigured voice ('für die Kreatur zeugenden').[28] However, by depicting how poetry's scales – an allusion to justice – are in ruins, 'Wir liegen schon unter den Trümmern der Waage...', he reveals that restitution is impossible. After the description of the broken scales, Celan cites for the first time Benjamin on Kafka's attentiveness.[29]

In addition to interspersing juridical imagery throughout his notes, Celan's reflections on the link between poetry and justice are filtered through his conversations with Martin Heidegger and Benjamin's respective analyses of poetic language, mortality and justice. While Heidegger links the question of justice to finding the balance between a coming to be and passing away through poetic thought, Benjamin explores how the messianic possibility of postponed justice involves a thoughtful reflection on the *Schuld* of the past. Celan forges his links to the two philosophers in his use of 'Aufmerksamkeit' and 'Kreatur', words Heidegger discusses in his analysis of Rilke's Eighth Elegy and which Benjamin examines in his study of Odradek. In 'Wozu Dichter?', which explores the

---

26 Ibid., p. 169.

27 Celan gestures to Adorno's 'Cultural Criticism and Society', where he pronounces the barbaric state of poetry after Auschwitz.

28 *Meridian*, p. 178.

29 Ibid., pp. 58 and 63.

creature in Rilke's Eighth Elegy, Heidegger examines the distinction between the death of humans ('sterben') and how animals perish ('verenden').[30] On the other hand, in his analysis of Odradek, Benjamin describes how Kafka's attentiveness to creatures includes humans and animals. While Rilke's elegies show a clear binary between life and death, Odradek is neither dead nor alive. In his turn to the creature in the *Meridian,* Celan neither follows Heidegger's path of uncovering Being nor Benjamin's messianic moment of redemption. Rather, Celan's Jewish creatures remain suspended between life and death. Owing to space constraints, I will focus on Celan's reflections on Odradek: a creature Benjamin links to the themes of forgetting, guilt, justice, prayer and attentiveness.

As mentioned earlier, Celan rejects the 'almond-eyed beauty' Sulamith and tells us to think about Auschwitz's 'krummnasigen, bucklichten, mauschelnden und kielkröpfigen Toten'. While Celan repeats this anti-Semitic description of the Jewish dead, he eventually replaces the word 'Toten' with 'Kreatur'. He writes, 'Ehrfurcht vor dem Geheimnis der krummnasigen Kreatur' [Respect for the secret of the hooked-nosed creature]and 'Es lebe die krummnasige Kreatur!' [Long live the hooked-nosed creature!].[31] Although depictions of the *Muselmann* vanish from the final draft, Celan's use of 'Kreatur' throughout his speech conveys this blurring between human/animal and living/dead. Moreover, with his use of 'Kreatur' alongside such words as 'Eingedenken', 'Aufmerksamkeit' and 'bucklichten', Celan discloses how the *Meridian's* reflections on mourning are encoded with elements of justice from Benjamin's Kafka study.

Soon after Celan entreats his audience to be mindful of 20 January, he references Kafka's *Aufmerksamkeit* to creatures. Similar to how Benjamin links Odradek's disfiguration to the forgetting of a past *Schuld,* Celan's Jewish creatures correspond to a *Schuld* that signifies both a forgotten past and the imperative to collect on a historical debt. By describing the deformed bodies in the death camps as 'bucklichten', Celan borrows another term from Benjamin. According to Benjamin, Odradek's deformed body is prefigured by 'Das bucklicht Männlein' [the hunchback] from German folklore: 'The hunchback is something that has been forgotten, something we once used to know, but he now blocks our way into the future'.[32] Describing how the hunchback implores the child in the folksong to include him in his prayers, Benjamin continues, 'The hunchback is at

---

30 Martin Heidegger, 'Wozu Dichter', in *Holzwege* (Frankfurt a.M. Main: Klostermann, 1950), pp. 248–95.

31 *Meridian*, p. 130 and p. 172.

32 Walter Benjamin, 'Franz Kafka. Beim Bau der Chinesischen Mauer', in *Selected Writings. 1927–1934*, ed. by Michael Jennings, trans. By Rodney Livingston (Cambridge, MA: Harvard University Press, 2005), p. 499.

home in a distorted [enstellten] life: he will disappear with the coming of the messiah, who will not wish to change the world by force but will make a slight adjustment [zurechtstellen].'[33] Prayer turns the hunchback's body into something 'zurecht'.

The messiah's act of justice ('Gerechtigkeit') does not radically change the world, but only makes a small shift: 'zurecht' conveys the sense of acting justly and setting aright what is askew. Benjamin concludes that even if Kafka did not pray, his 'Aufmerksamkeit' interceded on behalf of the most abandoned creatures.[34] However, this is where Celan's correspondence with Benjamin falters. While Benjamin's hunchback undergoes an adjustment with the messiah's arrival, there is no 'Zurechtstellen' for Celan. Devoid of redemption, his words and creatures remain disfigured, suspended between living and dead. Whereas traditional forms of justice entail a remuneration of *Schuld,* the debt in Celan's poems is transgenerational, perpetually passed into the future.

A Kaddish for Paul Celan

In this closing section on the shift from mourning to justice, Odradek again provides insight. In Kafka's comparison of Odradek's laugh without lungs to the rustling of falling leaves, Odradek is an 'Atemwende'. Caught between speech and silence, inorganic and organic, he departs and returns home. Kafka's narrator wonders if Odradek is a dead thing, but he concludes that Odradek will outlive him. Similarly, Celan himself functions as an Odradek-like figure in post-Holocaust discussions of poetry and philosophy. Like his description of a poem's oscillation between 'Schon-nicht-mehr' and 'Immer-noch' [already-no-longer and always-still], Celan's drowning is given poetological significance by such writers as Ingeborg Bachmann, Imre Kertész, Rose Ausländer, Primo Levi, Edmond Jabès, Yehuda Amichai and Edward Hirsch.[35] Within months of his death, poets began commemorating Celan in their writings.[36]

---

33 *Illuminations*, pp. 133–34.

34 The interplay between prayer and 'bucklicht' arises in Celan's poem 'Tenebrae' (1957); the word 'Bücken' describes the victims of genocide: 'Gegriffen schon, Herr, | ineinander verkrallt | [...] | gingen wir hin, uns zu bücken | nach Mulde und Maar.' In this scene of extermination, human figures become like animals bending over mass graves. In 'Gold', Celan includes a choir of insects: 'Der Chor | der Platanenstrünke | buckelt sich ein zum Gebet | gegens Gebet'. Again, creatures bend over in prayer. *Gedichte*, p. 97 and p. 350.

35 *Meridian*, p. 8.

Constituting a poetic lacuna for those who elegize him, Celan has come to embody the debt left behind in the submerged messages of the drowned. I know of no other modern poet who has been memorialized to the extent of Celan, who has been a catalyst for poems in German, Italian, French, Hungarian, Hebrew and English. While in traditional elegies poets often invoke the muses to help find proper words to mourn, Celan himself becomes the muse to recollect his own death. With Celan's transposition into the space of literature, his name signifies language's incapacity to find a proper measure for catastrophic loss. In the meridian between Celan's corporeal and poetic breathturns and those who meditate on his drowning, each poet probes how the signifying powers of language fall into a creaturely cry.

Reflecting on Celan's suicide, Primo Levi captures what is at stake when confronted with poetry he compares to an 'animal whine':

> [It is] the last inarticulate babel [...]. The gasps of a dying man [...]. It enthralls us as whirlpools enthrall us [...]. Celan the poet must be meditated upon and mourned rather than imitated. If his is a message, it gets lost in the 'background noise': it is not a communication, it is not a language, or at most it is a dark and maimed language, precisely like that of someone who is about to die and is alone, as we all will be at the point of death.[37]

Placing Celan's gasps next to the image of a whirlpool, Levi alludes to the momentary suffocation of Celan's 'Atemwende'. Emblematic of Levi's figure of the drowned, we hear in his description of Celan's poetry echoes of the *Muselmann*. Celan is like one of '[t]hose who have seen the face of the Gorgon, did not return, or returned wordless'.[38] Instead of imitating Celan's shift to silence, Levi contends that our responsibility must consist of a meditative mourning. But Levi waivers in his approach to Celan. Even though he admires 'Todesfuge's' 'raw lucidity', Levi remains captivated by the murkiness of his later compositions.

Counter to Levi's fears that Celan's message risked getting lost in his poetry's 'background noise', Edmond Jabès concentrates on the mere sounds of words,

---

36 For instance, Franz Wurm, Ernst Meister and Erich Fried repeatedly engage with Celan's poetry soon after his death. See the following poems: Franz Wurm's 'Du | entfernst dich' in *Die Horen* 83 (1971), p. 85; Ernst Meister's 'Kind keiner | Jahreszeit' in *Sage vom Ganzen den Satz* (Darmstadt und Neuwied: Hermann Luchterhand Verlag, 1972), p. 31. Erich Fried 'Beim Wiederlesen eines Gedichtes von Paul Celan' in *Gesammelte Werke, in Vier Bänden*, ed. by Volker Kaukoreit and Klaus Wagenbach (Berlin: Wagenbach, 1993), p. 65 (vol. 2). See also Ingeborg Bachmann's novel *Malina*, where Bachmann configures Celan's recovered body as *Flaschenpost* that washes up in the pages of her novel; *Malina* (Frankfurt a. M. Main: Suhrkamp, 1971).

37 Cited in Agamben, *Remnants*, pp. 36–37.

38 Primo Levi, *The Drowned and the Saved*, trans. by Raymond Rosenthal (New York, Vintage Books, 1989), pp. 83–84.

not on their definitive meaning in his essay, 'The Memory of Words. How I Read Paul Celan'. In his *in memoriam*, solicited by the *Frankfurter Allgemeine Zeitung* almost twenty years after Celan's death, Jabès shifts from the poet's physical absence to his poetic ruptures. Examining the different linguistic modes of how he encountered Celan's language through reading, listening and translation, Jabès concludes, 'Behind the silence of Paul Celan lies the never extinguished echo of another language [...]. [We must] interrogate the words of his memory, the words of his silence; to tunnel down into their past as "vocables"'.[39] Jabès is attuned to Celan's non-lexical utterances, which arise from the incomplete translations of his poems, which Jabès could only read in French. Upon this 'edge of two languages', Jabès listens closely to what translation withholds.

Just as Jabès listens to the gaps between two languages, we must occupy a similar position when confronted with poems that reflect on both Celan's death and his poetry. Rose Ausländer constructs such a space of dialogue in her poem 'In Memoriam Paul Celan' (1974), entering the whirlpool of his poems in order to trace the transformation of his elegiac voice. As she sets out to eulogize him, Ausländer constructs a corpse poem that allows Celan to transmit a message from his watery grave. Ausländer does not merely imitate Celan; rather, her poem opens up a space in which the reader listens to the distorted echoes between the two poets and reflects on how Ausländer interrogates the evolution of Celan's voice.

In Memoriam Paul Celan

'Meine blonde Mutter
kam nicht heim'
Paul Celan

Kam nicht heim
die Mutter

nie aufgegeben
den Tod

vom Sohn genährt
mit Schwarzmilch

39 Edmond Jabès, 'The Memory of Words', in *Paul Celan. Selections*, trans. by Pierre Joris (Berkeley: University of California Press, 2005), pp. 217–23.

die hielt ihn am Leben
das ertrank
im Tintenblut

Zwischen verschwiegenen Zeilen
das Nichtwort
im Leerraum
leuchtend[40]

['My blonde mother
didn't come home'
Paul Celan

Didn't come home
the mother

never gave up
death

nourished by her son
with blackmilk

which preserved his life
that drowned
in inkblood

Between silent lines
the not-word
in empty-space
blazing]

Ausländer begins with an epigraph from one of Celan's earliest poems on his mother's death, 'Espenbaum', sketching a continuity between her death and his drowning. But this conventional image of loss undergoes an estrangement. Shifting to the iconic image of 'Schwarze Milch' [black milk] from 'Todesfuge', now rendered into a compound word, Ausländer concludes her poem with reconfigured imagery from one of Celan's last poems, 'Die Posaunenstelle'.

Her heart ripped apart by lead in 'Espenbaum' – 'Meiner Mutter Herz ward wund von Blei' – Celan's murdered mother is now nourished by the son's constitutive image of the Holocaust: 'Schwarzmilch'.[41] Unlike Levi and Jabès, who focus on Celan's linguistic fissures, Ausländer draws on Celan's use of neologisms and fondness for compound words by constructing her own: 'Schwarzmilch' [blackmilk], 'Tintenblut' [inkblood], 'Nichtwort' [not-word] and 'Leerraum'

40 Rose Ausländer, *Gedichte und Prosa 1966–1975* (Frankfurt a. M. Main: Fischer Verlag, 1984), p. 138.
41 'Espenbaum', *Gedichte*, p. 30.

[empty-space]. Moving away from ventriloquizing Celan, Ausländer adapts his language and interprets the evolution of a poetics edging towards silence. In her condensation of imagery Ausländer traces the development of a dead figure who cannot return home to the metaphors of 'Schwarzmilch' mixed with 'Tintenblut'. She uncovers a 'Nichtwort' – an adaptation of Lucile's 'Gegenwort' from the *Meridian* – between lines rendered silent.

Nourishing the dead mother, blackmilk unites with the inkblood that both sustains and drowns the poet. Even though her poem lacks the topographic markings of the underworld, Ausländer encodes this realm with a mixture of milk and blood: Odysseus' libation for Teiresias in the underworld of *The Odyssey.* The prophet's voice can return only when he consumes this libation. While Teiresias concludes his prophecy by telling Odysseus that a gentle death will come to him at sea, this description is far from Celan's death in the Seine at the age of forty-nine.

Reminiscent of how Celan descends into the 'Salzflut' to rescue lost words in 'Die Schleuse', Ausländer enters the space of drowning to recuperate poetic fragments. Breathing new life into his words, she re-animates Celan's voice and turns him into a prophet. What does he say? Despite the Greek-like mixture of blackmilk and inkblood, Ausländer models her prophet in relation to another river poem by Celan. Interweaving Hölderlin's poetry in 'Tübingen, Jänner', Celan turns the mad poet into a prophet, whom he compares to Oedipus and Moses. Following the 'plunging words' beneath the water, Celan retrieves in the last line Hölderlin's word – or rather, 'Nichtwort' – of madness: 'Pallaksch. Pallaksch'. Similar to the recuperation of *Yizkor,* Celan ends with a foreign word that estranges the reader. If the poet/prophet were to arrive, he would only be able to stammer.[42]

Ausländer's poem concludes with a breathturn that she gleans from Celan's 'Die Posaunenstelle'. Instead of recovering a word, Ausländer listens for a specific sound: the blowing of the shofar. While Ausländer traces how the mother's figure transforms into the metonymy of blackmilk, her turn to 'Die Posaunenstelle' emphasizes the text's erasure and its replacement with an image of breath. I will examine briefly Celan's poem before turning to Ausländer's modification of its language.

Die Posaunenstelle
tief im glühenden
Leertext,

42 'Tübingen, Jänner', Ibid., p. 133. Hölderlin used 'Pallaksch' to mean both 'yes' and 'no'.

in Fackelhöhe
im Zeitloch:

hör dich ein
mit dem Mund.[43]

The Trumpet Place
deep in the glowing
text-void.

at torch height,
in the timehole:

hear deep in
with your mouth.

Die Posaunenstelle, or place of the shofar, refers to the ram's horn, which is blown on several occasions in the Jewish calendar. First and foremost, the shofar resounds during the Jewish New Year, Rosh Hashanah. The shofar interrupts the service's liturgical moments, whereby words of prayer give way to the three distinct sounds measured by exhalations and inhalations from the shofar. Comprised of multiple sounds, the first blast, or *tekiah*, is one long continuous burst. The second sound, named *shevarim*, consists of three shorter blasts. While *tekiah's* hopeful cry marks the time of redemption, *shevarim* symbolizes a cry of sorrow.

Although Celan's poem searches for the shofar's place, it withholds a description of sound. Instead, we are taken to a place devoid of time ('im Zeitloch:'). We expect to hear the shofar's call after the colon, but what unfolds is a double absence marked by a line and stanza break. Following this extended pause of breath, Celan ends with an imperative: 'hör dich ein | mit dem Mund'. The constricted last four lines of Ausländer's poem demonstrate that she hears this command both to listen and to respond. What does she hear?

In his insightful reading of the poem, Felstiner stresses the hopeful blast of *tekiah* during Rosh Hashanah, focusing on the resonances between the three staccato syllables in *te-ki-ah*, 'hör dich ein' and 'mit dem Mund'. [44] But Ausländer hears a different sound. Beneath her inclusion of the mournful fragments from 'Espenbaum' and 'Todesfuge', another creaturely sound emanates from the poem. Rather than *tekiah*, the three syllables on each of the last two lines demonstrate *shevarim*'s three short blasts, which convey weeping sounds or a

43 Ibid., p. 362. John Felstiner, *Paul Celan. Poet, Survivor, Jew* (New Haven: Yale University Press, 1995), p. 271.
44 Ibid., p. 274.

howl. Ausländer turns away from 'Todesfuge's' almond-eyed beauty and towards the moment of erasure of the creaturely voice that drowns and is set ablaze. Even though she gestures towards the propitious symbol of the shofar and ends with radiant brilliance ('leuchtend'), her closing words do not convey some redemptive light. Despite the constellation of word, void, light and breath, Genesis's potential scene of creation collapses into an incineration. The poem does not anticipate God's breath, but reveals the taking away of breath.

In addition to the sorrowful cry from the ram's horn, the shofar is blown at the beginning of the Jubilee year to mark the cancellation of past debts. Celan completed his poem a week before he turned forty-nine. Ilana Shmueli wrote in a letter: 'Today your birthday – among the Jews it is the actual jubilee [7x7] – I hope you know the meaning.'[45] However, there would be no respite for Celan, who drowned himself five months later. Celan indeed understood the significance of a Jubilee year, using the term in other poems to show the very impossibility of forgetting in relation to the Shoah.[46] Ausländer's poem takes up the debt left behind in the wake of Celan's death and transfers it to the reader.

Without directly citing the closing lines from 'Die Posaunenstelle', Ausländer fulfils its commands. By foregrounding the trajectory of how language approaches its negation, she heeds the imperative to pay attention. As the shofar's blast gives way to silence, Ausländer underscores how the poem's inhalations depict a drowning. While Celan rescues *Yizkor* and 'Pallaksch', Ausländer neither retrieves a word ('Nichtwort') nor the shofar's sound. Instead, she compels us to reflect on the meaning behind the breathturn beneath the water.

Similar to this play between breath and sound, Yehuda Amichai represents Celan's drowning as a breathturn: 'Paul Celan, toward the end your words grew fewer | and every word became so heavy in your body | that God set you down like a heavy load | for a moment, perhaps, to catch | His breath and wipe His brow | [...] | But the last bubbles that rose from your drowning mouth | were the final concentration, the frothy concentrate | of the heaviness of your life.'[47] As he imagines the poet's sinking body, the last vestige of breath, his bubbles, rise like *Flaschenpost* to the surface.

45 *The Correspondence of Paul Celan and Ilana Shmueli*, trans. by Susan H. Gillespie (Rhinebeck, NY: Sheep Meadow Press, 2011), p. 32.

46 'Und Kraft und Schmerz' and 'Die Fleissigen', in *Gedichte*, p. 338 and p. 236.

47 The poem appeared in 1998. Yehuda Amichai, *Open Closed Open. Poems*, trans. by Chana Bloch and Chana Kronfeld (New York: Harcourt, 2000), p. 130. See Na'ama Rokem, 'German-Hebrew encounters in the poetry and correspondence of Yehuda Amichai and Paul Celan', *Prooftexts*, 30.1 (2010), 97–127.

In the above texts Celan's physical absence is replaced with reflections on the de-evolution of a language turned into cries, gasps, bubbles or silence. Reminiscent of how Benjamin describes Kafka's novels as set in a swamp world brimming with atavistic creatures, Celan's creaturely poetics hearkens back to this swamp; it is a devolving language of mortals falling back into water.[48] As his language becomes amphibian and inclines into silence, Celan underscores an atavism behind his poems: 'We want to retain the thought of the "atavistic" return of the poem [*"atavistische" Wiederkehr des Gedichts*]'.[49] Celan's attentiveness to Auschwitz's broken Jewish figures that jabber with creaturely voice ('mauscheln') requires our own receptivity to such disarticulations within his poems.

I will conclude with a poem by Edward Hirsch, whose definition of elegy I cited earlier: '[Elegy] drives a wordless anguish toward the consolations of verbal articulation and ceremony.'[50] And yet, when his son died, Hirsch lamented his own estrangement from traditional poetic and liturgical forms of mourning.[51] The limits that Hirsch encountered when reflecting on his son's death, however, were already present two decades earlier in his poem 'In Memoriam Paul Celan' (1994). Like Ausländer and Amichai, Hirsch centres on Celan's drowning, his creaturely language and receiving his prophetic message.

Hirsch draws on Celan's lexicon by inscribing imagery from his oeuvre, too much to expand upon here:

> Lay these words into the dead man's grave
> next to the almonds and black cherries –
> tiny skulls and flowering blood-drops, eyes,
> and Thou, O bitterness that pillows his head.
>
> Lay these words on the dead man's eyelids
> like eyebrights, like medieval trumpet flowers
> that will flourish, this time, in the shade.
> Let the beheaded tulips glisten with rain.
>
> Lay these words on his drowned eyelids
> like coins or stars, ancillary eyes.
> Canopy the swollen sky with sunspots
> while thunder addresses the ground.

---

48 In another allusion to Kafka, Celan describes how his speech is an attempt to swim on dry land, thus comparing himself to a creature removed from its natural environment of water. *Meridian*, p. 186.

49 Ibid., p. 129.

50 See endnote 6.

51 Hirsch writes in 'Gabriel': 'It's not time to close the casket | Or say Kaddish for my son'. *Gabriel. A Poem* (New York: Knopf, 2014), p. 77.

> Syllable by syllable, clawed and handled,
> the words have united in grief.
> It is the ghostly hour of lamentation,
> the void's turn, mournful and absolute.
>
> Lay these words on the dead man's lips
> like burning tongs, a tongue of flame.
> A scouring eagle wheels and shrieks.
> Let God pray to us for this man.[52]

While hallmarks from 'Die Schleuse' are evident, there is no search for lost words; the poet descends into the grave to lay words like flowers upon the corpse. Instead of *Kaddish* – a prayer Hirsch rejects in 'Gabriel' – the poet places his words, which are themselves an amalgamation of Celan's poems, on drowned eyes. Thus, Hirsch performs the Greek ritual of Charon's obol: coins placed on the eyes to prevent the dead from haunting the living by transporting their souls to the beyond. In this act of charity, the poet attempts to pay Celan's fare across the river.

The Greek ritual of mourning is supplanted with a Jewish image from the Book of Isaiah. Hirsch's words touch the dead man's lips like a flame as if to consecrate his prophetic voice. But the scene of purification becomes holocaustal: the dead man's mouth is engulfed in flames. Emerging from his grave, the drowned poet's voice is not oracular. Instead, from his singed lips emanates a plaintive cry. What might intimate the return of the poet's voice – the fusing of syllables into words – eventually devolves into a creaturely scream: 'A scouring eagle wheels and shrieks'. Despite having his drowned eyelids replaced with the eagle's panoptic vision, the poet looks down on the world and can only emit a resounding non-human screech.

According to Hirsch, 'Every poetry has an element of lamentation, or the elegy, to ease the dead on their passage to the other world.'[53] But in his poem there is no transport of the dead to the other side. Hirsch suspends Celan and his language between life and death, human and creature, the grave and heaven. Like the missing *Kaddish* in 'Die Schleuse' and 'no | Second heaven', there is no transcendent space from which God remembers the departed. Instead of uttering

---

52 Edward Hirsch, *The Living Fire. New and Selected Poems 1975–2010* (New York: Knopf, 2010), p. 106. Hirsch alludes to the following poems: 'In Memoriam Paul Eluard', 'Zähle die Mandeln', 'Todtnauberg', 'Tenebrae' and 'Tübingen, Jänner'.

53 Edward Hirsch, 'The Sweetness of Nothing. Questions and Answers with Edward Hirsch at the Joshua Ringel Memorial Reading, May 2006', (http://twcresources.org/view-magazines.php?c=czoxNjoidjM4bjAxcDExXzE2LnBkZiI7)

a prayer extoling God, the poet commands God to pray *to us* for Celan. Adapting the injunction from 'Tenebrae', 'Bete, Herr | bete zu uns | wir sind nah', Hirsch guards over Celan's traces, revives his voice and allows him to utter his cry.

We behold in the previous texts Derrida's depiction of the precarious encounter between Celan and his readers: 'The poet is someone permanently engaged with a dying language that he resuscitates not by giving back to it a triumphant line, but by bringing it back like a phantom [...]. Nothing insures a poem against its death, because its archive can always be burned in crematory ovens or without being burned, is simply forgotten, not interpreted. Forgetting is always a possibility.'[54] Counter to how traditional elegies consist of compensatory acts, the poets who ponder the significance of Celan's drowning bear witness to this incomplete undertaking and watch over the body of his disfigured poetry. While each poet demonstrates that they received Celan's gift – he called his poems 'Geschenke an die Aufmerksamen' – they also take on a debt that cannot be paid off in their attempts to translate their meaning.[55] Celan underscored that such a balance was missing from his poetry, describing how 'the poem does not fit the measure' [das Ungemässe].[56] Whether approaching poetry as a work of mourning or a search for justice, both paths involve the breakdown of poetic measure. If poetry's scales collapse in ruins, what then does justice look like for Celan?

I would like to return to 'Die Schleuse's' closing words, where the poet rescues *Yizkor*. Although critics stress its relation to remembrance, *Yizkor* also requires from those left behind an act of *tzedakah:* a multivalent word conveying charity, righteousness and a justice that goes beyond its juridical connotations. Similar to Benjamin, who envisioned how the historian's task neither involves the retelling of the past nor an empathic relation with its victims, Celan sees the poet's task as enacting justice for the undead. *Yizkor* discloses a poetics of an incomplete justice. In this transition from poetry as a space of mourning to justice, the burden of the past transfers its *Schuld* into the future.

Evocative of how Benjamin refers to Odradek as an 'Entstellung', the Jewish word *Yizkor* both disfigures the German poem and signifies a *Schuld* left behind by Auschwitz's 'bucklichten' and 'mauschelnden' dead. By its conclusion, 'Die Schleuse' fulfils what Celan describes in his *Meridian* notes: it speaks a creature-

---

54 Jacques Derrida, *Sovereignties in Question. The Poetics of Paul Celan*, ed. by Thomas Dutoit and Outi Pasanen (New York: Fordham University Press, 2005), pp. 106–7.

55 See Celan's letter to Hans Bender in *Gesammelte Werke in Sieben Bänden*, ed. by Beda Allemann and Stefan Reichert (Frankfurt a.M. Main: Suhrkamp, 2000), p. 177 (vol. 3).

56 *Meridian*, p. 165.

ly language of 'Mauscheln' (a Jewish-German mixture) or 'Jüdeln'.[57] Thus, the poem speaks like a Jew. Unlike the Hebrew name 'Sulamith', which Celan worried his German audience had reduced to an empty metaphor, *Yizkor* resists such an appropriation.[58] Just as Benjamin locates Kafka's *Aufmerksamkeit* in relation to his forlorn creatures, *Yizkor* constitutes an interpretive lacuna that fosters our attentiveness to the figural distortions of language. As we watch over the poem's fragile body, each new interpretation serves as an act of resuscitation or what Levinas calls an 'extreme donation: attention – a mode of consciousness without distraction, i. e. without the power of escape'.[59] These forms of *tzedakah*, or small tokens ('kleine Aufmerksamkeiten'), do not ease the dead into the other world, but prevent the poet's language from perishing again.

---

57 Ibid., p. 128 and p. 129.
58 Celan lamented how contemporary German textbooks misappropriated 'Todesfuge' for classroom discussions. 'Black milk of morning' was not simply a genitive metaphor, but rather it conveyed for Celan reality. Ibid., p. 158.
59 Emmanuel Levinas, 'Paul Celan. From Being to the Other', in *Proper Names*, trans. by Michael B. Smith (Stanford, CA: Stanford University Press, 1996), p. 43.

Marko Pajević

Celan's Correspondence and Correspondence with Celan. Transfer Processes of Life

Letters, according to Walter Benjamin, are '"witnesses" belonging to the history of a person's "continued life"' [die "Zeugnisse" gehören zur Geschichte des "Fortlebens" eines Menschen].[1] They become witnesses, he writes, as, with growing chronological distance, the authors as subjects recede into the background in favour of a newly created 'third instance' which goes beyond the personal relationship between the correspondents (ibid.). What is this third instance that Benjamin does not define? To answer this question, instead of analysing the details of one piece of correspondence, this chapter will pursue the question of how to approach an author's correspondence as a whole: what can we make of it? What kinds of transfers take place throughout the process of corresponding and reading a correspondence? How does a correspondence live on?

These questions imply that, when talking about correspondence, we are also negotiating a construction of 'reality'. A letter is always a transfer between life and language as well, as are poems or any other form-giving activity; none of them should be confused with too simple an idea about 'reality'.[2] There is no clear-cut factuality; on the contrary: the given form shapes the events of the past and makes them what they are. Formulations in letters have a life-forming dimension, and the way we speak about correspondence – or translate letters into biographies, music or films, as we will see – also does something to the life in question, to the person and to how this person is perceived.

This chapter will first present the editorial circumstances relating to Celan's correspondence, enquire into the delicate relationship between life and language by discussing biographical and poetical approaches to Celan's work, and relate this to Celan's poetics. The second part will go beyond the discussion of Celan's correspondence to consider how we can access the poet's life today and what

1 Letter to Ernst Schoen, 19 September 1919, Walter Benjamin, *Gesammelte Briefe II* (Frankfurt a.M.: Suhrkamp, 1996), p. 48.

2 Mareike Stoll also points out that letters are not to be confused with what actually happened but are only one manifestation of the 'secret of encounter', in '"... und eine Schreibmaschine". Handgeschriebenes und Maschine-Geschriebenes bei Ingeborg Bachmann und Paul Celan', in *Ingeborg Bachmann und Paul Celan. Historisch-poetische Korrelationen*, ed. by Gernot Wimmer (Berlin: de Gruyter, 2014), pp. 122–37 (pp. 122–23).

https://doi.org/10.1515/9783110658330-016

transfer processes are at play when literary scholars and biographers, musicians and filmmakers use biographical material.

The correspondence

In the fifty years since Celan's death in 1970, an enormous amount of his correspondence has been published. This work began in the early 1990s,[3] with Barbara Wiedemann editing and thoroughly annotating several collections of letters between 1993 and 2001.[4] Further volumes of correspondence edited by Joachim Seng (2004) and Christoph König (2005) have revealed some more problematic dimensions of Celan's personality, his suspicions, irritability, intolerance and egocentricity, as well as his romantic relationships.[5] His voluminous French correspondence with his wife Gisèle Celan-Lestrange, very thoroughly annotated by Bertrand Badiou (2001), has been a milestone.[6] The publication of letters to and from his lovers began in 2002.[7] Other correspondence with friends, authors and

3 A key event triggering these publications was the transfer of Celan's papers to the German Literary Archive in Marbach in 1990 and, in 1991, the death of Celan's widow Gisèle Celan-Lestrange, the rights holder, and of his literary executor Beda Allemann. With all documents suddenly in the public domain, the scholarly community had plenty of material to work with, leading to a renewed interest in Celan and a boom in Celan scholarship.

Celan's son Eric became the official literary executor, but it is Bertrand Badiou who in fact took and still takes care of this task, with Barbara Wiedemann preparing most editions, often in close collaboration with Badiou. Wiedemann in particular wanted to make public the events and implications of the Goll affair – the accusations of plagiarism, initiated by Yvan Goll's widow Claire Goll, which had a profound and devastating impact on Celan's life.

4 Celan's correspondence with the poet Nelly Sachs (1993), with the writer and Celan's late friend, Franz Wurm (1996), and with his friends Hanne and Hermann Lenz (2001), combined with Wiedemann's meticulous documentation of the Goll affair (2000).

5 Both point to these dimensions in their afterwords, *Paul Celan Rudolf Hirsch Briefwechsel*, ed. by Joachim Seng (Frankfurt a. M.: Suhrkamp, 2004), p. 343; *Paul Celan Peter Szondi Briefwechsel*, ed. by Christoph König (Frankfurt a. M.: Suhrkamp, 2005), p. 108.

6 This was also the first opportunity to discover Celan as an author writing in French. His multilingualism is well known and significant for his poetry, but it is his letters that showcase it best. Since this correspondence was simultaneously published in German translation, however, that dimension was hardly perceived outside France.

7 Starting with Celan's brief correspondence with Diet Kloos-Barendregt (2002), followed by his exchanges with the friend from his childhood in Czernowitz and lover of the last part of his life Ilana Shmueli (2004), who had already published her Celan memoirs (2000). The correspondence with the poet Ingeborg Bachmann was kept strictly confidential until it was finally made public in 2008. Celan's long-term Austrian lover in Paris, Brigitta Eisenreich, wrote a voluminous book of memoirs about their relationship (2010). His correspondence with his lover Gi-

editors has received less attention.[8] His exchanges with the French poet René Char (2015) made more waves, probably owing to the importance of Char within the French-speaking context. Numerous other, more minor correspondence with editors, friends and writer-colleagues are also available in annotated form.[9] In 2019, Barbara Wiedemann edited 691 of Celan's letters in a single annotated volume of 1,286 pages.[10]

An equally impressive number of personal memoirs about Celan have been published,[11] alongside which several biographies have been written.[12] The story of Celan and Bachmann was also used as the basis of a detective story in *Die Kakerlakenstadt* [*Cockroach City*] by Uta-Maria Heim in 1993. An opera about Celan premiered in 2001 (Ruzicka/Mussbach), and the correspondence between Celan and Bachmann was made into a film (Beckermann 2016).

Taking a brief look at these activities and works demonstrates that an enormous amount of time and erudition has been invested in establishing precise knowledge about Celan's life. To what end? To what extent does it serve a better literary understanding or greater insight into cultural history? Or does it simply reflect a fascination with an exceptional person who might serve as an example? The interests of those working on and with Celan have strongly determined how his work and legacy have been received, and understandably so, but never without the risk of usurping the author.

Letter writing was a crucial activity for Celan for several reasons, one of which was the fact that he was a migrant. Many of his correspondents lived

---

sela Dischner remained unnoticed after being published in its first private edition until it was republished in 2012.

8 See Celan's correspondence with his editor Rudolf Hirsch (2004), with the literary scholar Peter Szondi (2005), with friends Klaus and Nani Demus (2009), with friends from his youth, Edith Silbermann (2010) and Gustav Chomed (2010), and with his German writer friends Heinrich Böll, Paul Schallück and Rolf Schroers (2011).

9 For a more extensive list of his correspondence, see Barbara Wiedemann's article on this topic in *Celan Handbuch. Leben – Werk – Wirkung*, ed. by Markus May, Peter Goßens and Jürgen Lehmann (Stuttgart: Metzler, 2008), pp. 215–26.

10 Paul Celan, *'etwas ganz und gar Persönliches'. Briefe 1934–1970*, ed. by Barbara Wiedemann (Berlin: Suhrkamp, 2019). Wiedemann's ambition was to present Celan's correspondence as co-equal to his poetry, 'seiner Dichtung ebenbürtig'. In her substantial introduction to her commentary, she gives an excellent introduction to the various forms and characters of the letters and insists that they represent Celan's life.

11 Written by Shmueli and Eisenstein, as already mentioned, alongside other important recollections by Edith Silbermann (1993) and Jean Daive (1996).

12 By John Felstiner (1995), Wolfgang Emmerich (1999), Andrea Lauterwein (2005) and Helmut Böttiger, the latter comprising three books and focussing on Celan's places (1996), on his life in Normandy (2016) and on his relationship with Ingeborg Bachmann (2017).

far away and were sometimes impossible to meet in person owing to the Iron Curtain. In addition, living in France but writing in German made it important for him to keep in contact with German life and letters, and to promote his poetry as well, all the more so after he was accused of plagiarism and felt the need to engage people in his defence. Of course, he was also in regular exchange with his publishers. In his final years, when he was living apart from his family, he had to increasingly rely on his friends. And a significant portion of the correspondence involved his lovers, with whom direct exchange was often difficult owing to the secrecy of the relationships. Such letters were sent to post office boxes or to his office at the École Normale Supérieure.

Celan was a very active writer of letters with a highly nuanced and subtle command of German, French and Romanian, but in almost all cases his addressees' contributions outweighed his own. Obviously, each correspondence is different depending on Celan's relation to the person and their respective circumstances. In his early years, his letters are much more playful and poetic, while later on they are often overshadowed by the Goll affair and its repercussions. With editors, topics are naturally more formal or technical; with other writers, they address more literary issues, poetics and the literary market; and with friends from his youth, they often evoke old times and friendships. But despite these differences, they are always about the connection between literature and life, if not the identity of life and literature, in the sense that literature makes life what it is. Celan's stance here is clearly related to the charged idea, of key importance to him, of a human 'encounter' in Martin Buber's understanding of the 'dialogical principle'.[13] Celan's letters are always written in the service of literature and encounter, where literature is the privileged place for such an encounter. This is evident, for instance, when, having received the address of his boyhood friend Gustav Chomed and re-established contact, he writes: 'You have no idea what it means to me to be able to write to you!' and later on about other friends from Czernovitz: 'If only I could count Tanja and Gustav amongst my readers.'[14] For Celan, letters as well as poems were life-defining, which is why he did not tolerate any separation between his poems and his life; for him, poems were manifestations of life and orientation points for his life – they gave him 'Richtung' [direction].[15] In particular, his correspondence

13 Martin Buber, *I and Thou*, trans. by R. G. Smith (London and NY: Continuum, 2004 [1937]).
14 Celan in letters to Gustav Chomed, 24 April 1962/23 June 1962, in Marina Dmitrieva-Einhorn, '"Einhorn: du weißt um die Steine ...". Zum Briefwechsel Celans mit Erich Einhorn', *Celan Jahrbuch*, 7 (1997–1998), 7–49.
15 In his *Bremer Rede* [*Bremen Speech*] from 1958, in *Gesammelte Werke in fünf Bänden* (Frankfurt a.M.: Suhrkamp, 1986), III: pp. 185–86.

with friends from his youth often invokes a tight bond which he misses in Paris and in the West. In this way, the letters reach out to others, just as Celan intends to do with his poems, which always address a 'you' – they are dialogical in nature and in search of an *encounter*.

The letters are also opportunities to establish and confirm such encounters or 'meridians', to use Celan's famous metaphor for a connection with someone else, and to find support, particularly after the destabilization caused by the Goll affair. An example of this self-stabilizing function can be found in a letter Celan wrote to Margarete Susman on 7 June 1963:

> Und Sie haben mir den Mut zugesprochen, mit meinen Worten unter die Menschen zu gehen, Sie haben mir geholfen, das Vertrauen zur Sprache zu bewahren, zu einer Sprache, die man mir – ich weiß, seit ich bei Ihnen war, daß ich es hier aussprechen darf –, die man mir zu vergällen versuchte (und noch immer zu vergällen versucht).
>
> [And your words have given me the courage to reach out to people with my words; you have helped me to keep my trust in language, in a language that people tried – I know, since visiting you, that I may express it here – that people tried to spoil for me (and are still trying to spoil).]

And he continues: 'Was Sie, verehrte Margarete Susman, geschrieben haben und noch schreiben, zählt für mich zu jenen einmaligen Begegnungen, aus denen man lebt' [What you, dear Margarete Susman, have written and still write, is for me one of the unique encounters that bring one to life].[16] Such encounters are at the core of Celan's conception of life, literature and letters. That a corresponding mindset between Celan and those with whom he is corresponding is often missing from these letters, particularly owing to Celan's suspicions in connection with the Goll affair, is another matter. In almost all cases, the correspondence could not assuage Celan's sufferings and he lost confidence in his writing partners.

Ilana Shmueli, in the afterword to her correspondence with Celan, in which poems by him were often included, writes:

> I still knew from our youth that in his poems Celan always needed a concrete You, a changing You, whom he addressed and by whom he wanted to be heard.
>
> I read the poems as part of his letters, I read them as letters to me. Most poems are identical with our experience, they tell our story, they talk about our walks through Jerusalem – they talk about Israel.

---

16 Lydia Koelle, '"Aufrechte Worte". Paul Celan – Margarete Susman. Eine "Cor-Respondenz"', *Celan-Jahrbuch, 8* (2001–2002), 7–32.

> Originally, I read his poems as a statement addressed specifically to me – he stressed in his letters that they were meant that way. I read them with a certain faith, as messages written exclusively to me. I felt they belonged to me, and it took a long time until I learned to give up this exclusivity.[17]

Shmueli confirms Benjamin's idea that a third instance emerges: even though the poems and letters are personal, they exceed this intimacy and become a literary document of more general concern, detached from the initial addressee. Her testimony clearly states that Celan's poems are like letters, which he suggested himself by referring to Osip Mandelstam's image of the poem as a message in a bottle, sent to an unknown reader.[18] However, in Celan's view, poems are *better* letters, the clearest and most direct way of sharing oneself, extremely 'explicit';[19] that is, poems even more so than letters are biographical documents. The boundaries between biography, correspondence and literature blur even further.

Christoph König contends that the letters serve the poems in a dialectical sense since Celan wrote them to give an initial linguistic form to the thoughts he then picked up in his poems. His letters are 'less concrete than his poems': they need interpretation to be connected to Celan's 'constructed' biography and are then 'radicalized' in the poems. The letters can thus be construed as exercises leading to poems.[20] Of course, some letters contain poems, or even consist of only one or several poems. Such cases break down the limits between letter and poem and show that the two genres can be one. König emphasizes the power relation in Celan's correspondences: everything was subordinated to Celan's conviction regarding the unique importance of his oeuvre, which is why empathy, sympathy and conversation usually played no role in his letters.[21] Taking Celan's correspondence with his wife as an example, König develops a dialectics of letters and poems, where Celan repeatedly uses certain formulations from poems as 'Losungen' [slogans/passwords] to construct his marriage within his poetics. This also implies some manipulation of his partners in correspondence.[22]

---

17 *Paul Celan – Ilana Shmueli. Briefwechsel*, ed. by Ilana Shmueli and Thomas Sparr (Frankfurt a.M.: Suhrkamp, 2004), p. 169.

18 In Celan's Bremen speech, GW 3, p. 186.

19 Shmueli in her memoirs: *Sag, dass Jerusalem ist. Über Paul Celan: Oktober 1969 – April 1970* (Eggingen: Edition Isele, 2000), p. 31.

20 Christoph König, 'Give the Word. Zur Kritik der Briefe Paul Celans in seinen Gedichten', *Euphorion*, 97 (2003), 473–97 (pp. 473–74).

21 König, afterword to the volume of Celan-Szondi correspondence, pp. 107–8.

22 König, 'Give the Word', p. 474.

With the biographical details they provide, the letters offer a wealth of information on Celan's work and guide the interpretation of this complex oeuvre, the poems included. He often writes about literature and his work, and many of his observations shed light on his poetics. When Celan includes poems in his letters, the context in the letters can provide clues for interpretation, even though he was reluctant to comment on them. It is remarkable that some formulations appear first in the letters and are then integrated into the poems. The letter context in such instances logically allows for a better understanding of the poem. A case in point is Celan's correspondence with his friend Erich Einhorn, whose name figures in the poem 'In Eins' ['All in one'], and this correspondence inspired the political implications of the poem.[23] Here, the letters he received clearly impact his poetry.

Badiou states that at times Celan says very simple things in his obscure poems which he expresses, also very simply, in his letters – but for poetry, Badiou claims with reference to Celan's poetics, some 'foreignness' is needed. On the other hand, Celan often uses a double movement in his letters: he says something and immediately withdraws from it, which turns his letter into a sort of prose poem.[24] Discussions of his translations, particularly with his editor Rudolf Hirsch, also provide good insights into his translating. But despite the fact that knowing Celan's correspondence helps one to understand his approach to poetry and translation, and to interpret his poems, the biographical approach remains flawed.

The biographical approach

The question of the author is a recurrent issue and we constantly need to negotiate anew the relation between biographical information and literary work. The author as a literary theory topic is definitely back[25] – the publications on Celan's life mentioned above are just one indication. In Celan studies, of course, the debate experienced its first peak in the early 1970s with the 'Gadamer-Szondi debate'. Hans-Georg Gadamer published a book of Celan readings in 1973, focusing

23 Cf. footnote 14.

24 Badiou, 'Au coeur d'une correspondance' (interview with Fernand Cambon, 15 June 2000), Special Issue on Celan, ed. by F. Cambon, *Europe*, 79/861–862 (2002), 191–208 (pp. 196–97).

25 With respect to Celan, Andrei Corbea-Hoisie made this point in 1999 with his conference on the relationship between biography and interpretation. Cf. his introduction in *Paul Celan, Biographie und Interpretation/Biographie et Interprétation*, ed. by A. Corbea-Hoisie (Konstanz: Hartung-Gorre, 2000), pp. 11–14 (p. 11).

exclusively on the poems themselves and putting his trust in a hermeneutic approach to make sense of Celan's poems, supposedly without any background knowledge.[26] Peter Szondi, however, had first shown how much concrete, lived experience – as well as geographical and historical references – are at work in these tightly-knit poems: after spending a day with Celan, he was able to identify the poem's references as places they had visited together and to events Celan related to those places.[27] Marlies Janz then expanded on their political aspects.[28] At the time, many critics perceived Celan as a writer whose texts were not only incomprehensible, 'hermetic', but also without any reference to real life. This has thoroughly changed: today, nobody can seriously deny this oeuvre its political dimension, and the biographical data drawn from Celan's correspondence has confirmed this shift.

This change in perception justifies the biographical approach; by now, its usefulness seems commonly accepted. We should never forget that the particular voice manifest in literature is the result of a unique life experience: great literature always results from one specific person experiencing life in this particular form.[29] Celan himself wrote in a letter to Gustav Chomed: 'ich habe in meinen Gedichten ein Äußerstes an menschlicher Erfahrung in dieser unserer Zeit eingebracht. So paradox das auch klingen mag: gerade *das* hält mich auch' [I have included in my poems an extreme of human experience in our times. As paradoxical as that might sound: it is precisely *this* that keeps me going].[30] The biographical approach can furthermore be legitimized by the fact that Celan himself stressed time and again how much his poems resulted from his concrete personal life experience.

However, even though details of the biographical circumstances provide relevant knowledge about the poem, this is not a sufficient justification for a biographical reading. It shows the authenticity of Celan's life/writing, but the poem is situated on another level. This becomes obvious, for instance, in the fact that he could send a love poem to several women, which shows that the poem takes

26 Hans-Georg Gadamer, *Wer bin Ich und wer bist Du? Ein Kommentar zu Paul Celans Gedichtfolge 'Atemkristall'* (Frankfurt a. M.: Suhrkamp, 1973).

27 Peter Szondi, 'Eden', in *Celan-Studien*, ed. by Jean Bollack (Frankfurt a. M.: Suhrkamp, 1973), pp. 113–25.

28 Marlies Janz, *Vom Engagement absoluter Poesie. Zur Lyrik und Ästhetik Paul Celans* (Frankfurt a. M.: Syndikat, 1976).

29 Uta Werner points out that Celan's life experience was always shaped by his readings as well, which become manifest in everything he writes: 'Aschenbildwahr. Celans Kunst "Avant la lettre" und die Verwandlung des Lebens in Schrift', in Corbea-Hoisie, *Paul Celan*, pp. 147–67.

30 In a letter from 29 January 1970, in *Paul Celan und Gustav Chomed, '... ich brauche Deine Briefe ...'*, ed. by Barbara Wiedemann and Jürgen Koppel (Berlin: Suhrkamp, 2010).

the described feeling beyond the concrete biographical background. Consequently, Celan always emphasized his opposition to the biographical approach and insisted that it is enough simply to read his poetry. He systematically refused to give any clues to help interpret his work. As he said, he was 'kein Freund der Vergesellschaftung des Innenlebens' [no advocate of opening inner life to society].[31] In a conversation with Franz Wurm, however, he said that there was a difference between publishing letters and writing about them – for him, only the latter represented an indiscretion.[32] Writing about his correspondence is therefore a very delicate endeavour. His wife confirmed that '100 per cent' of Celan's poems came from his own life experience but she nonetheless refused to provide details about his life, recommending instead that the focus remain on his work.[33] This contradictory position might also be one of self-interest, to keep critics at bay and in thrall at the same time. But what does this contradiction mean for us as readers? How should we deal with these letters and other biographical material? What is the relationship between biography and poetry in Celan's case?

The poetical approach

Biographical research has its merits and has established a new foundation for Celan research; however, when it distracts from the literariness of his work, it is counter-productive and serves neither Celan, literature, nor literary research. Even though it is tempting to work on historical data, with its appearance as solid, verifiable knowledge, literary scholarship should bear in mind the literariness of literature and not understand itself merely as a subdiscipline of history, sociology, psychology or other such forms of enquiry.

This problem was raised at the outset of the debate by Peter Szondi, who asked whether or not there is a counterbalance to Celan's references to reality – that is, to a determination from the outside – in the determination provided by the poem itself – that is, the interdependency of the single elements in the poem. And he added that the latter would modify the references to reality.[34] A poem

31 Hugo Huppert, *'Sinnen und Trachten'. Anmerkungen zur Poetologie* (Halle: Mitteldeutscher Verlag, 1973), p. 319.

32 Cf. Franz Wurm's postscript 'Erinnerung', in *Paul Celan. Briefwechsel mit Franz Wurm*, ed. by Barbara Wiedemann and Franz Wurm (Frankfurt a. M.: Suhrkamp, 1995), p. 251.

33 As John Felstiner reports in '"Wichtig?". Paul Celan et la question de la surjudaïsation', in Corbea-Hoisie, *Paul Celan*, pp. 91–97 (p. 91).

34 Cf. Szondi, *Celan-Studien*, pp. 120–21; also Janz, 'Text und Biographie in der Diskussion um Celan-Bachmann', in Corbea-Hoisie, *Paul Celan*, pp. 60–68 (p. 62). The biographical 'You', she

is not – at least not only – a historical document, and Celan's emphasis on the *acute* of presence in his Büchner speech should not be exclusively understood in the sense of his biographical and historico-political circumstances, as Barbara Wiedemann contends,[35] but also as the eternal 'here and now' of the poem and its unfolding power in each actualized reading.

This primacy of the poetical finds its confirmation in Celan's use of the term *Lebensschrift* [life-writing], which differs from *Biographie* and is more than this simple German translation of the Latin word for *biography.*[36] The poem takes as a point of departure specific dates, but, in Celan's poetics, it does not stay there, in the past of the event that has taken place, but carries it into the presence of each actualization of the poem. That is why he notes, '!! Nirgends von der Entstehung des Gedichts sprechen; sondern immer nur vom entstandenen Gedicht!!' [!! Do not speak anywhere of the genesis of the poem; but always only of the formed poem!!][37] Of the presence of the poem he writes: 'Die Gegenwart des Gedichts ist – und das <hat> nichts mit biographischen Daten zu <tun>, das Gedicht ist Lebensschrift – die Gegenwart des Gedichts ist die Gegenwart einer Person' [The presence of the poem is – and that is in no way related to biographical data, the poem is life-writing – the presence of the poem is the presence of a person].[38] A *person* is more than biographical data. With this term, Celan refers to Martin Buber: a human being is a person when in a dialogical encounter. Buber's dialogical principle builds on the constitutive power such moments of encounter have over life. Celan formulates this as follows: 'Im Gedicht: Vergegenwärtigung einer Person als Sprache, Vergegenwärtigung der Sprache als Person –' [In the poem: realization of a person as language, realisation of language as a person –].[39] For biographic data to become constitutive, they need to be realized in a poem; it is then the poem that writes life, as *Lebensschrift.* As Celan was therefore able to formulate it, 'meine Gedichte sind meine Vita' [my poems are my vita].[40]

---

states, transforms in the poem 'into the unique You of the individual poem, present only here and now, this You that constitutes itself *poetically* and that helps to write forth the *poetical* autobiography'.

35 Wiedemann, 'Das Jahr 1960', in Corbea-Hoisie, *Paul Celan*, pp. 44–59.

36 For a more detailed development of this notion, cf. Pajević, 'Paul Celans "Ich kenne dich". Das Gedicht als "Lebensschrift"', in Corbea-Hoisie, 2000, pp. 215–224.

37 Paul Celan, *Der Meridian. Endfassung Vorstufen Materialien*, ed. by B. Böschenstein and H. Schmull (Frankfurt a. M.: Suhrkamp, 1999), p. 94.

38 Ibid., p. 113.

39 Ibid., p. 114.

40 In Barbara Wiedemann, *Paul Celan – Die Goll-Affäre. Dokumente zu einer 'Infamie'* (Frankfurt a. M.: Suhrkamp, 2000), p. 522.

It is thus a question of what kind of literary research one wants to do: historical research, where literature is considered a document for the better understanding of a certain period in history, or poetical research, where one reflects on *signifiance*, that is, the meaning-making processes of language in *la chose littéraire*. In my view, both are legitimate and necessary and should not be played off against each other. They should convene in an anthropological perspective: how do we perceive the world and why in this form at a given moment? This would then be part of a *poetological anthropology* and *poetic thinking*.[41]

Celan's correspondence with Ingeborg Bachmann

I would like to illustrate this with reference to Celan's correspondence with Ingeborg Bachmann, which has provoked many reactions and has been widely considered as an apogee in German literary history, befitting of this dream couple. Bachmann herself described this relationships as 'exemplarisch' (*exemplary/ paradigmatic)* in a letter – and even though she crossed the word out, she was harshly criticized for it by Celan.[42] It can, however, be justified by the absolute claims both make about literature: they do indeed both incarnate this greatness of ambition.[43] Their correspondence is often touching, particularly owing to the inability of these giants of literature to find words; they struggle with language and against the difference in their backgrounds in the post-war years, between the Jew who lost everything and the successful daughter of a Nazi party member. Of course, the reader does not know how much was said on the phone – the published letters alone do not really give sufficient reasons for the constant misunderstandings. Years before the publication of their correspondence, many literary scholars had investigated their relationship, albeit in a necessarily speculative mode, as the correspondence was still being held back from the public. This state of affairs, however, was considered an advantage by the editors of a volume on their relationship, as it forced researchers to focus on the literary connections

41 For more about these ideas, see my monograph *Poetisches Denken und die Frage nach dem Menschen. Grundzüge einer poetologischen Anthropologie* (Freiburg im Breisgau: Karl Alber, 2012).

42 In her letter from 1 March 1951 and his reaction in a letter from 7 July 1951; in *Herzzeit. Ingeborg Bachmann – Paul Celan. Der Briefwechsel: Mit den Briefwechseln zwischen Paul Celan und Max Frisch sowie zwischen Ingeborg Bachmann und Gisèle Celan-Lestrange*, ed. by Bertrand Badiou et al. (Frankfurt a. M.: Suhrkamp, 2008).

43 On this correspondence and its 'exemplariness', cf. Marko Pajević, 'Die Korrespondenz Ingeborg Bachmann/Paul Celan – "exemplarisch"?', *Weimarer Beiträge*, 56/4 (2010), 519–43.

instead of on the letters.[44] Once the correspondence had been published, another volume was devoted to this couple, explicitly building on the new biographical knowledge that was finally available in order to gain historical insights without resorting to 'academic speculation'.[45]

Helmut Böttiger's recent account of Celan's and Bachmann's love story describes the various stations and aspects of this complex relationship, shedding light on the sometimes unfair and astonishing behaviour of both poets but also pointing out that, in Celan's case, more biographical knowledge can blur the picture.[46] Böttiger likewise draws attention to discrepancies in the biographical material, which are often due to the contradictory facets of personality in both Celan and Bachmann, but also to the conscious strategies employed to equate life with art. Bachmann strove to make her life readable in aesthetic terms. To this end, allusions to certain biographical matters and then the effacements thereof, as well as retroactive transformations, were common practice but nonetheless served some form of truth.[47] If authors are aware that their correspondence will be read at some point by literary scholars – and both Celan and Bachmann had their posteriority in mind from the earliest days – readers also have to be aware of this mixing of life and literature. The real basis for their relationship – Böttiger also states this explicitly[48] – was poems. The poems are more telling than the concrete dates of documents, and they become dates in a Derridean sense,[49] to which the authors could refer later on: as parts of their history and identity.

---

44 Cf. for instance Sigrid Weigel and Bernhard Böschenstein, 'Paul Celan/ Ingeborg Bachmann. Zur Rekonstruktion einer Konstellation', in *Ingeborg Bachmann und Paul Celan. Poetische Korrespondenzen: Vierzehn Beiträge* (Frankfurt a.M.: Suhrkamp, 1997), pp. 7–14; idem, *'Im Geheimnis der Begegnung'. Ingeborg Bachmann und Paul Celan*, ed. by Dieter Burdorf (Iserlohn: Institut für Kirche und Gesellschaft Iserlohn, 2003).

45 Gernot Wimmer, ed., *Ingeborg Bachmann und Paul Celan. Historisch-poetische Korrelationen* (Berlin: de Gruyter, 2014). The volume resulted from a conference held in Paris in 2012.

46 Helmut Böttiger, *Wir sagen uns Dunkles. Die Liebesgeschichte zwischen Ingeborg Bachmann und Paul Celan* (Munich: DVA, 2017), p. 26.

47 Ibid., p. 42.

48 Ibid., p. 51.

49 Cf. Jacques Derrida, *Shibboleth. Pour Paul Celan* (Paris: Galilée, 1986).

Ruth Beckermann's film *Die Geträumten* [*The Dreamed Ones*] about Celan and Bachmann's correspondence

According to Alain Badiou, Celan was the paradigmatic final figure of an age of poetry, of poets and thinkers, an age that started with Hölderlin.[50] Does that really mean that that age ended with Celan's death? Indeed, he still seems to serve as an example, inspiring others, including artists from other art forms, such as film.

The question of how to find a corresponding expression to this artist's life in another art form is tackled by Ruth Beckermann's recent film *Die Geträumten* [*The Dreamed Ones*], (2016),[51] a filmic representation of the correspondence between Paul Celan and Ingeborg Bachmann. Correspondence is primarily a phenomenon of the past. Few people still write real letters in our era of cheap and easy telephone and internet communication; the postal service today is slow, expensive and unreliable. Since the medium is at least part of the message, our contemporary media mode makes it difficult to imagine corresponding internationally by letter in the 1950s. The correspondents' exact circumstances were often elusive; rectifying misunderstandings could be complicated. Anxiety about (imagined) reactions was a consequence of this, much more so than today. Writing a letter is more charged than writing an email and implies a different form of engagement. When transferring such correspondence into our times, this has to be taken into consideration.

Beckermann wanted to see how young people today would react to these letters.[52] The film is, consequently, correspondence with the correspondence, transposing the emotion into our times. A film is always a commercial enterprise as well, and 'Celan' and 'Bachmann' are marketable brands – making it all the more important to avoid kitsch. Beckermann, wise to these considerations, proceeds by staging the letters in a radio station, where they are recorded, and then following the actors with the camera during the reading and the breaks. The screenplay, written with Ina Hartwig, conveys a good sense of the development of the relationship, with the cinematography commenting upon the effects of the letters. Hartwig specifies that she and Beckermann never intended to talk *about*

50 Alain Badiou, *Que pense le poème?* (Caen: Nous, 2016).

51 Beckermann, *Die Geträumten* (filmedition suhrkamp, Grandfilm 2016).

52 Interview with Beckermann, https://www.youtube.com/watch?v=Iwtd81jE1EU, accessed 9 June 2018.

the text, but *with* the texts.[53] Thus, the film enters into correspondence with the letters over time and space. How does it transform the textual manifestation of a personal relationship, the correspondence, into a visual manifestation?

The film starts with close-ups of the murals on the walls of an Austrian State Radio (ORF) broadcasting studio with a large domed ceiling. The camerawork is accompanied by extra-diegetic violin music,[54] creating an artistic atmosphere. After a cut, the camera shows a close-up of the actress's face as she listens to and looks (presumably) at the actor reading the poem *In Ägypten*, written by Celan for Bachmann for her twenty-second birthday shortly after they had first met in Vienna.

The viewer can see the young actors smirking about the pathos of the text at this early stage of their experience. The contemporaneity to our time and thus distance to the events described in the letters is manifest in the technicalities of the reading – the letters are explicitly mediated. They are from another time, read by other people in a different place, staged and technically recorded – the artificiality of the situation is clearly marked. All these deictic aspects are further corroborated by a sound technician appearing early in the film (00:08:00) to correct the actors' positions in relation to the microphone. And nonetheless, the film itself thematizes how in the process of the recording, the letters develop their own power and draw the actors in.

The choice of the radio setting is not arbitrary: radio was a key medium of Celan and Bachmann's time, and both of them had experience with such recordings. Bachmann wrote features and radio plays and at one point worked full-time for the radio station Rot-Weiß-Rot.[55] Both had at times been in the same position as the actors in the film, standing with a headset in front of a microphone. This position also symbolizes their isolation, focusing on voice/words as the only means of connecting with one another.

The filmmakers spent a lot of time casting the film in order to find actors with the necessary depth. They ultimately chose the remarkable musician Anja Plaschg (Soap&Skin) and the Burgtheater actor Laurence Rupp. In order to capture the readers' fresh reaction to the texts, Beckermann did not spend much time with rehearsals.[56] On one occasion, this approach results in Plaschg shed-

---

53 Brochure to the film, p. 49.

54 *Otoño Porteño*, from *Las Cuatra estaciones Porteñas*, written by Astor Piazzolla (1969), arranged for violin and strings by Leonid Desyatnikov.

55 Böttiger, *Wir sagen uns*, p. 81.

56 Interview with Beckermann, https://www.youtube.com/watch?v=W5SJpf6VJCw, accessed 9 June 2018.

ding tears and covering her face with her hands, asking the cameraman to stop filming: 'stop now, please' (00:12:45).

The apparently detached breaks in between the readings exhibit much emotional attachment to the letters and there are correspondences between the moods of the actors and the situation they have to enact during their reading. The relationship of the actors evolves together with the content of the letters they read. Their seemingly innocent conversations reflect indirectly the circumstances of the relationship between the poets. However, this develops naturally, without a script, thus subtly demonstrating the effects and the power of the letters.

Several aspects support this process, for instance, the position of the actors: at one point the film shows them listening to the recordings with headsets on: her, turned away, looking melancholically in another direction; him, standing a little behind her, looking pensively at her; both of them with their arms folded (00:15:20). This is a perfect illustration of the constellation in the correspondence of the time, when Bachmann was hesitating and Celan demanding and discontent with her indecision.

Such correspondences between the setting of the recording and the situation unfolding in the letters are created systematically: when the poets' relationship is close, the actors are positioned closely together, directly face-to-face, with only the microphones between them. When the poets have hurt each other and are distanced in their letters, the microphones are also at a distance, facing each other or even in parallel and so lacking any connection, lacking any possibility of a *meridian* connecting them.

The framing and editing underlines the relationship at each moment: it can assemble them both in one frame, showing their togetherness; crosscut from one to the other to demonstrate diverging positions; or sustain a close-up of one face to show the emotional effects of the letters. At times, image and reading become detached and comment upon each other.

The facial expressions upon which the camera lingers are often very telling. While she reads about the contradictions in Bachmann's heart, he stares blankly; then there is silence, he sighs and finally reads Celan's harsh reaction letter, in response to which her face again expresses desperation and indignation (00:23:30). Having read out the failure of their love, she hides her face behind the papers with the letters (00:28:10). After the correspondence has broken down, the camera shows him alone on the staircase, behind glass, while she is alone outside smoking while an off-screen voice reads a letter describing this separation (00:31:00). Then we see both actors sitting in the recording room, her rolling up the papers with the letters to form a telescope and looking at him through it. Here, the perspective the actors take of each other is shaped by the correspondence in a very literal manner.

The breakdown of the correspondence is marked by the camera filming the rain in the city at night from a driving car. Information about the separation in the form of Celan's marriage and Bachmann's move to Rome appears on these desolate images (00:38:30). After almost six years, they meet again, and Celan now woos Bachmann in his letters. He sends her poems, clearly referring in one of them to their recent encounter in 'Köln, am Hof' ['Cologne, Am Hof Hotel'], hence the title of the poem. He writes: 'Herzzeit, es stehn | die Geträumten für | die Mitternachtsziffer' [Time of hearts, the dreamed ones stand for the midnight cypher], which provides the title of the film, *Die Geträumten*, and superimposed on his reading we hear her asking 'but are we only the dreamed ones?' (00:40:20). Bachmann's question is repeated again shortly afterwards (00:41:50), thus creating an echo chamber of dreams. It stresses the questioning of the dream status and at the same time takes a dream-like form. This question actually appears in a letter in which Bachmann reacts to Celan's letters and poem (28 October 1957):

> Wenn ich an sie und das Kind denken muß – und ich werde immer daran denken müssen – werde ich Dich nicht umarmen können. Weiter weiß ich nichts. Die Ergänzung, sagst Du, muß heißen 'Ins Leben'. Das gilt für die Geträumten. Aber sind wir nur die Geträumten? Und hat eine Ergänzung nicht immer schon stattgehabt, und sind wir nicht schon verzweifelt im Leben, auch jetzt, wo wir meinen, es käme auf einen Schritt an, hinaus, hinüber, miteinander?
>
> [If I have to think of her and the child – and I will always have to – I won't be able to embrace you. I don't know any more than that. The addition, you say, must be 'Into life'. That is only valid for the dreamed ones. But are we only the dreamed ones? And has a complement not always taken place already, and are we not already desperate in life, even now, when we believe it depends on only one step, out, across, together?]

Celan pleads for them to live out their love, while Bachmann cautiously refers to the dimensions of dream and reality. She poses the question of life outside of literature, of combining their literary worlds with responsibilities towards other people, here Celan's family. An 'addition to life would then be the literary connection. This seems to be the crucial point for the relationship between the biographical and lived life for her. Both sides are necessary and have to coexist, producing each other and making life and literature possible. Being dreamed – this can also refer to us, the viewers, who try to bridge the gap between then and now, between them and us, and our empathetic efforts. What is real and what imagination in such letters?

During a break at this point, the camera observes the two actors eating in the cafeteria, but from a distance; the viewers see the couple talk, but without hearing them. They are behind a sliding glass door that keeps opening and closing (00:48:15), a symbol of the public getting only some distanced, fractured or veiled insights into what is really happening in this intimacy.

Shortly afterwards, during a cigarette break outside, they sit closely on the steps and joke about the sexually charged use of the verb 'komm' [come] (00:54:00). This topic is sustained as they talk about scars and tattoos and he touches her arm with the tattoo, establishing tender contact (00:54:50). Of course, despite its casualness in our present-day context, the topic of scars and tattoos as a symbol for marks of life (let alone tattoos on arms in the Jewish context!) is central to the Celan-Bachmann constellation.

Having documented the renewed distance between them, the film ends with a staged funfair photo of Bachmann's and Celan's heads in a cardboard plane (01:22:30). This final image could be interpreted as a self-ironic comment on the effect that this journey with the two poets was staged and cannot make any real claim to authenticity. In spite of the biographical dimension of the correspondence, all of this is only a representation, the film as well as the correspondence itself. The film thus clearly positions itself within the double bind of the biographical and the poetical. This is a point at which Benjamin's third instance becomes relevant.

Transfer into music

Many contemporary composers have been inspired by Celan's absolute demands on art and truth and have felt correspondences to Celan; an impressive number of musical pieces on his texts exists. Antoine Bonnet and Frédéric Marteau's ground-breaking volume on the relationship between Celan and music, published in 2015, lists several hundred compositions, some by famous composers such as Harrison Birtwistle, György Kurtág, Luciano Berio and Wolfgang Rihm, and includes chansons, and improvisational and electronic music.[57] What makes Celan so appealing to contemporary composers, according to Axel Englund, is that his texts enable 'the music to reflect on its own preconditions', combining 'the disbelief in language with the necessary subversion of this disbelief [...] thus putting notions of meaning, reference, and communication radically

57 *Paul Celan. La poésie, la musique. Avec une clé changeante*, ed. by Antoine Bonnet and Frédéric Marteau (Paris: Hermann, 2015).

into question while, in the same breath, creating a powerful apologia for those very aspects of music.'[58]

This oscillation between a direct biographical reference on the one hand and meaning and its transformation on the other is clearly evident in Peter Ruzicka's opera *Celan*, with a libretto by Peter Mussbach (2001). Given the title, *Celan*, one expects this opera to be a biography in musical form. However, its seven parts are only loosely inspired by Celan's biography and do not intend to represent his life realistically. The name of Celan's wife Gisèle becomes 'Christine' in the opera, an obvious allusion to the tense relationship between Christianity and Judaism in Celan's life. Celan figures twice, once as a young man and then later on in life. The opera does not use Celan's texts, nor does it pretend to be a 'biography in scenes' (Ruzicka); instead, it claims to remain abstract. The scenes constantly jump in time and space between Bucharest, Paris and Germany. They show the young Celan amongst friends and lovers, but also the poet's struggle and confrontations with the phantoms of his past, the death of his parents and anti-Semitism. There are also four film projections with the themes of a fleeing man, a love scene, childhood and war. The script first sets paranoiac behaviour and the reasons for it. It then mixes scenes of love with aggression.[59] Frédéric Marteau comments that the scenes represent rather diverse instances of a tragic destiny in snapshots or portraits that seek to grasp the psychological state of the poet.[60]

This procedure within the script is doubled by Ruzicka's music. Uwe Sommer-Sorgente demonstrates how the opera evolves musically from some of Ruzicka's earlier pieces and acquires a new quality here by playing with these musical forms and gestures. The entire piece is a series of variations that depart from and re-approach the initial scene, with modifications, re-compositions and overlaps, deformations, decompositions and condensations. These musical procedures familiarize the listener gradually with the sonorous material, which, at the same time, is constantly put into question. The listener therefore has to search for instances of coherence while being cautious about any definite form. This takes place in the interaction between music, text and acting. Sommer-Sorgente concludes that the music does not use a coherent narrative to ap-

58 Axel Englund, '(Im)possibilities of Communication. Celan, Ruzicka, Dittrich', *Perpectives of New Music*, 46/2 (2008), 5–32 (p. 28).

59 For the script and background information, see the brochure to the opera, Sächsische Staatsoper Dresden, March 2001.

60 Frédéric Marteau, 'Variations opératiques sur le nom de Celan. Aperçu d'un livret original. *Celan* de Peter Ruzicka et Peter Mussbach', in Bonnet and Marteau, *Paul Celan*, pp. 439–45 (p. 439).

proach its subject matter, but rather does so like a code, thus resembling the way Celan experienced the world – as a system of signs pointing at death.[61]

The opera clearly builds on material from Celan's correspondence and from textual witnesses about him, but it takes many liberties. Very little of the correspondence was accessible in 2000, when the opera was written; this fact may have contributed to the decision not to present *Celan* in the form of a coherent chronological life-story. But the more likely reason is that Ruzicka and Mussbach were more concerned with the drama of the psychological state and finding a contemporary artistic form for the simultaneity of opposing forces so characteristic of Celan's poetics, using Celan's life as a frame for showing a paradigmatic destiny of the twentieth century and for transferring to musical structures a polyvalent poetics.

Conclusion

If we want to do justice to Celan's poetry and to his life, we need to keep poetics in mind, and this is equally true when dealing with the biographical. Art is about *Lebensschrift*, with its entanglements between the documented, the represented, the real, lived, felt, imagined, the creative and created – unlike biography, with its tendency to delineate those dimensions and capture causal relations between them. And letters, similarly, cannot be reduced to biographical documents. The transfer from life to literature is also one from literature to life. In Celan's case, correspondence is part of this two-way street, but it also serves as an intermediary: it provides a space of dialogical exchange, centred around literature and human encounters, where formulations are developed that may eventually find their way into poems, which, for Celan, are more explicit forms of concrete life experience and human interaction. At the same time, the correspondence represents, as Benjamin states, a third instance, born of biographical experience but then transferred to a level at which personal life gains an open dimension, allowing the reader to relate to it. It becomes an example.

When we read letters this way, poetically and not exclusively as biographical data, they exceed a biographical interest in the author's life and become literature in their own right. As such, they trigger other processes, not only by inspiring readers but also, for example, through their transference into opera or film – which, in turn, trigger new reactions and make the correspondence live on,

---

61 Uwe Sommer-Sorgente, 'Des esquisses tendues vers la mort. Procédés musicaux dans *Celan* de Peter Ruzicka', in Bonnet and Marteau, *Paul Celan*, pp. 447–51.

transformed, in the mind of the audience. The third instance has then developed new forms of life as well.

We are dealing here with the question of the invention of a form of life by a form of language and the invention of a form of language by a form of life, as Henri Meschonnic defined the poem[62] – another two-way transfer. Life is to a considerable extent determined by the symbolic forms we develop to represent it; these include correspondence but also academic research on the lives of artists, on biographies, filmic adaptations or musical mises-en-scène. Correspondence and other biographical material is transformed in this process: it is detached from the personal dimension and becomes an element of the perception of the recipient, who in this transfer makes it part of his or her own life, thus carrying the past into the future in this present moment of reception. There is always interpretation at play, and the transfer processes start with the experience itself and continue from there. As long as they do, living experience continues as well.

62 For instance, in *Dans le bois de la langue* (Paris: Laurence Teper, 2008), p. 17.

Anselm Kiefer

Four Images

Fig. 1: *Aschenblume* | *Ash Flower* | *Fleur de cendre;* 2007 – 2012
Oil, emulsion, acrylic, shellac and chalk on canvas | Öl, Emulsion, Acryl, Schellack und Kreide auf Leinwand | Huile, émulsion, acrylique, gomme-laque et craie sur toile; 380 x 280 cm | 149 5/8 x 110 1/4 in

https://doi.org/10.1515/9783110658330-017

Fig. 2: *Oh Halme, ihr Halme, ihr Halme der Nacht* | *Oh stalks, you stalks, you stalks of the night* | *Oh épis, vous épis, vous épis de la nuit*; 2011
Oil, emulsion, acrylic, shellac and chalk on canvas | Öl, Emulsion, Acryl, Schellack und Kreide auf Leinwand | Huile, émulsion, acrylique, gomme-laque et craie sur toile; 280 x 380 x 7 cm | 110 1/4 x 149 5/8 x 2 3/4 in
Copyright: © Anselm Kiefer; Photo: Charles Duprat

Fig. 3: *Paul Celan: wir schöpften die Finsternis leer, wir fanden das Wort, das den Sommer heraufkam: Blume | Paul Celan : we scooped the darkness empty, we found the word that ascended summer: flower | Paul Celan : nous avons vidé l'obscurité, vous avons trouvé le mot qui venait de l'été : fleur*; 2012
Acrylic, emulsion, oil and shellac on photograph mounted on canvas | Acryl, Emulsion, Öl und Schellack auf Fotografie auf Leinwand | Acrylique, émulsion, huile et gomme-laque sur photographie contrecollée sur toile; 280 x 380 cm | 110 1/4 x 149 5/8 in
Copyright: © Anselm Kiefer; Photo: Charles Duprat

Fig. 4: *Streu deine Blumen Fremdling;* 2012
Oil, emulsion, acrylic, shellac on canvas | Öl, Emulsion, Acryl, Schellack auf Leinwand | Huile, émulsion, acrylique, gomme-laque sur toile; 280 x 570 x 10 cm | 110 1/4 x 224 3/8 x 4 in
Copyright: © Anselm Kiefer; Photo: Jörg von Bruchhausen

Peter Waterhouse

Memorial

Immensely green, overlooking Dover where
he lived, where I
heard him hesitate
touching and treading the surface
seeing the sea
he hesitating, tranquil.

Not immersing, not emerging,
holding a kite
up in the placid sky
he had no icebird and icebergs
and Mr Murdstone came into the house.
Mr Dick always up stairs
the Memorial lay on his desk
in the warmth of the desk and the deck.

I wish you'd go up stairs
and give
my compliments to Mr Dick.
And I'll be glad
to know how he gets on with his Memorial.

Written into the stillness
green, I am going to
ask you another question. Look at
this child.

What would you do with him, now?
Oh! Yes. Do with –

Whenever he lapsed into a smile and was
checked by a frown.
Sinking gradually through absence of effort
passing over the surface.
Dick was his name, Ric was his name, changed to Dick.
A florid, placid looking, gentle

https://doi.org/10.1515/9783110658330-018

gentleman who shut up one eye
nodded his head at me and shook it at
me as often and laughed and went.

*

His son? David's son? Indeed!
What shall you do with him?
Oh! do with him?
I should –
The contemplation of me seemed
to give him a sudden idea.
I should wash him.

He came
he came with no hand-writing
he walked on his hands.
Mr Dick, said my aunt, give me your hand.
He came
have him measured, have him clothed.
I shook hands with Mr Dick
who shook hands
with me time
and again.
Mr Dick, Mr Dixon
shook hands and hands again.
Laying down the pen. His
long pen.

Dick's paper.
His head almost lay upon the paper.
I had ample leisure to observe
the room, the
large paper
kite. The number
of pens, quantity of ink.
And nicks. I –
I believe I have made a start.
I think I have made a start.
Taking up his pen and asking

when the king had been killed.
Dick has a longer name
don't you ever call him by it.
He forgets to lay down his pen
and lays down his head.
Alone with the lamp.

*

The night inside
Dick
and silent bells were outside.
No melody
un
dee
do
dee
Mr Dick working
at his Memorial along and alone
I had seen him
working at it
through the open door
probably getting
on very well
I found him driving
at it
and the night was
inside Dick
silent bells were outside
I was one of Dick's bells
he saw me
and lay down his pen
casting anything
but a confident look
at the writing.
So the books say.
So they don't say.
Boy, walk into the bells
and hear what they want
and will.

*

With a withdrawing heart
a silent heart.
He could draw back to his mother
on top of Dover where
there is no Memorial.
Mr Murdstone was in the house.
No one was dead.
He saw Murdstone in the house.
I try to begin
my Memorial
but it is dead and no one
is dead. We all are
in mother
I'm walking towards birth
and birth.
Not reborn to be but born.

I wish you'd go up stairs
said my aunt, as she threaded her needle
and give my compliments to Mr Dick
and I'll be glad to know how
he gets on with his Memorial.

I'm growing younger.
There's a child.
Said the man with the dickname.
If it is to be an answer
it must be new,
a child.
Ask.

*

Mr Dick
what shall I do with this child.

Have
have a suit

made for
him a
tiny little suit.

Here, play with the boats, child,
those that I manned.

If, if,
so many of them.
If the wind.
If the world.
If the voices.
If the light.
If the kingfisher.
The fisher if.
If I.
Mr Dick, has been upwards
of ten years endeavouring to keep
King Charles the First out
of the Memorial. If King
Charles the First. King Charles I.

Did he say anything
to you about King Charles
the First, child
the First getting into it
into the Memorial
and was there now.

I have forgotten
to grow older.
And I look at this
old Memorial
which I write into.

I cannot remember the First.
I'm not old enough and
not clambering.

*

Kites.
While I don't write I fly
a large paper kite.
I live in an upstairs room
which I will leave
only now
and again.
When I see the kite flying I forget
sometimes to breathe. Breathe
the kite calls.
The kite looks, at me: Breathe.

*

In the most dangerous moment
the most unworldly, most unhappy
the most unfortunate man was asked
Mr Dick.
Mr Murdstone was in the house
to take the child, dispose of the child
deal with the child as he thought right.

When I write
my arch-memorial
I hear
no one returning
and am so confident.
No following, Only now.
No no. Only now.
No need to continue
to sink. What
was before, it
is before me?

*

Hesitating
and hesitating, squinting,
wakening, saying: What shall
you do with the child? Oh! do with him?

Why, if I was you,
I should –
The answer was given to me
as a present. The answer is
the present.
Wash him. He is.
Clothe him. He is.
Me listening, waiting, my wits wandering
God knows where
upon the wings of hard words –
I think of it
as one
of the pleasantest things
in a quiet way
that I have known.
As if a thousand things the world
makes a thousand noises about
were not one-half
so good.

Here, finally,
Charles the First, World the First.
The wound is not the memory.
The wound is me and meaning.
It's flowing; will not scar over.
From here we see the white scars of Dover.

Edmund de Waal

Breath

There is more white space than words in the last books of Paul Celan.

There are repetitions, gaps and hesitancies, fierce caesuras, attempts to start and attempts to resist ending. They are tough and jagged presences on the page. He creates new words, sometimes tenderly, sometimes with violence. Hence *light-duress, threadsuns, breathturn.* Your mind moves over the whiteness of the page and you try and sound what this whiteness means: its silence a place of redaction, or of held breath, or of exhalation.

Fig. 1: Making of *breath*, 2019. © Edmund de Waal. Courtesy the artist and Ivorypress. Photo: © Pablo Gómez-Ogando.]

Celan writes of how breath works 'Poetry: that can mean an *Atemwende*, a *breathturn.* Who knows, perhaps poetry travels this route – also the route of art – for the sake of such a breathturn?'

For the last year my studio has been a full of papers, liquid porcelain, scribbled poems on walls, gold leaf and vellum fragments. And I've made a book for Celan. It uses four different types of paper, each of a different weight and a different whiteness. They pace the book, so that you move and turn at different speeds. A book of different kinds of breath. A book that becomes a breathing in and out as you move between the lighter and heavier paper, the text repeating itself. His poems are here in German and in English translation, sometimes printed opposite each other, sometimes overlapping. You see the shadow of one poem

https://doi.org/10.1515/9783110658330-019

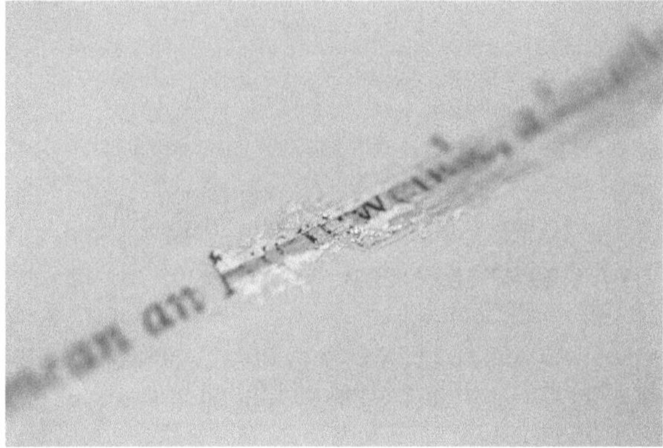

Fig. 2: *breath* (detail), 2019. © Edmund de Waal. Courtesy the artist and Ivorypress. Photo: © Pablo Gómez-Ogando.]

Fig. 3: *breath* (detail), 2019. © Edmund de Waal. Courtesy the artist and Ivorypress. Photo: © Pablo Gómez-Ogando.]

on another. It is letterpress so that you are aware of the pressure of the type, the bite of words, 'the dance of two words'.

And I've brushed porcelain slip over parts of Celan's poems so that they are whitened out and then rewritten his words again. Porcelain is my way of using white in the world. To bring it onto the whiteness of the page is exhilarating.

All books are palimpsests. As we read and re-read we re-create texts. Celan writes, and re-writes: *Breath* is my rewriting for him. And because we remake the world through books, I've collected medieval vellum manuscripts once used in bindings and re-used them in the vellum binding of this book. They are hidden

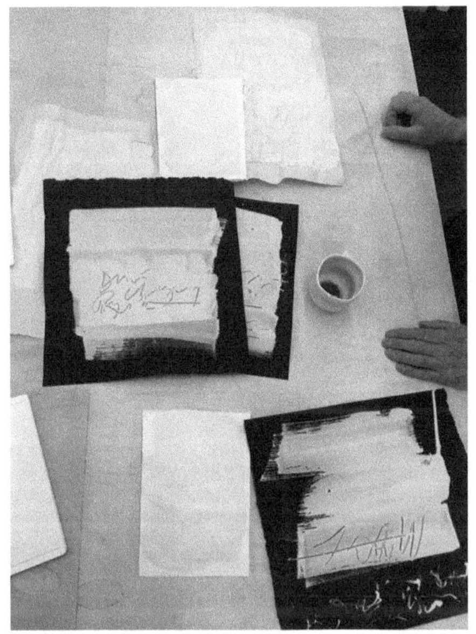

Fig. 4: Making of *breath*, 2018. © Edmund de Waal. Courtesy of the artist.]

Fig. 5: *breath* (detail), 2019. © Edmund de Waal. Courtesy of the artist and Ivorypress. Photo: © Pablo Gómez-Ogando.]

away again. This is how memory works, an iteration through our hands as well as our eyes.

Making this book is a journey into what books are, how they feel, their presence. *Breath* is as large as a medieval bible. It is held within a wooden box, to be opened with some care, read. Thinking of St Jerome reading in his study, the box turns into a lectern for my book to stand on.

Fig. 6: *breath* (installation view, Ivorypress Space Madrid), 2019. © Edmund de Waal. Courtesy the artist and Ivorypress. Photo: © Pablo Gómez-Ogando]

Fig. 7: *breath* (detail), 2019. © Edmund de Waal. Courtesy the artist and Ivorypress. Photo: © Pablo Gómez-Ogando.]

And then within the box there is a drawer. Open it and there is a small marble shelf, another lectern. And held within the drawer, paper-thin, translucent porcelain tiles with fragments of Celan's poems inscribed on them. Hold them to the light, place them on the marble shelf, hide them away like a held breath.

Breath is an attempt to make a book worthy of Celan, using porcelain, paper, marble, vellum, ink, gold. And words. To feel and sound his poems again.

Fig. 8: *breath* (installation view, Ivorypress Space Madrid), 2019. © Edmund de Waal. Courtesy the artist and Ivorypress. Photo: © Pablo Gómez-Ogando.]

Ulrike Draesner

'Huhediblu'

Translated by Thomas Marshall

(One)

He translated.

And retranslated.

Sometimes anger must have gripped him. Claire Goll in Paris, the Goll affair, gall and Gaelic and translations out of Gaelic. A dictionary in one's head, questions, rock types, formations of ice. In the kitchen the child sat with a star. You spoke French at the Celans', but in his poems the poet spoke German alone. Celan maintained that you could write poems in only one language. This he decreed, to himself and to others.

Most of the time other languages moved through his head. There, in the kitchen, there, on the street. There, while reading: Russian, French, Romanian, Italian, English. There, in his poetry – while translating. From all these languages. Wider und wieder. De nouveau.

Sometimes he rides a verse like a horse. Giddy up!, he enjoys it, makes words slide into each other, makes them move. It is his best and only game, the one he can count on: a mixture of trusting the letters and thawing them out. How he transforms these letters (ladders), makes them glide, fall, climb (*k-lettern* in German).

'Huhediblu'

Schwer-, Schwer-, Schwer-
fälliges auf
Wortwegen und -schneisen.

Und – ja –
die Bälge der Feme-Poeten

Note: The titles in round brackets are an exercise in (crypto)multilingualism, i. e. partial or entire anagrams of the title 'No One's Rose'.

https://doi.org/10.1515/9783110658330-020

lurchen und vespern und wispern und vipern,
episteln.
Geunktes, aus
Hand- und Fingergekröse, darüber
schriftfern eines
Propheten Name spurt, als
An- und Bei- und Afterschrift, unterm
Datum des Nimmermenschtags im September –:

Wann,
wann blühen, wann,
wann blühen die, hühendiblüh,
huhediblu, ja sie, die September-
rosen?

Hüh – on tue... Ja, wann?

Wann, wannwann,
Wahnwann, ja Wahn, –
Bruder
Geblendeter, Bruder
Erloschen, du liest,
dies hier, dies:
Dis-
parates –: Wann
blüht es, das Wann,
das Woher, das Wohin und was
und wer
sich aus- und an- und dahin- und zu sich lebt, den
Achsenton, Tellus, in seinem
vor Hell-
hörigkeit schwirrenden
Seelenohr, den
Achsenton tief
im Innern unsrer
sternrunden Wohnstatt Zerknirschung? Denn
sie bewegt sich, dennoch, im Herzsinn.

Den Ton, oh,
den Oh-Ton, ah,

das A und das O,
das Oh-diese-Galgen-schon-wieder, das Ah-es-gedeiht,

auf den alten
Alraunenfluren gedeiht es,
als schmucklos-schmückendes Beikraut,
als Beikraut, als Beiwort, als Beilwort,
ad-
jektivisch, so gehn
sie dem Menschen zuleibe, Schatten,
vernimmt man, war
alles Dagegen –
Feiertagsnachtisch, nicht mehr, –:

Frugal,
kontemporan und gesetzlich
geht Schinderhannes zu Werk,
sozial und alibi-elbisch, und
das Julchen, das Julchen:
daseinsfeist rülpst,
rülpst es das Fallbeil los, – call it (hott!)
love.

Oh quand refleuriront, oh roses, vos septembres?[1]

(Sere Noon)

The country doctor stands in Kafka's yard, braving the icy snowstorm. His horse has died on him; a new one must be sought. A borrowed horse, a life-saving steed. The man who wants to fight death, who must travel from village to village, from case to case: this is how Celan writes him into the first three versions of the poem that will finally be named 'Huhediblu', referring back to yet another Kafkaesque construction ('penal colony') and piling the three on top of one another: body, writing, pain.

1 Paul Celan, *Die Niemandsrose*, Tübinger Edition, ed. by Jürgen Wertheimer (Frankfurt a.M.: Suhrkamp, 1996), pp. 116–19.

> If one were only an Indian, instantly alert, and on a racing horse, leaning against the wind, kept on quivering jerkily over the quivering ground, until one shed one's spurs, for there needed no spurs, threw away the reins, for there needed no reins, and hardly saw that the land before one was smoothly shorn heath when horse's neck and head would be already gone.[2]

Giddy up. He wrote a poem? A verse. No, just a line. No: something he'd heard and picked up, something said by someone else. He wrote it down, crossed it out. What he had heard (in French), the memory of someone else's French verse (Verlaine), triggered the memory of the French verses of a third man (Apollinaire), of Russian verses (Brother Osip Mandelstam).[3] Crossing out, Red Indian, Kafka on horseback, 'horse's neck and head would be already gone' – a Nobody on horseback. Ulysses rode beneath the belly of a sheep to leave the cave of the battering, butchering giant Polyphemus. Polyphemus, literally 'the much-lauded one'. The butcher abounding in songs and legends, the butcher from whom Nobody escapes. By riding where there is no riding, because nobody rides upside down. On top, where he should be sitting, there's nothing but the shadow of his body. Legs clutching tightly, concealed under fleece. – Whoever grasps at him grasps at nothing. Celan writes, deleting the French beginning (it, too, must be overturned, beneath the fur). 'Only in German!' He scrawls, slashes – crossing out the language whose sounds initiated the writing (there are first lines in French over and over in Celan's work, then erased later on) in order to be able to turn around – to escape from beneath the slaughtering word – to flee hidden under an animal's belly, clinging to its fleece – since nobody speaks German.

Nobody speaks German.

In other words, the German spoken in the poem merely looks German. It is German in the shadow of the fleece. The flogging. The persecution by a dazzled figure clad all over in loud words of fame and awe, who had never had more than the one eye. The German of the poem is also spoken by the (wo)man who does not sit up top. It is a German unleashed by a movement in another language, by the last verse of Verlaine's poem 'L'espoir luit' ['Hope Shines'].

---

2 Franz Kafka, *The Wish to Be a Red Indian*, trans. by Willa Muir and Edwin Muir, *The Complete Stories*, ed. by Nahum N Glatzer (New York: Schocken Books, 1995), p. 390.

3 The first draft of 'Huhediblu' begins with the verse 'Oh, quand refleuriront les roses de septembre' (p. 116, left column), the last verse from the sonnet 'L'espoir luit' from the volume *Sagesse* by Paul Verlaine. It is followed (in the second line) by an allusion to the poem 'Schinderhannes' by Guillaume Apollinaire: '... à l'allemande, avant...' The 'brother' mentioned in verse 22 (p. 117) is specified both as Arnold (Arnold Zweig) and as Ossip (Osip Mandelstam) (p. 116, left column).

Still, the poet otherwise contends that 'you can't write a poem in a foreign language'.

...by which you understand him to mean 'only in one's own'.

But he says, 'Nobody can write poems in foreign languages.'

Nobody can. Mr Nobody can.

Both sentences are true. The figure on the horse's back also rides beneath its belly.

Nobody knows what he is talking about. He hides from Polyphemus and hides from himself that he is still hiding from him.

After having slid beneath the belly of a mute mount which is no mount at all, the non-German languages can be heard through the language that must be spoken from below, withdrawn from view, towards the butcher, because it is the language the butcher speaks. Insofar as butchers speak word-language at all.

The hum of these foreign words is not supposed to be heard, at the risk of not being understood. Yet these words must be used, because no others come close to speaking to a butchering, blinded being, feasting in a wood, a cave.

'Huhediblu' was written in September 1962. It is one of the poems in the collection entitled *Niemandsrose* [*No One's Rose*].

Its title is a multilingual word. In the poem Celan crosses the German verb 'blühen' with French 'tuer', kill. Bloom, kill. When written down 'tue', pronounced 'tü', is identical to 'tue', the (formally correct) imperative of German 'to do', 'tun'. The title word arises from the fact that the crossing of 'tuer' and 'blühen' becomes amalgamated with German 'hü', taken from the language used for horses. 'Hü' – 'go', 'hott' – 'stop'. 'Hü-hott' is what children say; it is one of their ways to play with contradiction, play with mastery. 'Hü'. 'Blüh'. 'Tü', vocally trans-posed and -lated into the quieter 'u'. Pronounced deeper down in one's mouth.

Deeper down in the wool. Its curly fleece. Just as the rose curls around its centre.

Niemandsrose. The rose that belongs to no one. The rose that is not someone's.

And nobody who is a rose.

Or somebody who is no rose?

Anybody who does not belong. Who still speaks up against Polyphemus. In the giant's very language.

Nobody, no-ever, no-lands.

(Sooner Nose)

Sometimes he must have been happy. It wasn't a blind f(l)ight after all, it was work and play, thinking and asking in one. The letter moved.

Trembling while riding, because he needed to give the horse the bridle, the hü-hott gives up (putting the allusion to Kafka's penal colony and country doctors into the third draft, yet again, and deleting it in the fourth).[4] In his prose, Kafka manages to turn the narrative screws of proximity and estrangement in a way nobody had known how to do before him. Nevertheless, his sentences follow smoothly onto each other, miraculously frictionless.

Celan's miracles (events) are of a different making. Letters keel over, shift, nose their way forwards. Hü-Hott. Who is riding through the night? It should not be the Erlkönig. A French verse gives 'Huhediblu' the spurs/thorns. Paul Celan does not simply speak out against multilingual poems. He opposes this multilingualism. Oppose: 'sich verwahren' in German. 'Wahren': to stay, protect, keep, each visibly crossed out by the prefix 'ver'. Sich verwahren: to close one's chest, to shrink back into oneself, to fend something off. Sitting on a mount, gliding beneath it. Fending off the multilingual poem, Celan tries to hide. Speaking against the multilingual poem, in German, he creates a German poem, erasing its origin in other languages, its (im)pulse.

The penultimate verse of 'Huhediblu' seems to mock those who do not understand the complex necessity of this process of counter-deletion – a deletion, necessitating creation in another language, which in turn subcutaneously refeeds into its multilingual impulses. Perhaps they (German poets like H. M. Enzensberger) don't need this reciprocal complexity of self-annihilation/creation. Wanting to open German up to English, for example, they just do it: hot love. According to Celan's poem, however, they're chasing an illusion: German will not be discarded like this. In German hands the new English 'hot' of these poets just becomes 'hott' again.

'Huhediblu' constitutes and negotiates a paradox: could a German poem discard German while still using it? Celan tries to be a riding nobody. To escape as nobody and to speak this German with another inf(l)ection, to emerge via the detour of a German poem from a linguistic sub-space, a hiding space in wool, refuge among roses.

Underfleece Ulysses. Un(der)consciously, un(der)awares, under-his-hand, in a process mastered and un-mastered in one, Celan binds himself back into this

---

4 'Straf- | kolonien und Land- | ärzte und Ritten ins nächsten | Dorf –' can be found in all versions but the final draft.

multilingual initiated writing. A writing whose second French impulse, Guillaume Apollinaire's 'Schinderhannes' poem, represents in turn a reaction to another part of the German history of violence, shifting and pushing German as a language by using it. 'Schiebe' [push], 'Schübe' [impulses, drawers, advances]. Echoing rhymes: 'Züge' [trains and traits]. 'Betrüge' [cheat].

Translating, yet again.

True, Celan does not write in different languages. He only ever comes from other languages into the language that is to be written.

From these others to his very 'own', from this own one back into the ones set as other.

'Oh, quand refleuriront les roses de septembre?' (beginning, deleted)

'Quand refleuriront, oh roses, vos septembres?' (end, found in writing)

In between: the entire poem unfolds.

Translating. Celan on the Parisian kitchen chair. In the end, Celan uses the German poem itself to translate Paul Verlaine's verse into the French closing lines of the very same German poem.

How many languages are we discussing now? On the surface even 'Huhediblu' looks German. Encountering it within the German body of *Niemandsrose*, authored by the 'German' writer Paul Celan, you might (internally) hear its title according to German spelling rules.

On the second surface, Celan's poems, above all 'Huhediblu', look multilingual.

In a third layer, in the evolution, they inevitably look multilingual.

At the fourth glance, they question the separation of languages. The French end of 'Huhediblu' is no longer French, but French-German. Over the course of the poem, which flees from Polyphemus the much-vaunted slaughterer, Verlaine's initiating verse has incorporated the 'à l'allemand, avant' from Apollinaire's poem about Schinderhannes the robber (multifariously famous for butchering people). It is French with German inside it. A sheep stepping out of the cave, 'no-body' clinging to its fur.

(*Ross!* On!)

German 'ü' (almost) exists as sound in French, though not as grapheme.

Hü-hott, huhediblu.

Hü-hott, one word, two directions. So this is how it works, the language between man and animal? No. That would be too nice. There's a bit in the horse's mouth. There it feels the master, the pull. Communication with a horse travels from mouth to mouth, administering pain.

Hü – on tue.

'Huhediblu' shatters the facade of monolingualism.

The rose appears in this poem only in French. It starts a further process of translation, a gliding or scooping, of which Celan, thinking-in-language, makes use again and again. 'Rose', French, flicks into German (almost identical to the eye, similar for the ear), just as the singular and the plural of the French word glide against each other (for the eye a difference in the 's', none for the ear). Sliding rhymes between languages ('blüh' – 'tue') are as much part of this linguo-poetic signature as the smooth melting of 'rose', French, into German 'Ross' (another word for horse). Thus, a circle is formed between rose and horse, blossom and kill. Celan transposes a bilingual field of word-similarities into a field of motifs to which a third language is connected via the 'hott' that supplements any 'hü': the English 'hot' (to the ear almost the same as 'hott', to the eye a difference in one letter). A constant transformation is implied. Giddy up! And the rose? Another instance of 'foreign' speech imported into each of these languages: the word stems from the Far East.

I count six languages: German, French, English, Latin, Italian and the language Huhediblu – a language of mixture and interrogation, of rhymes gliding between languages. To deadbloom, to bloomkill, imperative. By using an Italian 'di' as an interlink, one becomes the possession of the other. Flower from/to killing. Transposed into the darker register of the German 'u', whereby Celan manages to slip some English right into the title, already hybridized into that language which will be used explicitly only at the end of the poem. It shines back from that point right into its very beginning. In English /hu/ means 'who' (German 'wer'). Finally, the ear can catch the multilingual sentence hidden in a seemingly nonsensical word: who est di blue? Who is of the blue and talks, by speaking German, saying 'hü' and 'blüh', of killing?

In a trilingual shape – English, French and Italian – the poem's title hovers above the triple German 'schwer' [heavy] of its first verse.

'Who', transformed into 'sch-wer'.

Heavy the question, in German, as to the who.

(Noon-Seer)

Almost all formal means of a poem – metre, rhyme, stanzas, overall shape – are the gratifications and the gratuities of repetition. Celan works with interlingual rhymes, resonances, assonances; and he likes to double-record what he takes, because he wants to drop it on the way, hü-hott. It slips, is lost – and longed for ever after. The linguistic gestures of initiating and deleting, slanting and toppling, as used by the multilingual poem 'Huhediblu', present poems as spaces where any-some-no-body can be found. No, this is too affirmative. Rather found-shifted-crossed out. Poems are spaces where finding, concretely fantasized, is shown as an inconclusive process of a search for words, staging cunning and exile, fight and flight.

The poem ends on a twofold note in English and French. 'Call it (hott) love', alluding to Enzensberger's poem 'Call it Love',[5] sends us off across the sea into the next language and its who-est-di-blue surprise of flourishing, killing and the grief (the blues) the poem itself leaves behind. The language developed from the verse 'Oh, quand refleuriront les roses de septembre' finds the present gossipy, simulates spoiled speech, 'dies, dies: Dis- | parates', reaching for the anchor of their bygone common language, Latin ('tellus'): *Die Erde... ein Planet.*[6] The Schwer-Schwer-Schwerfälligkeit [clumsiness, heaviness, literally: a heavy way of falling] of the poem's very beginning, aiming at clairaudience, is taken up as a hearing that falls 'in seinem | vor Hell- | hörigkeit schwirrenden | Seelenohr'. The horse tears across the lake; borders between languages, mixed in the ear, rush together like earth and hell. Neither of these is named directly in the poem's first, German, idiom, but referred to in a second one (Latin 'tellus' for 'Earth' and English 'hell', 'bright' in German). Incessantly, non-German words interfere with the main body of the poem in German, usurping its signifiers, splitting them into Babel voices, speaking in two tongues simultaneously. Signification is 'fällig' – keeps stumbling, topples. 'Huhediblu' enacts this process as the very essence of what a poem *owes* (the second meaning of 'fällig' in German) to its readers and language(s): opening up the process of signification, it undermines the concept of monolingualism as such. The 'Oh-Ton, ah' as the 'A and O', alpha and omega, beginning and end of poetry, is an original (original tone, O-Ton) that has always been shifted.

(Seen, Soon, Or...?)

The word 'nobody' – the name used by cunning Ulysses for himself – is the word of a fraud. It serves to deceive a polysemic, bleeding man 'hung with words', who does not understand the difference between the semantic (referring to emptiness: nobody is there) and the performative levels (someone must have said it) within one language. Layers and gaps everywhere; any 'one language' reveals it-

5 Hans Magnus Enzensberger, *Verteidigung der Wölfe* (Frankfurt a. M.: Suhrkamp, 1957), p. 21.
6 'Tellus', the earth goddess.

self to be much less monolithic than the concept would imply. Monolingualism is – a myth. Each language presents itself in many shapes as voice and image, prosody and notation, reference and act. 'Nobody' presents itself as an inverted Shibboleth word: instead of inclusion, it generates exclusion. It pretends to be a name. But a name that does not name anyone is a linguistic means of deception. By suggesting a signifier which amounts to nothing but a 'no' it manages simultaneously to designate and to deny designation, turning into the name of a gap in the form of a (wo)man.

Rider on the Indian horse.

Again he tilts from the vertical, clings to coat, bundles against belly. Night falls, the coat-creature belly-beast carries him from the cave into light ('hell') and into bondage ('Hörigkeit'). To a place where there is nothing left but hearing? Or where you have to obey? Having fallen for something/someone?

Every way out seems blocked.

The German word 'Hellhörigkeit' [clairaudience] constitutes a paradox in itself. It seems to use what one sense (vision) can do to demarcate the other (hearing). But in fact, the German 'hell' deceives when it speaks of light. It originally belongs to the ear. Derived from the noun 'Hall' ('helli', 'hel' in Middle High German), it pertains, exclusively in Old High German and primarily in Middle High German, to voice and sound.[7]

'Hell' turns out to be a loanword: lent to the eye by the ear. The word tended increasingly towards speaking about light. With this tendency the eye returns the word to the ear, enabling it to perceive twofold: sound and light. Wave and wave. Such clairaudience (Hellhörigkeit) describes a space of exchange between senses and meanings. The reverberation and (sensual, organic) wandering of words on/in humans appear as poetic principles. They encompass more than one language.

(Noon SOS)

With the name 'Schinderhannes' another word of this kind becomes effective (treibt sein Wesen) in 'Huhediblu'. 'Frugal, | kontemporan und gesetzlich | geht Schinderhannes zu Werk'. Schinderhannes, German robber of the late eighteenth century, ringleader, terrorist, murderer. There are 211 crimes attested to him. He, too, is a much-lauded individual. Robber's bride Julchen 'daseinsfest rülpst | rülpst es das Fallbeil los, – call it (hott) | love.' Stout Germanness in the middle

7 *Deutsches Wörterbuch*, entry 'hell'.

of a German forest, having gorged itself on plunder and primitiveness. Schinderhannes, murder's servant, was the son of a 'Schinder' [a 'knacker']. Hott indeed: here the horse is killed. The Schinderhannes of 'Huhediblu' is the result of a double migration across linguistic borders. Through Apollinaire's poem 'Schinderhannes', the historic figure has been converted back into German territory as a robber who crouches and drinks in the woods but forswears love because he still has to kill a Jew on the Rhine. Because German, in the end, falls back on German, even if it dreams of escaping from its very own Hott to hot.

Again, something is due (fällig). Words fall: 'Beiworte, Beilworte'. German as language is due. In the end, the poem zooms away from the language in which it was conceived (in which it created itself). Which it had reached, clinging beneath some animal's fur.

And now – what remains? Has nobody saved himself?

Having entered the altered French of the poem's final line, where he cannot be 'grasped' as Polyphemus, blinded, hungry and enraged, he steps out of the cave, searching for his sheep.

Nobody has saved himself. At the cost of dissolution into another idiom.

(Noose Ore)

Later poems trigger earlier ones. That the multilingualism which surfaces so clearly in 'Huhediblu' did not do so in earlier poems doesn't mean that it was absent from them. Resonances, sliding rhymes can also be found within the entire work of an author, between texts, from 'wann' to 'wannwann'.

> Ein Holzstern, blau,
> aus kleinen Rauten gebaut. Heute, von
> der jüngsten unserer Hände.
>
> Das Wort, während
> du Salz aus der Nacht fällst, der Blick
> wieder die Windgalle sucht:
>
> – Ein Stern, tu ihn,
> tu den Stern in die Nacht.
>
> (– In meine, in
> meine.)[8]

---

8 Paul Celan, *Sprachgitter*, Tübinger Edition, ed. by Jürgen Wertheimer (Frankfurt a.M.: Suhrkamp, 1996), pp. 78–79.

As Celan's drafts reveal, this poem, written in August 1958 and published in the volume *Sprachgitter* [*Speech-Grille*], also sprung from a French sentence: 'Cette étoile, mets-la dans la nuit.'

A sentence spoken in Paris at the kitchen table where a star was built 'by the youngest of our hands'?

Building a star: travelling from one language to another. From one form (wooden rhombuses) to the other (words).

'Ein Wort, während' the eye looks for the star in the sky as 'Windgalle'.

Another word, translated by Celan. He took it from two technical languages, medicine (specifically: diseases with horses) and astronomy, where 'Windgalle' refers to a bright glow in the sky opposite the sun.[9]

> – Ein Stern, tu ihn,
> tu den Stern in die Nacht.

'Tu ihn': 'do it' – put it there, take it, throw it. But also 'tu' (in French): kill it. Having read 'Huhediblu', the 'killing' in 'doing' cannot possibly not be heard.

Save and kill, in one. Construct and annihilate, in one. The poem ends on two lines in parentheses. Only limited speaking can follow on from killing. A withdrawal?

> (– In meine, in
> meine.)

Into the night that belongs to me. To which I belong. Into 'meine' (German 'meinen': to mean it, to refer to): into the very process of referring/relating. The process of wanting to express something. For in each German 'Tun' [action], in each action performed in relation to the star, killing still has its say.

(*En Rose*)

The question of multilingualism in Paul Celan's poems leads deep into the subtexts of their formation, into the 'Hellhörigkeit' of poetic thinking, that hellish brightness of hearing. It is a thinking that genuinely conceives of poetry as trans-

9 *Deutsches Wörterbuch*, entry 'windgalle': 'heller schein am himmel der sonne gegenüber, ein anzeichen von sturmwind' Adelung; steir. Unger-Khull 635; 'little cloud at the sky', also ox-eye, weather gall. And: windgall, winddog, meaning wassergalle; engl. windgall, 'fuszgeschwulst der pferde'.

lation. Again and again the stimulus for the poetic text comes from translation; it continually creates the matrix for the evolving poem.

In its final line 'Huhediblu' hauls itself up onto the bank of another language. Prepared by the multiple intersections of blossom, *tuer* and hü(-hott), it completes its movement by fighting its way back into French. French represents a different kind of sub-language to English, a sub-sub-language adjacent to one of Celan's earliest languages: Romanian. 'Huhediblu' aims at the centre of Celan's guest language – French – by tackling its poetic canon: the original verse is rewritten, written anew, in the light of the poet's own (owned? fällig?) German. The many-worded ride of a long poem – touching on derision, self-protection, ridicule, woundedness and doubt – results in a linguistic space where one language contains another one and is changed by it.

There are no harmless encounters with German and its new and old characters, no antipathy or apathy towards them, no innocence of them: 'quand refleuriront, oh roses, vos septembres?'

September, the month the German Reich invaded Poland, the month Paul Celan's mother was deported by the National Socialists. In the poem the 'quand' slips when translated into 'wann, wannwann, Wahn'.

By now, the *Niemandsrose* of the volume's title has itself been translated. 'Huhediblu' acts out what a Niemandsrose might be: nobody, clinging into curls, hiding in a process of folding/unfolding. The word 'rose' glides. 'Huhediblu', the French counterpart of nobody's rose, albeit in German, is a programmatic, poetological poem that becomes adjectivally 'hell-hörig': it listens to hell and light, to hü and hott, to blossom and kill. Ad-jekt – abject – glued to the abyss.

'Huhediblu': who comes from the blue? Who was or is blue-eyed? 'Aryan'? In German to be blue-eyed also signifies to be ignorant. Through 'blühen' we might also hear 'buhen' (to boo, to hoot). Has the poem's speaker been booed whilst looking for words? Is he using his poem to boo the booers back? Celan contrasts the illusion of escaping the German language with the cunning, non-riding riding, the multiple deletion of the name by a new Ulysses. To all appearances this movement maintains monolingualism. It must: the language of violence itself is the only language that Polyphemus knows – though badly enough. So that the cunning and jest, embodied in someone who wants to be no one calling out 'nobody', actually works.

The process of continuous shifting that has been set in motion demands a price. 'Üben' [practising], 'buhlen' [courting in a rather disgusting way] and 'lügen' [lying] also resound in an ever-shifting 'blühen' [blooming]. All these word fields vibrate within the heavy-heavy-heaviness of the German language, repeatedly set in motion by Celan's 'Huhediblu'. Because clairvoyance is 'clair' only when it perceives even the echo of echoes.

Paul Celan, the poet, translated poems by others over and over. And went on translating, in writing. In his poems, multilingualism 'treibt sein Wesen'. The German phrase literally means 'to drive one's essence/being, rationally as much as by instinct'.

Only in German do you 'drive your soul'.
You drive it in language.
Drive it into it. You ride on it. Flying, without neck, overhead.

Michael Eskin and Durs Grünbein

We Are All Migrants of Language. A Conversation

Translated from the German by Michael Eskin

Michael Eskin: When and where did you first hear Celan's name? Do you still remember its impact on you? What you felt? What you thought?

Durs Grünbein: I came across the name 'Celan' for the first time in the works of the philosopher Theodor W. Adorno. He always spoke about a poet who tried to save the German language after Auschwitz, single-handedly shouldering, it appeared, the burden of history. I hadn't yet read anything by him, but from then on I had the most profound respect for this name. Even though it wasn't really a name so much as a secret code among the initiated – a catchword almost, that also had the ring of a chemical element. When I finally did read 'Death Fugue', I was surprised. I don't know exactly what I had been expecting – dark, hermetic texts of extreme difficulty perhaps, but not that. Celan, by the way, was not part of the school curriculum in East Germany. No teacher had spoiled his singsong for me through rote didacticism, which is why I encountered Celan's magical, shamanistic lines utterly unprepared, in a state of complete innocence, so to speak.

The word 'shamanistic' comes to mind involuntarily here, by way of nonsensical word play: for what I grasped then was that for Celan everything revolved around shame, great shame – the shame of one who was ashamed that hardly anyone among his contemporaries was ashamed. At that time, I also learned everything about his life: about his parents' death; about his conscription to forced labour; about his move to Paris and his reading at the Gruppe 47 gathering; about the Goll Affair and his suicide on the Seine. Since then, I haven't stopped thinking about the painful question of shame. Why was this sensitive, sophisticated human being so ashamed for his fellow men that he grew ever more thin-

---

Note: This conversation is a heavily abbreviated English version of 'Der Spiritus des Lebendigen', first published – also in shortened form – in *Sinn & Form* (January 2020) and, in its entirety, in: Michael Eskin, *'Schwerer werden. Leichter sein'. Gespräche um Celan mit Durs Grünbein, Gerhard Falkner, Aris Fioretos und Ulrike Draesner* (Göttingen: Wallstein Verlag, 2020). Translated from the German by Michael Eskin;

https://doi.org/10.1515/9783110658330-021

skinned, ever more suspicious to the point of paranoia, until he could finally no longer stand it and only wished to disappear?

You could approach his works from several perspectives. As an accusation directed at Germans for murdering Jews and for repressing the crime after the war. As an attempt to escape from the horrors of history into poetry by claiming language for himself like a child – the child that mumbles and talks to itself. Or as a relentless battle with shame – a shame of many colours: the shame of the survivor who couldn't protect his parents; the shame of the speaker who felt at home in the language of the murderers because it was the language of his mother; the shame of the poet who knows instinctively that modern poetry always only speaks of itself – evincing strong affinities with the pathology of narcissism – and who senses that he can never fully grow up because his uniquely profound experience of language cuts him off from life; shame for all the false notes in the poems of others; shame for the imitators; the shame of one who can trust himself as little as all the others, of one who ever lives on the brink of depression and is ashamed of it; the shame, finally, of the 'idiosyncratician' of language whose linguistic sensitivity drives him into ever deeper isolation, who is literally revulsed by conversation with others and who feels miserable about it. 'The hollowed-out heart, | wherein they install feeling. | Homeland Ready- | made parts'. You can't say it any more clearly. I've never understood why Celan has been accused of hermeticism. But I've also always wondered how so many could so easily relate to him. It didn't work for me.

Michael Eskin: What I find particularly interesting here is the link that can be established between your reflections on Celan's shame and your own treatment of the subject. The word you often use in your poetry and essays to express your own shame regarding your historical-existential emplacement is 'Peinlichkeit', 'embarrassment'.

Do you see a connection between yourself and Celan? Do *you* feel a certain embarrassment or shame for your fellow men, which might be akin to the shame you perceive in Celan?

Durs Grünbein: In Berlin, I only have to step outside to trip over one of those *Stolpersteine* – 'stumbling stones' – scattered across the city's sidewalks, and it starts all over again. I often take the time to read the names of our former neighbours – deported, all of them. Many were retirees, but there were also small children and newlyweds. Then I think to myself: what a dirty rotten mess. Apartments confiscated, people crammed into cattle cars never to return. 'Murdered in Minsk' it might say, and we think of the Belorussian capital of today. But the actual place of death was Maly Trostinec, where most were shot on arrival. Not many know the place, it doesn't figure prominently in the nomenclature of the extermination archipelago. Many Germans today would be surprised if they were told what happened to those erstwhile Berliners after *they* had arrived. Those were the killing fields in the East, random execution pits behind the Eastern front. Much of this Holocaust chapter still lies in the dark. And it is then that I feel shame and rage welling up inside me about how little is still generally known. So much on the subject of dealing with the past – *Vergangenheitsbewältigung* – also one of those verbal monstrosities cooked up by post-war Germany.

I feel shame for the overall lack of a sense of injustice, shame for the shocking absence of imagination. Defenceless human beings, civilians slaughtered in the wings of the theatres of war, and still most apparently find it hard to imagine themselves in their place. The non-Jew becomes an Aryan again by remaining unaffected by the whole thing. It's not *his* family's business, it only concerned the others. That's not a good foundation for a society. And more and more often voices can be heard that wish to put all that behind – it was, after all, only a drop of 'bird shit' on Germany's otherwise glorious history. It's precisely here, at this juncture, that every single one of Celan's words sets in. It is difficult for him to compose a poem because the language in which he writes is poisoned. I am ashamed of the apathy, the coldness of heart, the often clumsy and cramped language of the politicians who officially deal with these issues. The matter, meanwhile, is fairly simple from a human and civil rights perspective: murder is murder is murder. And no one has to be Jewish to say to himself: the other – that's you. Look in the mirror: you too don't want to be murdered. Shame also for the actions of a state that ordered the extermination of fellow citizens in the name of the nation. It's embarrassing to say this, but it must be said again and again until the very last one among us sees himself in the place of the murdered.

Heiner Müller once told me a Jewish joke whose black humour stuck in my craw: 'That Auschwitz business – the Germans will never forgive us for it'. Why not make shame the starting point of understanding? That's how Kafka's Josef K. ends. The last sentence in *The Trial*, the moment of execution, reads: '[...] it was as though shame would survive him'. I, for one, will be survived by this shame.

Michael Eskin: Claude David, the renowned French Germanist, once called Celan the 'greatest French poet of the German language'. Do you agree with this characterization? Or do you see him as a German poet who happened also to have lived in France? Is it important to you to site Celan in terms of nationality?

Durs Grünbein: The truly fascinating thing about his poetry is its *Ortlosigkeit*, its 'placelessness' – understood not as a deficiency so much as a moral stance. His is the state of the universal migrant who had never been granted a home. As a German-speaking Jew, he was driven out of his culture of origin – call it Romania or Ukraine, depending on how you look at it. Or rather: he couldn't stay where his parents had been murdered. He doesn't want to go to

Germany, where he can be present, at most, through his books, but he can't physically live there. There, the murderers ran free or acted with unheard-of brazenness at their trials. I dare you to re-watch the footage of the Frankfurt Auschwitz Trial. Our own air is still poisoned with Nazism; he would suffocate in it.

A rhetorical question: why didn't Celan move to the GDR? Because they would have clamped down on him as a formalist and bourgeois *l'art-pour-l'art* poet. No one would have published his books. Even his dalliance with the Russian Revolution wouldn't have helped him.

In France, he remains the stranger, the foreigner, even though he completely assimilates in term of language. As a poet, he turns his ear towards tidings carried his way by German radio waves. They deliver signals from the dear departed, and he in turn responds from his own secret station. To the French, he remains an exotic character writing poetry in German. They discover him later by way of philosophy – ironically in connection with the work of a much-contested thinker who was deeply complicit in Hitler's tyranny: Martin Heidegger. Jacques Derrida, the French-Algerian, will recognize his own fate in Celan's and induct him once and for all into the sacred halls of philosophy. I once attended one of his lectures in Paris, in which he spoke about Celan's precarious standing in the German-speaking lands for two hours. 'No one witnesses for the witness' and 'Pontic nothing' were mentioned. I can still hear the lines in the philosopher's wonderful diction and French accent. I understood then: for Celan, language itself constitutes exile. He is the essentially banished, who can never arrive, and as such he identifies with all the other exiles in poetry. Their proximity is immediate. And so we encounter Ovid, Dante, Mandelstam, Tsvetayeva – the dialogue in the transit spaces commences. A Frenchman Celan never was. And in contemporary German poetry, he is in his own league.

Michael Eskin: Is there an affinity between you and Celan as far as the question of *Ortlosigkeit* is concerned? Being 'underway' – the person's in general as well as the poem's – is one of the core motifs in Celan's oeuvre. Your own work in turn is shot through with the motif of 'transit': in your poems and essays, you speak of airports, waiting areas, real and imagined journeys across the globe, and even into outer space and all the way to the bottom of the sea. At one point, you depict yourself as 'ever underway, ever busy checking watches and translating from one life sphere into the next', as 'nowhere at home and never arriving'. And yet, contrary to Celan, you somehow remain in 'your' country, the land of your origin (even though the GDR no longer exists).

Do you view yourself as a *German* poet or as a poet who writes *in German*, one who is at home everywhere and nowhere, living in a state of universal migration?

This question is important to me because I, for one, have never experienced your poetry as properly and strictly 'German' – whatever this may mean. I've always perceived something quite 'non-German' in your imagery, use of language, sense of phrasing and melody, in the very 'set' – to use Roman Jakobson's term – of your poetics; something that casts a somewhat bitter, ironic light on the geographical contingency of your birth. I have a similar sense reading Celan's poetry.

Durs Grünbein: I don't feel uncomfortable with your impression. The poems *should* feel a bit strange, different from everything else, perhaps even historically atypical. Which isn't to say anachronistic. Preferably exotic or, even better, 'foreign'.

I experimented a lot before publishing my first poem. I was quite dissatisfied with the banal *Normaldeutsch* of many of my contemporaries. It was only much later that I discovered its appeal. And it took a long time until I learned to appreciate the deviations of so-called *Pop-Lyrik* – only after I had come across Apollinaire and recognized him as the source of some of the currents in international post-war poetry (American, French and German). It was the exotic that impressed me most in the poems I liked to read. I liked Hölderlin's 'Kalamatta language', Gottfried Benn's import-export trade with colonial metaphors, Frank O'Hara's 'catchiness'. I always liked the runaways, for instance Elizabeth Bishop, who first moved to Paris and then to Brazil, to free herself from the linguistic conventions of New England. And of course: Wallace Stevens, who developed his poetics of the American South in Florida, the 'Secretary of the moon' with his longing for the order of the vegetative ('The Order of Key West'). That the *key* to Western thought must have washed up on the shores of other continents after all the waves of globalization – Asia, the tropics, Africa – was something I immediately understood.

All of which was very much in tune with Carl Einstein, the smartest of avant-gardists, whose sole aim was to re-enchant a disenchanted world by dint of new myths and totems. That's how, one fine day, antiquity in all of its freshness wafted my way, as if after a long sea voyage that allowed me to see the coast in a new light. I know that this meant going out on a limb, catapulting myself out of my own narrow cultural confines. But it had to be done, for time and space had long been universally jumbled. We are all migrants of language. Every state library is, to quote Benn, 'a brothel of sentences', a 'delirious paradise', and in the midst of the din of the metropolis, leafing through atlases and picture books, you come across a 'dream-laden word'.

Apparently, the GDR was, from the very beginning, much too small for the flights of my imagination. Later on, concrete daily life in the West would also become too stifling. And so, I had to take a deep dive into antiquity, into the baroque age, into ancient Rome, Baudelaire, Lautréamont and so on. Suddenly, Columbus was looking over my shoulder, flying fish were jerking in the gutter, and the West Indies were at my doorstep.

Michael Eskin: You once said that 'not much will remain of the poetry of that insane twentieth century, but certainly some Benn and Celan'. Could you explain this a bit further?

Durs Grünbein: The juxtaposition of these two names – questionable in itself to many – simply means: these two, contemporaries of the German-Jewish catastrophe, irreducibly *belong*. After all, it's the poets that a language community holds onto. You can't intentionally organize it through a politics of memory – it simply is what it is. As long as we have data carriers – yesterday's book, today's internet – the poems of these two will travel through time. We sense the flame that burns in our collective memory, we sense what reliably lights up in our moments of longing. Celan is one and Benn the other, that's it.

Benn will most likely show up on the reading lists of the conservative Right (it's already happening), while Celan will probably find himself in the camp of Germany's critics. True poetry, however, survives the civil war, or any schism for that matter, because it is animated by something that overcomes all elements of opposition. It may be easy for an unaffected German to sweep aside Celan's grief. As long, though, as we are endowed with a sensitivity to language and possess a sense of our own history with all its vagaries, no one will be able to avoid Celan. Benn, conversely, is good for certain (blue) hours. Both boast explosive compounds, bold chemical word formulas that are preserved in free radicals of expression independently of their poems. 'Winged words' they used to be called. Both poets have left us a rich thesaurus of such winged words.

Michael Eskin: Benn famously argued that poetry is (and ought to be) strictly 'monological', 'addressing no one', concerned exclusively 'with the poet himself', articulating the poet's 'self-encounter'. Celan, on the other hand, argued the exact opposite: poetry is by its very nature 'dialogical' and always strives to encounter the other ...

Your own poetics seems to oscillate between these two poles: on the one hand, you characterize poetry as a 'tangle of the voices of many ages' and, thus, as dialogical; on the other hand, you underline the 'monological nature' of poetry and call it 'monophonic'. Echoing Benn, you even go so far as to suggest that 'poetry is above all self-encounter'.

How does this work? Could you comment on this tension in your poetics?

I am asking in particular because you and Celan are, to the best of my knowledge, the only two German-language poets to have adopted the legacy of Russian-Jewish poet Osip Mandelstam as a centrepiece of your own respective poetics. The lynchpin of Mandelstam's poetics in turn, which supplied Celan with the crucial metaphor of poetry as 'Flaschenpost', a 'message in a bottle', is that both man and poem are essentially *dialogical*, oriented towards an interlocutor. How does one square Benn, Celan and Mandelstam?

Durs Grünbein: Your question is quite devious. I feel cornered, and I don't know how to get out. It'll only be possible by breaking up the very concepts of *monologue* and *dialogue*. One would have to show that even the most monological poem (in Benn's sense) is subterraneously animated by call and response, by a longing for the unknown reader who will one day embrace it. The monologist would be one who no longer wishes to be meddled or interfered with; he banks away from speech, getting high on the flights of his own soul. But he never fully succeeds, and he knows it. One would then have to show that even the dialogic exchange with a 'you', with another person, harbours a caveat: the fear of being misunderstood, deceived, accused of intellectual theft.

After *Die Niemandsrose* [*No One's Rose*] Celan has an ever-greater sense of being hunted down by the literary posse, the lyric police, who suspect him of plagiarism. His dialogue with the persecuted poets, those who were chafing among their contemporaries (Büchner and Heine, Hölderlin, Tsvetayeva and Mandelstam) becomes his safe space where he can speak freely, more freely than with almost any of his many epistolary interlocutors. His dialogue with the dead gives him stability throughout the political ice age of the 1950s and 1960s, during which the murdered were murdered all over again amid the intoxication of oblivion on the part of the busy survivors in the nation of murderers. In this situation, he sends out poems as bottled messages in the hope that they might one day wash up on 'heartland', wherever that may be.

I consider Celan the greatest post-war poet. If, however, you are asking to whom his poems are addressed, you will find yourself in dire straits. Who might this 'Other' be? The distant person or the next best, the neighbour, the sceptical contemporary, perhaps even the enemy next door? Or is it one of the unreachable departed, representative of all of them? The wandering Jew in the Mandorla or a cloud of smoke? An absent God?

Michael Eskin: You are absolutely right, one has to question the very notions of monologue and dialogue, if only because language itself is anything but monological. Still, though, going along with Celan and Mandelstam, the distinction does carry existential and ethical value: for isn't it precisely about Celan's repudiation of the monologist's gesture of 'splendid isolation'?

But to return to your own poetry, which, in my view, is ever open to 'meddling': in the cycle 'Ashes for Breakfast' from the volume *After the Satires*, you openly engage in multiple dialogues with various poetic forebears – Baudelaire ('Thus he languidly acted the dandy [...] | And saw how it croaked in the gutter, the limping swan'), Rilke ('No Apollo, every lowlife on the corner tells you you have to change your life') and Hölderlin ('But the poets, you know it, are difficult folk | Who no longer found anything'), to name only a few. Celan, too, appears to address the reader through the mask of Grünbein: in the signal word 'Ashes' for instance, which, as far as German post-war poetry is concerned, cannot but invoke Sulamith's 'ashen hair' from 'Death Fugue'. Celan's voice is even more strongly audible in lines such as 'I have eaten ashes for breakfast, the dust | that falls from the dailies ... || I have eaten ashes for breakfast. My daily diet'. It's virtually impossible not to read these lines as a rewriting of, or a variation on, Celan's 'Black milk of dawn we drink it at night | we drink at noon and in the morning' – again from 'Death Fugue'.

Are these allusions to Celan intentional or coincidental? Could you comment on this? Are we witnessing a truly bold identification of Grünbein's poetic 'I' with the 'we' of the victims commemorated in 'Death Fugue' on the one hand and, on the other hand, an ironic appropriation of Celan's Holocaust legacy in the ostensibly trivial context of daily news?

Durs Grünbein: Banal you say. I would rather say 'transitory' – in the sense of the transitoriness of all words and phenomena. Words travel, that is their scandalous destiny. A word like 'ashes' is, in and of itself, owing to its very meaning, untethered. It wafts and breezes through texts, just like those ashes that the wind blew away and that mixed with the dust ... Nothing to be done: these dead (and their ashes) are on the conscience of an entire nation. Am I being sufficiently clear? 'The truth is concrete: I breathe stones', Heiner Müller once wrote. One could change it to: 'I breathe ashes'.

Michael Eskin: You couldn't be more clear, especially in our shared 'tender ... mother tongue' that 'silently | Swallowed everything', as you write in *Porcelain*, in which 'ashes' also constitutes a central motif.

What about the 'ashes' of *Porcelain?* A poetic cycle of forty-nine ten-liners in which you conjure the destruction of your native city, Dresden, in February 1945, from the perspective of, among others, the 'girl Rosi (a tender four)', and which palpably quakes with Celanian overtones. *Are* we justified in hearing Celan in the background? For instance in your reference to the 'May Beetle Song', which also prominently figures in the final poem, 'In the air', of Celan's *The No One's Rose* and which is about war, conflagration and loss? Or in a phrase such as '*This* booming', which immediately summons, through all the Allied squadrons' din, Celan's poem 'A Booming', which in turn speaks of the (historical, existential) 'truth' that has 'stepped forth' amid humanity. Or in your recourse to musical compositions such as Bach's 'The Art of the Fugue', which cannot but invoke Celan's 'Death Fugue'? Or in your frequent use of the phrase 'in one' ('Here, many in one, the city shows itself as the one'), which palpably harks back to Celan's poem 'In One', which in turn commemorates *many* a fight for freedom *in one* poem (the French and Russian revolutions as well as the Spanish Civil War, among others)? Or in your strategic placement of the word 'happened' – as in the oft-repeated narrative formula 'What happened then', or the following hemistich: 'It happened here. What?' – which cannot but take us back to Celan's poem 'What happened'? Or in a verse like 'Descend, once again, into the air-raid shelter', which ostensibly cites a famous line from Celan's early poem 'Corona': "My eye descends to the sex of the lover'? Or in the cycle's very title, which, as I have argued elsewhere, can be read as a subtle dedication to Celan ('pour Celan')? Or, last but not least, in the very name of your mother – 'Rosi' – through whose 'tender' four-year-old eyes we cannot help glimpsing Celan's own *The No One's Rose*, which in turn invokes the 'Rose' of Rilke's epitaph – 'Rose, oh pure contradiction, desire | To be no one's sleep beneath so many | Lids' – which you in turn summon as one of the motifs of the 'destruction of your city' in a 'clearing of time', 'on the lids, inside', whenever *you* close your 'eyes'?

Is all this but a mirage, or are we witnessing, in *Porcelain* – arguably, your most personal and autobiographically intimate work – an intense and intentional dialogue with Celan?

Durs Grünbein: I see. We're getting down to business now. You're touching the raw spot here. Much has been written on the destruction of Dresden, historians have argued about it. Some have questioned the justification for choosing the city as a target. Even though it had served a strategic military purpose as an arms industry and transportation hub, et cetera. The GDR's official narrative went as follows: 'Anglo-American bomber planes' perfidiously destroyed a defenceless city, the baroque pearl on the Elbe, in a kind of *overkill*. Which was pretty close to the propaganda speak spouted during the war by Goebbels, who liked to refer to 'Anglo-American air terror' and 'perfidious attacks'.

Dresden has become a sealed space since falling under the sway of revisionism, which abuses the abiding grief over the city's destruction for its own purposes. Every year, come February 13, the fight over who has the interpretive prerogative flares up again. We know that the city is a favoured gathering spot of the extreme Right. A case of failed, deformed mourning or the inability to mourn?

Porzellan reflects, and reflects on, all that, I hope. It was supposed to be a personal intervention on the subject, a meditation on a familiar position in the context of a much broader history.

Brecht was right when he wrote: 'Our cities are only a part | Of all the cities we destroyed'. That was in a poem of 1944, written one year before the bitter end. From a purely statistical viewpoint, what one of the standard histories on *Dresden during the Air War* tells us is true: 'Dresden – that was the most violent conventional bombing attack on the European continent, with the biggest conflagrations'. But Rotterdam, Coventry, London and Warsaw – not to mention

Guernica – preceded Dresden. So, let's not confuse cause and effect. The very gesture of tallying up victims and comparing degrees of destruction is obscene. Certainly, for many civilians the tragic aspects of Hitler's reign only fully swam into ken in the course of the destruction of German cities. It was much too late for an about-face. A bitter 1943 quip by Brecht says it all: 'Long before enemy bombers appeared above | Our cities had become uninhabitable'.

Why uninhabitable? Because they were all governed by the terror of the Nazi surveillance state. Because people could no longer breathe freely, because their lives had been 'booked'.

In a rare poetic moment Celan captures his impression of Nazi Germany: in 1938, en route to France, during a stopover in Berlin, only a few days before the Night of Broken Glass. The episode is commemorated in the poem 'La Contrescarpe':

> Via Krakow
> You came, at the Anhalter
> Bahnhof
> a smoke floated toward your gaze,
> it was already of tomorrow [...]

Porzellan, too, contains multiple irruptions of the biographical. And that's where my dialogue with Celan, to whom – let's just say it, once and for all – the entire cycle is dedicated without my explicitly having made a note of it, gets going. A convoluted homage ...

This *Poem on the Demise of My City*, as the subtitle reads, is an embrace of and into the void. Ten lines of exposure each to conjure the ghosts. It's a dialogue with many participants – Brecht and Thomas Mann, Goethe and Auden, Bach and Richard Strauß, Samuel Beckett, who visited Dresden during the Nazi era, calling it the 'porcelain Madonna' – and, above all, Celan ...

Paul Celan. A Select Bibliography

Collated by Jana Maria Weiß

Primary Works

Collected Works

Celan, Paul, *Werke. Historisch-kritische Ausgabe*, ed. by *Rolf Bücher and others, 16 vols* (Frankfurt a. M. and Berlin: Suhrkamp, 1990–2017):
Vol. I: *Frühe Gedichte*, ed. by Andreas Lohr with Holger Gehle and Rolf Bücher (2003).
Vol. II/III: *Der Sand aus den Urnen. Mohn und Gedächtnis*, ed. by Andreas Lohr with Holger Gehle and Rolf Bücher (2003).
Vol. IV: *Von Schwelle zu Schwelle*, ed. by Holger Gehle with Andreas Lohr and Rolf Bücher (2004).
Vol. V: *Sprachgitter*, ed. by Holger Gehle with Andreas Lohr and Rolf Bücher (2002).
Vol. VI: *Die Niemandsrose*, ed. by Axel Gellhaus with Holger Gehle and Rolf Bücher (2001).
Vol. VII: *Atemwende*, ed. by Rolf Bücher (1990).
Vol. VIII: *Fadensonnen*, ed. by Rolf Bücher (1991).
Vol. IX: *Lichtzwang*, ed. by Rolf Bücher with Andreas Lohr and Axel Gellhaus (1997).
Vol. X: *Schneepart*, ed. by Rolf Bücher with Axel Gellhaus and Andreas Lohr-Jasperneite (1994).
Vol. XI: *Verstreut gedruckte Gedichte. Nachgelassene Gedichte bis 1963*, ed. by Holger Gehle and Thomas Schneider with Andreas Lohr and Rolf Bücher (2006).
Vol. XII: *Eingedunkelt*, ed. by Rolf Bücher and Andreas Lohr with Hans Kruschwitz and Thomas Schneider (2006).
Vol. XIII: *Nachgelassene Gedichte 1963–1968*, ed. by Rolf Bücher and Andreas Lohr with Hans Kruschwitz (2011).
Vol. XIV: *Nachgelassene Gedichte 1968–1970*, ed. by Hans Kruschwitz and Thomas Schneider (2008).
Vol. XV: *Prosa I. Zu Lebzeiten publizierte Prosa und Reden*, ed. by Andreas Lohr and Heino Schmull with Rolf Bücher, prepared by Axel Gellhaus (2014).
Vol. XVI: *Prosa II. Zu Lebzeiten unpublizierte Prosa*, ed. by Andreas Lohr with Heino Schmull and Rolf Bücher (2017).

Celan, Paul, *Werke. Tübinger Ausgabe*, ed. by *Jürgen Wertheimer and others, 9 vols* (Frankfurt a. M.: Suhrkamp, 1996–2004):
Vol. I: *Mohn und Gedächtnis. Vorstufen – Textgenese – Endfassung*, ed. by Jürgen Wertheimer with Heino Schmull and Christiane Braun (2004).
Vol. II: *Von Schwelle zu Schwelle. Vorstufen – Textgenese – Endfassung*, ed. by Jürgen Wertheimer with Heino Schmull, Christiane Braun and Markus Heilmann (2002).
Vol. III: *Sprachgitter. Vorstufen – Textgenese – Endfassung*, ed. by Jürgen Wertheimer with Heino Schmull and Michael Schwarzkopf (1996).

https://doi.org/10.1515/9783110658330-022

Vol. IV: *Die Niemandsrose. Vorstufen – Textgenese – Endfassung*, ed. by Jürgen Wertheimer with Heino Schmull and Michael Schwarzkopf (1996).
Vol. V: *Atemwende. Vorstufen – Textgenese – Endfassung*, ed. by Jürgen Wertheimer with Heino Schmull and Christiane Wittkop (2000).
Vol. VI: *Fadensonnen. Vorstufen – Textgenese – Endfassung*, ed. by Jürgen Wertheimer with Heino Schmull, Markus Heilmann and Christiane Wittkop (2000).
Vol. VII: *Lichtzwang. Vorstufen – Textgenese – Endfassung*, ed. by Jürgen Wertheimer with Heino Schmull, Markus Heilmann and Christiane Wittkop (2001).
Vol. VIII: *Schneepart. Vorstufen – Textgenese – Reinschrift*, ed. by Jürgen Wertheimer with Heino Schmull, Markus Heilmann and Christiane Wittkop (2002).
Vol. IX: *Der Meridian. Endfassung – Vorstufen – Materialien*, ed. by Bernhard Böschenstein and Heino Schmull with Michael Schwarzkopf and Christiane Wittkop (1999).

Celan, Paul, *Gesammelte Werke in sieben Bänden*, ed. by Beda Allemann and Stefan Reichert with Rolf Bücher, 7 vols, 2nd rev. edn (Frankfurt a. M.: Suhrkamp, 2000):
Vol. I: *Gedichte I.*
Vol. II: *Gedichte II.*
Vol. III: *Gedichte III. Prosa – Reden.*
Vol. IV: *Übertragungen I. Zweisprachig.*
Vol. V: *Übertragungen II. Zweisprachig.*
Vol. VI: *Das Frühwerk.*
Vol. VII: *Gedichte aus dem Nachlaß.*

Celan, Paul, *'Mikrolithen sinds, Steinchen'. Die Prosa aus dem Nachlaß*, ed. by Barbara Wiedemann and Bertrand Badiou (Frankfurt a. M.: Suhrkamp, 2005).

Celan, Paul, *Die Gedichte. Kommentierte Gesamtausgabe*, ed. by Barbara Wiedemann (Berlin: Suhrkamp, 2018).

Translations by Celan

The majority of Paul Celan's translations published during his lifetime are printed in

Celan, Paul, *Gesammelte Werke in sieben Bänden*, ed. by Beda Allemann and Stefan Reichert with Rolf Bücher, 7 vols, 2nd rev. edn (Frankfurt a. M.: Suhrkamp, 2000):
Vol. IV: *Übertragungen I. Zweisprachig.*
Vol. V: *Übertragungen II. Zweisprachig.*

For a complete list of Celan's translations see:

Goßens, Peter, 'Bibliographie der Übersetzungen Paul Celans', *Celan-Jahrbuch*, 8 (2001/2002), 353–89.

Letters

Celan, Paul, *"etwas ganz und gar Persönliches". Briefe. 1934–1970,* ed. by Barbara Wiedemann (Berlin: Suhrkamp, 2019).

Celan, Paul, and Theodor W. Adorno, 'Briefwechsel. 1960–1968', ed. by Joachim Seng, *Frankfurter Adorno-Blätter*, 7 (2003), 177–200.

Celan, Paul, and Ingeborg Bachmann, *Herzzeit. Ingeborg Bachmann – Paul Celan, Der Briefwechsel. Mit den Briefwechseln zwischen Paul Celan und Max Frisch sowie zwischen Ingeborg Bachmann und Gisèle Celan-Lestrange*, ed. by Bertrand Badiou and others (Frankfurt a. M.: Suhrkamp, 2008).

Celan, Paul, and Hans Bender, *Briefe an Hans Bender*, ed. by Volker Neuhaus with Ute Heimbüchel (Munich: Hanser, 1981).

Celan, Paul, and Gisèle Celan-Lestrange, *Correspondance. 1951–1970: Avec un choix de lettres de Paul Celan à son fils Eric*, ed. by Bertrand Badiou with Eric Celan, 2 vols (Paris: Seuil, 2001).

Celan, Paul, and René Char, *Correspondance. 1954–1968: Avec des lettres de Gisèle Celan-Lestrange, Jean Delay, Marie-Madeleine Delay et Pierre Deniker. Suivie de la Correspondance René Char – Gisèle Celan-Lestrange, 1969–1977*, ed. by Bertrand Badiou (Paris: Gallimard, 2015).

Celan, Paul, and Gustav Chomed, *'Ich brauche Deine Briefe'. Der Briefwechsel*, ed. by Barbara Wiedemann and Jürgen Köchel (Berlin: Suhrkamp, 2010).

Celan, Paul, and Klaus and Nani Demus, *Briefwechsel*, ed. by Joachim Seng (Frankfurt a. M.: Suhrkamp, 2009).

Celan, Paul, and Gisela Dischner, *'Wie aus weiter Ferne zu Dir'. Briefwechsel*, ed. by Barbara Wiedemann with Gisela Dischner (Berlin: Suhrkamp, 2012).

Celan, Paul, and Erich Einhorn, *'du weißt um die Steine…'. Briefwechsel*, ed. by Marina Dmitrieva-Einhorn (Berlin: Friedenauer Presse, 2001).

Celan, Paul, and Rudolf Hirsch, *Briefwechsel*, ed. by Joachim Seng (Frankfurt a. M.: Suhrkamp, 2004).

Celan, Paul, and Hanne and Hermann Lenz, *Briefwechsel. Mit drei Briefen von Gisèle Celan-Lestrange*, ed. by Barbara Wiedemann with Hanne Lenz (Frankfurt a. M.: Suhrkamp, 2001).

Celan, Paul, and Alfred Margul-Sperber, 'Briefe von Paul Celan an Alfred Margul-Sperber', *Neue Literatur*, 26.7 (1975), 50–63.

Celan, Paul, and Nelly Sachs, *Briefwechsel*, ed. by Barbara Wiedemann (Frankfurt a. M.: Suhrkamp, 1993).

Celan, Paul, and Ilana Shmueli, *Briefwechsel*, ed. by Ilana Shmueli and Thomas Sparr (Frankfurt a. M.: Suhrkamp, 2004).

Celan, Paul, and Peter Szondi, *Briefwechsel. Mit Briefen von Gisèle Celan-Lestrange an Peter Szondi und Auszügen aus dem Briefwechsel zwischen Peter Szondi und Jean und Mayotte Bollack*, ed. by Christoph König (Frankfurt a. M.: Suhrkamp, 2005).

Celan, Paul, and Franz Wurm, *Briefwechsel*, ed. by Barbara Wiedemann (Frankfurt a. M.: Suhrkamp, 1995).

Celan, Paul, *'Du mußt versuchen, auch den Schweigenden zu hören'. Briefe an Diet Kloos-Barendregt. Handschrift – Edition – Kommentar*, ed. by Paul Sars with Laurent Sprooten (Frankfurt a. M.: Suhrkamp, 2002).

Celan, Paul, *Briefwechsel mit den rheinischen Freunden. Heinrich Böll, Paul Schallück und Rolf Schroers*, ed. by Barbara Wiedemann (Berlin: Suhrkamp, 2011).

English Translations of Celan

Celan, Paul, 'Corona' and 'Chanson of a Lady in the Shadow', trans. by Michael Bullock, *Modern Poetry in Translation*, 3 (1967), 20–21.

Celan, Paul, 'Tenebrae', 'There was Earth', 'Zurich, the Stork Inn', 'Psalm' and 'You Were my Death', trans. by Michael Hamburger, *Modern Poetry in Translation*, 7 (1970), 27–28.

Celan, Paul, *Speech-Grille and Selected Poems*, trans. by Joachim Neugroschel (New York: Dutton, 1971).

Celan, Paul, *Nineteen Poems*, trans. by Michael Hamburger (South Hinksey: Carcanet, 1972).

Celan, Paul, *Selected Poems*, trans. by Michael Hamburger and Christopher Middleton (Harmondsworth: Penguin, 1972).

Celan, Paul, *65 Poems*, transl. by Brian Lynch with Peter Jankowsky (Dublin: Raven Arts Press, 1985).

Celan, Paul, *Collected Prose*, trans. by Rosemary Waldrop (Manchester: Carcanet, 1986).

Celan, Paul, *Glottal Stop. 101 Poems*, trans. by Nikolai Popov and Heather McHugh (Middletown: Wesleyan University Press, 2000).

Celan, Paul, *Selected Poems and Prose of Paul Celan*, trans. by John Felstiner (New York: Norton, 2001).

Celan, Paul, *'Fathomsuns' and 'Benighted'*, trans. by Ian Fairley (Manchester: Carcanet, 2001).

Celan, Paul, *Poems. Revised and Expanded,* trans. by Michael Hamburger (New York: Persea Books, 2002).

Celan, Paul, *Lichtzwang/Lightduress*, trans. by Pierre Joris (Los Angeles: Green Integer, 2005).

Celan, Paul, *Paul Celan. Selections*, ed. and trans. by Pierre Joris (Berkeley: University of California Press, 2005).

Celan, Paul, *Poems of Paul Celan*, trans. by Michael Hamburger (London: Anvil, 2007).

Celan, Paul, *Snow Part/Schneepart*, trans. by Ian Fairley (Manchester: Carcanet, 2007).

Celan, Paul, *The Meridian. Final Version – Drafts – Materials*, ed. by Bernhard Böschenstein and Heino Schmull, trans. by Pierre Joris (Stanford: Stanford University Press, 2011).

Celan, Paul, *Corona. Selected Poems of Paul Celan*, trans. by Susan H. Gillespie (Barrytown: Station Hill, 2013).

Celan, Paul, *Breathturn Into Timestead. The Collected Later Poetry,* trans. by Pierre Joris (New York: Farrar, Straus and Giroux, 2014).

Celan, Paul, and Nelly Sachs, *Correspondence*, ed. by Barbara Wiedemann, trans. by Christopher Clark (New York: Sheep Meadow, 1995).

Celan, Paul, and Ingeborg Bachmann, *Correspondence, with the Correspondences between Paul Celan and Max Frisch and between Ingeborg Bachmann and Gisèle Celan-Lestrange*, trans. by Wieland Hoban (Calcutta: Seagull Books, 2010).

Celan, Paul, and Ilana Shmueli, *The Correspondence of Paul Celan and Ilana Shmueli*, ed. and trans. by Susan H. Gillespie (New York: Sheep Meadow, 2010).

Secondary Literature

Amthor, Wiebke, *Schneegespräche an gastlichen Tischen. Wechselseitiges Übersetzen bei Paul Celan und André du Bouchet* (Heidelberg: Winter, 2006).

André, Robert, *Gespräche von Text zu Text. Celan, Heidegger, Hölderlin* (Hamburg: Felix Meiner, 2001).

Arnold, Heinz Ludwig, *Die Gruppe 47* (Reinbek bei Hamburg: Rowohlt, 2004).

Arnold, Heinz Ludwig, ed., *Paul Celan, Text + Kritik*, 53/54 (2002), 3rd rev. edn.

Auerochs, Bernd, 'Gründung und Auslöschung des Judentums. Zu Paul Celans Gedicht "Psalm"', *Literaturwissenschaftliches Jahrbuch*, 45 (2004), 261–81.

Auerochs, Bernd, Friederike Felicitas Günther and Markus May, eds, *Celan-Perspektiven 2019* (Heidelberg: Winter, 2019).

Badiou, Bertrand, '*D'une main – de l'autre main. Préface*', in Paul Celan and René Char, *Correspondance: 1954–1968. Avec des lettres de Gisèle Celan-Lestrange, Jean Delay, Marie-Madeleine Delay et Pierre Deniker. Suivie de la Correspondance René Char – Gisèle Celan-Lestrange: 1969–1977*, ed. by Bertrand Badiou (Paris: Gallimard, 2015), pp. 9–31.

Baer, Ulrich, *Remnants of Song. Trauma and the Experience of Modernity in Charles Baudelaire and Paul Celan* (Stanford: Stanford University Press, 2000).

Baer, Ulrich, 'The Perfection of Poetry. Rainer Maria Rilke and Paul Celan', *New German Review*, 91 (2004), 171–89.

Bahti, Timothy, 'A Minor Form and its Inversions. The Image, the Poem, the Book in Celan's "Unter ein Bild"', *Modern Language Notes*, 110 (1995), 565–78.

Bahti, Timothy, "Dickinson, Celan, and Some Translations of Inversion", in *Poetik der Transformation. Paul Celan – Übersetzer und übersetzt*, ed. by Alfred Bodenheimer and Shimon Sandbank (Tübingen: Niemeyer, 1999), pp. 117–28.

Bambach, Charles, *Thinking the Poetic Measure of Justice. Hölderlin – Heidegger – Celan* (Albany: State University of New York Press, 2013).

Barnert, Arno, *Mit dem fremden Wort. Poetisches Zitieren bei Paul Celan* (Frankfurt a.M.: Stroemfeld, 2007).

Barnert, Arno, Chiara Caradonna and Annika Stello, '"Im Reich der mittleren Dämonen". Paul Celan in Freiburg und sein Briefwechsel mit Gerhart Baumann', *Text. Kritische Beiträge*, 15 (2016), 15–115.

Bekker, Hugo, *Paul Celan. Studies in his Early Poetry* (Leiden: Brill, 2008).

Bevilacqua, Giuseppe, *Auf der Suche nach dem Atemkristall. Celan-Studien*, trans. by Peter Goßens and Marianne Schneider (Munich: Hanser, 2004).

Beyer, Marcel, 'Landkarten, Sprachigkeit, Paul Celan', *Text + Kritik*, 53/54 (2002), 3rd rev. edn, 48–65.

Blum-Barth, Natalia, and Christine Waldschmidt, eds, *Celan-Referenzen. Prozesse einer Traditionsbildung in der Moderne* (Göttingen: V&R unipress, 2016).

Boase-Beier, Jean, 'Interpretation and Creativity in the Translation of Paul Celan', in *Kreativität und Hermeneutik in der Translation*, ed. by Larisa Cercel, Marco Agnetta and María Teresa Amido Lozano (Tübingen: Narr Francke Attempto, 2017), pp. 59–76.

Bodenheimer, Alfred, and Shimon Sandbank, eds, *Poetik der Transformation. Paul Celan – Übersetzer und übersetzt* (Tübingen: Niemeyer, 1999).

Bohm, Arnd, 'Landscapes of Exile. Celans "Gespräch im Gebirg"', *The Germanic Review*, 78.2 (2003), 99–111.

Bollack, Jean, *Herzstein. Über ein unveröffentlichtes Gedicht von Paul Celan*, trans. by Werner Wögerbauer (Munich: Hanser, 1993).
Bollack, Jean, *Paul Celan. Poetik der Fremdheit*, trans. by Werner Wögerbauer (Vienna: Zsolnay, 2000).
Bollack, Jean, *Dichtung wider Dichtung. Paul Celan und die Literatur*, trans. by Werner Wögerbauer (Göttingen: Wallstein, 2006).
Bonnet, Antoine, and Frédéric Marteau, eds, *Paul Celan. La poésie, la musique. Avec une clé changeante* (Paris: Hermann, 2015).
Böschenstein, Bernhard, 'Anmerkungen zu Celans letzter Übersetzung. Jean Daive: Weisse Dezimale', *Text + Kritik*, 53/54 (1977), 69–73.
Böschenstein, Bernhard, 'Paul Celan und die französische Dichtung', in Bernhard Böschenstein, *Leuchttürme. Von Hölderlin zu Celan: Wirkung und Vergleich* (Frankfurt a. M.: Insel, 1977), pp. 307–30.
Böschenstein, Bernhard, and Sigrid Weigel, eds, *Ingeborg Bachmann und Paul Celan. Poetische Korrespondenzen: Vierzehn Beiträge* (Frankfurt a. M.: Suhrkamp, 1997).
Böttiger, Helmut, *Celan am Meer*, 2nd edn (Göttingen: Wallstein, 2017).
Böttiger, Helmut, *Wir sagen uns Dunkles. Die Liebesgeschichte zwischen Ingeborg Bachmann und Paul Celan* (Munich: DVA, 2017).
Boyd, Thimothy, *'Dunkeler gespannt'. Untersuchungen zur Erotik der Dichtung Paul Celans* (Heidelberg: Winter, 2006).
Braun, Michael, *'Hörreste, Sehreste'. Das literarische Fragment bei Büchner, Kafka, Benn und Celan* (Cologne: Böhlau, 2002).
Briegleb, Klaus, *Missachtung und Tabu. Eine Streitschrift zur Frage: 'Wie antisemitisch war die Gruppe 47?'* (Berlin: Philo, 2003).
Buck, Theo, *Celan-Studien*, 7 vols (Aachen: Rimbaud, 1993–2005).
Buck, Theo, '"Sonnenflechten" und "azurner Schleim" – Celan übersetzt Rimbaud', *Text + Kritik*, 53/54 (2002), 3rd rev. edn, 66–98.
Burdorf, Dieter, ed., *'Im Geheimnis der Begegnung'. Ingeborg Bachmann und Paul Celan* (Iserlohn: Institut für Kirche und Gesellschaft Iserlohn, 2003).
Cameron, Esther, *Western Art and Jewish Presence in the Work of Paul Celan. Roots and Ramifications of the 'Meridian' Speech* (Lanham: Lexington Books, 2014).
Chalfen, Israel, *Paul Celan. Eine Biographie seiner Jugend* (Frankfurt a. M.: Insel, 1979).
Colin, Amy-Diana, ed., *Argumentum e Silentio. International Paul Celan Symposium* (New York: De Gruyter, 1987).
Colin, Amy-Diana, *Paul Celan. Holograms of Darkness* (Bloomington: Indiana University Press, 1991).
Colin, Amy-Diana, and Edith Silbermann, eds, *Paul Celan – Edith Silbermann. Zeugnisse einer Freundschaft: Gedichte, Briefwechsel, Erinnerungen* (Munich: Wilhelm Fink Verlag, 2010).
Connolly, Thomas C., *Paul Celan's Unfinished Poetics. Readings in the Sous-Oeuvre* (Cambridge: Legenda, 2018).
Corbea-Hoișie, Andrei, ed., *Paul Celan. Biographie und Interpretation/Biographie et Interprétation* (Konstanz: Hartung-Gorre, 2000).
Corbea-Hoișie, Andrei, *Paul Celans 'unbequemes Zuhause'. Sein erstes Jahrzehnt in Paris* (Aachen: Rimbaud, 2017).
Dembeck, Till, '"No pasaran" – Lyrik, Kulturpolitik und Sprachdifferenz bei T.S. Eliot, Paul Celan and Rolf Dieter Brinkmann', *arcadia*, 48.1 (2013), 1–41.

Derrida, Jacques, *Schibboleth. Pour Paul Celan* (Paris: Galilée, 1986).

Derrida, Jacques, 'Shibboleth. For Paul Celan', in Jacques Derrida, *Sovereignties in Question. The Poetics of Paul Celan*, ed. and trans. by Thomas Dutoit and Outi Pasanen (New York: Fordham University Press, 2005), pp. 1–64.

Dogà, Ulisse, *'Port Bou – deutsch?'. Paul Celan liest Walter Benjamin* (Aachen: Rimbaud, 2009).

Eisenreich, Brigitta, *Celans Kreidestern. Ein Bericht: Mit Briefen und anderen unveröffentlichten Dokumenten* (Berlin: Suhrkamp, 2010).

Emmerich, Wolfgang, *Paul Celan* (Reinbek bei Hamburg: Rowohlt, 1999).

Encarnação, Gilda Lopes, *'Fremde Nähe'. Das Dialogische als poetisches und poetologisches Prinzip bei Paul Celan* (Würzburg: Königshausen & Neumann, 2007).

Englund, Axel, *Still Songs. Music in and around the Poetry of Paul Celan* (Farnham: Ashgate, 2012).

Eshel, Amir, 'Paul Celan's Other. History, Poetics, and Ethics', *New German Critique*, 91 (2004), 57–77.

Eshel, Amir, 'Paul Celan's Other Reconsidered', *Yearbook for European Jewish Literature Studies*, 2.1 (2015), 306–21.

Eskin, Michael, *Ethics and Dialogue. In the Works of Levinas, Bakhtin, Mandel'shtam, and Celan* (Oxford: Oxford University Press, 2000).

Eskin, Michael, *Poetic Affairs. Celan, Grünbein, Brodsky* (Stanford: Stanford University Press, 2008).

Fassbind, Bernard, *Poetik des Dialogs. Voraussetzungen dialogischer Poesie bei Paul Celan und Konzepte von Intersubjektivität bei Martin Buber, Martin Heidegger und Emmanuel Levinas* (Munich: Fink, 1995).

Febel, Gisela, 'Gibt Paul Celans *Sprachgitter* wirklich nur den Blick auf einen hermetischen René Char frei? Überlegungen zur Wirkung von Übersetzungen und zur Macht von Rezeptionsmustern', in *Literarische Übersetzung. Formen und Möglichkeiten ihrer Wirkung in neuerer Zeit*, ed. by Wolfgang Pöckl (Bonn: Romanistischer Verlag, 1992), pp. 179–209.

Felstiner, John, 'Mother Tongue, Holy Tongue. On Translating and not Translating Paul Celan', in *Comparative Literature*, 38.4 (1986), 113–36.

Felstiner, John, *Paul Celan. Poet, Survivor, Jew* (New Haven: Yale University Press, 1995).

Felstiner, John, 'Translating as Transference. Paul Celan's Versions of Shakespeare, Dickinson, Mandelshtam, Apollinaire', in *Translating Literatures, Translating Cultures. New Vistas and Approaches in Literary Studies*, ed. by Kurt Müller-Vollmer and Michael Irmscher (Berlin: Erich Schmidt, 1998), pp. 165–75.

Felstiner, John, '"Here we go round the Prickly Pear" or "Your Song, what does it know?". Celan vis-à-vis Mallarmé, in *Poetik der Transformation. Paul Celan – Übersetzer und übersetzt*, ed. by Alfred Bodenheimer and Shimon Sandbank (Tübingen: Niemeyer, 1999), pp. 79–86.

Ferran, Bronac, '"A Language that No-One Speaks". Celan and the Concrete Poets', in *Celan-Perspektiven 2019*, ed. by Bernd Auerochs, Friederike Felicitas Günther and Markus May (Heidelberg: Winter, 2019), pp. 107–25.

Fioretos, Aris, ed., *Word Traces. Readings of Paul Celan* (Baltimore: The Johns Hopkins University Press, 1994).

Friedrich, Hugo, *Die Struktur der modernen Lyrik* (Reinbek bei Hamburg: Rowohlt, 1956).

Gadamer, Hans-Georg, *Wer bin Ich und wer bist Du? Ein Kommentar zu Paul Celans Gedichtfolge 'Atemkristall'* (Frankfurt a. M.: Suhrkamp, 1973).
Gaisbauer, Hubert, Bernhard Hain and Erika Schuster, eds, *Unverloren. Trotz allem. Paul Celan-Symposion Wien 2000* (Vienna: Mandelbaum, 2000).
Gellhaus, Axel, ed., *Paul Antschel/Paul Celan in Czernowitz, Marbacher Magazin*, 90 (2000).
Gellhaus, Axel, and Karin Hermann, eds, *'Qualitativer Wechsel'. Textgenese bei Paul Celan* (Würzburg: Königshausen & Neumann, 2010).
Gellhaus, Axel, and others, eds, *'Fremde Nähe'. Eine Ausstellung des Deutschen Literaturarchivs im Schiller-Nationalmuseum Marbach am Neckar und im Stadthaus Zürich* (Marbach am Neckar: Deutsche Schillergesellschaft, 1987).
Glazova, Anna, 'Poetry of Bringing About Presence. Paul Celan translates Osip Mandelstam', *Modern Languages Notes*, 123.5 (2008), 1108–26.
Glazova, Anna, 'Paul Celan in Conversation with Walter Benjamin. "The Secret Open"', *The Germanic Review*, 91.3 (2016), 277–93.
Graubner, Hans, *'Unter dem Neigungswinkel'. Celans biographische Poetologie* (Würzburg: Königshausen & Neumann, 2018).
Greisch, Jean, '*Zeitgehöft et Anwesen.* La dia-chronie du poème', in *Contre-jour. Études sur Paul Celan*, ed. by Martine Broda (Paris: Éditions du Cerf, 1986), pp. 167–83.
Günther, Friederike Felicitas, *Grenzgänge zum Anorganischen bei Rilke und Celan* (Heidelberg: Winter, 2018).
Günzel, Elke, *Das wandernde Zitat. Paul Celan im jüdischen Kontext* (Würzburg: Königshausen & Neumann, 1995).
Hainz, Martin A., *Masken der Mehrdeutigkeit. Celan-Lektüren mit Adorno, Szondi und Derrida*, 2nd rev. edn (Vienna: Braumüller, 2003).
Hallberg, Robert von, 'Celan's Universality', *Michigan Quarterly Review*, 45.2 (2006), 348–58.
Hamacher, Werner, 'The Second of Inversion. Movements of a Figure through Celan's Poetry', in *Word Traces. Readings of Paul Celan Fioretos*, ed. by Aris Fioretos, (Baltimore: The Johns Hopkins University Press, 1994), pp. 219–65.
Hamacher, Werner, *Entferntes Verstehen. Studien zu Philosophie und Literatur von Kant bis Celan* (Frankfurt a. M.: Suhrkamp, 1998).
Hamacher, Werner, *Keinmaleins. Texte zu Celan* (Frankfurt a. M.: Klostermann, 2019).
Hamacher, Werner, and Winfried Menninghaus, eds, *Paul Celan* (Frankfurt a. M.: Suhrkamp, 1988).
Hamburger, Michael, 'On Translating Celan', in *Poems of Paul Celan*, trans. by Michael Hamburger (London: Anvil, 2007), pp. 405–22.
Harbusch, Ute, *Gegenübersetzungen. Paul Celans Übertragungen französischer Symbolisten* (Göttingen: Wallstein, 2005).
Hawkins, Beth, *Reluctant Theologians. Franz Kafka, Paul Celan, Edmond Jabès* (New York: Fordham University Press, 2003).
Hillard, Derek, *Critical Moments. Paul Celan and Figurations of Madness* (Ann Arbor: University Microfilms International, 2002).
Hillard, Derek, *Poetry as Individuality. The Discourse of Observation in Paul Celan* (Lewisburg: Bucknell University Press, 2010).
Hillard, Derek, 'Paul Celan in America', *Compar(a)ison*, 1 (2013), 61–84.
Hirsch, Marianne, and Leo Spitzer, *Ghosts of Home. The Afterlife of Czernowitz in Jewish Memory* (Berkeley: University of California Press, 2010).

Hoelzel, Alfred, 'Paul Celan. An Authentic Jewish Voice?', in *Argumentum e Silentio. International Paul Celan Symposium*, ed. by Amy-Diana Colin (New York: De Gruyter, 1987), pp. 352–58.

Hofer, Matthew, '"Between Worlds". W.S. Merwin and Paul Celan', *New German Critique*, 91 (2004), 101–15.

Hollander, Benjamin, ed., *Translating Tradition. Paul Celan in France* (San Francisco: Acts, 1988).

Huppert, Hugo, '"Spirituell". Ein Gespräch mit Paul Celan', in *Paul Celan*, ed. by Werner Hamacher and Winfried Menninghaus (Frankfurt a. M.: Suhrkamp, 1998), pp. 319–24.

Italiano, Federico, *Translation and Geography* (London: Routledge, 2016).

Ivanovic, Christine, *Das Gedicht im Geheimnis der Begegnung. Dichtung und Poetik Celans im Kontext seiner russischen Lektüren* (Tübingen: Niemeyer, 1996).

Ivanovic, Christine, *"Kyrillisches, Freunde, auch das...". Die russische Bibliothek Paul Celans im Deutschen Literaturarchiv Marbach* (Marbach am Neckar: Deutsche Schillergesellschaft, 1996).

Jakob, Michael, ed., *Paul Celan Today, Compar(a)ison*, 1 (2013).

Janz, Marlies, *Vom Engagement absoluter Poesie. Zur Lyrik und Ästhetik Paul Celans* (Frankfurt a. M.: Syndikat, 1976).

Janz, Marlies, 'Text und Biographie in der Diskussion um Celan – Bachmann', in *Paul Celan. Biographie und Interpretation/Biographie et Interprétation*, ed. by Andrei Corbea-Hoișie (Konstanz: Hartung-Gorre, 2000), pp. 60–68.

Janz, Marlies, '"Judendeutsch". Paul Celans "Gespräch im Gebirg" im Kontext der "Atemwende"', *Celan-Jahrbuch*, 9 (2003–2005), 75–102.

Joris, Pierre, "Celan/Heidegger. Translation at the Mountain of Death", in *Poetik der Transformation. Paul Celan – Übersetzer und übersetzt*, ed. by Alfred Bodenheimer and Shimon Sandbank (Tübingen: Niemeyer, 1999), pp. 167–74.

Karr, Ruven, *Die Toten im Gespräch. Trialogische Strukturen in der Dichtung Paul Celans* (Hannover: Wehrhahn, 2015).

Karr, Ruven, ed., *Celan und der Holocaust. Neue Beiträge zur Forschung* (Hannover: Wehrhahn, 2015).

Kligerman, Eric, *Sites of the Uncanny. Paul Celan, Specularity and the Visual Arts* (Berlin: De Gruyter, 2007).

Kligermann, Eric, 'Celan's Cinematic. Anxiety of the Gaze in "Night and Fog" and "Engführung"', in *Visualizing the Holocaust. Documents, Aesthetics, Memory*, ed. by David Bathrick, Brad Prager and Michael D. Richardson (Rochester: Camden House, 2008), pp. 185–210.

Klink, Joanna, 'You. An Introduction to Paul Celan', *The Iowa Review*, 30.1 (2000), 1–18.

Koch, Julian, 'The Image in Celan's Poetics', *German Life and Letters*, 71.4 (2018), 434–51.

Koelle, Lydia, *Paul Celans pneumatisches Judentum. Gott-Rede und menschliche Existenz nach der Shoah* (Mainz: Matthias Grünewald, 1997).

Koelle, Lydia, '"Aufrechte Worte". Paul Celan – Margarete Susman: Eine "Cor-Respondenz"', *Celan-Jahrbuch*, 8 (2001/2002), 7–32.

Kohl, Katrin, '"Nach Celan?" Die Bedeutung Celans in der Geschichte deutschsprachiger Lyrik und Poetik nach 1945', *Jahrbuch für Internationale Germanistik*, 43.1 (2011), 35–55.

König, Christoph, 'Give the Word. Zur Kritik der Briefe Paul Celans in seinen Gedichten', *Euphorion*, 97 (2003), 473–97.

König, Frank, *Vertieftes Sein. Wahrnehmung und Körperlichkeit bei Paul Celan und Maurice Merleau-Ponty* (Heidelberg: Winter, 2014).

Korte, Hermann, 'Säulenheilige und Portalfiguren? Benn und Celan im Poetik-Dialog mit der jüngeren deutschsprachigen Lyrik seit den 1990er Jahren', in *Schaltstelle. Neue deutsche Lyrik im Dialog*, ed. by Karen Leeder (Amsterdam: Rodopi, 2007), pp. 111–37.

Krings, Marcel, 'Botanische Dichtung. Theophanie und Sprache in Celans "Gespräch im Gebirg"', *Germanisch-Romanische Monatsschrift*, 54 (2004), 411–31.

Lacoue-Labarthe, Philippe, *Poetry as Experience*, trans. by Andrea Tarnowski (Stanford: Stanford University Press, 1999).

Lefebvre, Jean-Pierre, 'La Correspondance entre René Char et Paul Celan', *Études Germaniques*, 71.1 (2016), 159–64.

Lehmann, Jürgen, '"Dichten heißt immer unterwegs sein". Literarische Grenzüberschreitungen am Beispiel Celans', *arcadia*, 28.2 (1993), 113–30.

Lehmann, Jürgen, 'Karnevaleske Dialogisierung. Anmerkungen zum Verhältnis Mandel'štam – Celan', in *Germanistik und Komparatistik. Germanistische Symposien Berichtsbände*, ed. by Hendrik Birus (Stuttgart: Metzler, 1995), pp. 541–55.

Lehmann, Jürgen, and Christine Ivanovic, eds, *Stationen. Kontinuität und Entwicklung in Paul Celans Übersetzungswerk* (Heidelberg: Winter, 1997).

Lehmann, Jürgen, with Christine Ivanovic, eds, *Kommentar zu Paul Celans 'Die Niemandsrose'* (Heidelberg: Winter, 1997).

Lehmann, Jürgen, and others, *Kommentar zu Paul Celans 'Sprachgitter'* (Heidelberg: Winter, 2005).

Levine, Michael G., '"Pendant". Büchner, Celan, and the Terrible Voice of the Meridian', *Modern Languages Notes*, 3.122 (2007), 573–601.

Levine, Michael G., *A Weak Messianic Power. Figures of a Time to Come in Benjamin, Derrida, and Celan* (New York: Fordham University Press, 2014).

Levine, Michael G., *Atomzertrümmerung. Zu einem Gedicht von Paul Celan* (Vienna: Turia + Kant, 2018).

Liska, Vivian, *Die Nacht der Hymnen. Paul Celans Gedichte: 1938–1944* (Bern: Peter Lang, 1993).

Liska, Vivian, '"Roots against Heaven". An Aporetic Inversion in Paul Celan', *New German Critique*, 91 (2004), 41–56.

Liska, Vivian, *German-Jewish Thought and its Afterlife. A Tenuous Legacy* (Bloomington: Indiana University Press, 2017).

Lyon, James K., 'Paul Celan and Martin Buber. Poetry as Dialogue', *Publications of the Modern Languages Association*, 86 (1971), 110–20.

Lyon, James K., *Paul Celan and Martin Heidegger. An Unresolved Conversation. 1951–1970* (Baltimore: The Johns Hopkins University Press, 2006).

MacDonald, Ian, 'Returning to the "House of Oblivion". Celan between Adorno and Heidegger', in *Adorno and Literature*, ed. by David Cunningham and Nigel Mapp (London: Continuum, 2008), pp. 117–30.

Martín Gijón, Mario, and Rosa Benéitez Andrés, *Lecturas de Paul Celan* (Madrid: Abada Editores, 2017).

May, Markus, *'Ein Klaffen, das mich sichtbar macht'. Untersuchungen zu Paul Celans Übersetzungen amerikanischer Lyrik* (Heidelberg: Winter, 2004).

May, Markus, Peter Goßens, and Jürgen Lehmann, eds, *Celan-Handbuch. Leben – Werk – Wirkung*, 2nd rev. edn (Stuttgart: Metzler, 2012).

Meinecke, Dietlind, ed., *Über Paul Celan* (Frankfurt a. M.: Suhrkamp, 1973).

Menninghaus, Winfried, *Paul Celan. Magie der Form.* (Frankfurt a. M.: Suhrkamp, 1980).

Menninghaus, Winfried, 'Wissen oder Nicht-Wissen. Überlegungen zum Problem des Zitats bei Celan und in der Celan-Philologie', in *Datum und Zitat bei Paul Celan. Akten des Internationalen Paul Celan-Colloquiums Haifa 1986*, ed. by Bernd Witte and Chaim Shoham (Bern: Peter Lang, 1987), pp. 81–96.

Miglio, Camilla, *Celan e Valéry. Poesia, traduzione di una distanza* (Naples: Edizioni Scientifiche Italiane, 1997).

Miglio, Camilla, 'Celan – Ungaretti – Celan. Die Suche nach der eigenen Sprache "in eines Anderen Sache"', *Text + Kritik*, 53/54 (2002), 3rd rev. edn, 132–44.

Miglio, Camilla, *Vita a fronte. Saggio su Paul Celan* (Macerata: Quodlibet, 2005).

Miglio, Camilla, '"Wiederholung ist eine Erinnerung in Richtung nach vorn". Ein Kierkegaardsches Muster in Celans Poetik der Übersetzung', in *Fremdes wahrnehmen, aufnehmen, annehmen. Studien zur deutschen Sprache und Kultur in Kontaktsituationen*, ed. by Barbara Hans-Bianchi and others (Frankfurt a. M.: Peter Lang, 2013), pp. 97–108.

Neumann, Gerhard, 'Die "absolute" Metapher. Ein Abgrenzungsversuch am Beispiel Stéphane Mallarmés und Paul Celans', *Poetica*, 3 (1970), 188–225.

Neumann, Gerhard, *Selbstversuch* (Freiburg im Breisgau: Rombach, 2018).

Olschner, Leonard, *Der feste Buchstab. Erläuterungen zu Paul Celans Gedichtübertragungen* (Göttingen: Vandenhoeck & Ruprecht, 1985).

Olschner, Leonard, 'Anamnesis. Paul Celan's Translations of Poetry', *Studies in 20th Century Literature*, 12.2 (1988), 163–97.

Olschner, Leonard, 'Fugal provocation in Paul Celan's "Todesfuge" and "Engführung"', *German Life and Letters*, 43 (1989/1990), 79–89.

Olschner, Leonard, *Im Abgrund Zeit. Paul Celans Poetiksplitter* (Göttingen: Vandenhoeck & Ruprecht, 2007).

Olschner, Leonard, 'Celans poetologisches Verstummen und Weiter-Sprechen', *Jahrbuch für Internationale Germanistik*, 43.1 (2011), 57–78.

Pajević, Marko, 'Erfahrungen, Orte, Aufenthalte und die Sorge um das Selbst', *arcadia*, 32.1 (1997), 148–61.

Pajević, Marko, 'Paul Celans "Ich kenne dich". Das Gedicht als "Lebensschrift"', in *Paul Celan. Biographie und Interpretation/Biographie et Interprétation*, ed. by Andrei Corbea-Hoişie (Konstanz: Hartung-Gorre, 2000), pp. 215–24.

Pajević, Marko, *Zur Poetik Paul Celans. Gedicht und Mensch – die Arbeit am Sinn* (Heidelberg: Winter, 2000).

Pajević, Marko, 'Die Korrespondenz Ingeborg Bachmann/Paul Celan – "exemplarisch"?', *Weimarer Beiträge*, 56.4 (2010), 519–43.

Pajević, Marko, *Poetisches Denken und die Frage nach dem Menschen. Grundzüge einer poetologischen Anthropologie* (Freiburg im Breisgau: Karl Alber, 2012).

Patka, Markus G., and Peter Goßens, eds, *'Displaced'. Paul Celan in Wien 1947/1948* (Frankfurt a. M.: Suhrkamp, 2001).

Pennone, Florence, *Paul Celans Übersetzungspoetik. Entwicklungslinien in seinen Übertragungen französischer Lyrik* (Tübingen: Niemeyer, 2007).

Perrey, Beate, 'Visual Musical Poetry. The Feeling of Pallaksch in Bacon, Celan, and Kurtág', *Comparative Criticism*, 25 (2004), 123–59.

Pickford, Henry W., *The Sense of Semblance. Philosophical Analyses of Holocaust Art* (New York: Fordham University Press, 2013).

Pöggeler, Otto, *Spur des Wortes. Zur Lyrik Paul Celans* (Freiburg im Breisgau: Karl Alber, 1986).

Pöggeler, Otto, and Christoph Jamme, eds, *'Der glühende Leertext'. Annäherungen an Paul Celans Dichtung* (Munich: Fink, 1993).

Pöggeler, Otto, *Der Stein hinterm Aug. Studien zu Celans Gedichten* (Munich: Fink, 2000).

Reuss, Roland, *Im Zeithof. Celan-Provokationen* (Frankfurt a. M.: Stroemfeld, 2001).

Richter, Alexandra, Patrik Alac and Bertrand Badiou, eds, *Paul Celan – La bibliothèque philosophique* (Paris: Editions Rue d'Ulm, 2004).

Rokem, Na'ama, 'German-Hebrew Encounters in the Poetry and Correspondence of Yehuda Amichai and Paul Celan', in *Prooftexts*, 30.1 (2010), 97–127.

Ryan, Judith, 'Monologische Lyrik. Paul Celans Antwort auf Gottfried Benn', *Basis. Jahrbuch für deutsche Gegenwartsliteratur*, 2 (1971), 260–82.

Ryland, Charlotte, *Paul Celan's Encounters with Surrealism. Trauma, Translation and Shared Poetic Space* (Oxford: Legenda, 2010).

Ryland, Charlotte, 'Keeping Faith. Michael Hamburger's Translations of Paul Celan's Poetry', *Jahrbuch für Internationale Germanistik*, 43 (2011), 63–76.

Sanmann, Angela, *Poetische Interaktion. Französisch-deutsche Lyrikübersetzungen bei Friedhelm Kemp, Paul Celan, Ludwig Harig, Volker Braun* (Berlin and Boston: De Gruyter, 2013).

Schmitz-Emans, Monika, *Poesie als Dialog. Vergleichende Studien zu Paul Celan und seinem literarischen Umfeld* (Heidelberg: Winter, 1993).

Schmull, Heino, 'Übersetzen als Sprung. Textgenetische und poetologische Beobachtungen an Celans Übersetzungen von Shakespeares Sonetten', *arcadia*, 32 (1997), 119–47.

Schuster, Marc-Oliver, 'Dismantling Anti-Semitic Authorship in Paul Celan's "Gespräch im Gebirg"', *Modern Austrian Literature*, 35.1/2 (2002), 23–42.

Seng, Joachim, 'Von der Musikalität einer "graueren" Sprache. Zu Celans Auseinandersetzung mit Adorno', *Germanisch-Romanische Monatsschrift*, 45.4 (1995), 19–30.

Shmueli, Ilana, *Sag, daß Jerusalem ist. Über Paul Celan: Oktober 1969-April 1970* (Eggingen: Edition Isele, 2000).

Sideras, Agis, *Paul Celan und Gottfried Benn. Zwei Poetologien nach 1945* (Würzburg: Königshausen & Neumann, 2005).

Silbermann, Edith, *Begegnung mit Paul Paul Celan. Erinnerung und Interpretation* (Aachen: Rimbaud, 1993).

Sparr, Thomas, *Celans Poetik des hermetischen Gedichts* (Heidelberg: Winter, 1989).

Speier, Hans-Michael, ed., *Interpretationen. Gedichte von Paul Celan* (Stuttgart: Reclam, 2002).

Speier, Hans-Michael, ed., *Celan-Jahrbuch*, I–IX (Heidelberg: Winter, 1987–2005), X (Würzburg: Königshausen & Neumann, 2018).

Steiner, George, *After Babel. Aspects of Language and Translation*, 3rd edn (Oxford: Oxford University Press, 1998).

Stewart, Corbert, 'Paul Celan's Modes of Silence. Some Observations on "Sprachgitter"', *Modern Language Review*, 67.1 (1972), 127–42.

Strelka, Joseph P., ed., *Psalm und Hawdalah. Zum Werk Paul Celans. Akten des Internationalen Paul Celan-Kolloquiums New York 1985* (Bern: Peter Lang, 1987).
Szondi, Peter, *Celan-Studien*, ed. by Jean Bollack (Frankfurt a.M.: Suhrkamp, 1972).
Szondi, Peter, 'Eden', in Peter Szondi, *Celan-Studien*, ed. by Jean Bollack (Frankfurt a.M.: Suhrkamp, 1972), pp. 83–92.
Tawada, Yoko, 'Das Tor des Übersetzers oder Celan liest Japanisch', *Zeitschrift für Interkulturelle Germanistik*, 4.2 (2013), 171–77.
Tawada, Yoko, 'Die Krone aus Gras. Zu Paul Celans "Die Niemandsrose"', *Text + Kritik*, 53/54 (2002), 3rd rev. edn, 170–83.
Tawada, Yoko, 'Rabbi Löw und 27 Punkte. Physiognomie der Interpunktion bei Paul Celan', *arcadia*, 32.1 (1997), 283–86.
Terras, Victor, and Karl S. Weimar, 'Mandelstamm and Celan. A Postscript', *Germano-Slavica*, 2 (1978), 353–70.
Thomas, Nicola, 'Stark, Necessary and Not Permanent. Huts in the Work of Paul Celan and J.H. Prynne', *German Life and Letters*, 69.3 (2016), 350–64.
Tobias, Rochelle, *The Discourse of Nature in the Poetry of Paul Celan. The Unnatural World* (Baltimore: The Johns Hopkins University Press, 2006).
Tophoven, Elmar, 'Translating Celan Translating', in *Argumentum e Silentio. International Paul Celan Symposium*, ed. by Amy-Diana Colin (New York: De Gruyter, 1987), pp. 377–83.
Waterhouse, Peter, 'Un, an, Amen, atmen, Deutschland. Versuch über Paul Celans Gedicht "Wolfsbohne"', *Text + Kritik*, 53/54 (2002), 3rd rev. edn, 38–47.
Weigel, Sigrid, and Bernhard Böschenstein, 'Paul Celan/Ingeborg Bachmann. Zur Rekonstruktion einer Konstellation', in *Ingeborg Bachmann und Paul Celan. Poetische Korrespondenzen: Vierzehn Beiträge*, ed. by Bernhard Böschenstein and Sigrid Weigel (Frankfurt a.M.: Suhrkamp, 1997), pp. 7–14.
Weller, Shane, 'From "Gedicht" to "Genicht". Paul Celan and Language Scepticism', *German Life and Letters*, 69.1 (2016), 69–91.
Welling, Florian, *'Vom Anblick der Amseln'. Paul Celans Kafka-Rezeption* (Göttingen: Wallstein, 2019).
Werner, Uta, *Textgräber. Paul Celans geologische Lyrik* (Munich: Fink, 1998).
Werner, Uta, 'Aschenbildwahr. Celans Kunst "Avant la lettre" und die Verwandlung des Lebens in Schrift', in *Paul Celan. Biographie und Interpretation/Biographie et Interprétation*, ed. by Andrei Corbea-Hoişie (Konstanz: Hartung-Gorre, 2000), pp. 147–67.
Wertheimer, Jürgen, and John Neubauer, eds, *Celan und/in Europa*, *arcadia*, 32.1 (1997).
Wiedemann, Barbara, *Antschel Paul – Paul Celan. Studien zum Frühwerk* (Tübingen: Niemeyer, 1985).
Wiedemann, Barabara, ed., *Die Goll-Affäre. Dokumente zu einer 'Infamie'* (Frankfurt a.M.: Suhrkamp, 2000).
Wiedemann, Barbara, '"Lesen Sie! Immerzu nur lesen!" Celan-Lektüre und Celans Lektüren', *Poetica*, 36.1/2 (2004), 169–91.
Wiedemann, Barbara, *'Sprachgitter'. Paul Celan und das Sprechgitter des Pfullinger Klosters*, 2nd rev. edn (Marbach am Neckar: Deutsche Schillergesellschaft, 2014).
Wimmer, Gernot, ed., *Ingeborg Bachmann und Paul Celan. Historisch-poetische Korrelationen* (Berlin: De Gruyter, 2014).

Witte, Bernd, and Chaim Shoham, eds, *Datum und Zitat bei Paul Celan. Akten des Internationalen Paul Celan-Colloquiums Haifa 1986* (Bern: Peter Lang, 1987).
Zach, Matthias, *Traduction littéraire et création poétique. Yves Bonnefoy et Paul Celan traduisent Shakespeare* (Tours: Presses universitaires François-Rabelais, 2018).
Zanetti, Sandro, *'zeitoffen'. Zur Chronographie Paul Celans* (Munich: Fink, 2006).

Contributors

Helmut Böttiger is a German writer, literary critic and essayist.

Chiara Caradonna is post-doctoral fellow at the Martin Buber Society, Hebrew University of Jerusalem, Israel.

Amy Diana Colin is Associate Professor of German at the University of Pittsburgh, USA.

Thomas C. Connolly is Associate Professor of French at Yale University, USA.

Andrei Corbea-Hoisie is Professor of German at the University of Iași, Rumania.

Ulrike Draesner is a German writer and essayist.

Cherilyn Elston is Lecturer in Latin American Cultural Studies at the University of Reading, UK.

Michael Eskin is an author, philosopher and literary critic, and cofounder of Upper West Side Philosophers, Inc., New York, USA.

Durs Grünbein is a German writer and essayist.

Christine Ivanovic teaches comparative literature at the University of Vienna, Austria.

Anselm Kiefer is a German artist.

Eric Kligerman is Associate Professor of German at the University of Florida, USA.

Karen Leeder is Professor of Modern German Literature at the University of Oxford and Fellow and Tutor in German at New College, Oxford, UK.

Charlie Louth is Fellow and Tutor in German at Queen's College, Oxford, UK.

Áine McMurtry is Senior Lecturer in German at King's College, London, UK.

Kristina Mendicino is Associate Professor of German Studies at Brown University, USA.

Camilla Miglio is Professor of German Studies at Sapienza University in Rome, Italy.

Marko Pajević is Astra-Professor of German Studies, funded by the European Union, at the University of Tartu, Estonia.

Denis Thouard is Research Director in Philosophy at the CNRS (Centre national de la recherche scientifique) in Paris, France, and Berlin, Germany.

Sue Vice is Professor of English at the University of Sheffield, UK.

Edmund de Waal is a British artist, master-potter and writer.

Peter Waterhouse is an Austrian writer.

Index